RED, WHITE, AND KIND OF BLUE?

The Conservatives and the Americanization of Canadian Constitutional Culture

Situated between two different constitutional traditions, those of the United Kingdom and the United States, Canada has maintained a distinctive third way: federal, parliamentary, and flexible. Yet in recent years it seems that Canadian constitutional culture has been moving increasingly in an American direction. Through the prorogation crises of 2008 and 2009, its Senate reform proposals, and the appointment process for Supreme Court judges, Stephen Harper's Conservative government has repeatedly shown a tendency to push Canada further into the U.S. constitutional orbit.

Red, White, and Kind of Blue? is a comparative legal analysis of this creeping Americanization, as well as a probing examination of the costs and benefits that come with it. Comparing British, Canadian, and American constitutional traditions, David Schneiderman offers a critical perspective on the Americanization of Canadian constitutional practice and a timely warning about its unexamined consequences.

DAVID SCHNEIDERMAN is a professor in the Faculty of Law at the University of Toronto.

Red, White, and Kind of Blue?

The Conservatives and the Americanization of Canadian Constitutional Culture

DAVID SCHNEIDERMAN

UNIVERSITY OF TORONTO PRESS
Toronto Buffalo London

© University of Toronto Press 2015
Toronto Buffalo London
www.utppublishing.com
Printed in the U.S.A.

ISBN 978-1-4426-2947-9 (cloth)
ISBN 978-1-4426-2948-6 (paper)

∞

Printed on acid-free, 100% post-consumer recycled paper with vegetable-based inks.

Library and Archives Canada Cataloguing in Publication

Schneiderman, David, 1958–, author
Red, white, and kind of blue? : the conservatives and the Americanization
of Canadian constitutional culture/David Schneiderman.

Includes bibliographical references and index.
ISBN 978-1-4426-2947-9 (cloth). – ISBN 978-1-4426-2948-6 (paper)

1. Constitutional law – Canada – American influences. 2. Constitutional
law – United States. I. Title.

KE4226.S36 2015   342.71   C2015-904683-1
KF4482.S36 2015

This book has been published with the help of a grant from the Federation
for the Humanities and Social Sciences, through the Awards to Scholarly
Publications Program, using funds provided by the Social Sciences and
Humanities Research Council of Canada.

University of Toronto Press acknowledges the financial assistance to its
publishing program of the Canada Council for the Arts and the Ontario
Arts Council, an agency of the Government of Ontario.

 **Canada Council
for the Arts** **Conseil des Arts
du Canada**

 **ONTARIO ARTS COUNCIL
CONSEIL DES ARTS DE L'ONTARIO**
an Ontario government agency
un organisme du gouvernement de l'Ontario

 Funded by the   Financé par le
Government   gouvernement
of Canada   du Canada |  Canada

To Kiran and Anika

Contents

Acknowledgments

It was shortly after I returned from a three-year sojourn in the United States that the idea for this book was hatched. I had been teaching U.S. constitutional law to U.S. law students during the second term of President George W. Bush. Confidence in the president had reached all-time lows. The advantages of the parliamentary system over the presidential one were increasingly apparent, at least to me. Upon my return to Canada, I could hear arguments during the course of two controversial prorogations reminiscent of those that had issued out of the Bush II White House. Then, there were initiatives like Senate reform and a new procedure for Supreme Court of Canada nominations. All of this appeared to mimic U.S. constitutional rules or practice. *Red, White, and Kind of Blue?* was born out of this intuition.

This book has been a great deal of fun to write. Its initial arguments were developed on the run, as events were running their course. I am grateful to my home institution, the Faculty of Law at the University of Toronto, and to former Dean Mayo Moran and to the current dean, Edward Iacobucci, for their steadfast support. I am also grateful to colleagues at Georgetown University Law School, and to past dean Alex Aleinikoff, for their gracious hospitality and willingness to allow a Canadian to instruct U.S. law students about their own constitution.

I presented an early version of chapter 5 at the "Workshop on Media and Courts," Onati Socio-Legal Studies Institute in June 2013, at the University of Toronto Faculty of Law / University of Montreal "Beetz-Laskin Inaugural Conference" in September 2012, and at the Osgoode Hall Law School "Constitutional Cases Conference" in May 2012. Early versions of other chapters were presented at the "Parliamentary Democracy" panel at the David Asper Centre for Constitutional Rights, in January 2009, at a Faculty of Law, University of Toronto event on Senate reform in March 2009, and Faculty of Law seminars at the University of Toronto in February and November 2013. A book panel was organized at the University of Toronto Faculty of Law in late September 2014, where Peter Russell, Jean Leclair, and Yasmin Dawood commented upon a draft of the book. In addition to their thoughtful advice, I received helpful comments from Ben Berger, Mark Walters, Rob Walsh, and Nelson Wiseman. I also had the benefit of Martin Friedland's sage advice and encouragement at key moments. Daniel Quinlan of University of Toronto Press provided valuable encouragement and feedback early on. I also had the benefit of excellent research assistance from Matthew Burns, Aria Laskin, Sarah McLeod, Benjamin Miller, Krista Nerland, Zaire Puil, and Chava Schwebel, all former law students at the University of Toronto. Aria Laskin not only helped code newspaper accounts, she generated the data that appear in chapter 5. All throughout, I had the loving support of Pratima, Kiran, and Anika.

A small portion of chapter 2 previously appeared in the *Canadian Parliamentary Review* and an early version of the latter half of chapter 5 appeared online at *Oñati Socio-legal Series*.

As I indicate in the introduction, this is not meant to be a polemic directed at the Harper Conservative government. There are a number of those sorts of books already in circulation. Instead, I take seriously the arguments in support of shifts in practice in an American direction made by the Conservative government. Though I happen to disagree with these shifts, I do not disagree that we are in need of reform in each of the areas under discussion. Each of the topics taken up here, particularly insofar as they concern concentration of power in the executive branch, should preoccupy Canadians into the future.

I have dedicated this book to my children, who will be given their own opportunity to contribute to the ongoing experiment of Canadian constitutionalism. I am hoping that they will have learned something from their dad along the way.

RED, WHITE, AND KIND OF BLUE?

The Conservatives and the Americanization
of Canadian Constitutional Culture

Introduction

"Canadians are conditioned from infancy to think of themselves as citizens of a country of uncertain identity, a confusing past, and a hazardous future," observed Northrop Frye.[1] Canadians might be an impressionable lot – they might be open to influences from elsewhere – but this does not render their past unknowable. Nor does it deliver them up to an indefinite future in which they have no hand in the shape of things to come. Instead, we might insist that Canadians, within limits, have an ability to choose the changes they want, so long as they are adequately informed about them.[2]

Being open to influences from elsewhere renders Canadians particularly vulnerable to the weight of their overbearing neighbour to the south. This susceptibility includes being influenced by aspects of American constitutional governance. When Canada's Conservative government sought to separate out and enhance executive authority during two prorogation crises, initiating Senate reform and revamping the Supreme Court of Canada judicial appointment process, it appeared that the Conservatives were succumbing to the force of America's gravitational pull. If successful, the outcome of these constitutional initiatives would have been to push Canada further into the orbit of U.S. constitutional influence.

This book examines these innovations with a view to evaluating the extent to which they disturb traditions and practices associated with

---

1 Northrop Frye, "Sharing the Continent," in Northrop Frye, *Divisions on a Ground: Essays on Canadian Culture*, ed. James Polk (Toronto: House of Anansi, 1989), 57.
2 See W.H. New, *Borderlands: How We Talk About Canada* (Vancouver: UBC Press, 1996), 102.

Canada's constitutional culture. It is not that many aspects of constitutional self-governance are not in need of reform. To the contrary, many of the practices and institutions that were the target of the Harper government's reforms are in dire need of rethinking. The concern animating this book is that the prime minister and his government proposed that Canada mimic some of the most problematic aspects of U.S. governance, with its separate executive branch, divided and gridlocked congressional government, and dysfunctional judicial confirmation hearings. It would have been less objectionable if it had been suggested that Canadians take up elements of U.S. constitutional practice that are worthwhile replicating. Change, in other words, should be welcome, but not under conditions that inhibit argument and innovative thinking.

An overriding problem with these initiatives is that they were not intended to engage the Canadian public very much. Many of them were not difficult to initiate, but for Senate reform, they could be initiated simply by executive edicts. From the government's perspective, these innovations needn't have triggered the use of Canada's constitutional amending formulae. They could, for this reason, fly somewhat under the constitutional radar. It is this flexibility – in contrast to the rigidity of Canada's amending formulae – the prime minister hoped to exploit in pursuit of his constitutional plans.

It was not that the prime minister or his Cabinet openly acknowledged that Canada's constitutional order should look more like the U.S. one. We do have, however, statements and legislative enactments – their "performative utterances" – that were intended to have certain effects or "uptake."[3] We also have a context – a "pre-existing conversation"[4] – for understanding the meaning of these utterances, namely, over 225 years of American and almost 150 years of Canadian constitutional experience. The available evidence indicates that the prime minister admires U.S.-style limited government.[5] As some initiatives are

---

3 J.L. Austin, *How to Do Things with Words*, 2nd ed. (Cambridge, MA: Harvard University Press, 1975), 109, 117.

4 Quentin Skinner, "Interpretation and the Understanding of Speech Acts," in Quentin Skinner, *Visions of Politics*. Vol. 1, *Regarding Method* (Cambridge: Cambridge University Press, 2002), 103–27, 115–16.

5 Stephen J. Harper, "Text of Stephen Harper's Speech to the Council for National Policy, June 1997," Canada Votes 2006, www.cbc.ca/canadavotes2006/leadersparties/harper_speech.html. Harper said to this U.S. conservative think tank, "Your country, and particularly your conservative movement, is a light and an inspiration to people in this country and across the world."

traceable to proposals initiated by the Conservative Party's forerunner, the Reform Party, we also know that U.S. precedent helped to prompt and shape these earlier proposals.[6] They all happen to fit well into a larger pattern of taking from what is familiar and close at hand, a process of constitutional borrowing that Mark Tushnet associates with the idea of constitutional "bricolage."[7]

The object of this book is to examine the implications of these innovative practices for Canadian constitutional culture. It is not intended to be an anti-Harper polemic. The purpose is to take seriously the ideas associated with the proposals advanced by the Harper Conservatives. The hope is that by isolating each of these proposed innovations, Canadians will be in a better position to consciously direct the political momentum in which they have been caught up. They may choose to embrace these innovations, of course. They may have done so, implicitly, by having elected Prime Minister Harper on three prior occasions. They should choose to do so, however, only on the basis of full disclosure of their consequences and in open debate.[8] This book is intended to be a modest contribution to this element of Canada's ongoing project of self-rule.

Some might be reassured by the knowledge that the prime minister has not had substantial success in driving Canadian constitutional culture in an American direction. The Supreme Court constitutionally forbade the pursuit of Senate reform via unilateral federal legislation. The prime minister abandoned holding judicial nomination hearings for his last two Supreme Court nominees.[9] As the prime minister mostly relied upon executive edict, few of these innovations would have been secure enough to outlast him in any event. Whenever change is sought solely by executive action, much will depend on the behaviour of

6 Roger Gibbins, "The Impact of the American Constitution on Contemporary Canadian Constitutional Politics," in *The Canadian and American Constitutions in Comparative Perspective*, ed. Marian C. McKenna, 131–45 (Calgary: University of Calgary Press, 1993).

7 Mark Tushnet, "Comparative Constitutional Law," *Yale Law Journal* 108 (1999): 1304.

8 Rounds of failed constitutional reform in the 1990s indicate that Canadians likely will no longer tolerate not being consulted about major constitutional change. See Peter H. Russell, *Constitutional Odyssey: Can Canadians Become a Sovereign People?* 2nd ed. (Toronto: University of Toronto Press, 1993), 234.

9 His last two appointments, Justices Clément Gascon and Suzanne Côté, unlike his previous ones, were made without their appearing first before a special House of Commons Committee. See Sean Fine, "Harper Appoints New Judge, Passes Over Public Hearing," *Globe and Mail*, 28 November 2014.

successive political leaders and their party platforms. Such is the risk of proceeding by unilateral executive order and legislation rather than by constitutional reform. What has been done can endure, but can also be undone, with time. We should worry, however, that such initiatives might be more lasting, even where the government changes hands. Claims that the prime minister is directly elected continues to inhibit the prospect of future coalition governments; the executive continues to treat the House of Commons disdainfully as a separate branch; many still yearn for an elected Senate; and judicial confirmation processes are likely develop further along the lines already laid down. In other words, future governments may choose to guide constitutional practice in similar directions. We can reasonably anticipate, then, that arguments made here will have salience in the future.

The Necessary Comparative Dimension

This book also is an exercise in comparative constitutional law. Undertaking this task calls for the examination of not just one but three distinct constitutional traditions – of the United Kingdom, United States, and Canada over time. There is, of course, more than a family resemblance between them. Understanding Canadian constitutional culture requires that it be traced back to its origins in English constitutional thought and imperial policy. This tradition heavily influences developments in British North America and in what would become the United States. The American (or U.S. – I use them interchangeably) experience shapes both the fortunes and constitutional predicament of the British rump in North America – the counterfactual to the revolutionary polity to the south – in what would become Canada. If the English constitutional experience has been formative, Canadians have always been under an American influence, continually being drawn into its orbit. Canada, in this sense, has been the product of these two empires. Taking the long view, we can say that the sorts of pressures examined in this book are not new, that Canadian constitutional developments always have been intertwined with the United States, and that Canadians continually have been tempted to deepen that relationship. Canadians, in short, always have been at the front lines of the movement towards greater integration and harmonization with its populous and powerful neighbour to the south.

Taking up comparative constitutional law methods has the advantage of isolating both similarities and differences. Claims to constitutional distinctiveness, Sujit Choudhry has argued, are "inherently relative,"[10] in which case we might find movement towards convergence, based on regional or universal standards, or divergence, even resistance, away from prevailing patterns. The approach adopted here resembles a "dialogical"[11] or "engagement" model'[12] of comparison that facilitates, through self-reflection, the identification of similarity and of difference. It also "facilitates constitutional choice" insofar as it clarifies the implications of adopting constitutional change in one direction or another.[13]

The Perennial Identity Question

Inevitably, the book engages with enduring Canadian identity questions, such as, "Who are we" and "What distinguishes us from the United States?" Asking such questions remains a healthy Canadian preoccupation. Otherwise, why insist on policing Canada's borders? Why not just fold up Canadian tents and join in the political project to the south. Canadian philosopher George Grant appeared to be of the view that Canadians and Americans were practically joined together at the hip. Canada's demise was inevitable – a "necessity" – because of the "impossibility of conservatism" in an age when all that matters is the "capacity to consume." There was "nothing," Grant declared, "essential [that] distinguishes Canadians from Americans – no 'deep division of principle.'"[14] For his purposes, Canada has ceased to exist as a nation. "The disadvantages of being a branch-plant satellite rather than in having a full membership in the Republic will become obvious," Grant predicted.[15] Why not, then, have a more direct say in who rules over Canada?

---

10 Sujit Choudhry, "The *Lochner* Era and Comparative Constitutionalism," *International Journal of Constitutional Law* 2 (2004): 52.

11 Sujit Choudhry, "Globalization in Search of Justification: Toward a Theory of Comparative Constitutional Interpretation," *Indiana Law Journal* 74 (1999): 856–7.

12 Vicki C. Jackson, *Constitutional Engagement in a Transnational Era* (New York: Oxford University Press, 2010), 72.

13 Choudhry, "*Lochner* Era," 52.

14 George Grant, *Lament for a Nation: The Defeat of Canadian Nationalism* (Toronto: McClelland & Stewart, 1965), 90, 54, 76. This was considered a positive development for an earlier generation of historians. See discussion in Carl C. Berger, "Internationalism, Continentalism, and the Writing of History: Comments on the Carnegie Series on the Relations of Canada and the United States," in *The Influence of the United States on Canadian Development: Eleven Case Studies*, ed. Richard A. Preston, 32–54 (Durham, NC: Duke University Press, 1972).

15 Grant, *Lament for a Nation*, 86, 90.

Rather than giving up on the Canadian project of democratic self-rule, this book holds out the hope that it is worthwhile to sustain that project. In thinking about the content of Canadian constitutional culture, one should be able to do more than develop understandings that are "pragmatic, ad hoc, and a response to the needs of the moment."[16] Though democratic patterns and practices in Canada look increasingly like American ones,[17] I argue in chapter 1 that Canadian constitutional culture at least continues to hold out the prospect of channelling collective political wills better than does American practice. So rather than folding up tents, Canadians might instead want to celebrate this distinctive feature of their constitutional culture.

Yet there is no need to condemn ongoing American influences.[18] This book is not intended to be an anti-American polemic. It is not premised upon "ritualistic expressions of deeply held assumptions" about the United States[19] or a species of "hatred, bias, and deliberately contrived fear mongering."[20] Instead, the book's arguments rely upon a U.S. historical record as well as interpretations of that experience by leading academics in the field. Increasing numbers of scholars are expressing dismay at the state of constitutional democracy in the U.S.[21] As two co-authors put it in the title of their recent book, "It's Even Worse Than It Looks."[22] So there is no need for a Canadian scholar to evaluate

16 Allan Smith, *Canada: An American Nation? Essays on Continentalism, Identity, and the Canadian Frame of Mind* (Montreal and Kingston: McGill-Queen's University Press, 1994), 10.
17 S.F. Wise, "The Annexation Movement and Its Effect on Canadian Opinion, 1837–67," in S.F. Wise and Robert Craig Brown, *Canada Views the United States: Nineteenth-Century Political Attitudes* (Toronto: Macmillan Canada, 1967), 95.
18 Frank H. Underhill, *The Image of Canada* (Fredericton: University of New Brunswick Press, 1962), 14.
19 Wise, "Annexation Movement and Its Effect," 95.
20 J.L. Granatstein, *Yankee Go Home? Canadians and Anti-Americanism* (Toronto: Harper-Collins, 1996), 286.
21 For example, Bruce Ackerman, *The Decline and Fall of the American Republic* (Cambridge, MA: Harvard University Press, 2010); Robert A. Dahl, *How Democratic Is the American Constitution?* (New Haven, CT: Yale University Press, 2001); Lawrence Lessig, *Republic, Lost: How Money Corrupts Congress – and a Plan to Stop It* (New York: Twelve, 2011); Sanford Levinson, *Our Undemocratic Constitution: Where the Constitution Goes Wrong (and How We the People Can Correct It)* (New York: Oxford University Press, 2006).
22 Thomas E. Mann and Norman J. Ornstein, *It's Even Worse Than It Looks: How the American Constitutional System Collided with the New Politics of Extremism* (New York: Basic Books, 2012).

that experience in light of the voluminous record. Nor do I purport to introduce a novel account of the English constitutional experience or of British imperial policy in North America. Rather, I hope to contribute to an understanding of Canadian constitutional practice and culture, fore-grounding contemporary debates in light of that inheritance. The book is not about being buried by or resurrecting that tradition. Instead, I hope to lay the groundwork for "new departures" in the direction of sensible, democratically legitimate change.[23]

A Distinctive Culture?

It is not that there will be only a single idea that shapes Canadian con-stitutional culture. Instead, we are likely to find an ensemble of prac-tices and understandings that are continually evolving. For instance, I have argued that Canadian constitutional culture presently channels middle-class values in its understanding of equality rights, is hostile towards the idea that income assistance rises to the level of constitu-tional right, but contemplates a robust role for the state to facilitate market exchange and the redistribution of wealth.[24] It might well be, as Grant maintains, that even in these respects Canadian political and legal institutions only are marginally different from those in the United States. On the pressing questions facing industrial civilization, Grant argued, there are no differences between the two systems "sufficiently important to provide the basis for an alternative culture on the north-ern half of this continent."[25] There might be nothing that is "unique or exclusive," Northrop Frye agreed, only a difference in "matter[s] of

23 Margaret Atwood, *Survival: A Thematic Guide to Canadian Literature* (Toronto: House of Anansi, 2012), 278.
24 See David Schneiderman, "Universality vs Particularity: Litigating Middle-Class Values under Section 15," *Supreme Court Law Review* (2nd) 33 (2006): 367–87; Sch-neiderman, "Property Rights, Investor Rights, and Regulatory Innovation: Com-paring Constitutional Cultures in Transition," *International Journal of Constitutional Law* 4 (2006): 371–91; Schneiderman, "Social Rights and Common Sense: *Gosselin* through a Media Lens," in *Social and Economic Insecurity: Rights, Social Citizenship and Governance*, ed. Margot Young, Susan B. Boyd, Gwen Brodsky, and Shelagh Day, 57–73 (Vancouver: UBC Press, 2007); Schneiderman, "Human Needs above Property Rights? Rethinking the Woodsworth Legacy in an Era of Economic Globalization," in *Human Welfare, Rights and Social Activism: Rethinking the Legacy of J.S. Woodsworth*, ed. Jane Pilkington, 161–79 (Toronto: University of Toronto Press, 2009).
25 Grant, *Lament for a Nation*, 74.

emphasis and of degree."[26] It is these differences – small ones, some say[27] – that many Canadians stubbornly cling to. If America has historically been the crucible of our distinctiveness,[28] are there differences worth preserving? Perhaps so, if we improve upon them under conditions of informed and public deliberation.

Nor do I intend to draw any sharp distinction between English-Canadian, Quebec, and Aboriginal constitutional cultures. It is true that there are competing narratives about the Constitution issuing out of these differing "national" communities – they each draw upon different (and sometimes similar) histories and legal traditions.[29] In other work,[30] I have tried to have due regard for this phenomenon. There seems less reason to be attentive to such differences here, largely because the conception of constitutional culture relied upon insists on a mythical unity. It rests on the belief that there is a single community upon which this culture operates,[31] an abstraction common to much "modern" constitutionalism.[32] It is a conception that imposes a common vision and common principles upon fragmented polities.[33] It is, from this angle, a "unitary discourse."[34] It also is a productive one,[35] a project of social

---

26 Frye, "Sharing the Continent," 59.
27 Generally, see David Card and Richard B. Freeman, *Small Differences That Matter: Labor Markets and Income Maintenance in Canada and the United States* (Chicago: University of Chicago Press, 1993).
28 Ian Angus, *A Border Within: National Identity, Cultural Plurality and Wilderness* (Montreal and Kingston: McGill-Queen's University Press, 1997), 116.
29 See Jean-François Gaudreault-DesBiens, "The Quebec Secession Reference and the Judicial Arbitration of Conflicting Narratives about Law, Democracy, and Identity," *Vermont Law Review* 23 (1999): 797–8; and John Borrows, *Canada's Indigenous Constitution* (Toronto: University of Toronto Press), who calls this intermingling a "mistake" (15).
30 For example, David Schneiderman, "Dual(ling) Charters: The Harmonics of Rights in Canada and Quebec," *Ottawa Law Review* 24 (1992): 235–63.
31 Paul Kahn, *The Cultural Study of Law* (Chicago: Chicago University Press, 1993), 113; Carl Schmitt, *The Concept of the Political*, trans. George Schwab (Chicago: University of Chicago Press, 1996).
32 James Tully, *Strange Multiplicity: Constitutionalism in an Age of Diversity* (Cambridge: Cambridge University Press, 1995), 58; see Jacob T. Levy, "Montesquieu's Constitutional Legacies," in *Montesquieu and His Legacy*, ed. Rebecca Kingston, 115–37 (Albany, NY: State University Press of New York, 2009).
33 Pierre Bourdieu, "Rethinking the State: Genesis and Structure of the Bureaucratic Field," in Pierre Bourdieu, *Practical Reason* (Stanford, CA: Stanford University Press, 1998), 46.
34 Michel Foucault, "Two Lectures," in Michel Foucault, *Power/Knowledge: Selected Interviews and Other Writings 1972–77*, ed. Colin Gordon (New York: Pantheon, 1980), 82.
35 Ibid., 93.

integration and "active *dis*integration" of competing formulations[36] that are reduced merely to local or particularistic aberrations. For this reason, the task of identifying elements that make up Canada's constitutional culture is a challenging, even a delicate, one. In some ways, it is as difficult as the question asked of First Nations when making an Aboriginal rights claim. Writing for a majority of the Supreme Court of Canada in the Van der Peet case, Chief Justice Antonio Lamer limited constitutional Aboriginal rights to those unextinguished pre-contact practices, customs, and traditions that are "integral" to the distinctive Aboriginal culture making the claim. By "distinctive," the Court said it was referring not to what was different about Aboriginal culture but to what made the culture "what it was."[37]

The question asked here is similar, yet different. It is not a question to be answered by a purportedly authoritative and neutral tribunal like the Supreme Court of Canada. Rather, it is a question requiring an answer from the self-governing community to whom the question is addressed: the polity called Canada. The question is not posed in order to narrow the range of values and institutions considered distinctive, as in Van der Peet. Instead, the question is intended to provoke a fulsome response that does not inhibit, but provokes, debate and deliberation. John Borrows describes indigenous law as "developed through people talking with one another."[38] Ideally, it is developed via deliberation and consultation by all those affected in both formal and informal settings. In asking this sort of question, I am calling upon mainstream constitutional law and culture to cultivate similar practices.

Lastly, a search for the indicators of a "distinctive" constitutional culture need not be fixed on differences between that culture and all others in the world. Rather, the object is to identify salient differences between Canadian and U.S. constitutional cultures, understanding that they hold much in common. Some will call this a "small, practical question"[39] concerning the "narcissism of small differences."[40] It is

36 Phillip Corrigan and Derek Sayer, *The Great Arch: English State Formation as Cultural Revolution* (Oxford: Basil Blackwell, 1985), 195.
37 *R v Van der Peet* [1996] 2 SCR 507, para 71. For a penetrating critique, see John Borrows, *Recovering Canada: The Resurgence of Indigenous Law* (Toronto: University of Toronto Press, 2002), chap. 3.
38 Borrows, *Canada's Indigenous Constitution*, 35.
39 George Grant, *Technology and Empire* (Toronto: House of Anansi, 1969), 78.
40 Wise, "Annexation Movement and Its Effect," 96.

inspired, however, by a concern that Alan Cairns identified thirty years ago: "The hypnotic presence of the American version [of nationalism] militates against understanding of the very different Canadian situation and contributes to a failure to perceive alternative bases of systems of survival."[41]

Constitutional Culture

What makes up what I am calling constitutional culture? I think of it as being much more than what constitutional text provides or what courts say the constitutional text means. It encompasses more than the body of unwritten constitutional conventions (rules common to parliamentary systems of government) or constitutional principles (the "vital unstated assumptions upon which the text is based").[42] Constitutional culture refers to the compendium of fundamental values and norms that are represented in law, custom, and popular culture. It gives expression to dominant understandings of constitutional values that are widely shared within the constitutional order. Constitutional culture is intended to illuminate the ways in which constitutional norms are put into practice by a variety of institutions and groups, generating the imaginative possibilities that lie embedded within them.[43]

It is to be distinguished from the more encompassing idea of "political culture." According to Almond and Verba, the study of political culture is concerned with public attitudes that help to sustain successful political systems.[44] Breaking from the theoretical tradition of treating political regimes as shaped solely by their constitutions,[45] Alexis de Tocqueville's *Democracy in America* helped to define the field of political culture. Tocqueville famously catalogued the "practical experience, habits, and opinion – in a word, ... the mores [*mouers*] – of the

---

41 Alan C. Cairns, "Political Science in Canada and the American Issue," *Canadian Journal of Political Science* 8 (1975): 231.

42 *Reference re Secession of Quebec* [1998] 2 SCR 217, para 49.

43 Kahn, *Cultural Study of Law*, 95; also Benjamin L. Berger, *Law's Religion: Religious Difference and the Claims of Constitutionalism* (Toronto: University of Toronto Press, 2015), chap. 1.

44 Gabriel A. Almond and Sidney Verba, *Civic Culture* (Boston: Little Brown, 1965), 121; David J. Elkins and Richard E. Simeon, "A Cause in Search of Its Effect, or What Does Political Culture Explain?" *Comparative Politics* 11 (1979): 127–45.

45 Sheldon S. Wolin, *Tocqueville between Two Worlds: The Making of a Political and Theoretical Life* (Princeton, NJ: Princeton University Press, 2001), 207.

Americans in maintaining their laws."[46] Political culture therefore refers to a range of ideologies, policies, and practices of which constitutions and institutions will be but one element.[47] Public values and attitudes may be important considerations, but the study of constitutional culture focuses on a narrower set of norms and institutions than the panoply of values and actors that sustain a political regime. Nor is this project meant to isolate social values that distinguish Canada from the United States. Such studies tap into public opinion polling about a host of measurements by which citizens conduct themselves and interact with each other.[48] In common with some of these social values studies, however, this book seeks to identify constitutional values that distinguish Canada from the United States. It also aims to isolate the avenues by which they may become more alike.

Others have used understandings of constitutional culture in somewhat similar ways. Robert Post, for instance, ascribes to constitutional culture extrajudicial beliefs about what the U.S. Constitution means. He argues that U.S. judges contend with these values and beliefs in the course of making constitutional law.[49] His Yale colleague Reva Siegel invokes constitutional culture in order to explain how interpretation of the U.S. Constitution changes over time without having recourse to constitutional amendments. Change occurs, Siegel maintains, because of popular engagement (mainly social movements) with constitutional

46 Alexis de Tocqueville, *Democracy in America*, trans. Arthur Goldhammer (New York: Library of America, 2004), 356.
47 Nelson Wiseman, *In Search of Canadian Political Culture* (Vancouver: UBC Press, 2007), 14, 18. Verney distinguishes between "civilization" and "culture," arguing that Canadians have resisted being absorbed into American civilization while retaining a distinctive political culture based upon French-English duality. For my purposes, this distinction does not hold up if American influence is being felt in Canadian political culture. See Douglas V. Verney, *Three Civilizations, Two Cultures, One State: Canada's Political Traditions* (Durham, NC: Duke University Press, 1986).
48 For example, Michael Adams, with Amy Langstaff and David Jamieson, *Fire and Ice: The United States, Canada and the Myth of Converging Values* (Toronto: Penguin Canada, 2003); also, with a wider lens, Edward Grabb and James Curtis, *Regions Apart: Four Societies of Canada and the United States* (Don Mills, ON: Oxford University Press, 2006).
49 Robert C. Post, "Foreword: Fashioning the Legal Constitution – Culture, Courts, and Law," *Harvard Law Review* 117 (2003): 8; also Matthew S.R. Palmer, "New Zealand Constitutional Culture," *New Zealand Universities Law Review* 22 (2007): 565. "Judge-made law is constantly interpreting ambient culture to separate the reasonable from the unreasonable, the offensive from the inoffensive, the private from the public, and so forth" (Post, "Foreword," 80).

arguments and traditions.[50] Ernest Young works a similar binary in distinguishing between the canonical constitution – the text as codified in 1787 and its subsequent amendments – and the extracanonical constitution, made up of a variety of statutes, executive material, and practices – "legal norms existing outside of what we traditionally think of as the 'Constitution.'"[51] Ferejohn, Rakove, and Riley suggest a different binary, between a higher order of culture associated with judges and legalists, and a lower order associated with the community at large. Their working definition of constitutional culture has the advantage of being capacious: a "web of interpretive norms, canons and practices which most members of a particular community accept and employ (at least implicitly)."[52]

In contrast to these other formulations, the approach adopted here does not distinguish sharply between inside and outside the "official" constitution or between public opinion and judicial and legal opinion. Rather, understandings of constitutional culture are conjoined into a melange that represents widely shared and dominant understandings of the constitution's workings.[53] The advantage of such a conception is that it brings power and influence into the discussion[54] – not all participants in a constitutional order have equal access to contributing to its content – as well as the possibility of change – as cultures are rarely

---

50 Reva B. Siegel, "Constitutional Culture, Social Movement Conflict and Constitutional Change: The Case of the De Facto ERA," *California Law Review* 94 (2006): 1347. Constitutional culture "supplies the practices of argument that channel the expression of disagreement into claims about the meaning of a shared tradition, teaching advocates to express claims of partisan conviction in the language of public value" (1350).

51 Ernest A. Young, "The Constitution outside the Constitution," *Yale Law Journal* 117 (2007): 411.

52 John Ferejohn, Jack N. Rakove, and Jonathan Riley, "Editor's Introduction," in *Constitutional Culture and Democratic Rule*, ed. John Ferejohn, Jack N. Rakove, and Jonathan Riley (Cambridge, MA: Cambridge University Press, 2001), 10.

53 Dominant opinion, however, will be contestable. The construction of Canadian national identity is explained by Mildred Schwartz: the "definition given by the public to its national identity is the result of social divisions within the society, roles and institutions associated with leadership and guidance on national objectives, and the shifting circumstances of social groups and the nation as a whole." See Mildred Schwartz, *Public Opinion and Canadian Identity* (Scarborough, ON: Fitzhenry and Whiteside, 1967), 239.

54 Pierre Bourdieu, *Pascalian Meditations* (Stanford, CA: Stanford University Press, 2000), 70.

static entities.[55] Alan Cairns approximates the conception advanced here, where constitutional culture stands for the "values, cultural assumptions, identities, and implicit meanings that lie behind its official, public face."[56] Whereas Cairns sees this as a source of "difficulty" for achieving comprehensive constitutional change, it is offered here as a resource for understanding how the constitutional project moves forward through incremental and piecemeal change.

I consider Montesquieu the first to have integrated these elements into a complex understanding of constitutional regimes, in his *Spirit of the Laws*. In order to fully understand a regime, one must examine not only its legal institutions (its nature) but also the principles (the "reasons" for its maxims)[57] that lie behind its institutions.[58] These are the laws derived "from the nature of things," each particular arrangement best relating to the "disposition of the people in whose favor it is established" having reference to religion, political economy, climate, geography, and its *moeurs* and customs.[59] Weimar-era legal theorist Hermann Heller worked this synthetic understanding of constitutionalism in his work on state theory.[60] Heller described a country's constitution as a "normatively formed being," influenced by "natural and cultural factors." What Heller called

55 James Farr, "Conceptual Change and Constitutional Innovation," in *Conceptual Change and the Constitution*, ed. Terence Ball and J.G.A. Pocock (Lawrence: University Press of Kansas, 1988), 14. For instance, Nikolai Wenzel understands constitutional culture as encompassing a wide range of norms, attitudes, belief, and opinion "that individuals (and preponderant groups within a country) hold about the nature, scope, and function of constitutional constraints," but he says little about how that culture will change over time, in "From Contract to Mental Model: Constitutional Culture as a Fact of the Social Sciences," *Review of Austrian Economics* 23 (2010): 65.

56 Alan C. Cairns, "Barriers to Constitutional Renewal in Canada: The Role of Constitutional Culture," in *Reconfigurations: Canadian Citizenship and Constitutional Change, Selected Essays by Alan C. Cairns*, ed. Douglas E. Williams (Toronto: McClelland and Stewart, 1995), 142.

57 Baron de Montesquieu, *The Spirit of the Laws*, trans. Thomas Nugent (New York: Hafner, 1949), lxviii; Montesquieu, *Oeuvres Complètes*. Vol. 2, ed. Roger Caillois (Paris: Librarie Gallimard, 1951), 230.

58 Sharon Krause, "The Spirit of Separate Powers in Montesquieu," *Review of Politics* 62 (2000): 231–65. The "force of principle," Montesquieu wrote, "pulls everything along" (in *Spirit of the Laws*, 8, 11; Montesquieu, *Oeuvres Complètes*, 2:357).

59 Montesquieu, *Spirit of the Laws*, lxvii, 6; Montesquieu, *Oeuvres Complètes*, 2:229, 237, 238.

60 Hermann Heller, "The Nature and Structure of the State," trans. David Dyzenhaus, *Cardozo Law Review* 18 (1996): 1185–6, 1187, 1191, 1174. See David Dyzenhaus, *Legality and Legitimacy: Carl Schmitt, Hans Kelsen and Herman Heller in Weimar* (Oxford: Oxford University Press, 1997), chap. 4, for a valuable discussion of Heller's legal theory.

the "normed constitution" was made up of "customs, ethics, religion, tact, fashion, and so on" – the "whole natural and cultural milieu, the anthropological, geographic, national, economic and social normalities." According to Heller, the "content and validity of a norm are never determined merely by its text, and never solely by the standpoints and characteristics of its legislators, but above all by the characteristics of the norm addressees [the citizens and institutions] who observe them."[61] It is an understanding of constitutional norms as a system of rules developed by the "participants" themselves that I wish to emphasize. Citizens, as much as politicians and courts, generate the content of constitutional culture.

We would want to include within its compass shared understandings about the relationships between state, market, and citizen (what we might call political economy). As Heller admits, "The proposition that the actual constitution resides in actual relationships of power always proves itself true in the end."[62] Social and economic power, in other words, will help to frame the constitutional order. In this context, it is helpful to think about institutions that generate the values and norms of constitutional culture as exercising a form of cultural authority. The media, for this reason, play a considerable role in the analysis that follows. The media perform critical functions in defining and circulating a dominant consensus about the meaning of the constitution.[63] They are one of the principal agents for the dissemination of dominant views.

These norms might not be shared equally among all citizens or branches of the state – indeed, numerous subcultures might give expression to different or variable foundational rules. Some will be predominant, however, and they will be portrayed as representing "shared values." The custodians of constitutional culture – the press, the courts, national and subnational political actors, and NGOs – help to outline the parameters of the dominant social consensus on pressing questions that reflect these basic rules.[64] If the project of identifying the parameters of constitutional culture is to seek out dominant norms, it is imperative that we remain attentive to the fact that such an exercise always will be partial and exclusionary.[65]

---

61 Ibid., 1190–1.
62 Heller, "Nature and Structure of the State," 1194.
63 Stuart Hall, "The Rediscovery of Ideology: The Return of the Repressed in Media Studies," in *Culture, Society and the Media*, ed. Michael Gurevitch, Tony Bennett, James Curran, and Janet Woolacott (London: Routledge, 1985), 64.
64 Ibid., 85.
65 Seyla Benhabib, *The Claims of Culture: Equality and Diversity in the Global Era* (Princeton, NJ: Princeton University Press, 2002), 8.

Relatedly, constitutional culture will change over time. Culture is "contested, temporal and emergent" and so always is in "transition."[66] Culture is a "contrapuntal ensemble," according to Edward Said, "for it is the case that no identity can ever exist by itself and without an array of opposites, negatives, oppositions."[67] Constitutional culture, in other words, is open continuously to contestation. We must be alert to processes by which "official" culture represses and displaces alternative accounts that can give rise to a break in tradition.[68] Yet polities require some form of closure so as to preserve a semblance of order and identity. These very acts of closure, however, should prompt questions about the possibilities that are foreclosed by constitutional settlement. This then can precipitate new forms of imagining political community. In this way, culture is more accurately both "order-maintaining" and "order-transforming."[69] Methodologically, this suggests that we should be able to identify, with some degree of confidence, dominant views about constitutional culture in any given period. Though these views should be considered in transition, they will seldom change as suddenly as do the identities of social actors who view culture as a toolkit with which to continually transform themselves.[70] Nevertheless, the dynamism inherent in this process makes it a difficult task to pin down constitutional culture – a task that is elusive and always partial.

An Example

Though much of the discussion that follows will be about top-down processes that inform its content, one way to get a handle on constitutional culture is to think about popular understandings of constitutional rights. Consider, for instance, the rights available to the criminal accused prior to the entrenchment of the Canadian Charter of

---

66 James Clifford, *The Predicament of Culture: Twentieth-Century Ethnography, Literature, and Art* (Cambridge, MA: Harvard University Press, 1988), 19; Margaret Jane Radin, *Reinterpreting Property* (Chicago: University of Chicago Press, 1993).
67 Edward W. Said, *Culture and Imperialism* (London: Chatto and Windus, 1993), 60.
68 Ian Angus, *Identity and Justice* (Toronto: University of Toronto Press, 2008), 47.
69 E.N. Eisenstadt, "The Order-Maintaining and Order-Transforming Dimensions of Culture," in *Theory of Culture*, ed. Richard Münch and Neil J. Smelser (Berkeley: University of California Press, 1992), 71, 83; also Alan Keenan, *Democracy in Question: Democratic Openness in a Time of Political Closure* (Stanford, CA: Stanford University Press, 2003), 69.
70 John Fiske, *Understanding Popular Culture* (London: Routledge, 1989), 29.

Rights and Freedoms in 1982. Until then, a criminal accused had the benefit of a number of common law and statutory privileges – such as the presumption of innocence – but very few "rights" to protect accused persons during interrogation by police or in the course of collecting evidence.[71] Sociologist Seymour Martin Lipset labels this the "crime control" model, which he contrasts with the "due process" model dominant in the United States.[72] The rights of the criminal accused pre-1982 barely mirrored the rights that are now available to an accused person under the Charter, which borrows heavily from the U.S. due process model as it developed under U.S. Supreme Court Chief Justice Earl Warren. In the eyes of a large number of Canadians (particularly English-speaking ones), however, an accused would have had a variety of rights available to him or her when encountering the criminal justice system prior to 1982, including rights against "unreasonable search and seizure" and to "retain and instruct counsel without delay" that the Warren Court had initiated. This is because a generation of Canadians would have been raised on the stock of U.S. television police shows, such as *Dragnet*, *Adam-12*, and *Hawaii Five-O*, each of which would have reinforced the common-sense idea that an accused engaging with the criminal justice system had rights. The idea that when an accused is arrested in Canada, he gets the same treatment as those read their rights by U.S. authorities, resonated well with Canadians.[73] This helps to explain why those rights were not so controversial at the time of the

71 M.L. Friedland, "Reforming Police Powers: Who's in Charge?," in *Police Powers in Canada: The Evolution and Practice of Authority*, ed. R.C. Macleod and David Schneiderman, 100–18 (Toronto: University of Toronto Press, 1994).
72 Seymour Martin Lipset, *Continental Divide: The Values and Institutions of the United States and Canada* (New York: Routledge, 1990).
73 A 1980 study of 640 individuals in three Canadian cities (Montreal, Toronto, and Winnipeg) revealed respondents were "reasonably well informed" about "knowledge of law on everyday concerns," but a "number of misconceptions centred around differences between American and Canadian law (e.g. 'pleading the Fifth Amendment,' 'being informed of your rights')." The inclusion of Montreal in this survey suggests that American cultural production also influenced French-speaking public opinion in Quebec. See Robert J. Moore, "Reflections of Canadians on the Law and the Legal System: Legal Research Institute Survey of Respondents in Montreal, Toronto and Winnipeg," in *Law in a Cynical Society? Opinion and Law in the 1980s*, ed. Dale Gibson and Janet K. Baldwin (Calgary: Carswell, 1985), 48. The point that Canadians expected to have their "rights read" pre-Charter also has been made in Harry Arthurs, "Constitutional Courage," *McGill Law Journal* 49 (2003): 8n24; and Gibbins, "Impact of the American Constitution," 139.

drafting of the Charter in 1980–1 – that is, outside of the opposition of police associations and prosecutors.[74] Canadian constitutional culture had arrived in this place well before the entrenchment of the rights of the accused under the Charter.

What Follows

The following chapters of this book aim to draw out salient differences by examining discrete features of Canadian and U.S. constitutional practice. Admittedly, the United States has long been open to influences from different corners of the world – it arguably is one of the most pluralist places in the world. This openness is premised, however, on a homogeneity of purpose and identity – the constitution is treated as a covenant running across generations to which fidelity is required by every citizen – though disagreement about its meaning arises continuously over the course of its history.[75] At bottom, U.S. constitutional culture is about an ever-expanding egalitarian and universalist understanding of liberty. Thomas Jefferson viewed the U.S. constitutional project as an imperialist project to which the Western hemisphere voluntarily would succumb by virtue of its universal appeal to freedom.[76] For these reasons, the U.S. Constitution has been described as being an "inclusive" rather than an "exclusive" project: "It does not annex or destroy the other powers it faces but on the contrary opens itself to them, including them in the network."[77] But some scepticism about this global project is called for. Given the sort of freedom U.S. constitutionalism purports to export around the globe, with its accompanying baggage of consumerism, absolutist property rights, and low-level democracy, there is reason to worry about its deleterious influence on alternative constitutional visions around the world. Undoubtedly this influence is being felt in Canada.

---

74 Kent Roach, *Due Process and Victims Rights: The New Law and Politics of Criminal Justice* (Toronto: University of Toronto Press, 1999).
75 Sanford Levinson, *Constitutional Faith* (Princeton, NJ: Princeton University Press, 1988), 17; H. Jefferson Powell, *A Community Built on Words: The Constitution in History and Politics* (Chicago: Chicago University Press, 2002), 5.
76 Daniel Boorstin, *The Lost World of Thomas Jefferson* (Boston: Beacon, 1948), 231–2.
77 Michael Hardt and Antonio Negri, *Empire* (Cambridge, MA: Harvard University Press, 2000), 166.

The first chapter explores constitutional differences over time. Tracing patterns of constitutional behaviour since the British conquest of 1759, a key component of that narrative, and which plays a central role in the formation of Canadian constitutional culture, is the dream of democratic self-rule.[78] By inheriting the royal prerogatives previously exercised by the monarch and subsequently by parliamentary authority in London, Canadians were able to achieve levels of self-government surpassing that available in the United States without having recourse to a bloody revolution. What emerges over time is a robust species of parliamentary self-government that is constrained by bicameralism, the federal division of powers, and a charter of rights – meaningful constraints, to be sure – but is otherwise unlimited. This enables Canadians to better translate their preferences into law. It also gives rise to troubling centralization of authority in the executive.

Exploiting this concentration of authority, Prime Minister Harper has, by his conduct, been nudging Canadian constitutional culture in the direction of U.S.-style limits. Chapter 2 concerns the 2008 prorogation of Parliament in the face of threats of a coalition government, composed of two opposition parties, taking power. Just as the president of the United States is elected, the prime minister maintained that the people elect him. Consequently, any change in government requires a new election. This proposition rubs against a foundational principle of responsible government – that the executive is drawn from the ranks of the House of Commons. In order to gauge the prime minister's success in shifting public perceptions, I undertake a qualitative evaluation of media reports from four leading newspapers. The empirical evidence suggests that the prime minister had some success in shifting public perceptions in the direction of the presidential model.

Chapter 3 takes up a second prorogation in 2009 prompted by the government's stubborn resistance to disclose documents that may have implicated Canadian Armed Forces in torture by handing over detainees to Afghan security forces. Rather than producing the requested documents, the prime minister preferred to shutter Parliament. I assess the legal arguments made by both sides in the debate and conclude that the prime minister erroneously claimed executive-style privilege from parliamentary processes. What is striking is that these are constitutional

---

78 "Self-rule is the emergent dream of the periphery, a dream that must be dampened by the centre, with the redcoats, if necessary" (Angus, *Identity and Justice*, 85).

arguments reminiscent of those issuing out of the White House in response to similar requests to divulge information, arguments having to do with the so-called unitary executive.

Chapter 4 concerns the aborted rollout of Senate reform. Unlike other initiatives discussed in this book, the Harper government introduced legislation to facilitate provincial elections to identify persons fit for appointment to the Canadian Senate. The proposals echoed the Reform Party of Canada platform that promoted a U.S.-style Senate that would be equal, elected, and effective ("Triple E") (the Reform Party, for this reason, plays a predominant role in this and the next chapter in channelling features of the U.S. constitutional experience).[79] The Harper government proposals were not connected to securing formal constitutional amendment and left the proposed Senate extremely powerful and without any reciprocal checking mechanisms available to the House of Commons. This would secure a key aim of U.S. constitutional design, which is to limit government by constraining legislative energy issuing out of the lower house. Ultimately, the Supreme Court of Canada declared the scheme beyond the capacity of the federal government to enact, as a result of the Constitution's amending formulae.[80] I evaluate the positions taken up by the provinces, together with the Supreme Court opinion, and conclude that their positions yield a form of constitutional gridlock, one that impedes constitutional experimentation and innovation, however ill advised they may be, of parliamentary institutions.

The last initiative, taken up in chapter 5, concerns the adoption of judicial nomination hearings. This, once again, mimics some of the dysfunctional features of U.S. constitutional practice. The U.S. Senate advises and consents to executive branch appointments, including appointments to the United States Supreme Court. Senate confirmation hearings have been characterized as national seminars on constitutional law, yet the process today amounts to little more than lengthy soliloquys on the Constitution delivered by senators and non-replies from nominees, broadcast live on national television. In Canada, judicial appointments to high courts constitutionally are the sole preserve

---

79 "There is a greater receptivity," observes Gibbins, "to American ideas, and indeed to non-Canadian ideas in general, within the Reform Party than there is within the more established parties," in "Impact of the American Constitution," 144.

80 *Reference re Senate Reform* [2014] 1 SCR 704.

of the prime minister. Judicial confirmation hearings before a revamped Canadian Senate were a key component of the Reform Party of Canada's platform. The object of the proposal at that time appears to have been precipitated by the expansive authority accorded to the judiciary under the Charter of Rights. For Reform Party stalwarts, judicial confirmation hearings would expose an illegitimate and unrepresentative judicial branch that was promoting almost exclusively the interests of powerful minorities such as women and gays and lesbians. For both the Reform and the present-day Conservative Party, a revamped appointment process would have the benefit of performing an educative function of a different kind – one of politicizing judicial functions that often have flown under the radar of Canadian public opinion. The chapter focuses on the first five hearings in which nominees to the Court appeared before a special committee of the House of Commons. With the objective of evaluating the educative function performed by the committee hearings, I undertake both a qualitative and quantitative analysis of media reporting by a cross section of leading Canadian newspapers in both official languages. I conclude that the public learned very little about the judicial process in Canada. Instead, media reports tend to depoliticize judging, preferring to focus on judicial personalities. I suggest that we look elsewhere for reform proposals that better balance the institutional demands for judicial independence and the increasing desire for democratic accountability.

By way of conclusion, I return to the theme of constitutional culture and change. The practices and institutions discussed in prior chapters are desperately in need of reform. Drawing guidance from Edmund Burke, we should envisage constitutional change not merely for its own sake but as advancing a constitutional project worth preserving. That feature of Canadian constitutional culture isolated earlier – a capacity to more easily express the popular will through law – can be associated with a culture of openness. Valuing this culture of openness, however, could have the effect of preserving executive dominance – which facilitates policy nimbleness – and also renders Canada vulnerable to the influence of the United States. Canadians might be so open that we will drift further into American arms.

A few words should be said about a countervailing tendency, also evident during Prime Minister Harper's tenure, of enhancing Canada's British connections. The Queen's portrait was ordered to be displayed prominently in all Canadian embassies and consulates, the Canadian Navy was renamed the Royal Canadian Navy, and attempts were made to revive historical memory at the two hundredth anniversary of the War of 1812, the botched American invasion of what remained of British North America.[81] These efforts surely problematize claims about the Americanization of Canadian constitutional culture. They look to be, however, mostly in the realm of the symbolic. They are not initiatives intended to alter the expectations of Canadian citizens about what their governments can do or cannot do – it is not about institutionalizing a version of limited, divided, presidential-style government. These are not initiatives to alter the substance of constitutional practice. Instead, they divert us from an agenda that tilts Canadian practice further in U.S. directions. They are, in short, distractions.

On the other hand, one could easily marshal other evidence of a drift into American arms. There are indications that Canada is being nudged in the direction of U.S.-style government in the domains of crime control, environmental regulation, and foreign affairs, among other policy fields. More broadly, this shift is consistent with larger trends towards continental integration and further absorption within the U.S. orbit. Indeed, Peter Russell cautions, it "would have been a miracle if Canada had been immune to the global appeal of the American model."[82] What is most worrying is that this shift threatens to do away with the few things that make Canada distinctive, constitutionally speaking, from its much larger and powerful neighbour to the south. Moreover, this is being done with little public discussion. This book is intended to inform and contribute to that critical debate. My hope is that this book revives interest in Canadian constitutionalism at a time of potentially significant transition.

---

81 John Ibbitson, "The Remaking of the Canadian Myth," *Globe and Mail*, 2 May 2012; Jennifer Ditchburn, "Canada's 1812 Overtures," *Globe and Mail*, 13 September 2011. See Ian McKay and Jamie Swift, *Warrior Nation: Rebranding Canada in an Age of Anxiety* (Toronto: Between the Lines, 2012), for the attempt at rebranding Canada as a "warrior nation."

82 Peter H. Russell, *Constitutional Odyssey: Can Canadians Become a Sovereign People?*, 2nd ed. (Toronto: University of Toronto Press, 1993), 11.

1 "No Servile Copy": Constitutional Differences That Matter

In the case of the federal government, the problems are big and easy to recognize ... government is unlimited.

Stephen Harper[1]

In the first edition of his classic treatise on English constitutional law, *The Law of the Constitution*, Albert Venn Dicey declared that, in its distribution of powers between national and sub-national legislatures, the Constitution of the United States was the "exact opposite of the English constitution, the very essence of which is ... the unlimited authority of Parliament." In the case of Canada, it also was "clear," he maintained, "that the Constitution of the Dominion is modelled on that of the Union."[2] It followed that the Canadian Constitution also was the "exact opposite" of the English – it was not about "unlimited authority."

Canadian commentators were enraged by Dicey's characterization of the Canadian model.[3] The Constitution was certainly not modelled on that of the United States in the organization of the executive

---

1 Stephen J. Harper, "One Crucial Flaw in Canadian Government Is the Ineptitude of Federal Cabinets," *Report Newsmagazine*, 28 May 2001, 13.
2 A.V. Dicey, *Introduction to the Study of the Law of the Constitution* (London: Macmillan, 1885), 127, 153; also Goldwin Smith, *Canada and the Canadian Question* (London: Macmillan, 1891), 157.
3 H. Jenkyns, "Remarks on Certain Points in Mr Dicey's 'Law of the Constitution,'" *Law Quarterly Review* 3 (1887): 206–7; John G. Bourinot, *Canadian Studies in Comparative Politics* (Montreal: Dawson Brothers, 1890), 21–7; A.H.F. Lefroy, *The Law of Legislative Power in Canada* (Toronto: Toronto Law Book, 1897–8), lxv–lxvi.

in Parliament, urged his Canadian critics. Dicey acknowledged these criticisms in later editions – the distinction between its British parliamentary and federal features were "just and valuable," he admitted – but stood his ground on the federal features of the regime – "we must inevitably regard it as a copy, though no means a servile copy, of the Constitution of the United States."[4]

This late nineteenth-century comparative constitutional exercise sheds light on distinctive features of Canadian constitutional culture I emphasize here, features not fully captured by the debate between Dicey and his critics. If, as Dicey claimed, the type of federalism adopted in Canada looked very much like that adopted in the United States, then federal legislative authority would have been strictly confined in Canada, power reserved for the provinces or the people, and hemmed in by a Bill of Rights. In Canada, legislative power was premised upon a different idea: that of legislative omnipotence, in federal, and also provincial, fields of authority. The imperial parliament retained authority in some matters, but otherwise, as between the two levels of government, nothing was withheld. The upshot is that, although federalism divides authority, it does not bar policy development. Though it delays legislative change, federalism rarely "frustrates the popular will."[5] Relatedly, if the British parliamentary inheritance unequivocally shaped Canada's constitutional frame, as Canadian critics maintained, it also endowed the executive, both federal and provincial, with ample authority to direct the nation- and province-building project. By contrast, in the United States, executive authority is separated out and hemmed in by the premise that excessive concentration of authority is a dangerous thing.

The aim of this chapter is to highlight distinctive constitutional differences between the U.S. and Canadian regimes at the level of constitutional culture. The object is not to express a preference for one system over the other – even if denigration of the United States has been a

---

4 Dicey, *Introduction to the Study of the Law of the Constitution*, 162. "This is indeed denied," he asserted, "but in my judgment without adequate grounds, by competent Canadian critics" (ibid.). Dicey described as "official mendacity" the act's preamble, declaring that this was a constitution "similar in principle to that of the United Kingdom" (153). In the last revised edition of his text, the Canadian preamble was described as a "diplomatic inaccuracy" (161).

5 Frederick J. Fletcher and Donald C. Wallace, "Federal-Provincial Relations and the Making of Public Policy in Canada: A Review of the Case Studies," in *Division of Powers and Public Policy*, ed. Richard Simeon (Toronto: University of Toronto Press, 1985), 132–3.

defining feature of Canadian identity[6] – but to identify those things that are distinctive and, if valuable, worth preserving. Not all differences will be highlighted. Rather, in order to push forward with the book's argument, I emphasize the origins of its robust authority that also gives rise to a problematic aspect of that distinctiveness, namely, the concentration of power in the office of the prime minister.[7] In doing so, I also inevitably touch upon the perennial "Canadian identity" question: What, if anything, makes Canada distinctive from the United States? Answers range across time, from the rise of a viable left politics in the early twentieth to the recognition of same-sex marriage in the late twentieth century. I answer that question by emphasizing constitutional differences that evolve into "malleable" Canadian institutions of self-government that rarely frustrate the popular will.[8]

The first part of the chapter highlights constitutional text and structure – an exercise of comparison at the level of formal constitutional differences. In the second part, I scour explanations for these constitutional differences. Traditionally, this source of differences has been fought over the terrain of "ideological origins." I suggest that a better explanation can be found in "constitutional origins," an approach I consider analogous to a "historical institutionalist" explanation,[9] which understands institutions and their feedback mechanisms as structuring the range of possibilities that can be pursued by actors and groups to "do things."[10] This is no discussion of culture at the expense of institutions, but a synthesis of both,[11] an exercise I undertake in a lengthy discussion in part 3. What should become apparent is that Canadians

6 Seymour Martin Lipset, *The First New Nation: The United States in Historical and Comparative Perspective* (Garden City, NY: Anchor Books, 1967), 293; Patricia K. Wood, "Defining 'Canadian': Anti-Americanism and Identity in Sir John A. Macdonald's Nationalism," *Journal of Canadian Studies* 36 (2001): 65.

7 Donald J. Savoie, *Governing from the Centre: The Concentration of Power in Canadian Politics* (Toronto: University of Toronto Press, 1999).

8 David E. Smith, *The Republican Option in Canada, Past and Present* (Toronto: University of Toronto Press, 1999), 27.

9 Paul Pierson and Theda Skocpol, "Historical Institutionalism in Contemporary Political Science," in *Political Science: State of the Discipline*, ed. Ira Katznelson and Helen V. Milner, 693–721 (New York: W.W. Norton, 2002).

10 Theda Skocpol, *Protecting Soldiers and Mothers: The Political Origins of Social Policy in the United States* (Cambridge, MA: Harvard University Press, 1992), 47.

11 Janet Ajzenstat, *Discovering Confederation: A Canadian's Story* (Montreal and Kingston: McGill-Queen's University Press, 2014), 32–3.

were able to achieve similar levels of self-government over time, as in the United States, without a revolution, while inheriting the outlines of an institutionally strong and therefore uninhibited state.

1. Text and Structure as a Source of Difference

1867

In order to give content to Canada's distinctive constitutional culture, it is fruitful to look for initial guidance in constitutional text and structure. The framers of the 1867 British North America Act (now called the Constitution Act, 1867) declared they were enacting a new constitution for Canada "similar in principle to that of the United Kingdom." Therefore key features of the British system came to be reflected in Canada's constitution: the British monarch is both head of state and a constituent element of Parliament, which is made up of two houses, an elected lower house and an appointed upper house. One element deviated significantly from that model, as Dicey emphasized: the division of legislative power between national and provincial units based upon lists of "classes of subjects" that are allocated to each level of government. Here, Canadian constitutional design drew upon the U.S. experience, although the framers wanted to avoid pitfalls that had resulted in the recently concluded American civil war.[12] This would be achieved, in part, by creating a federal government that was "relatively stronger" than its U.S. counterpart.[13]

To this end, the federal government was endowed with significant authority to guide the new political and economic union. A single currency, a uniform banking system and customs union,[14] together with federal supervision under a "trade and commerce" power, all ensured adequate authority to steer the national ship of state. A federal power

---

12 Edgar W. McInnis, "Two North American Federations: A Comparison," in *Essays in Canadian History: Presented to George Mackinnon Wrong for His Eightieth Birthday*, ed. R. Flenley, 94–118 (Toronto: Macmillan Canada, 1939); Jennifer Smith, "Canadian Confederation and the Influence of American Federalism," *Canadian Journal of Political Science* 21 (1988): 443–63.

13 William Bennett Munro, *American Influences on Canadian Government* (Toronto: Macmillan, 1929), 23.

14 The customs union (section 121) deprived provinces of the power to erect tariff barriers to the movement of manufactured and agricultural goods.

to reserve and disallow provincial laws, together with a power to declare works or undertakings situated within a province to be to the "general advantage of Canada," gave supervisory breadth and scope to the new national authority. Provincial power would also be robust within its own spheres. It included omnibus authority over "property and civil rights," intended to cover the "private law" domains (typically described as the law of property, torts, and contracts, in the common law provinces outside of Quebec). The area was comprehensively treated in a new Civil Code for Lower Canada, enacted in the year before Confederation, in anticipation of the jurisdictional room the province of Quebec would exercise in these domains.[15] There remained authority for Parliament to make uniform the laws in respect of property and civil rights for the three provinces outside of Quebec. However, this could be achieved only with their consent, which would never be forthcoming. Underscoring this ample authority available to both levels of government, the federal and provincial governments were authorized to incur public debt in order to finance the development of local and national economic infrastructure, a prerequisite for the new economic unit.[16] Almost every one of the powers with which the two levels of government are endowed can be described as enabling rather than disabling. In the words of Alfred Stepan, Canadian federalism is less "demos-constraining" and more "demos-enabling."[17]

The debilitating effects of sectionalism based upon language and religion would be addressed by dividing Canada up into provinces and by recognizing denominational education rights for Protestants in Quebec and for Roman Catholics in Ontario. Factions based upon property – addressing the threat of economic levelling precipitated by "class" politics – would be checked by the Senate, where a significant property qualification ensured that propertied interests could act as a brake on parliamentary excess. "The rights of the minority must be protected," proclaimed John A. Macdonald at the Quebec Conference in support of his Senate proposal, "and the rich are always in fewer number than

15 Thomas McCord, *The Civil Code of Lower Canada Together with a Synopsis of the Changes in the Law Effected by the Civil Code of Lower Canada*, 2nd ed. (Montreal: Dawson, 1870), i–ii.

16 J.G.A. Pocock, *Virtue, Commerce and History* (Cambridge: Cambridge University Press), 68–9.

17 Alfred Stepan, *Arguing Comparative Politics* (Oxford: Oxford University Press, 2001), 331.

the poor."[18] Its checking functions would be tempered, in part, by the fact that senators were appointed and not elected. In addition, the federal power of reservation and disallowance, already mentioned, could function as a check on provincial excesses.[19] One of the pioneers in constitutional scholarship at the University of Toronto, W.P.M. Kennedy, detected parallels between the Canadian constitutional power of disallowance and U.S. constitutional property rights. In the period 1867–93, Kennedy found the power "consistently used during these years to protect those spheres of provincial civic life which are protected explicitly or by implication" in the United States.[20]

Lastly, democratic excess could be stifled by adopting the British model of the "mixed constitution," which struck a harmonious balance between monarchy, aristocracy, and democracy.[21] Each of these distinct interests, the common law chronicler Blackstone observed, "jointly impel the machine of government in a direction different from what either acting by itself, would have done."[22] Governing did not belong to any single constituent element but was "shared or mixed between several elements."[23] This was different from the "separation of powers," another element of the British inheritance. According to the separation of powers model, the executive, legislative, and judicial branches serve separate

---

18 G.P. Browne, ed., *Documents on the Confederation of British North America* (Toronto: McClelland & Stewart, 1969), 98.

19 McInnis, "Two North American Federations," 106.

20 W.P.M. Kennedy, *Essays in Constitutional Law* (London: Oxford University Press, 1934), 49. John Willis similarly described how operation of the common law presumptions of statutory interpretation perform constitution-like functions. These presumptions, such as the requirement, absent clear and plain language, of compensation in the event of an expropriation, acted as an "ideal constitution" for England and Canada. John Willis, "Statute Interpretation in a Nutshell," *Canadian Bar Review* 16 (1938): 21. By the beginning of the twentieth century, however, the federal power largely fell into disuse. See G.V. La Forest, *Disallowance and Reservation of Provincial Legislation* (Ottawa: Department of Justice, 1955).

21 Janet Ajzenstat, "Modern Mixed Government: A Liberal Defence of Inequality," *Canadian Journal of Political Science* 18 (1985): 119–34; Philip Resnick, *The Masks of Proteus: Canadian Reflections on the State* (Montreal and Kingston: McGill-Queen's University Press, 1990), 71–87.

22 William Blackstone, *Commentaries on the Laws of England* (1765; Chicago: University of Chicago Press, 1979), 1:151; also Lord Henry Brougham, *Political Philosophy*. Part 3, *Of Democracy, Mixed Monarchy* (London: Charles Knight, 1844), 302.

23 Martin Diamond, *As Far as Republican Principles Will Admit*, ed. William A. Schambra (Washington: AEI, 1992), 60.

and distinct functions.[24] Though I will have more to say about this in subsequent chapters, it suffices to emphasize here that the separation of powers between executive and legislative branches in parliamentary systems is only "partial," in contrast to the more comprehensive separation between president and Congress in the United States[25]

Canadian constitutional design suggests a pattern intended to endow both levels of government with ample power to both facilitate and instigate economic activity and integration.[26] This was a constitutional design intended to enhance the "facilitative state":[27] public power with sufficient legal authority to generate conditions for the growth of private economic power upon which the success of the new Canadian state would depend.[28] There was little that could stand in the way of legislative authority other than the enumerated limitations divided between the two orders of government, limits that would be jealously guarded and preserved by the provinces.[29] The framers, wrote A.H.F. Lefroy, one of Canada's early constitutional treatise writers, "recognized no reserve power either in the people of the Dominion at large, or in the people of the provinces in particular." "There is, then, no possible kind of legislation relating to the internal affairs of Canada," Lefroy observed, "which cannot be enacted either by the Dominion parliament or by the provincial legislatures."[30] This was a direct inheritance from the British parliamentary tradition. As Dicey memorably put it, Parliament had "the right make or unmake any law whatever."[31] British parliamentary supremacy was "the very keystone of the law of the constitution," wrote

---

24 Baron de Montesquieu, *The Spirit of the Laws*, trans. Thomas Nugent (New York: Hafner, 1949), 151–2.

25 M.J.C. Vile, *Constitutionalism and the Separation of Powers*, 2nd ed. (Indianapolis: Liberty Fund, 1998), 81.

26 Peter J. Smith, "The Ideological Origins of Canadian Confederation," *Canadian Journal of Political Science* 20 (1987): 25.

27 David Sugarman and G.R. Rubin, "Towards a New History of Law and Material Society in England, 1750–1914," in *Law, Economy and Society, 1750–1914: Essays in the History of English Law*, ed. G.R. Rubin and David Sugarman (Oxford: Professional Books, 1984), 10–11.

28 James Willard Hurst, *Law and the Conditions of Freedom in Nineteenth-Century United States* (Madison: University of Wisconsin Press, 1956).

29 Robert C. Vipond, *Liberty and Community: Canadian Federalism and the Failure of the Constitution* (Albany, NY: State University of New York Press, 1991), 135.

30 A.H.F. Lefroy, *Canada's Federal System Being a Treatise on Canadian Constitutional Law under the British North America Act* (Toronto: Carswell, 1913), 266, 96.

31 Dicey, *Introduction to the Study of the Law*, 38, 68.

Dicey, though its powers were practically limited by what he called the "rule of law," namely, the policing of legislative power by courts.

The idea of parliamentary supremacy itself is an inheritance of the "excessive power" originally enjoyed by the British Crown.[32] This was a "treasury of omnipotence" equivalent to the sum of "elasticity" and "undefined possibilities" available to the Crown under the royal prerogative.[33] Prerogative authority – the undefined and unconstrained discretion held in reserve by the monarch – was wrested by degrees from the Crown by Parliament. Over time it conferred extraordinary power on Parliament, the prime minister, and his Cabinet.[34] Having inherited a semblance of this omnipotence, the British legal historian James Bryce described the Canadian system as "more democratic than that in the U.S."[35] Some Canadians boasted, reported journalist Goldwin Smith, that their system was "more democratic" and "less monarchical and even autocratic" than the American one.[36] Were there any revolutionary impulse, Bryce wrote, "desiring to carry sweeping changes by a sudden stroke, these could be carried swiftly by Parliamentary legislation."[37] This is an exaggeration, of course (as is Stephen Harper's quote that appears as an epigraph to this chapter). Nevertheless, the sentiment captures an important feature of Canadian constitutional design. Though limits to legislative action are built into the system at both levels of government, the overall pattern is one of muscular law-making authority, what might be called one of "energetic federalism."[38] Although disciplined by a division of powers, legislative energy was largely unbounded.

It could be said that the Canadian Charter of Rights and Freedoms entirely upsets this scheme. The entrenchment of a bill of rights in 1982,

32 J.L. De Lolme, *The Constitution of England or, An Account of the English Government: In Which It Is Compared Both with the Republican Form of Government and the Other Monarchies of Europe*, new ed. by John McGregor (London: Henry G. Bohn, 1853), 20–1.

33 John Neville Figgis, *The Divine Right of Kings*, 2nd ed. (Cambridge: Cambridge University Press, 1922), 237; Charles Howard McIlwain, *The High Court of Parliament and Its Supremacy: A Historical Essay on the Boundaries between Legislation and Adjudication in England* (1910; Hamden: Anchor Books, 1962), 53–1.

34 Dicey, *Introduction to the Study of the Law*, 460–1.

35 James Bryce, *Canada: An Actual Democracy* (Toronto: Macmillan Canada, 1921), 41, originally a chapter in James Bryce, *Modern Democracies* (London: Macmillan, 1921), 1:455–508.

36 Smith, *Canada and the Canadian Question*, 161.

37 Bryce, *Canada: An Actual Democracy*, 41.

38 David Schneiderman, "Constitutional Interpretation in an Age of Anxiety: A Reconsideration of the Local Prohibition Case," *McGill Law Journal* 41 (1996): 414.

Seymour Martin Lipset claims, is the "most important step that Canada has taken to Americanize itself."[39] Insofar as the Charter entrenches constitutional limits on both federal and provincial governments, even at times incorporating language of U.S. Supreme Court decision-making, Canada will have moved far in in the direction of U.S.-style constitutional limitations. There are important textual distinctions between the rights documents, however. They concern the absence of express economic rights, including property rights, from Canada's Charter. Admittedly, however, business firms have been able to avail themselves of some constitutional rights indirectly, with some success, so as to undermine state regulation of business.[40] The Charter's notwithstanding clause (section 33) also gives voice to Canada's statist tradition by enabling governments to override many rights and freedoms for five-year renewable periods,[41] preserving a semblance of "omnipotence" that has raised cause for concern.[42] On occasion, judicial interpretation also has been attentive to the capacity of the Charter to act as a bulwark for limiting legitimate state regulation. In Edwards Books, Chief Justice Dickson famously declared that in applying the Charter, "courts must be cautious to ensure that it does not simply become an instrument of better situated individuals to roll back legislation which has as its object the improvement of the condition of less advantaged individuals."[43] Sometimes the Supreme Court has advanced libertarian conceptions of constitutional rights, too.[44] For this reason, the legacy

39 Seymour Martin Lipset, *Continental Divide: The Values and Institutions of the United States and Canada* (New York: Routledge, 1990), 235.
40 Richard W. Bauman, "Business, Economic Rights, and the Charter," in *Charting the Consequences: The Impact of Charter Rights on Canadian Law and Politics*, ed. David Schneiderman and Kate Sutherland, 58–108 (Toronto: University of Toronto Press, 1997).
41 Peter Lougheed, "Why a Notwithstanding Clause?," *Points of View / Points de vue* 6 (Centre for Constitutional Studies, 1998); Peter H. Russell, "Standing Up for Notwithstanding," *Alberta Law Review* 29 (1991): 293–309.
42 John D. Whyte, "On Not Standing for Notwithstanding," *Alberta Law Review* 28 (1990): 348–57.
43 *Edwards Books and Art Ltd v R* [1986] 2 SCR 713, para 141.
44 *Chaoulli v Quebec* [2005] 1 SCR 791. The Charter has the potential, of course, to disable both levels of government in a wide range of policy areas. Supreme Court decision-making, but for a handful of cases (e.g., Chaoulli), has cautiously declared itself uninterested in second-guessing legislative policy choices, particularly where government is protecting vulnerable groups, mediating between the claims of competing groups, allocating scarce resources, or interpreting complex scientific evidence. See *Irwin Toy Ltd v Quebec (AG)* [1989] 1 SCR 927.

of the Charter is not ambivalent as regards state capacity – it will have significantly retarded it. The same could be said about the impact of the North American Free Trade Agreement (NAFTA) investment chapter (chapter 11), which makes available to foreign investors U.S.-style constitutional property rights that can be claimed against Canada before international investment tribunals. The adoption of a constitution-like property rights regime for foreign investors drives Canada further in the direction of embracing U.S.-style constitutional limits.[45]

1787

One could also tell a "demos-enabling" story about U.S. constitutionalism.[46] The generation that framed the 1787 Constitution proposed replacing the Articles of Confederation, which had governed the independent colonies after the revolution, with a new and more powerful national government. They could not have been obsessed solely with limiting government; rather, there was a powerful current of centralization underlying their plan.[47] The Articles were premised on a distrust of centralized authority, so states were allocated the preponderance of legislative authority, including an exclusive capacity to levy taxes and to regulate trade.[48] The 1787 Constitution, by contrast, was intended to enable a new "energetic" federal government.[49] If this is a story not

---

45 David Schneiderman, "Property Rights, Investor Rights, and Regulatory Innovation: Comparing Constitutional Cultures in Transition," *International Journal of Constitutional Law* 4 (2006): 371–91.

46 Stephen L. Elkin, *Reconstructing the Commercial Republic: Constitutional Design after Madison* (Chicago: Chicago University Press, 2006), chap. 2; Brian Balogh, *A Government Out of Sight: The Mystery of National Authority in Nineteenth-Century America* (Cambridge: Cambridge University Press, 2009); Samuel H. Beer, *To Make a Nation: The Rediscovery of American Federalism* (Cambridge, MA: Harvard University Press, 1993), 386.

47 Beer, *To Make a Nation*, 380; Max M. Edling, *A Revolution in Favor of Government: Origins of the U.S. Constitution and the Making of the American State* (New York: Oxford University Press, 2008). Elkin admits that "Madison was not always as clear as he might have been about the central importance of active government to liberty," in *Reconstructing the Commercial Republic*, 47.

48 Merrill Jenson, *Articles of Confederation: An Interpretation of the Social-Constitutional History of the American Revolution, 1774–1781* (Madison: University of Wisconsin Press, 1963).

49 Pauline Maier, *Ratification: The People Debate the Constitution, 1788–1787* (New York: Simon and Shuster, 2010).

unlike the Canadian one, the difference is the presence of a competing narrative of binding constraints that was available throughout and has been dominant during long stretches of U.S. constitutional history.[50] According to this "constitution-as-constraining" narrative, the U.S. design is said to facilitate mostly limited government by virtue of its checking mechanisms of federalism, the separation of powers, and a Bill of Rights.[51] From this angle, the design's presuppositions are best explained by its principal theoretician, James Madison, who provided an exposition of its founding principles in the *Federalist Papers*, a collection of newspaper articles by Madison, Alexander Hamilton, and John Jay, published with the objective of convincing New York state voters to ratify the 1787 Constitution.[52] The *Federalist Papers* may have had little influence in the subsequent ratification of the 1787 Constitution,[53] but the collection of essays has the merit of providing us with the best publicly available reasons for New Yorkers to approve of the scheme.

The "various and unequal distribution of property," observed Madison in the "Federalist No. 10," is "the most common and durable source of factions."[54] Factionalism had riven the United States during the period of the Articles of Confederation (1776–87) as states enacted laws to protect local debtors from out-of state-creditors. It is these "vices" that prompted a sequence of meetings, leading ultimately to the constitutional convention in Philadelphia, and the offer of a new republican form of government. Factionalism could not be cured, observed Madison, but only checked, by an ingenious constitutional design.[55]

---

50 Harry N. Scheiber, "Private Rights and Public Power: American Law, Capitalism, and the Republican Polity in Nineteenth-Century America," *Yale Law Journal* 107 (1997): 840.

51 Cass R. Sunstein, *The Partial Constitution* (Cambridge, MA: Harvard University Press, 1993), 23.

52 Madison did not get his way in many respects, however, as revealed by the rejection of many aspects of his "Virgina Plan," the main focus of discussion at the Constitutional Convention. See the discussion in Gordon S. Wood, *Revolutionary Characters: What Made the Founders Different* (New York: Penguin Press, 2006), 157ff; and F.H. Buckley, *The Once and Future King: The Rise of Crown Government in America* (New York: Encounter Books, 2014), chap. 2.

53 Maier, *Ratification*, 84.

54 Alexander Hamilton, James Madison, and John Jay, *The Federalist Papers*, ed. Clinton Rossiter (New York: New American Library, 1961), 79.

55 James Madison, *Writings*, ed. Jack N. Rakove (New York: Library of America, 1999), 69–80.

Sovereignty would lie not in the hands of a "favoured class" or a "handful of tyrannical nobles," but in the "great body of the people." Federalism, following the logic of this account, would break society up "into so many parts," making unlikely any combination of interests that was dangerous to the "minority."[56] Central governmental authority would be limited by a short list of enumerated subjects with "residual and inviolable sovereignty" reserved, by implication, to the states and to the people (this reservation would come to be acknowledged in the Tenth Amendment). States too would be denied authority in a "remarkable number" of key areas, including in the printing of paper money, enacting debtor-relief laws or laws impairing the obligation of contracts.[57] This would result in a central authority that was neither "national" nor "federal" (as in a confederation of states), but "mixed" – a "composition of both," declared Madison.[58] This was not to be a mixed or balanced constitution of the British constitutional sort, however. Though there was much admiration expressed by the revolutionaries for the mixed constitution,[59] Congress's upper chamber would represent the states and not a fledgling aristocracy.[60]

The separation of powers between the executive, legislative, and judicial branches would ensure that each "department" jealously guarded its jurisdiction and so would "resist encroachments" from rival branches: "Ambition must be made to counteract ambition," observed Madison. The methods and timing of elections would vary across the legislative and executive branches. Senators would hold their seats for terms of six years, representatives would have a tenure of two years, and presidents, four years. Moreover, the president would not be directly elected by the people but by "a small number of persons" appointed by states – an electoral college – "most likely to possess the information and

---

56 Hamilton, Madison, and Jay, *Federalist Papers*, 241, 324. The idea of popular sovereignty is an innovation Pauline Maier attributes to James Wilson at the Pennsylvania ratifying convention (in *Ratification*, 109–10).

57 Gordon S. Wood, *Empire of Liberty: A History of the Early Republic, 1789–1815* (New York: Oxford University Press, 2009), 33.

58 Hamilton, Madison, and Jay, *Federalist Papers*, 244–6.

59 Lance Banning, "Republican Ideology and the Triumph of the Constitution, 1789 to 1793," *William and Mary Quarterly* 31 (1974): 167–88; Elaine K. Swift, *The Making of the American Senate: Reconstitutive Change in Congress, 1787–1841* (Ann Arbor: University of Michigan Press, 1996), 20.

60 Gordon S. Wood, *The Creation of the American Republic, 1776–87* (Chapel Hill: University of North Carolina Press, 1969), 203, 557.

discernment requisite to such complicated investigations."[61] The genius of Madison's design of republican government, Nedelsky argues, was its reliance on institutional mechanisms to facilitate rule by a "competent elite." These mechanisms would ensure that interests would mutually check each other, but this alone would not yield decision making in the public interest. Rather, it would enable "those who have the requisite abilities to undertake the difficult task of discerning it – without having to suppress their self-interest at the same time."[62]

Madison was ambivalent about attaching a bill of rights to the 1787 Constitution for fear that it would imply federal authority where none had been granted.[63] He came around to support the effort, as various states insisted that a bill of rights be attached to the new constitution as a prerequisite to ratification[64] and after running a hard-fought campaign for a seat in the House of Representatives, during which he publicly pledged to support it.[65] Though it is doubtful Madison intended the judicial branch to bind other departments on questions of constitutional consistency, he believed a bill of rights would be useful to the extent it performed an educative function.[66] If such "fundamental maxims" became absorbed within the "national sentiment," to "counteract the impulses of interest and passion," Madison observed, rights would check intemperate political behaviour.[67]

To be sure, there are elements in U.S. constitutional design that the Canadians were happy to borrow. There is an elite upper chamber protecting propertied interests, for instance, and a list of enumerations endowing the federal government with sufficient "energy" upon which the Canadians would model their federal enumerations.[68] Indeed, it has been said that the Canadian scheme so far carried Hamilton's ideas

61 Hamilton, Madison, and Jay, *Federalist Papers*, 322, 412.
62 Jennifer Nedelsky, *Private Property and the Limits of American Constitutionalism: The Madisonian Framework and Its Legacy* (Chicago: University of Chicago Press, 1990), 176.
63 Madison, "Vices of the Political System of the United States," 420.
64 Richard K. Matthews, *If Men Were Angels: James Madison and the Heartless Empire of Reason* (Lawrence: University Press of Kansas, 1995), 128.
65 Wood, *Empire of Liberty*, 68.
66 James Madison, "To Edmund Pendleton," 21 June 1789, in *Madison*, 465–7, 464; Jack N. Rakove, *Original Meanings: Politics and Ideas in the Making of the Constitution* (New York: Vintage Books, 1996), 336.
67 James Madison, "To Thomas Jefferson," 17 October 1788, in *Madison*, 422.
68 Munro, *American Influences on Canadian Government*, 18.

into effect that he would have been envious.[69] Americans borrowed as well: the presidential veto has been likened to the royal prerogative in Great Britain, which was rendered obsolete by a politically accountable executive in the British Parliament.[70] As for limits on the federal government, political practice and judicial interpretation would expand national federal authority beyond its original bounds, making the U.S. system look more like the Canadians' handiwork. The strict cabining of government, however, which lies at the core of the U.S. constitutional project, appears foreign to the Canadian frame.

That the U.S. project simultaneously established and then limited government helps to explain the continuing appeal to the intentions of the framers in U.S. political and legal discourse (in recent times, rather successfully, by the Tea Party), an appeal that falls flat in Canadian circles. By contrast, Canadians saw little need to be overly anxious about excessive legislative activity, which is not to say that the Canadian framers trusted democracy.[71] Rather, they exhibited the "superb confidence of the Victorian middle class" in crafting their constitutional design.[72] The English constitutional lawyer Dicey expressed this confidence well. There was little reason to worry about the expansion of the franchise, as "the formal possession of political power" would not make the "poor the rulers of the nation." "Property, somehow or other," Dicey observed, "asserts its weight everywhere."[73] Political power inherently would be trustworthy as it was to be held exclusively by the class best suited to wield it.

---

69 Edgar W. McInnis, *The Unguarded Frontier: A History of American-Canadian Relations* (Garden City, NY: Doubleday, Doran, 1942), 254; Smith, "Ideological Origins of Canadian Confederation," 28.

70 Herbert Arthur Smith, *Federalism in North America: A Comparative Study of Institutions in the United States and Canada* (Boston: Chipman Law, 1923), 32; and Eric Nelson, *The Royalist Revolution: Monarchy and the American Founding* (Cambridge, MA: Harvard University Press, 2014), chap. 5.

71 McInnis, "Two North American Federations," 95; Robert Craig Brown, "Canadian Opinion after Confederation, 1867–1914," in *Canada Views the United States: Nineteenth-Century Political Attitudes*, ed. S.F. Wise and Robert Craig Brown, 98–120 (Toronto: Macmillan Canada, 1967).

72 Edward P. Thompson, *The Poverty of Theory and Other Essays* (London: Merlin, 1978), 264.

73 A.V. Dicey, "Why Englishmen Are Not Alarmed at the Political Crisis," *Nation*, 22 October 1885, 341; Bernard Manin, *The Principles of Representative Government* (Cambridge: Cambridge University Press, 1997). For a less than optimistic account in this same period, see Walter Bagehot's 1872 introduction to the second edition of *The English Constitution* in *The Collected Works of Walter Bagehot*, ed. Norman St John-Stevas (London: Economist, 1974), 5:165–202.

Property Rights

An instructive way to contrast the design of the two systems is to focus on property rights. This is considered to represent a "primary legal difference" between Canada and the United States,[74] yet is a critical element of every liberal legal order.[75] For the most part, property rights are absent from Canadian constitutional design. Though, as mentioned, the Canadian Senate was intended to protect such interests, and though the federal power of reservation and disallowance initially served as a proxy for constitutional property rights, legislative energy in this field has been largely unbounded. As A.H.F. Lefroy put it in his first constitutional law text, once a law is passed by the appropriate level of government, "it is not competent for any Court to pronounce the Act invalid because it may affect injuriously private rights."[76] Canadian constitutional design was not so much limited as empowered to secure existing entitlements, liberate economic enterprise, and generate new wealth. Rather than removing the state from certain levers of economic power, the state would be expected to have its hands on those levers. This design not only facilitated economic productivity through state enterprise but also sanctioned legislative incursions into the realm of property rights as a motor for economic development. This power was felt particularly by First Nations when the federal government insisted upon the compulsory dispossession of their lands in pre- and post-Confederation Canada, prior to the entrenchment of Aboriginal rights in 1982.[77]

This does not mean that every legislative incursion into the realm of property is tolerated. Common law presumptions require judges to construe such incursions strictly and to insist upon compensation unless a statute expressly forbids it. These presumptions are reflected in statutory regimes at both national and sub-national levels that require compensation in cases of physical takings. So in instances where real property is expropriated, compensation usually is required to be paid, though not

---

74 John Brigham, *Property and the Politics of Entitlement* (Philadelphia: Temple University Press, 1990), 136; Kason Kaufman, *The Origins of Canadian and American Political Differences* (Cambridge, MA: Harvard University Press, 2009), 16.

75 Ian McKay, "The Liberal Order Framework: A Prospectus for a Reconnaissance of Canadian History," *Canadian Historical Review* 81 (2000): 627.

76 Lefroy, *Law of Legislative Power in Canada*, 279.

77 The definitive work on this subject is Darlene Johnston, *The Taking of Indian Lands in Canada: Consent or Coercion?* (Saskatoon: University of Saskatchewan Native Law Centre, 1989).

constitutionally so.[78] The presumption also can be expressly displaced, so that what might look like a compensable taking at common law can be deemed not to be a taking requiring compensation.[79] Canadian courts, then, are highly deferential to legislative incursions into the realm of property rights. Denying a permit, for instance, to build a single-family dwelling on environmentally sensitive beachfront property does not give rise to an obligation to pay compensation under the Nova Scotia law. "In this country, extensive and restrictive land use regulation is the norm. Such regulation has, almost without exception, been found not to constitute compensable expropriation," observed Justice Thomas Cromwell. Only in cases where a regulation results in a denial of all reasonable use of real property will compensation be expected to be paid, and only if a claimant meets the "exacting" standards of the provincial statute.[80]

By contrast, constitutional culture in the United States is portrayed as organized around solicitude towards private property rights.[81] The federalist project in 1787 "safeguarded all in a homogeneous commercial environment of secure property and free exchange."[82] Property rights were incorporated into the Fifth Amendment to the U.S. Constitution (the "takings" clause) for the purpose of limiting the federal government. After the civil war, states no longer were trustworthy sites of authority and so property rights limitations were extended to them via the Fourteenth Amendment. State constitutions also adopted similar language,[83] making the discourse of "vested rights" a significant feature of U.S. constitutional culture.

Despite the framers' avowed commitment to private property and natural liberty, they were not, insists Bruce Ackerman, "blind worshippers" of the free market.[84] Americans got into the "governmental

---

78 Bruce Ziff, "'Taking' Liberties: Protections for Private Property in Canada," in *Modern Studies in Property Law*, ed. Elizabeth Cooke (Oxford: Hart, 2005), 3:347.

79 *Canadian Pacific Railway Co v Vancouver (City)* [2006] 1 SCR 227, para 37.

80 *Mariner Real Estate Ltd v Nova Scotia (AG)* (1999) 68 LCR 1, 18, 22 (NSCA); also *Canadian Pacific Railway v Vancouver*, para 30.

81 Nedelsky, *Private Property*; Laura S. Underkuffler, *The Idea of Property: Its Meaning and Power* (Oxford: Oxford University Press, 2003).

82 Carol M. Rose, *Property and Persuasion: Essays on the History, Theory, and Rhetoric of Ownership* (Boulder, CO: Westview, 1994), 81.

83 Thomas M. Cooley, *A Treatise on the Constitutional Limitations Which Rest upon the Legislative Power of the States of the American Union* (Boston: Little, Brown, 1883), 431.

84 Bruce A. Ackerman, *Private Property and the Constitution* (New Haven, CT: Yale University Press, 1977), 7.

habit" early on.[85] Hence, there have arisen competing interpretations of property rights, favourable to markets and governments alike.[86] These competing conceptions have allowed government intervention in markets, which conceptualizes property as mutable, and, on the other hand, have heightened property protections, treating them as distrustful interferences with market processes. Hence, in the mid-nineteenth century (the "commonwealth" period), legislators and courts tolerated all variety of intrusions into private property so as to promote economic improvement and development. State governments made "strong, positive use of law to maintain such conditions as [they] thought essential" in order to render private property productive. Lacking sources of new capital, legal regulation helped to facilitate economic development by promoting the "allocation of capital to transport, the development of commercial agriculture and to the encouragement of industry." It is only in the late nineteenth century that what Novak calls a "cult of constitutionalism" took hold, which enthusiastically policed the lines between public power and private right.[87] In a case analogous to the Nova Scotia one – barring development on sensitive beachfront property – Justice Antonin Scalia could draw on the property rights tradition and find that the state prohibition was "inconsistent with the historical compact recorded in the Takings Clause that has become part of our constitutional culture."[88] Compensation would be due to the owner.

No such claim could plausibly be made in the Canadian constitutional context. Gregory Alexander, in a book-length comparison of

---

85 Jonathan R.T. Hughes, *The Governmental Habit: Economic Controls from Colonial Times to the Present* (New York: Basic Books, 1977).

86 Underkuffler, *Idea of Property*; Gregory S. Alexander, *Commodity and Propriety: Competing Visions of Property in American Legal Thought* (Chicago: University of Chicago Press, 1997). This is the side of the American property rights regime that Christopher Manfredi and Mark Rush emphasize, relying upon Justice Breyer's account of "active liberty" at the expense of the continuing discursive power of the vested rights tradition that is more solicitous of property, in *Judging Democracy* (Peterborough, ON: Broadview, 2008), 24–8. As Underkuffler emphasizes, both are operative in U.S. constitutional culture. On the regulatory side of the equation, see Stephen Breyer, *Active Liberty: Interpreting Our Democratic Constitution* (New York: Alfred A. Knopf, 2005).

87 William J. Novak, *The People's Welfare: Law and Regulation in Nineteenth-Century America* (Chapel Hill: University of North Carolina Press, 1996), 846; Hurst, *Law and the Conditions of Freedom*, 26, 53; also Oscar Handlin and Mary Flug Handlin, *Commonwealth: A Study of the Role of Government in the American Economy: Massachusetts, 1774–1861*, rev. ed. (Cambridge, MA: Harvard University Press, 1969); and Leonard W. Levy, *The Law of the Commonwealth and Chief Justice Shaw* (Cambridge, MA: Harvard University Press, 1957), 306.

88 *Lucas v South Carolina Coastal Council*, 505 US 1003, 1025 (1992).

constitutional property systems, nevertheless concludes that Canadian law regarding the protection of property is "substantially on par with that in the United States." There are similarities in the practical working out of property problems in the two jurisdictions, Alexander rightly claims. Canadians, like Americans, mostly express solicitude towards property rights. Yet, outside of Aboriginal property rights, property in Canada has not risen to the order of constitutional right. In overstating the degree of similarity, Alexander relies on a "Canadian academic" who writes that "constitutional and quasi-constitutional" protections in Canada are in some instances "equal [to and] ... even surpass ... the American [U.S.] regime."[89] Bruce Ziff speaks here of NAFTA's protections for foreign investors that resemble U.S.-style constitutional property rights. Ziff's discussion underscores the point that, with the adoption of property rights for foreign investors under NAFTA, there has been movement in the direction of embracing U.S. constitutional limits on property rights.[90] There are, then, "fundamental" differences[91] between the two property regimes that have implications, as I argue below, beyond the law of property itself.

2. Ideological Origins as a Source of Difference

Tory Touch

What is it about the U.S. and Canadian constitutional systems that marks them as so similar yet different? Invariably, the answer to such a question lies in interpretation of the past.[92] Much research has focused upon "ideological origins," that is, whether Canada at its origins was committed ideologically to a political order different from that emanating out of the United States. The debate has generated fault lines over whether differences between the two systems ever existed or persist.[93] The dominant frame was provided by Louis Hartz's "fragment" theory. Hartz claimed that European settlers in British North America brought

---

89 Gregory S. Alexander, *The Global Debate over Constitutional Property: Lessons for American Takings Jurisprudence* (Chicago: Chicago University Press, 2006), 42, quoting Ziff, "'Taking' Liberties," 341.

90 Schneiderman, "Property Rights, Investor Rights, and Regulatory Innovation."

91 Alexander, *Global Debate over Constitutional Property*, 42.

92 Lipset, *Continental Divide*, 16.

93 Of course there are other sources of differences between the two states – geography, economic wealth, party system, etc. – which are not the subject of discussion here.

with them only a fragment – an unrepresentative sample – of the ideo-logical spectrum available in the home country.[94] These mostly were "liberal" bourgeois fragments, Hartz maintained, uncompromised by competing "feudal" forces, the exception being Quebec, where feudal fragments prevailed. As a consequence, Lockean liberalism mostly took root in North America.[95] The process described by Hartz is deceptively simple: "A part detaches itself from the whole, the whole fails to renew itself, and the part develops without inhibition."[96]

How does this explain differences between the two political cul-tures, in particular, the presence of a viable social democratic politics in Canada? The oft-cited explanation, developed by Hartz's student Gad Horowitz, has been that the presence of a "Tory touch" gave rise to a political culture different from that in the United States.[97] According to the Tory touch thesis, a collectivist orientation emerged from Canada's conservative political origins traceable back to the arrival of numbers of loyalists escaping from the American Revolution. This "fragment" of toryism nurtured both a right-wing and later a left-wing politics.

The tory touch thesis encounters many bumps along the road. First, it generalizes Canadian political culture from a single case – its gen-esis is the ideological preference of emigrants to Upper Canada – while failing to explain ideological diversity at provincial and regional lev-els. Instead, there might be multiple ideological influences, including an Aboriginal one, intermingling with European founding cultures.[98] It also presumes a single homogeneous political culture in the United States that is single-mindedly opposed to the use of state power. As

---

94 Gad Horowitz, *Canadian Labour in Politics* (Toronto: University of Toronto Press, 1968), 4.

95 Louis Hartz, *The Liberal Tradition in America: An Interpretation of American Political Thought since the Revolution* (San Diego: Harcourt Brace Javanovich, 1955), 20–1. Hartz is not too precise about what he means by Lockean liberalism. He associates this with liberal individualism (in ibid., 12) and looks not unlike the dismal picture offered by C.B. Macpherson in *Political Theory of Possessive Individualism: Hobbes to Locke* (London: Oxford University Press, 1962).

96 Louis Hartz, *The Founding of New Societies: Studies in the History of the United States, Latin America, South Africa, Canada, and Australia* (New York: Harcourt, Brace & World, 1964), 9.

97 Gad Horowitz, "Conservatism, Liberalism, and Socialism in Canada: An Interpreta-tion," *Canadian Journal of Economics and Political Science* 32 (1966): 143–71.

98 Nelson Wiseman, *In Search of Canadian Political Culture* (Vancouver: UBC Press, 2007), 24; Gérard Bouchard, *Genèse des nations et cultures du Nouveau Monde* (Montreal: Boréal, 2001).

mentioned, in the mid- to late nineteenth-century United States, national and state governments made use of lawful authority to facilitate economic development in an era of capital scarcity. Lastly, there is the empirical question of whether loyalists escaping the revolution really carried with them the political values of organic collectivism.[99] S.F. Wise argues, for instance, that loyalists escaping to Canada from the American Revolution were "conservatives" in the name of liberal individualism and not in the name of collectivism.[100] Similarly, Janice Potter describes loyalist thought as "remarkably modern" and politically pluralist.[101] Hartz's student Kenneth McRae similarly contends that there is a "wealth of empirical evidence" to sustain the proposition the loyalists did not represent a "Tory aristocracy or privileged class," as "the American experience was basically a liberal one."[102]

An examination of this past leads others to deny there is any significant difference between the two countries. For Janet Ajzenstat the Canadian Constitution is not so unlike the U.S. one – it is no "second-rate thing" but "an excellent example of an Enlightenment constitution." The entrenchment of parliamentary democracy in 1867 secured the classical liberal political virtues of "equality, non-discrimination, the rule of law, and the mores of representative government."[103] It would be a distortion of their handicraft to attribute anything more to the founders' constitution than a desire to entrench Lockean liberal values. It would not have been their intention, for instance, to entrench a Tory collectivist identity that could then be hijacked by a left-socialist

---

99 H.D. Forbes, "Hartz-Horowitz at Twenty: Nationalism, Toryism and Socialism in Canada and the United States," *Canadian Journal of Political Science* 20 (1987): 287.

100 S.F. Wise, *God's Peculiar Peoples: Essays on Political Culture in Nineteenth-Century Canada* (Ottawa: Carleton University Press, 1993), 199–212.

101 Janice Potter, *The Liberty We Seek: Loyalist Ideology in Colonial New York and Massachusetts* (Cambridge, MA: Harvard University Press, 1983), 60; Peter J. Smith, "Civic Humanism versus Liberalism: Fitting the Loyalists In," in *Canada's Origins: Liberal, Tory, or Republican?*, ed. Janet Ajzenstat and Peter J. Smith (Ottawa: Carleton University Press, 1995), 127. Potter claims that Loyalists were attuned to the problems of self-interest and political faction, which were "inevitable and unalterable" and so looked to institutions of government to check factionalism's effects (Potter, *Liberty We Seek*, 49, 55). This mirrors Madison's thinking about factions in *Federalist*, 10.

102 Kenneth D. McRae, "The Structure of Canadian History," in Hartz, *Founding of New Societies*, 235.

103 Janet Ajzenstat, *The Canadian Founding: John Locke and Parliament* (Montreal & Kingston: McGill-Queen's University Press, 2007), 47, 8.

political agenda. There never was "a significant Tory influence," she maintains with co-author Peter J. Smith, in which case we should find nothing distinctive in Canada's constitutional design. This has the advantage of freeing up the possibility that U.S. and Canadian political cultures are "similar" in that they are "both heir to the liberal constitutionalism that originated with John Locke."[104] If George Grant bemoaned that symmetry, Ajzenstat celebrates it. This account, however, does little work to explain the significant constitutional differences that persist.

Civic Humanism

Others have preferred to emphasize another sort of similarity with U.S. origins. This work focuses upon a "civic humanist" discourse – with an emphasis on independent and virtuous political leadership uncorrupted by the machinations of aristocratic "court" government[105] – that was prominent in the American revolutionary era.[106] This political orientation migrated north, making its presence felt in nineteenth-century Canadian debates in Upper and Lower Canada.[107] The evidence here is equivocal. Kelley claims that, at the time of the American Revolution, the majority of the *habitants* of what would later become Lower Canada were in agreement with republicanist claims about abuses perpetrated

---

104 Peter J. Smith and Janet Ajzenstat, "Canada's Political Culture Today: Liberal, Republican, or Third Wave?," in *Canada's Origins: Liberal, Tory, or Republican?*, ed. Janet Ajzenstat and Peter J. Smith (Ottawa: Carleton University Press, 1995), 266, 265.
105 J.G.A. Pocock, *The Machiavellian Moment: Florentine Political Thought and the Atlantic Republican Tradition* (Princeton, NJ: Princeton University Press, 1975), 407.
106 Wood, *Creation of the American Republic, 1776–87*. Republicanism has had a "wildfire popularity" among historians of the early American republic; see Joyce Appleby, *Liberalism and Republicanism in the Historical Imagination* (Cambridge, MA: Harvard University Press, 1992), 279. On the republican revival in historiography, see Daniel T. Rodgers, "Republicanism: The Career of a Concept," *Journal of American History* 79 (1992): 11–38.
107 Smith, "Ideological Origins of Canadian Confederation"; Louis-George Harvey, "The First Distinct Society: French Canada, America and the Constitution of 1791," in *Canadian Constitutionalism 1791–1991*, ed. Janet Azjenstat, 123–47 (Ottawa: Canadian Study of Parliament Group, 1992); Louis-George Harvey, *Le printemps de l'Amérique française: americainité, anitcolonialisme et républicainsime dans les discours politique québécois, 1805–1837* (Montreal: Boréal, 2005); Michel Ducharme, *The Idea of Liberty in Canada during the Age of Atlantic Revolutions, 1776–1838*, trans. Peter Feldstein (Montreal and Kingston: McGill-Queen's University Press, 2014).

by British authorities.[108] By the time of the Lower Canadian rebellion, an American-style republicanism was predominant among the *patriotes*, as evidenced by their calls for a constitutional convention and an elective upper chamber.[109] The most recent study of the period suggests, however, that even these Lower Canadian reformers were faithful to parliamentary institutions established by the Constitution Act, 1791. By the mid-nineteenth century, republicanism all but ceased to have a presence in Lower Canadian constitutional politics.[110] Peter Smith maintains that the North American discourse of civic virtue, if not sufficiently widespread to generate British North American unity, had a presence in framing Canada's ideological origins. He admits, however, that it was commercial ideology that won out over the discourse of civic virtue in 1867 constitutional arrangements.[111] So the claim, at bottom, is a very modest one: republicanist discourse was not a predominant force in nineteenth-century Canada.

There even is some doubt about its influence in revolutionary America. Isaac Kramnick contends that by that time colonists had reconciled themselves to the market economy – "Now the moral and virtuous man was defined not by his civic activity but by his economic activity."[112] The scholarly consensus at present accepts that there was no stark binary between liberalism and republicanism and that the rhetoric of the revolutionary era reveals "traces of diverse intellectual influences," including those of Locke.[113]

Aboriginal Origins

John Ralston Saul rejects the proposition that Canada's origins are traceable to Victorian-era values of 1867, an error that "lies at the heart of

---

108 Stéphane Kelley, *La petit loterie: comment la Couronne a obtenu la collaboration du Canada français après 1837* (Montreal: Boréal), 85. Kelley refers to the 1774 "Address of the General Congress to the Inhabitants of the Province of Quebec," reprinted in W.P.M. Kennedy, *Statutes, Treaties and Documents of the Canadian Constitution, 1713–1929*, 2nd ed. (Toronto: Oxford University Press, 1930), 143–7.

109 "Petition of House of Assembly of Lower Canada, 1833," in Kennedy, *Statutes, Treaties and Documents*, 264, 266.

110 Ducharme, *Idea of Liberty in Canada*, 55, 185.

111 Smith, "Ideological Origins of Canadian Confederation," 29; John W. Dafoe, *Canada: An American Nation* (New York: Columbia University Press, 1935), 77.

112 Isaac Kramnick, *Republicanism and Bourgeois Radicalism: Political Ideology in Late Eighteenth-Century England and America* (Ithaca, NY: Cornell University Press, 1990), 196; Appleby, *Liberalism and Republicanism in the Historical Imagination*, chap. 5.

113 Edling, *Revolution in Favor of Government*, 39.

many of our difficulties today." Saul instead maintains that Canada's origins should be traced back to earlier Aboriginal-European encounters. Our "deep roots ... are far more indigenous than liberal" and so a return to the practices of this early encounter era generate resources with which to imagine Canada anew. In this early period Aboriginals welcomed, accommodated, and fostered a European presence on a continent that otherwise was harsh and uninviting. It is there that we began to develop "ways of relating to the other and ways of doing things [that] settled in, became habit, became culture." It is this Aboriginal "undercurrent" of openness that helps to explain contemporary "Canadian civilization." There are direct linkages, he maintains, between Aboriginal notions of shared welfare and shared practices that lie at the centre of Canadian identity, such as "equalization payments and single-tier health care and public education." The disjuncture between the early encounter era and much of post-Confederation history (e.g., reducing Aboriginal peoples to merely a subject of federal legislative power in section 91(24)) is never really explained. On the imperial side, Saul contends, an Aboriginal culture of sharing is reflected in governor's instructions to make laws for the "peace, *welfare* and good government" of their subject colonies rather than for "peace, *order* and good government," which ultimately gets taken up in the British North America Act. "Welfare, after all, appears 'more often' in early drafts of the confederation act."[114] Refreshing as Saul's approach may be, it is methodologically unsound. Saul relies on the language of generic instructions – constitutionally speaking, exercises of the royal prerogative – that granted to royal governors in British North America almost complete and unfettered discretion to rule over their appointed colonies.[115]

114 John Ralston Saul, *A Fair Country: Telling Truths about Canada* (Toronto: Viking Canada, 2008), 15, 63, 57, 20, 69.
115 Leonard Wood Labaree, *Royal Government in America: A Study of the British Colonial System before 1783* (New York: Frederick Ungar, 1958), 218; Christopher Tomlins, "Necessities of State: Police, Sovereignty, and the Constitution," *Journal of Policy History* 20 (2008): 48. Saul relies on Jordan Birenbaum's survey of these terms in statutory imperial statutes concerning the Australian colonies, in *A Fair Country*, 332, notes to 153, 155. Birenbaum's findings, however, are significantly at odds with Saul's hypothesis. He observes that "welfare" most often appears in imperial documents when referring to a specific colony (e.g., the New South Wales Constitution Act, 1842), while "order" most often appears with reference to colonies collectively (e.g., the South Australia Act, 1834). See Jordan Birenbaum, "Canada Instaurata 1867 – Imperial Perceptions of Provincial Autonomy: Rereading the 1867 Confederation Settlement" (Master's thesis, University of Alberta, 2004), 283–4.

This amounted to the delegated exercise of the "Crown prerogative" (that unfettered realm of monarchical discretion) greater than even that available to the Crown in England.[116] Saul's method falls into the trap of relying too much on the opening phrase in section 91 of the 1867 Act – the purported source of plenary federal legislative authority – as representing a defining feature of Canada's political culture.

Constitutional Origins

Rather than looking to ideological origins, it might be more fruitful to focus on the constitutional paths taken by both imperial and local actors in early Canadian history. This is an inquiry that might be called a "constitutional origins" approach, which has the benefit of focusing the discussion on a narrower set of values associated with constitutional culture. Emphasizing the development of institutions and practices over time is a productive way of tapping into Canada's distinctive constitutional culture.[117] A focus on institutional history brings to light the ways in which a constitutional system generates rules *and* resources for the operation of political processes.[118] A focus on these structures and processes helps to isolate the range of political possibilities on offer, generating patterns of interaction that determine political outcomes over time that can be assimilated under the rubric of constitutional culture.

The recent revival of interest in imperial constitutional history aids in this enterprise. Elizabeth Mancke maintains that strong state institutions in the territory that was to become Canada generated a political culture distinct from that found in the United States. She observes "two distinct patterns of imperial governance" that developed in British North America. Colonies established on the eastern seaboard, in what would become the United States, were endowed with considerable autonomy from imperial authority, at least in their internal affairs. By contrast, dependencies in what later would become Canada, were subject to "greater state control, either as conquered colonies or as commercial territories controlled by metropolitan-based firms." The latter type

---

116 Chester Martin, *Empire & Commonwealth: Studies in Governance and Self-Government in Canada* (Oxford: Clarendon, 1929), 23.
117 Kaufman, *Origins of Canadian and American Political Differences*, 20; Pierson and Skocpol, "Historical Institutionalism in Contemporary Political Science."
118 John Dearlove, "Bringing the Constitution Back in Political Science and the State," *Political Studies* 37 (1989): 512–39.

provided a firm foundation for the exercise of vigorous political control by the metropolitan centre. This helps to explain the distinctiveness of Canadian political culture. It was not a fragment of the U.S. one "but a distinct and separate branch of the British trunk," she observes.[119]

Mancke surely is right that an analysis of constitutional culture begins, at the very least, with British imperial policy in British North America. Such an endeavour requires, however, that attention be paid to how those policies generated both the complicity and antipathy of the colonists themselves over time. Mancke's emphasis on external control – on "colonial and constitutional frameworks determined in Britain" – elides local interaction with, and even resistance to, colonial intentions.[120] Stretching the narrative forward in time has the advantage of both explaining contemporary controversies over ideological origins and the concentration of political power in the executive branch.

3. Constitutional Origins: From Royal to Legislative Omnipotence

When Rex Was Lex

The King is "over-lord of the whole land, so he is master of every person that inhabiteth the same, having power over the life and death of every one of them," so claimed James I. Parliament, by comparison, declared the King, was "nothing else but the head court of the king and his vassals."[121] Because monarchical authority was derived from God, no competing authority would be tolerated. After all, how could parliamentarians expect to have their way over God's own "anointed viceregent"?[122] In the seventeenth century, government by royal prerogative – premised on the King's sole and absolute discretion – was the rule.

---

119 Elizabeth Mancke, "Early Modern Imperial Governance and the Origins of Canadian Political Culture," *Canadian Journal of Political Science* 32 (1999): 8, 20. On the self-government regarding internal affairs, see Ken MacMillan, *The Atlantic Imperial Constitution: Center and Periphery in the English Atlantic World* (Basingstoke: Palgrave Macmillan, 2011), 175.

120 Ibid., 8, 20. In contrasting Canadian and American colonists, Mancke admits that "British North Americans negotiated the function, control and growth of those [colonial] institutions, more than contested their legitimacy" (ibid., 19).

121 G.W. Prothero, ed., *Select Statutes and Other Constitutional Documents, 1558–1625* (Oxford: Clarendon, 1913), 400.

122 Harvey Mansfield, "Party Government and the Settlement of 1688," *American Political Science Review* 58 (1964): 937.

As the King's prerogative authority widened, the task was to find ways to cabin its growth, if not roll back its scope. Lawyers invoked the common law – referring to a law older than the monarch – as a limit on the King's prerogative.[123] The common law's rule of "reason" facilitated a discourse of limited government, alongside an anti-monarchical republican account, that could constrain monarchical absolutism.[124] As it turned out, common law judges were unreliable allies in limiting prerogative power.[125] Instead, it was a discourse of parliamentary sovereignty that emerged victorious over the royal prerogative. According to the victor's account, the monarch operates in conjunction with Parliament, namely, the Lords and the Commons, serving to "balance" (or "mix") the constitution (hence, the notion of "King-in-Parliament"). Not only could Parliament tame prerogative power, it could also take control of public revenues. The right of the people to tax themselves and to control subsidies to the Crown, observed de Lolme in 1784, ensured that the Crown would not govern without the guiding advice of the people's representatives.[126] It was this fulsome conception of parliamentary sovereignty that generated "a treasury of omnipotence not inferior in elasticity and controversial convenience to the undefined possibilities of royal prerogative."[127]

The extravagant claims of prerogative rule by Charles I resulted in rebellion, his beheading, a republican interlude, and, with time, the restoration of the English Crown on terms that assured the supremacy of Parliament (associated with the "Glorious Revolution").[128] Over the course of the next fifty years, the Crown's executive functions would be assumed by legislation. So that they would be of the "same mind" as the legislative majority, the Crown's advisors would be drawn from the

---

123 J.G.A. Pocock, *The Ancient Constitution and the Feudal Law: A Study of English Historical Thought in the Seventeenth Century* (Cambridge: Cambridge University Press, 1987), 46.

124 Allan Cromartie, "The Constitutionalist Revolution: The Transformation of Political Culture in Early Stuart England," *Past and Present* 163 (1999): 76–120; Quentin Skinner, "Classical liberty, Renaissance Translation, and the English Civil War," in Quentin Skinner, *Visions of Politic* (Cambridge: Cambridge University Press, 2002), 2:308–43.

125 Adam Tomkins, *Our Republican Constitution* (Oxford: Hart, 2005), 69–87.

126 De Lolme, *Constitution of England,* 325.

127 Figgis, *Divine Right of Kings,* 237.

128 Whereby, simply put, the English and Scottish Parliaments replaced James II with William and Mary and determined that succession of the Crown would be confined to Protestants.

ranks of the Commons.[129] What was emerging via "remarkably indirect" means was a new conception of Parliament as omnipotent, exemplified by Blackstone's characterization of Parliament as "the place where that absolute despotic power, which must in all governments reside somewhere, is intrusted."[130] While acknowledging rival theories propounded by Locke and others that there remained "inherent" limits on Parliament's authority, Blackstone maintained otherwise: "So long therefore as the English constitution lasts, we may venture to affirm, that the power of parliament is absolute and without control."[131] Paley put the matter with less flourish: "An act of parliament in England, can never be unconstitutional, in the strict and proper acceptation of the term."[132] Parliament could now assume the absolute powers formerly exercised by the King in accordance with divine right. De Lolme captures the development well in this paradoxical formulation that it "was the excessive power of the king which made England free."[133]

The course of constitutional history from the sixteenth through to the nineteenth centuries is a movement, then, from one theory of omnipotence to another. It is this legacy that is transmitted through British imperial policy and its legal texts and that helps to explain the strong state tradition as it emerges in Canadian constitutional culture after the attainment of responsible government.

Empire's Edges

In the decades prior to the American Revolution, the British remained cautious about intruding into the internal affairs of the colonies. By contrast, matters of more direct interest to the metropole concerning

---

129 William R. Anson, *The Law and Custom of the Constitution, Part I: Parliament*, 3rd ed. (Oxford: Oxford University Press, 1897), 29. It is this practice that eventually gives rise to the convention that Cabinet should be responsible to the House.

130 Blackstone, *Commentaries on the Laws of England*, 156; also J.W. Gough, *Fundamental Law in English Constitutional History* (Oxford: Clarendon, 1961), 80.

131 Blackstone, *Commentaries on the Laws of England*, 157. These passages are difficult to reconcile with Blackstone's commitment to natural law principles. See David Lieberman, *Province of Legislation Determined: Legal Theory in Eighteenth-Century Britain* (Cambridge: Cambridge University Press, 1989), 50–1; and Gough, *Fundamental Law in English Constitutional History*, 188–92. He resolves this difficulty by rendering English law entirely consistent with natural law (see *Commentaries on the Laws of England*, 123).

132 Willam Paley, *The Principles of Moral and Political Philosophy*, 2nd ed. (London: Printed by J. Davis, for R. Faulder, 1786), 301.

133 De Lolme, *Constitution of England*, 21.

extra-colonial affairs, such as trade and commerce, had long been of interest.[134] As a consequence, the imperial Parliament exhibited no caution in February 1765 when it passed the Stamp Act, forever changing the course of imperial history. Having nothing to do with commerce or navigation (viz., external affairs), the act imposed a tax on legal and commercial documents, newspapers, pamphlets, cards, and even dice in order to raise revenue to support British troops in North America.[135] Though the Stamp Act was withdrawn eventually, the overriding constitutional question now concerned the scope of British parliamentary authority over the colonies.[136]

Colonists in British North America had been exercising fulsome self-government for some time over the objections of metropolitan-appointed governors.[137] With governors dependent upon local legislatures for the provision of supplies to cover government expenditures, colonists were under the impression that they had secured the same quality of self-government as had Britons following the Glorious Revolution.[138] Any attempt at "engrossing all power" into the hands of the royal governor was, so pleaded a cadre of Virginians in the early eighteenth century, "a great alteration of government, much to the dissatisfaction of this country."[139] Colonists did not initially refute the theoretical omnipotence of Parliament but came around to the view that Parliament could not have untrammelled authority over their lives and estates, at least not without the consent of the governed.[140]

---

134 MacMillan, *Atlantic Imperial Constitution*, 1175.
135 Edmund S. Morgan and Helen M. Morgan, *The Stamp Act Crisis: Prologue to a Revolution* (London: Collier Books, 1963); William Holdsworth, *A History of English Law* (London: Methuen, 1938), 11:110.
136 Arthur Berriedale Keith, *Constitutional History of the First British Empire* (Oxford: Clarendon, 1930), 344; Bernard Knollenberg, *Origin of the American Revolution, 1759–1766*, new rev. ed. (New York: Collier Books, 1961), 208.
137 Jack P. Greene, "The Origins of New Colonial Policy, 1748–1763," in *The Blackwell Encyclopedia of the American Revolution*, ed. Jack P. Greene and J.R. Pole (Cambridge, MA: Blackwell, 1991), 98.
138 Jack P. Greene, *Peripheries and Center: Constitutional Development in the Extended Polities of the British Empire and the United States, 1607–1788* (Athens: University of Georgia Press, 1986), 64.
139 J. Lightfoot, Matthew Page, Benj. Harrison, Robert Carter, James Blair, and Phil. Ludwell, "Charges against Governor Nicholson," *Virginia Magazine of History and Biography* 3 (1896): 375; Nelson, *Royalist Revolution*, chap. 1.
140 Jack P. Greene, *The Constitutional Origins of the American Revolution* (Cambridge: Cambridge University Press, 2011), 81.

Though colonists might have had "up to half a dozen theories [of] why parliamentary sovereignty had [its] limits,"[141] they embraced an older, legal vision of custom and common law that operated as a constraint on power.[142] This amounted to a repudiation of parliamentary authority resulting in an odd hybrid in constitutional theory: a return to rule by Stuart Kings coupled with colonial legislative autonomy. By contrast, the emerging dominant constitutional discourse relied upon by imperial authorities was the newer one of a supreme Parliament with as capacious a law-making authority as had the Crown in the exercise of its royal prerogative.[143]

British North American colonists apparently would have been content, initially, if metropolitan authorities had merely kept to their own sphere of concern by respecting the distinction between "internal" and "external" affairs. Colonial leadership maintained that local legislative bodies had fulsome authority over internal affairs of the colony, such as the power to tax. These were matters of "internal police" within the colony, urged the colonists, addressing matters of everyday concern.[144] The imperial Parliament had authority only over the colony's external affairs, things commonly associated with trade regulation, such as excise duties on trade.[145] This binary figured centrally in Richard

---

141 John Phillip Reid, *Constitutional History of the American Revolution: The Authority to Legislate* (Madison: University of Wisconsin Press, 1991), 80.

142 John Philip Reid, *Constitutional History of the American Revolution: The Authority of Law* (Madison: University of Wisconsin Press, 1993), 4–5. The old colonial system, observes Seeley, was "an irrational jumble of two opposite conceptions": "It claimed to rule the colonists because they are Englishmen and brothers, and yet it ruled them as if they were conquered Indians." J.R. Seeley, *The Expansion of England* (London: Macmillan, 1888), 69. This is a late nineteenth-century anachronism – imperial authority did not yet, in the mid- to late eighteenth century, deign to "rule" First Nations. More precisely, Seeley admits, the American colonists were self-governing in most matters but for trade (67, 68).

143 Nelson, *Royalist Revolution*, 55.

144 Bernard Bailyn, *The Ideological Origins of the American Revolution* (Cambridge, MA: Harvard University Press, 1976), 214, 203; Alison L. LaCroix, *The Ideological Origins of American Federalism* (Cambridge, MA: Harvard University Press, 2010), chap. 2.

145 Edmund Burke observed that these sorts of regulations, associated with the navigation acts, were tolerated by the colonists until 1764, the year of the Revenue Act, at which point Britons began contemplating new sources of parliamentary revenue. See Burke, "Speech on Moving the Resolutions for Conciliation with the Colonies" (22 March 1775), in *The Works of the Right Honourable Edmund Burke* (Oxford: Oxford University Press, 1906), 2:113. The controversial Stamp Act was introduced in the following year. See Keith, *Constitutional History of the First British Empire*, 343–4.

Bland's 1760 riposte against the exercise of the King's prerogative power in Virginia[146] and, subsequently, in Benjamin Franklin's 1765 testimony before the House of Commons on the eve of passage of the Stamp Act,[147] as well as Daniel Dulany's tract of that same year.[148]

Burke also pleaded with fellow parliamentarians to respect the distinction between internal and external affairs "originally moved by the Americans themselves" and in which they acquiesced.[149] British Whigs, by contrast, maintained that such a division of labour was impossible. Parliamentary authority was not divisible: either the colonies were subject to imperial authority or they had an independent existence that dissolved their union with the British Crown.[150] In fact, the colonies had no independent constitutional existence, their authority being no greater than domestic corporations within Britain with the power to make by-laws.[151]

Pushed to the brink, the internal-external distinction was rendered old-fashioned within a decade, and colonial leadership drew the line elsewhere – at independence.[152] Colonial representatives in their "Declaration of Independence" (1776) accused governors of, among other things, having "suspended" the operation of laws, "dissolved" representative houses of assembly, making judges "dependent" on executive patronage, "imposing" taxes without consent, "abolishing" English law in the province of Quebec, "establishing therein an Arbitrary government," and rendering Quebec "at once an example and fit instrument for introducing the same absolute rule into these Colonies." Each of these complaints would later echo in the colonies

---

146 Craig Yirush, *Settlers, Liberty, and Empire: The Roots of Early American Political Theory, 1675–1775* (Cambridge: Cambridge University Press, 2011), 177.

147 Holdsworth, *History of English Law*, 112.

148 Daniel Dulaney, *Considerations on the Propriety of Imposing Taxes in the British Colonies for the Purpose of Raising Revenue, by the Act of Parliament* (Annapolis: North American, 1765), in Bernard Bailyn, ed., *Pamphlets of the American Revolution, 1750–1765* (Cambridge, MA: Belknap, 1965), 1:607–58.

149 Burke, "Speech on American Taxation," 149, 145–6.

150 Bailyn, *Ideological Origins of the American Revolution*, 218.

151 Greene, *Constitutional Origins of the American Revolution*, 97.

152 Gordon Wood describes such attempts at dividing Parliament's power as "futile." Given the choice between the doctrine of parliamentary sovereignty and no authority, most Americans decided that Parliament had no power to make any laws for them. Gordon S. Wood, *The Americanization of Benjamin Franklin* (New York: Penguin, 2004), 123–4.

that would join together to become the Dominion of Canada. Most would be managed by working out a version of the internal-external distinction in constitutional affairs.[153] Imposing dependency, however, would prove less problematic, as a strong statist orientation gained ground early on that would contain political developments there.

A Better "Balanced" Constitution

Marking the end of the "first empire,"[154] the American Revolution shaped immeasurably the progress of constitutional government in Canada. British imperial authorities had learned their lessons – even if the wrong ones – from those events. The policy emerging in, this, the "second empire," was less one of benign neglect and one of "more direct control." Though events on the ground, such as a large conquered French-speaking population resisting the imposition of English law, language, and religion, mitigated absorption, the British "instinct for empire continued" unabated.[155] It would prove impossible for imperial authorities, however, not to acquiesce ultimately to Canadian claims to self-government. As Burke insisted in his 1775 speech on conciliation with America, there inevitably would come a time "to admit the people of our colonies into an interest in the constitution."[156]

The conditions giving rise to rebellion in America would be carefully avoided for as long a time as possible. Loyalist refugee Chief Justice William Smith of Montreal characterized "All America ... at the very outset ... [as being] abandoned to Democracy."[157] In America, "full Scope & Vigour were given to the principles of Democracy by the establishment of a popular representation, in their houses of Assembly, [where] no care was taken to preserve a due mixture of the

153 Dafoe, *Canada: An American Nation*, 20.
154 Seeley, *Expansion of England*, 14.
155 Vincent T. Harlow, *The Founding of the Second British Empire, 1763–1793* (London: Longmans Green, 1964), 2:785.
156 Burke, "Speech on Moving the Resolutions for Conciliation with the Colonies," 2:203.
157 "Chief Justice Smith to Dorchester" (5 February 1790), in Adam Shortt and Arthur G. Doughty, eds., *Documents Relating to the Constitutional History of Canada, 1759–1791* (Ottawa: J. de L. Taché, 1907), 1018; also in Kennedy, *Statutes, Treaties and Documents*, 191.

Monarchical, & Aristocratical parts of the British Constitution."[158] The establishment of uncontrollable "little Republics"[159] would be avoided in what remained of British North America by creating institutions for representative government "carefully hedged about."[160]

The program for concentrated political authority was well underway before the American revolt. With formal peace secured between France and Britain via the Treaty of Paris (1763), the Royal Proclamation of 1763 (an exercise of the royal prerogative) directed the governor to establish representative assemblies only "so soon as the state and circumstances" of the colony would admit. Given that it "may be the impracticable" to do so, Governor James Murray was instructed to "make rules and regulations necessary for the peace, order and good government of the Province." A new council, made up of lieutenant governors, the chief justice, surveyor general, and eight other local notables would assist in the administration of government.

Governing from the metropole by royal prerogative, however, appeared no longer sufficient to the meet the needs of Britain's "new subjects." Francis Maseres offered a convincing case for parliamentary intervention in his 1766 "Considerations on the Expediency of Procuring an Act of Parliament for the Settlement of the Province of Quebec." He complained that the toleration of Roman Catholicism, even though acknowledged by the Treaty of Peace 1763, was not permitted by the laws of Great Britain; that the extent to which English law displaced local Canadian law was ambiguous; that securing a durable public revenue via taxation was without firm foundation; and that

---

158 "Discussion of Petitions and Counter Petitions *Re* Change of Government in Canada," enclosed with correspondence from William W. Grenville, Secretary of State, to Lord Dorchester, Governor of Canada (20 October 1789), in Shortt and Doughty, *Documents*, 983. The Constitution had been rendered out of balance without the presence of the dignified parts of the British Constitution. The lesson to be learned and applied forcefully to the remaining British colonies was that "every kind of Authority that is not inconsistent with the Constitution given to the Province, ought, therefore be concentred in his [the executive's] hands" – nothing would be introduced "tending to lessen the Authority which the Parent State ought to possess over it." See "Letter from the Third Duke of Portland, Secretary for War and the Colonies, to Lieutenant Governor John Graves Simcoe" (20 May 1795), in Kennedy, *Statutes, Treaties and Documents*, 217.

159 "Discussion of Petitions," in Shortt and Doughty, *Documents*, 983.

160 Oscar D. Skelton, *The Canadian Dominion: A Chronicle of Our Northern Neighbour* (New Haven, CT: Yale University Press, 1919), 31.

the establishment of an assembly, even if premature, properly required the authority of Parliament.[161] Swayed by Maseres's legal argument,[162] imperial masters took the unusual step of constituting civil authority in Quebec by an Act of Parliament.[163] The Quebec Act of 1774, "railroaded" through Parliament on the eve of American rebellion,[164] though intended to provide a more "active constitution,"[165] practically carried on the same arrangement as before.[166]

Continued political rule by governors and appointed councillors, however, proved intolerable to the colonists. "Ancient subjects," like English-speaking traders in Montreal and Quebec, petitioned for representative institutions.[167] There were now a "sufficient number of [Protestant] freeholders" who were qualified to sit – those who were ready and willing to take the "oath of abjuration of the pope's power" – so as to constitute a house of assembly.[168] If it was not a house constituted solely of Protestants, it was one where a preponderance of Protestants would have control and "a few of the most moderate sort of Roman Catholicks" could sit. The absorption of American loyalists into western Quebec intensified this demand, calling for an evolution in colonial policy that would make what remained of British North America attractive to newly arriving Protestant settlers and traders.[169] Governor Carleton, Murray's successor, resisted these developments. Despite the metropole's best intentions, it was improper to transplant British forms of government, "because it is impossible for the Dignity of the Throne, or Peerage to be represented in the American Forests."

---

161 Francis Maseres, *Occasional Essays on Various Subjects Chiefly Political and Historical* (London: Robert Wilks, 1809), 333, 337, 339, 343.

162 Reginald Coupland, *The Quebec Act* (Oxford: Clarendon, 1999), 67.

163 Harlow, *Founding of the Second British Empire*, 703.

164 Alfred Leroy Burt, *The Old Province of Quebec*. Vol. 1, *1760–1778* (Toronto: McClelland and Stewart, 1968), 169.

165 Lord Thurlow in "Debates in the British Parliament on the Quebec Act, 1774," in Kennedy, *Statutes, Treaties and Documents*, 102.

166 W.P.M. Kennedy, *The Constitution of Canada: An Introduction to Its Development and Law* (Oxford: Oxford University Press, 1922), 52.

167 "Petition for House of Assembly; To the King's Most Excellent Majesty" (24 November 1784), in Shortt and Doughty, *Documents*, 743.

168 "Case of the British Merchants Trading to Quebec, 1774," in Kennedy, *Statutes, Treaties and Documents*, 87.

169 "Petition of the Western Loyalists" (15 April 1787), in Shortt and Doughty, *Documents*, 949; also Harlow, *Founding of the Second British Empire*, 724.

Establishing a popular assembly "in a Country where all Men appear nearly upon a Level, must give strong bias to Republican principles."[170] The proposed assembly would be a "dangerous experiment," observed Solicitor General Wedderburn.[171]

Popular assemblies remained a threat, given the hard lessons learned by the American revolt.[172] At the same time, proposals for repeal of the Quebec Act were being entertained in Parliament. Secretary of State William Wyndham Grenville was convinced, that there was merit to such a proposal in light of a curious legislative lacuna: the absence of any power to tax what remained of British North America, despite Maseres's best advice.[173] As a way of solving this conundrum and of appeasing demands for representative institutions, Grenville proposed the division of the province into "two districts, having distinct Legislatures, in which the separate interests of the old, & new Subjects might preponderate, according to the respective proportion of population, & of wealth."[174] Anything short of that would not be tolerated for much longer: "The neighbourhood of the United States, & even of the remaining British colonies seems to make it impossible that the people

---

170 "Carleton to Sherburne" (20 January 1768), in Kennedy, *Statutes, Treaties and Documents*, 78.
171 "Report of Solicitor General Alex. Wedderburn" (6 December 1772), in Shortt and Doughty, *Documents*, 426.
172 Fears associated with the French Revolution did not play a role in the events leading up to the 1791 Constitution – it simply was too early to have caused real alarm. See Burt, *Old Province of Quebec*, 2:200; F. Murray Greenwood, *Legacies of Fear: Law and Politics in Quebec in the Era of the French Revolution* (Toronto: University of Toronto Press, 1993), 61–3.
173 Burt, *Old Province of Quebec*, 2:198–202; E.A. Cruilshank, "The Genesis of the Canada Act," *Ontario Historical Society Papers and Records* 28 (1932): 233–5. The Quebec Act, 1774, denied to the Legislative Council an ability to impose taxes and duties, except for those approved by inhabitants of a town or district for the purpose of building roads, public buildings, etc. (Art. XIII). Late in the Revolutionary War, Parliament enacted the Colonial Tax Repeal Act, 1778 (18 Geo. III, c 12) denying to the King and Parliament an ability to impose any tax but for duties associated with the regulation of international commerce. See Carl Stephenson and Frederick George Marcham, eds., *Sources of English Constitutional History: A Selection of Documents from A.D. 600 to the Present* (New York: Harper & Brothers, 1937), 663. Taken together, Grenville observed, nowhere could be found "so essential a power as that of assessing, levying, & applying the contributions of individuals in order to execute those objects which are of general necessity, or advantage to the community" (in Shortt and Doughty, *Documents*, 974).
174 "Discussion of Petitions," in Shortt and Doughty, *Documents*, 976.

of Canada should acquiesce, for any considerable length of time, in the continuance of a system at all resembling that under which they are now governed," he observed.[175]

By the Constitution Act, 1791 (the third constitution in a little more than three decades),[176] Quebec was divided into two Canadas – Upper and Lower – and each was given a constitution purportedly modelled on the British one: a carefully "balanced" constitution that maintained a "due mixture" of democratic, aristocratic, and monarchical elements.[177] There would be an elected lower assembly, analogous to the House of Commons, and a hereditary legislative council, analogous to the House of Lords, made up of "discreet and proper persons."

Constitutional veto points remained plentiful. The whole scheme is nicely captured in English lawyer Charles Clark's treatise *A Summary of Colonial Law*.[178] "In general," he writes, "the local power of making laws is vested in the governor, acting with the advice of a council of government." The governor wields power not unlike the Crown in pre-revolutionary England. He "possesses a negative voice in the legislature; for without his consent no bill passes into a law" and may, "at his own discretion, adjourn, prorogue and dissolve the Assemblies." "On the whole," Clark acknowledges, "it appears that the powers with which colonial governors are instructed are most ample and transcendent, and more extensive than those which the laws of England allow the sovereign himself to exercise."[179] Democracy, indeed, was carefully hedged about by the 1791 Act. The "affirmative voice of the people in their representatives is opposed by three negatives," Clark concludes, "the first in the Council, the second on the Governor, and the third in the Crown."[180] No thought was given to making the executive responsible to the elected assembly, a practice that was becoming a standard one in the mother country.

---

175 "Grenville to Dorchester," in Shortt and Doughty, *Documents*, 987.
176 I am following Russell's numerical chronology in *Constitutional Odyssey: Can Canadians Become a Sovereign People?*, 2nd ed. (Toronto: University of Toronto Press), 13.
177 "Discussion of Petitions," in Shortt and Doughty, *Documents*, 983.
178 Charles Clark, *A Summary of Colonial Law* (London: S. Sweet, A. Maxwell, and Stevens & Sons, 1834).
179 Ibid., 34.
180 Ibid., 25, 30, 34, 46. Clark acknowledges that this authority "appears at first quite irreconcilable with English notions of the rights and privileges of such an assembly." It is, nevertheless, he points out, expressly provided for in the Governor's commission (ibid., 30).

Permitting an Interest in the Constitution

Nevertheless, control over executive power emerged as a principal concern for Canadian assemblies. Appeals to an executive accountable to the elected legislature were channelled into claims over control of the public purse, just as it had been both for Britons and Americans before them.[181] Having local assemblies reject supplies for civil government (the "civil list") proved embarrassing to the "honour of the Crown." A rash of Crown prorogations ensued. Claims of "an inalienable right not to be taxed without the consent" of the governed issued from the lower houses. Control over expenditure and patronage appointments, including a judicial branch holding multiple salaried offices, were at the heart of the conflict.[182]

Increasing their appeals to republican forms of government, and despondent about the prospects of change, Upper and Lower Canadian political leadership eventually resorted to violent rebellion, which in both provinces were easily quashed. Lord Durham was dispatched to inquire into prospects for an "enduring tranquility" and, after an embarrassingly short stay of five months as governor, issued the most important colonial document of the era. In his report, Durham recommended the immediate institution of responsible government – the "wise principle" secured by the revolution of 1688 – and the joining together of the two Canadas into a single province in order to achieve the long-hoped-for assimilation of French Canadians.[183] Colonial authorities were in no rush to embrace Durham's recommendation regarding responsible government.[184] The imperial Parliament instead eagerly pursued the assimilationist project – "Anglo-Saxons ... always [being] ... prone to

---

181 Holdsworth writes that the "history of the evolution of the civil list is the financial parallel of the history of cabinet." Holdsworth, *History of English Law*, 10:485.

182 W.R. Lederman, "The Independence of the Judiciary," Part II, *Canadian Bar Review* 34 (1956): 1139–79, 1149–50; C.P. Lucas, ed., *Lord Durham's Report on the Affairs of British North America*. Vol. 1, *Introduction* (Oxford: Clarendon, 1912), 225–6. "Let them not be all at once judges, and legislators and administrators," declared Louis-Joseph Papineau. Quoted in Yvan Lamonde, *The Social History of Ideas in Quebec, 1760–1896*, trans. Phyllis Aronoff and Howard Scott (Montreal and Kingston: McGill-Queen's University Press, 2013), 79.

183 The Earl of Durham, *Lord Durham's Report on the Affairs of North America*, Vol. 2, ed. C.P. Lucas (Oxford: Clarendon, 1912), 79.

184 Arthur Berriedale Keith, *Responsible Government in the Dominions* (Oxford: Clarendon, 1912), 1:15.

overestimate their absorptive capacity."[185] The two colonies were fused into a single province with "one Legislative Council and one assembly" to make laws for the "peace, welfare and good government of the Province" in, this, Canada's fourth constitution.[186]

Durham's call for responsible government fell firmly within established British constitutional practice at the time (Durham, as mentioned, traces its origins to 1688).[187] It departed, instead, from British imperial practice. A governor could not follow both the desires of an elected assembly and that of his political master in matters such as foreign affairs, declared the secretary of state for the colonies, Lord John Russell.[188] Any division of authority was resisted by imperial governors, just as it was in the decade leading up to American independence. The brilliant Nova Scotia politician Joseph Howe claimed no such conflict would arise if "British statesmen ... confine themselves to those general arrangements affecting the whole empire, of which we admit them to be the best judges, and of which we never asked to take a part." Howe's pragmatism (portended by Edmund Burke in the House of Commons) anticipates the ensuing compromise: "If the duties and responsibilities of government are fairly and judiciously divided between the Imperial and Colonial authorities, no such case as that assumed by your Lordship can occur; and if it should, surely the

---

185 Harlow, *Founding of the Second British Empire*, 668.
186 Act of Union, 1840, 3 & 4 Victoria, c 35, Art III.
187 Holdsworth, *History of English Law*, 10:642; Durham, *Lord Durham's Report*, 79. It has been claimed that Canadians were in the vanguard in calling for responsible government: "Such a clear principle [of responsible government] had not yet been established in Britain," even by the 1830s (John Ralston Saul, *Louis-Hippolyte LaFontaine and Robert Baldwin* [Toronto: Penguin Canada, 2010], 55; also Aileen Dunham, *Political Unrest in Upper Canada, 1815–1836* [Toronto: McClelland & Stewart, 1963], 154). This cannot be correct. Pierre Bédard, leader of the Canadian Party in the Assembly of Lower Canada and editor of the influential *Le Canadien*, articulated the principle of responsible government as early as 1807 (see Ajzenstat, *Canadian Founding*, 129; Ducharme, *Idea of Liberty in Canada*, 58; Lamonde, *Social History of Ideas in* Quebec, 33). This is consistent with the contemporaneous correspondence of Governor Craig wherein he advises Secretary of State Castelreagh that French Canadians in the Lower Canadian Assembly "either believe or affect to believe that there exists a Ministry here, and that in imitation of the Constitution of Britain that Ministry is responsible to them for the conduct of government." See "Craig to Castlereagh" (5 August 1808), in Kennedy, *Statutes, Treaties and Documents*, 224.
188 "Lord John Russell on Canadian Affairs, June 1839" (speech delivered on the Act of Union, 3 June 1839), in Kennedy, *Statutes, Treaties and Documents*, 383.

good sense of all parties concerned may safely be trusted, to avoid any violent or unpleasant collision."[189]

Indeed, Durham recommended just such a division of labour in his report. Durham proposed a distinction between internal and external spheres in a new constitution that would unite Upper and Lower Canada. "I know not in what respect it can be desirable that we should interfere with their [Canada's] internal legislation in matters which do not affect their relations with the mother country," he observed.[190] The matters of concern to imperial authority were "very few" and included the "constitution of the form of government," "the regulation of foreign relations, and of trade with the mother country, other British colonies and foreign nations," and the "disposal of the public lands."[191]

Despite resistance from London, a succession of governors general conceded ground to Canadian reformers.[192] With the appointment of Lord Elgin in 1848, self-government was secured, resulting in the first Cabinet government under the leadership of La Fontaine and Baldwin.[193] In the words of Lord Elgin, Canadians finally could expect the head of government to "shew that he has the confidence in the loyalty of all the influential parties with which he has to deal." "That Ministers and oppositions should occasionally change places is the very essence of our Constitutional system," he wrote to Colonial Secretary Lord Grey.[194] It was at this point that the governor's role receded into the background, resembling that of the British monarch.[195] It also is at this point that the head of government in Canada assumed almost all of

---

189 "Joseph Howe to Lord John Russell" (September 1839), in Kennedy, *Statutes, Treaties and Documents*, 399.

190 Durham, *Lord Durham's Report*, 282.

191 Ibid., 282. Janet Ajzenstat maintains, by laying down a division of powers, Durham laid out no "new law, policy, or scheme of any kind," in *The Political Thought of Lord Durham* (Montreal and Kingston: McGill-Queen's University Press, 1988), 43. His intention was not to lay down a "line," as argued in Chester W. New, *Lord Durham: A Biography of John George Lambton, First Earl of Durham* (Oxford: Clarendon, 1929), 508, but to loosen imperial constraints on the colony (in Ajzenstat, *Discovering Confederation*, 114).

192 Barbara Messamore, *Canada's Governors General, 1847–1878: Biography and Constitutional Evolution* (Toronto: University of Toronto Press, 2006), 42–6.

193 John G. Bourinot, *Lord Elgin* (Toronto: Morang, 1906); Saul, *Louis-Hippolyte LaFontaine and Robert Baldwin*.

194 Arthur G. Doughty, ed., *The Elgin-Grey Papers, 1846–52* (Ottawa: J.-O. Patenaude O.S.I., 1937), 1:47, 46.

195 Kennedy, *Constitution of Canada*, 271.

the prerogatives formerly exercised by the Crown in Canada. Limits on Canadian parliamentary government were rendered practically obsolete by the triumph of responsible government.[196]

With the arrival of eagerly sought responsible government, and as the metropolitan centre slowly lost authority and colonists gained control of the levers of government, Canadians inherited the shell of an institutionally strong state. Within twenty years of Durham's report, the colony claimed authority to fix its own tariffs in 1859, despite its stark departure from the free trade policy of the mother country.[197] Finance Minister Galt famously declared, in response to the threatened disallowance of his fiscal policy, that "Self-government would be utterly annihilated if the views of the Imperial Government were to be preferred to those of the people of Canada" in matters concerning "the internal government of the country."[198] Other elements of Durham's external sphere would slip out of imperial hands. The disposal of public lands had been a subject of great controversy ever since the Constitution Act, 1791 mandated setting aside lands to finance establishment of the Protestant church in Canada (the "clergy reserves"). It was the "most mischievous practical cause of dissension," declared Durham,[199] making it inevitable that this jurisdiction would soon come under local control.[200] As for trade and relations with foreign powers, this too, but more slowly, devolved into Canadian hands. Immediately prior to Confederation, Canadian delegations

---

196 Paul Romney, "From Constitutionalism to Legalism: Trial by Jury, Responsible Government, and the Rule of Law in Canadian Political Culture," *Law and History Review* 7 (1989): 158.

197 Oscar Skelton, *Life and Times of Sir Alexander Tilloch Galt*, ed. Guy Maclean (Toronto: McClelland & Stewart, 1966), 118.

198 H.E. Egerton and W.L. Grant, *Canadian Constitutional Development* (London: John Murray, 1907), 350–1.

199 Durham, *Lord Durham's Report*, 179.

200 Non–Church of England affiliates felt – "degraded" and in "a position of legal inferiority," reported Lord Durham. Giving security to a favoured sect, Durham feared, "endanger[ed] the loss of the Colony" to the United States (ibid., 177). He therefore recommended that Parliament adopt the "voluntary principle," a "tone of thought prevalent" in the United States that "has exerted a very considerable influence over the neighbouring provinces" (ibid.). See also Alan Wilson, *The Clergy Reserves of Upper Canada: A Canadian Mortmain* (Toronto: University of Toronto Press, 1968), 198–9. After Durham's recommendations on the matter, the British Parliament in 1853 acknowledged Canada's authority to settle the question of the clergy reserves. Parliament enacted such a law in 1854 (18 Vict, c 2), paying out existing claims, with the balance paid out to municipalities (in Kennedy, *Statutes, Treaties and Documents*, 521).

participated actively in the negotiation of international treaties in which Canada had an interest, having the effect of conferring upon them an "international status as separate and sovereign states."[201] There was, pre- and post-Confederation, a "steadily broadening horizon" of Canadian involvement in trade relations.[202] With Canadian representation in the Imperial War Cabinet in 1917,[203] overt demands for Canadian independence in matters of war and peace surfaced. Even constitutional amendments, though under the control of the imperial Parliament, would be prompted only on the initiative of Canadian political actors.[204]

Room for Growth

Metropole authority receded into the background as fulsome self-government was conceded to the colony.[205] The 1867 Act gave formal expression to this change in imperial policy, though colonial masters continued to share a semblance of power.[206] It was, after all, the fountainhead of authority for the two new levels of government.[207] Among the new features of Canada's fifth constitution, the British North America Act, 1867, was a federal government, styled after the British Parliament with an upper and lower chamber, and which divided up, in some detail, legislative authority between the federal and four provincial governments. Having secured continued access to a rich resource base in the northwest, colonial policy on Aboriginal peoples would be less generous, consigning them to a federal enumeration.[208]

---

201 Edward Porritt, *The Fiscal and Diplomatic Freedom of the British Overseas Dominions* (Oxford: Clarendon, 1992), 193, 195, quoting the marquess of Ripon.

202 Martin, *Empire & Commonwealth*, 333.

203 Robert Laird Borden, *Canadian Constitutional Studies* (Toronto: University of Toronto Press, 1922), 109–11.

204 Paul Gérin-Lajoie, *Constitutional Amendment in Canada* (Toronto: University of Toronto Press, 1950), 137. Thus, it could be claimed that by 1929 "all of Durham's reservations have gone by the board in whole or in part, in practice if not in theory" (in Martin, *Empire & Commonwealth*, 334).

205 Ged Martin, *The Durham Report and British Policy* (Cambridge: Cambridge University Press, 1972), 61; John Stuart Mill, *Utilitarianism, Liberty & Representative Government* (1861; London: J.M. Dent & Sons, 1910), 378.

206 D.A. O'Sullivan, *Government in Canada*, 2nd ed. (Toronto: Carswell, 1887), 8.

207 Alexander T. Galt, *Speech on the Proposed Union of the British North American Provinces* (Montreal: M. Longmoore, 1864), 8.

208 J.R. Miller, *Compact, Contract, Covenant: Aboriginal Treaty Making in Canada* (Toronto: University of Toronto Press, 2009), 191, 232.

In a typical federal state, power is divided once. In a federal *colonial* state, power is divided twice.[209] The first division concerned law-making authority over Canada's internal affairs as between federal and provincial governments. The borders between imperial and Canadian authority constituted the second division. In addition to rights of reservation and disallowance, imperial authority held onto the reins of formal constitutional amendment, together with final judicial authority lodged in the Judicial Committee of the Privy Council (until appeals to that body were abolished in 1949). The "regulation of foreign relations" also was reserved for the metropolis in a "miscellaneous provision," numbered section 132 in the 1867 Act, conferring on "the parliament and government of Canada ... all powers necessary or proper for performing the obligations of Canada or of any province thereof, as part of the British Empire, towards foreign countries, arising under treaties between the Empire and such foreign countries." It was contemplated that imperial authorities would conduct foreign affairs on behalf of the Dominion of Canada, a state of dependency that would come to an end only with the Statute of Westminster in 1931. It probably is no coincidence that section 132 is similar to the language of the U.S. Constitution's "necessary and proper" clause, which authorizes Congress to "make all laws necessary and proper" for carrying into execution congressional authority.[210] It must have been contemplated that everything necessary to put into effect obligations undertaken on behalf of the empire be done irrespective of the internal division of powers. The withdrawal of imperial authority in putting into effect international obligations created a void that continues to preoccupy constitutional interpretation in Canada. The entering into international obligations, by contrast, remains a matter of executive discretion, namely within the purview of the Prime Minister's Office, as a remnant of the Crown prerogative over foreign relations.[211]

---

209 O'Sullivan, *Government in Canada*, 20.

210 Article I, section viii, clause 18. Congress was given the widest ambit by Chief Justice John Marshall of the U.S. Supreme Court early in the nineteenth century, rejecting a restrictive interpretation of the clause: "Let the end be legitimate, let it be within the scope of the constitution, and all means which are appropriate, which are plainly adapted to that end ... are constitutional," he declared in *McCulloch v Maryland*, 17 US 316, 421 (1819).

211 In a comparative study of four Commonwealth jurisdictions, McLachlan finds that Canada's has the "least developed" process for parliamentary review of the executive's treaty-making power. See Campbell McLachlan, *Foreign Relations Law* (Oxford: Oxford University Press, 2014), 171–3.

The evolving frame of government resulted in a constitutional order, Viscount Bryce concluded, that was "rather more democratic" than anything else on the continent. For Bryce, the nation was preoccupied with matters belonging to the "sphere of commercial and industrial progress, the development of material resources of the country by rendering aid to agriculture, by the regulation of mining, by constructing public works and opening up lines of railway and canal communication." Moreover, these were things over which political parties were not divided, "for the policy of laissez faire has few adherents in a country which finds in governmental action or financial support to private enterprise the quickest means of carrying out every promising project."[212] Given the few impediments to policy choices that remained, this constitutional inheritance allowed for different political possibilities to emerge, though foreclosed at various times in the United States. It is this muscularity and flexibility, I argue in subsequent chapters, that Prime Minister Harper has exploited.

In the United States, by contrast, constitutional law had the noticeable result of limiting possibilities for political change. The discussion typically is framed by addressing the absence of a viable left democratic politics in the United States. Though a variety of factors have been offered – American exceptionalism,[213] absence of a feudal inheritance,[214] the promise of social mobility,[215] or the siphoning effects of radical republicanism[216] and the New Deal[217] – the Constitution "has been comparatively neglected," observes Daniel Lazare. Yet the Constitution, he continues, "would create and shape the people ... Rather than of society, it would be over it." Lazare points particularly to the protection of property rights in the Fifth and Fourteenth Amendments as standing in the way of any

212 Bryce, *Canada: An Actual Democracy*, 41, 17.
213 Eric Foner, "Why Is There No Socialism in the United States?," *History Workshop Journal* 17 (1989): 57–80; Werner Sombart, *Why Is There No Socialism in the United States?*, trans. Patricia M. Hocking (1905; London: Macmillan, 1976).
214 Hartz, *Liberal Tradition in America*, 60.
215 Irving Howe, *Socialism and America* (San Diego: Harcourt Brace Jovanovich, 1985), 134; Lipset, *First New Nation*, 202.
216 Sean Wilentz, *Chants Democratic: New York City and the Rise of the American Working Class, 1788–1850* (New York: Oxford University Press, 2004), 247.
217 Seymour Martin Lipset, *Agrarian Socialism: The Cooperative Commonwealth Federation in Saskatchewan – A Study in Political Sociology* (Berkeley: University of California Press, 1968), 32.

social-democratic experimentation.[218] Theda Skocpol canvasses extant explanations for the sluggish establishment of nationwide pensions and social insurance in the United States and concludes that "long-standing political structures," including constitutional forms, "have not encouraged U.S. industrial workers to operate as class-conscious political forces."[219] Selig Perlman, in answering why there is not an American labour party, pointed to federal and state bills of rights "which embody in fullness the eighteenth century philosophy of economic individualism and governmental *laissez faire.*" This stifled the emergence of labour party politics and "compelled the American labor movement to develop a sort of non-partisan political action with limited objectives thoroughly characteristic of American conditions."[220] William Forbath's study of the American labour movement confirms the inhibiting effects of American constitutional culture. He finds that judicial review of the Constitution during the Lochner era (discussed below) "shaped labor's strategic calculus," prompting labour's claim-making strategies to be limited by what was tolerable according to the constraining standards of the common law and constitutional discourse.[221]

Why is there no similar culture of attenuated claim-making strategizing in Canada? After all, American labour leadership, claiming to represent Canadian workers early in the twentieth century, attempted to stifle trade union calls for intervention in the economy on behalf of workers. Instead, Canadians were inspired by the election of fifty-four trade unionists in British parliamentary elections in 1905. Samuel

---

218 Daniel Lazare, "America the Undemocratic," *New Left Review* 232 (1998): 32, 15. Michael Lind criticizes Lazare's reliance on a simple majoritarianism in contrast to the more complex "consociational" framework represented by the U.S. Constitution. Offering an alternative explanation for the failure of socialism in the U.S., Lind writes that a "key variable may be, not constitutional design, but political culture" – "the form of the constitution is less important than cultural attitudes toward law and government," in Michael Lind, "Why There Will Be No Revolution in the US: A Reply to Daniel Lazare," *New Left Review* 233 (1999): 112. As mentioned in the introduction, I prefer to distinguish between political and constitutional culture while acknowledging that some elements of political culture will be caught by the idea of constitutional culture.

219 Skocpol, *Protecting Soldiers and Mothers*, 50.

220 Selig Perlman, *A History of Trade Unionism in the United States* (New York: Macmillan, 1923), 285, 289.

221 William E. Forbath, *Law and the Shaping of the American Labor Movement* (Cambridge, MA: Harvard University Press, 1991), 7.

Gompers, head of the American Federation of Labor, maintained, nevertheless, that labour's experience in Europe did not translate well in the New World.[222] The alliance between socialist activists and the trade union movement, however, would not be forestalled in Canada. In Canada, as in Britain, the labour movement entered the political arena and had some success in electing representatives in both provincial and federal legislatures. In 1944, the first social democratic government was elected in Canada in the province of Saskatchewan, the product of an agrarian radicalism opposed to large enterprise,[223] in which labour had "an appreciable influence." The socialism of the Co-operative Commonwealth Federation (CCF) was limited to the regulation of big business and the nationalization of natural resources and public utilities.[224]

In the U.S. Supreme Court brief filed on behalf of Joseph Lochner in the infamous Lochner case,[225] successfully claiming that a New York state law limiting the daily and weekly hours of work for bakery workers interfered with liberty and due process rights under the Fourteenth Amendment, lawyers argued that regulating hours of work for adult labourers, outside of railways and mines, was unusual and arbitrary. Among the only analogues available was An Act Respecting Bakeshops enacted in Ontario in 1896 limiting the weekly hours of work for bakery workers. Even the English law on the subject, the English Bakehouse Act of 1863, limited hours of work only for those under the age of eighteen.[226]

For much of its history, Canada admittedly did not exploit this legislative capacity.[227] It lagged in the introduction of many important pieces of social legislation as compared to other transatlantic states.[228]

---

222 Robert H. Babcock, *Gompers in Canada: A Study in American Continentalism before the First World War* (Toronto: University of Toronto Press, 1974), 155, 165, 179.

223 David Schneiderman, "Human Needs above Property Rights? Rethinking the Woodsworth Legacy in an Era of Economic Globalization," in *Human Welfare, Rights, and Social Activism: Rethinking the Legacy of J.S. Woodsworth,* ed. Jane Pulkington, 161–79 (Toronto: University of Toronto Press, 2010).

224 Lipset, *Agrarian Socialism,* 278, 164–5.

225 *Lochner v New York,* 198 US 45 (1905).

226 "Brief for Plaintiff in Error" in the Supreme Court of the United States in *Lochner v New York* (1904) 44, 40–1.

227 Harold J. Laski, "Canada's Constitution," *New Republic* 35 (4 July 1923): 159.

228 M.J. Coldwell, *Left Turn, Canada* (London: Victor Gollancz, 1945), 102; Bryce M. Stewart, *Canadian Labor Laws and the Treaty* (New York: Columbia University Press, 1926).

That Canada is portrayed as the more advanced welfare state as compared to the United States rankles Canadian conservatives. Not only was Canada late to the game, "*laissez faire* ideology and the private sector have been quite important in Canada's history," grumbles William Watson.[229] Turning the table on Canada's alleged collectivism, Brian Lee Crowley argues that one of the features that distinguished Canada from the United States was "Canadians' unbreakable attachment to a demanding work ethic and a strong distaste for any kind of dependence on the public purse."[230] Though framed in general terms (note the language of "importance" and "distaste"), the historical claims seem to fly in the face of facts like the imposition of protective tariffs by Alexander Galt in 1859 (previously mentioned), and, again, in 1879 to promote Canadian domestic industry (associated with the "national policy"). It also flies in the face of Bryce's early twentieth-century observation that "the policy of laissez faire has few adherents."[231] It is not my intention to settle this dispute here, only to observe that it is our "unused" constitutional capacity that helps to explain why a social democratic alternative arose in Canada but not in the United States. The "strong state presence" associated with Canadian constitutional culture "widened the range of political discourse and ideologies."[232]

The Research Committee of the League for Social Reconstruction asked in 1935 the constitutional question that any socialist government in Canada would have to face: "Did the fathers of Confederation rivet a particular economic system upon the backs of the Canadian people in 1867, or did they merely provide a political framework within which Canadian democracy was to work out its own destiny, socialist or capitalist?" They concluded that the "essence of the Confederation arrangement" would not stand in the way of establishing what they called a cooperative commonwealth. Without guaranteed property rights,

---

229 William Watson, *Globalization and the Meaning of Canadian Life* (Toronto: University of Toronto Press, 1998) 128.

230 Brian Lee Crowley, *Fearful Symmetry: The Fall and Rise of Canada's Founding Values* (Toronto: Key Porter Books, 2009) 44.

231 Bryce, *Canada: An Actual Democracy*, 17.

232 Mancke, "Early Modern Imperial Governance," 19. It is curious that Janet Ajzenstat, who is otherwise careful about such things, would claim that a "glance at their national debates in Congress, a glance at their national newspapers and journals shows that the United States entertains a broader range of political ideas than does Canada," in *The Once and Future Canadian Democracy: An Essay in Political Thought* (Montreal and Kingston: McGill-Queen's University Press, 2003), 113.

protection of the sanctity of contracts, a due process clause, or "rights reserved to the people," the state at both federal provincial levels "can do anything" – "Theoretically any economic change is possible."[233]

The LSR group perhaps overstated the capacity to achieve legislative and constitutional change in Canada. The division of legislative authority among eleven governments has given rise to what has been solicitously called the "difficulties of divided jurisdiction."[234] Yet parcelling up jurisdiction has not prevented the emergence of institutional mechanisms of intergovernmental cooperation (i.e., cooperative federalism and administrative inter-delegation) to overcome these difficulties. Numerous studies suggest that federalism did not obstruct the realization of important national objectives, though it may have delayed them.[235] In their review of the impact of federalism on policy outcomes for the Macdonald Commission, Frederick Fletcher and Donald Wallace write, "It is not unreasonable to conclude that both governments have found ways and means to accomplish many, perhaps most, of their objectives." Rather than acting as a bar to policy development, the pattern of Canadian federalism "has been more one of delay and frustration than of paralysis ... the system rarely frustrates the popular will."[236]

It is true that in the United States, for some fifty years (1937–95), the Supreme Court pretty much abdicated judicial review on federalism lines in favour of the play of political forces. Recently, however, the Court has signalled a return to policing jurisdictional limits (the "new federalism") in ways that may discourage the production of new national policies.[237] Beginning in 1995, the Court indicated it would no longer simply yield to just any exercise of the federal commerce clause. The Tenth Amendment resurfaced as yet another resource for the Court to limit federal action. President Obama's signal congressional

---

233 Research Committee of the League for Social Reconstruction, *Social Planning for Canada* (Toronto: Thomas Nelson and Sons, 1935), 501, 502.

234 J.A. Corry, *"Difficulties of Divided Jurisdiction": A Study Prepared for the Royal Commission on Dominion-Provincial Relations* (Ottawa: King's Printer, 1939).

235 For example, see Keith Banting, *The Welfare State and Canadian Federalism* (Montreal and Kingston: McGill-Queen's University Press, 1982), on income assistance; and Richard Simeon, *Federal-Provincial Diplomacy: The Making of Recent Policy in Canada* (Toronto: University of Toronto Press, 1973), on the Canadian pension plan.

236 Fletcher and Wallace, "Federal-Provincial Relations," 132–3, 131, 151.

237 Breyer, *Active Liberty*, 62. "Delay and deliberate confusion in government," observes Hartz, "become intolerable in communities where men have decisive social programs that they want to execute," in *Liberal Tradition in America*, 85.

achievement, the Affordable Care Act, for instance, failed to convince a majority of the justices on the Court that it fell within the Court's increasingly narrow interpretation of federal commerce clause authority. The majority, instead, took a narrow view of federal power under the commerce clause that may imperil future national programs.[238] This is not to say that, in the U.S. tradition, one cannot conceive of federalism as power conferring – as a mode for empowering, rather than limiting, government action[239] – only that its power-limiting function remains a central part of the U.S. constitutional narrative.

4. Property Rights (Again)

This idea of institutional agility via a strong state can be illustrated by an episode in early twentieth-century Ontario concerning, again, property rights.[240] The Ontario government, led by Minister without Portfolio Adam Beck, was proceeding with a program for public hydroelectric power in Ontario by entering into a series of contracts with southern Ontario municipalities. Private providers consequently would lose contracts worth millions of dollars, as would investors in these companies in Canada and abroad, while lawsuits challenged the validity of these contracts.[241] In a number of these cases it was claimed

---

238 Andrew Koppelman, *The Tough Luck Constitution and the Assault on Health Care Reform* (New York: Oxford University Press, 2013), 119–20.

239 Erwin Chemerinsky, *Enhancing Government: Federalism for the 21st Century* (Stanford: Stanford University Press, 2008).

240 Much of this history is drawn from Christopher Armstrong, *The Politics of Federalism: Ontario's Relations with the Federal Government 1867–1942* (Toronto: University of Toronto Press, 1981), 55–64; and H.V. Nelles, *The Politics of Development: Forests, Mines and Hydro-Electric Power in Ontario, 1894–1941* (Toronto: Macmillan of Canada, 1974), 256–306. I elsewhere visited this episode in David Schneiderman, "Canadian Constitutionalism, the Rule of Law and Economic Globalization," in *Participatory Justice in a Global Economy: The New Rule of Law?*, ed. Patricia Hughes and Patrick A. Molinari, 65–85 (Montreal: Les Éditions Themis, 2004). Paul Romney also invokes it, though to illustrate the decline of the federal power of disallowance and the rise of "constitutionalism" or a common law of constitutional limitations as between the federal and provincial governments, in "From Constitutionalism to Legalism," 160. George Grant (curiously) makes reference to this episode, as well, as an example of conservatism acting in behalf of the "social doctrine that public order and tradition, in contrast to freedom and experiment, were central to the good life," in *Lament for a Nation*, 71.

241 *The Credit of Canada: How It Is Affected by the Ontario Power Legislation: Views of British Journals and of English and Canadian Writers and Correspondents* (Toronto: R.G. McLean, 1909).

that the contracts were void, as the assent of the local electorate was not secured in advance, as required by enabling legislation. Facing recalcitrant company opposition and endless litigation, Beck pushed through a 1909 statute validating all municipal contracts, even those without the requisite authorization, and denying to the courts any jurisdiction to question the initiative.[242] This, according to W.E. O'Brien, was legislative interference with "vested rights" in the interests of "carry[ing] out some object of supposed public utility" (Canadian constitutional culture not being immune to the influence of dominant U.S. constitutional discourse).[243] English journalist Goldwin Smith, residing in Toronto at the time, decried the province's "confiscation" of "our right to property" and the plunder and oppression of private interests.[244] He and others maintained that the legislation was beyond the constitutional capacity of the province and that, in any event, it should be disallowed by the federal minister of justice for being "unconstitutional in a political" sense.[245] On an application to declare the contracts and legislation void, Justice William Renwick Riddell declared the powers of the provincial legislature "the same in intention, though not in extension, as those of the Imperial Parliament" and so stayed the action.[246]

It appears that it was Goldwin Smith who secured the opinion of Professor Dicey on the controversy.[247] If, as mentioned above, Dicey insisted that British parliamentary supremacy was the "very keystone" of English constitutional law,[248] would he not view Canadian constitutional authority, though divided, equally fulsome?[249] If, on the other hand, he had been correct to regard the British North America Act as "a copy, though no means a servile copy, of the Constitution of the United

---

242 Armstrong, *Politics of Federalism*, 57–8. They should "not be open to question and shall not be called into question on any ground whatever in any court but shall be held and adjudged to be valid and binding." See Power Commission Amendment Act, 1909, 9 Edw VII, c 19, s 4.

243 W.E. O'Brien, "What Are the Functions of a Provincial Legislature? – The Distinction between Public and Private Purposes," *Canada Law Journal* 45 (1909): 137–44.

244 Goldwin Smith, in *The Credit of Canada*, 48.

245 Francis Henry Chrysler, *A Question of Disallowance: Argument before the Privy Council on the Petitions for Vetoing of the Power Legislation of Ontario – The Credit of Canada, the Supreme Issue* (Ottawa, 1909), 66.

246 *Smith v London* (1909) 20 Ontario Law Reports 133, 137 (Ont Div Ct).

247 Chrysler, *Question of Disallowance*, 40.

248 Dicey, *Introduction to the Study of the Law of the Constitution*, 68.

249 The Judicial Committee of the Privy Council already had done so. See *Bank of Toronto v Lambe* [1887] 12 Appeal Cases 575 (JCPC).

States" in its federal features,[250] might there be limits to exercises of legislative authority unknown to English constitutional law?

Predictably,[251] Dicey called the provincial measures "unjust and impolitic" but opined there was nothing in the 1867 Act "which provides that a law passed by a provincial legislature shall not be palpably unjust." The "obvious unfairness of a law can hardly affect its validity if the law falls within the terms of the BNA Act," observed Dicey. In his view, the only remedy available was to petition the governor general for disallowance; indeed, he could hardly "conceive [of] a stronger case." Alternatively, Canadians could seek an amendment to the 1867 Act from the imperial Parliament incorporating U.S.-style constitutional constraints, "limiting the power of legislatures to interfere with acquired rights and with the validity of contracts," though such an amendment would "hardly be obtained ... unless it were obviously desirable by the people of Canada."[252] Despite concerns expressed by British financial opinion – Canadian Finance Minister Fielding was warned repeatedly that failure to intervene would damage Canada's credit in London's financial houses[253] – and the sympathy of Prime Minister Laurier,[254] the power of disallowance would not be exercised in these circumstances, "even though confiscation of property without compensation, and so an abuse of legislative power" had occurred, according to the report of the minister of justice responding to the request for disallowance.[255] The Ontario government could proceed with its plan for public power under a constitutional regime that would not significantly hinder provincial or federal experimentation.

How might this Canadian culture of openness to legislative innovation be contrasted with that in the United States? Justice Riddell drew out the "salient distinction" between English and U.S. constitutional law in his 1909 ruling. Retroactive legislation staying a pending action is

---

250 Dicey, *Introduction to the Study of the Law of the Constitution*, 162.
251 For reasons having to do with several decades of Judicial Committee of the Privy Council jurisprudence dealing with Canadian federalism. See, for example, Lefroy, *Law of Legislative Power in Canada*, 279.
252 A.V. Dicey, "Unjust and Impolitic Provincial Legislation and Its Disallowance by the Governor-General," *Canada Law Journal* 45 (1909): 459, 461, 462.
253 Credit of Canada, *How It Is Affected by the Ontario Power Legislation;* Armstrong, *Politics of Federalism*, 58.
254 Laurier is quoted as describing the provincial measures as "highly improper and prejudicial," in Armstrong, *Politics of Federalism*, 61.
255 C.B. Labatt, "The Scope of the Power of the Dominion Government to Disallow Provincial Statutes," *Canada Law Journal* 45 (1909): 297.

considered a judicial act in the United States and so beyond the capacity of the legislative branch.[256] Things are more complicated when denying courts jurisdiction to hear a case – what is called "jurisdiction stripping." Stripping courts of jurisdiction particularly is contentious when the adjudication of constitutional rights, such as property or due process rights, are barred from a judicial hearing. If state courts are available – not creatures of the constitution, though with jurisdiction to hear federal constitutional claims – it may be that constitutionality is less problematic. What is problematic in the United States is that if no court, state or federal, is allowed to hear constitutional claims. There will be a "strong argument" that due process rights have been denied in such cases.[257]

The situation in Canada likely has changed, in some respects, with the passage of the Charter of Rights and Freedoms. We know that the judiciary will not tolerate the closure of courts insofar as it prevents the vindication of constitutional claims.[258] As for jurisdiction stripping of non-constitutional claims, some law professors were of the opinion in 1994 that a Liberal government bill, rolling back Prime Minister Mulroney's privatization of Pearson Airport, stripping the courts of jurisdiction to hear the claim for lost profits (providing compensation for sunk costs but not future profits), ran afoul somehow of the Charter's "rule of law." The government settled the matter with the private consortium and so the matter never came to court. I was of the view then, in a submission jointly authored with Joel Bakan to a Senate Committee (instigated by the late Senator and law professor Gerald Beaudoin), that there was nothing in the Charter or the Canadian Bill of Rights to prevent the government from proceeding in this fashion.[259] The impression I had then was that we represented the minority view among law professors.[260] If so, one might say that convergence with U.S. constitutional culture on this front already was underway.

---

256 *Smith v London*, 163.
257 Erwin Chemerinsky, *Constitutional Law: Principles and Policies* (New York: Aspen, 2006) 152, 175.
258 *BCGEU v British Columbia (AG)* [1988] 2 SCR 214.
259 Joel Bakan and David Schneiderman, "Submission to the Standing Senate Committee on Legal and Constitutional Affairs concerning Bill C-22" (unpublished). An abbreviated version of the argument can be found in Joel Bakan and David Schneiderman, "The Pearson Bill Would Pass Legal Muster," *Globe and Mail*, 2 January 1995.
260 For a representative view, see Patrick J. Monahan, *Constitution Law* (Toronto: Irwin Law, 1996), 414.

2 President or Prime Minister? Prorogation 2008

Anyone who has seriously studied the parliamentary system knows that the House of Commons has long ceased to be a serious legislative body. It is first an electoral college to maintain the power of the incumbent Prime Minister and second a debating forum for partisan alternatives to the current dictator.

Stephen Harper[1]

The minority government of Prime Minister Stephen Harper was about to plummet into the abyss in late 2008. Only six weeks had passed since the last federal election[2] – only two since the speech from the throne.

---

1 Stephen Harper, "Other People's Money," *Bulldog*, 8 January 1997.
2 An election had been necessary, declared Prime Minister Harper, because the minority Parliament was "not working." There was little evidence of this. Rather, it appeared that a looming global financial crisis, for which the Conservatives did not want to take the blame, helped to precipitate the early election call. Compounding the awkwardness for the prime minister was that the last federal election flew in the face of the prime minister's prior legislative commitment to elections at fixed intervals. An amendment to the Canada Elections Act fixed the date of general elections to the third Monday in October, four years after the last general election. See "An Act to Amend the Canada Elections Act," SC 2007, c 10 (assented to 3 May 2007). This would have entailed holding off on the September 2008 election for another two years. Prime Minister Harper was unapologetic about abandoning this commitment. The fixed election law had no application to minority governments, the prime minister claimed. In any event, it could not bind future Parliaments as the power of the governor general to dissolve Parliament, acting under the advice of the prime minister, remained unaffected (s 56.1[1]). The question was litigated in *Conacher*, and both at trial and on appeal, the Federal Court of Canada declined to find that a constitutional convention had been established that could politically constrain the prime minister's discretion. See *Conacher v Canada (Prime Minister)* [2010] 3 FCR 411 (TD); aff'd [2011] 4 FCR 22 (CA).

One hundred and forty three Conservatives were elected to Parliament. Three opposition parties – the Liberals, New Democrats, and Bloc Québécois – controlled the plurality of seats (163).[3] They were determined to topple the newly installed government.

The first act of any significance by the Harper minority government was to issue a financial statement on Thursday, 27 November 2008. Rather than addressing a mounting global economic crisis, the government threatened to withdraw per-vote political subsidies for all federal political parties, cap public service wages, temporarily suspend the right to strike, and remove pay equity claims from the Canadian Human Rights Commission.[4] Seemingly out of touch with current events, Finance Minister Flaherty predicted there would even be small budget surpluses in the coming years.[5] While acknowledging that the country was likely to enter into recession, no new economic stimulus was introduced to help buffer its effects on the Canadian economy.[6] This was "widely seen as a terrible miscalculation" leaving the opposition parties hopping mad.[7] Rumours spread that they were scheming in advance of a budget vote scheduled for the following Monday (1 December)[8] – budget votes are "confidence" motions over which the government could fall. As English- and French-language columnists observed, the opposition parties smelled blood.[9] Talk of a new Liberal-led coalition

3 Seats were held by Liberal (seventy-seven), New Democrat (thirty-seven), and Bloc Québécois (forty-nine) members of Parliament. Two seats were held by independents. On the 2008 federal election results, see Andrew Heard, "The Governor-General's Decision to Prorogue Parliament: Parliamentary Democracy Defended or Endangered?," *Points of View / Points de vue* (Centre for Constitutional Studies Discussion Paper No. 7) (January 2008).

4 Finance Canada, "Economic and Fiscal Statement 2008," 27 November 2008, www.fin. gc.ca/ec2008/speech/speech-eng.html.

5 Les Whittington and Bruce Campion-Smith, "Showdown Looms over 'Mean' Tory Blueprint," *Toronto Star*, 28 November 2008.

6 Les Whittington, "Finance Minister Won't Back Down on Vote Subsidies," *Toronto Star*, 29 November 2008.

7 Tonda McCharles, Bruce Campion-Smith, and Joanna Smith, "Harper Scrambles to Retain Power," *Toronto Star*, 29 November 2008; Don Martin, "Who Will Blink on the Brink," *Calgary Herald*, 29 November 2008.

8 John Geddes and Aaron Wherry, "Inside the Crisis That Shook the Nation," *Maclean's*, 29 December 2008, 13–22.

9 Vincent Marissal, "Un coup d'État tranquille," *La Presse*, 30 November 2008; Thomas Walkom, "Hard-Right Tory Ideology Has Put the PM in a Bind," *Toronto Star*, 29 November 2008.

government was rife.[10] In order to forestall a vote of "no confidence," Prime Minister Harper retreated from most every one of the objectionable elements contained in the November financial statement, but this last-minute concession, announced by Transportation Minister John Baird two days later, seemed unlikely to delay the inevitable fall of the government.[11]

Liberal leader Stéphane Dion, however, had suffered a humiliating defeat in the October election, receiving the lowest share of the popular vote ever in the party's history.[12] One long week after the election, Dion announced he would step down and hand over the party reins after a May leadership convention.[13] As leader of Her Majesty's official opposition, it was Dion who led the charge in favour of the proposed coalition, writing directly to Governor General Michaëlle Jean on behalf of the other opposition leaders. Dion advised that, jointly with the New Democrats, we "are resolved to form a new government and to this end we have the support of the Bloc Québécois for a period of 18 months." Dion requested of the governor general that a "new government ... be allowed to demonstrate it has the confidence of the House of Commons."[14]

Dion's gambit to take on the mantle of prime minister – a matter of some internal debate within the Liberal Party caucus[15] – so soon after underperforming in the federal election offered up vulnerabilities the governing Conservatives would successfully exploit. Shifting governing authority from the Conservatives to a Liberal-NDP coalition

---

10 Joanna Smith, "Several Options Exist under Constitution," *Toronto Star*, 29 November 2008; Gilles Toupin, Joël-Denis Bellavance, and Hugo De Grandpré, "Prêts pour d'autres élections?," *La Presse*, 28 November 2008.

11 Les Whittington, Tonda McCharles, and Bruce Campion-Smith, "Tories Blink in Showdown," *Toronto Star*, 30 November 2008.

12 Michael, Valpy, "Key Liberals Send Out Feelers for Dion's Job," *Globe and Mail*, 17 October 2008.

13 Jane Taber, "Dion Twice Believed He Had a Chance to Survive," *Globe and Mail*, 21 October 2008.

14 Stephane Dion, "Coalitions Normal Event throughout the World: Dion," *Edmonton Journal*, 4 December 2008.

15 Joanna Smith and Bruce Campion-Smith, "Who Should Take the Helm of the Coalition, *Toronto Star*, 29 November 2008; Canwest News Service, "Harper Staves Off Defeat, Constitutional Crisis," *Calgary Herald*, 29 November 2008; Juliet O'Neil and Andrew Mayeda, "PM Postpones Probable Defeat of Government, *Edmonton Journal*, 29 November 2008.

with Bloc support, Prime Minister Harper alleged, was outrageously undemocratic without a new election.[16] In the House of Commons, Harper lambasted the opposition for "working on a back room deal to reverse the results of the last election."[17] "They want to take power rather than earn it," he added. "The opposition is in its right to bring down the government, but Stephane Dion does not have the right to take power without an election," declared the prime minister:[18] "The highest principle of Canadian democracy is that if one wants to be prime minister, one gets one's mandate from the Canadian people, and not from Quebec separatists."[19] In his televised address to the nation the following Wednesday night (3 December), the prime minister condemned the "opposition [for] attempting to impose this deal without your say, without your consent, and without your vote."[20] According to Conservative Party talking points, the claim was that a "socialist-separatist driven coalition is attempting to overturn the results of the last election and impose a Prime Minister that Canadians rejected."[21] Tom Flanagan, Harper's former political advisor, summed up the coalition proposal as a "head-spinning violation of democratic norms of open discussion and majority rule."[22] The prime minister pledged in the House to use every "legal means" at his disposal "to protect our democracy."[23]

All paths to foiling a loss of confidence motion in the House led to Rideau Hall and the governor general, Michaëlle Jean. Harper could advise the governor general to exercise the Crown's personal prerogative of dissolving Parliament, resulting in a fresh election. Conservative strategists feared that the governor general would turn Harper down if he asked for dissolution.[24] The less drastic solution that would buy some time but not forestall a confidence vote was to seek prorogation,

---

16 McCharles, Campion-Smith, and Smith, "Harper Scrambles to Retain Power."
17 Canada, *Parliamentary Debates*, 28 October 2008.
18 McCharles, Campion-Smith, and Smith, "Harper Scrambles to Retain Power."
19 David Akin, Andrew Mayeda, and Juliet O'Neill, "Harper Seeks to Suspend House; Tories' Destiny in Hands of Governor General," *Calgary Herald*, 3 December 2008.
20 Stephen Harper, "Opposition Imposing Deal 'Without Your Say': PM," *Edmonton Journal*, 4 December 2008.
21 CNET Database (Conservative Party of Canada), 2008.
22 Tom Flanagan, "Only Voters Have the Right to Decide on the Coalition," *Globe and Mail*, 9 January 2009.
23 Harper, "Opposition Imposing Deal."
24 Lawrence Martin, *Harperland: The Politics of Control* (Toronto: Viking Canada, 2010), 186.

which would terminate the current parliamentary session and resume a new one sometime in 2009. Harper's advisors were quite confident that this request would not be denied – it was the "only sound course of action," one anonymous source advises.[25] On Thursday, 4 December 2008, the governor general granted the prime minister's request to prorogue Parliament and so shuttered the House of Commons. It would resume its business on 26 January 2009.

The object of this chapter is not to place blame upon or praise the governor general (though I will have something to say about the correctness of the governor general's decision in the chapter's conclusion). Instead, I revisit these events with a view to understanding the proposed shift in Canada's constitutional culture promoted by Stephen Harper and his supporters. Conservative talking points maintained there could be no change of government without an election. Anything short of a new election flouted democratic principles. After all, it was claimed, the "most important decision in modern politics is choosing the executive of the national government."[26] It simply was illegitimate to convene a coalition without going to the people. The opposition politicians' conceit was that "they can legally succeed in what millions of Canadians see as the overturning of the outcome of the democratic election, and do it without giving Canadians the ultimate say in the matter."[27] Russell coined the term "Harper's new rules" to describe these new terms of engagement.[28]

Though there have been few coalition governments federally in post-1867 Canada,[29] this is a view deeply at odds with Canada's parliamentary tradition. The claim better reflects U.S. constitutional practice than the Canadian one. Executives change hands in the United States only by

---

25 Martin, *Harperland*, 186. *Erskine May's Treatise on the Law, Privileges, Proceedings and Usage of Parliament*, 23rd ed. (London: LexisNexis UK, 2004). Erskine May's treatise describes prorogation as having the effect of "at once suspend[ing] all business, including committee proceedings, until Parliament shall be summoned again, and to end the sittings of Parliament" (274).

26 Flanagan, "Only Voters Have the Right to Decide on the Coalition."

27 Michael Bliss, "Playing Footsie with the Enemy," *National Post*, 4 December 2008.

28 Peter Russell, "Learning to Live with Minority Parliaments," in *Parliamentary Democracy in Crisis*, ed. Peter Russell and Lorne Sossin (Toronto: University of Toronto Press, 2009), 141.

29 Heard, "Governor-General's Decision"; Lawrence Leduc, "Coalition Government: When It Happens, How It Works," in *Parliamentary Democracy in Crisis*, ed. Peter Russell and Lorne Sossin (Toronto: University of Toronto Press, 2009), 129.

election and as a result of a vote of the college of electors (note the reference to the House of Commons as an electoral college in the epigraph to this chapter). Short of the occasion when the vice president assumes the presidency, there can be no change of leadership without a fresh election. The prime minister and his friends appear to have been fostering the perception that the prime minister, like the U.S. president, is a separate and distinct branch of government that is elected by the citizens and constitutionally insulated from the entreaties of Parliament, including from motions of no confidence.

Conservatives uncharacteristically were slow to identify the parliamentary traditions that were at stake. Rainer Knopff and Dave Snow attend to this deficiency by denying that Harper and Flanagan make any claim that a change of government necessitated a fresh election in every case, only in *this* case. "Harper's new rules," they conclude, "turn out to be rather mythical."[30] I turn to a more detailed discussion of these claims and situate them in a larger literature concerning the presidentialization of prime ministerial authority in part 1. It turns out, however, that "Harper's new rules" are not so mythical when considered in light of media reports, an analysis that I undertake in part 2. There I consider how well Conservative talking points "took" by scrutinizing media reports of the 2008 prorogation episode published by four newspapers. Because much of the vociferous opposition to the coalition emerged out of Alberta,[31] I ask how well two of Alberta's leading newspapers (the *Calgary Herald* and *Edmonton Journal*) treated this question in contrast to both Canada's largest circulation English-language newspaper, the *Toronto Star*, and Quebec's largest-circulation French-language newspaper, *La Presse*. The concern is that this episode, as it played out in the press, may have helped contribute to a shift in the direction of U.S. constitutional style and practice.

Such a concern is not misplaced. An Ipsos Reid poll commissioned by the Dominion Institute shortly after these events reported that 51 per cent of respondents believed the prime minister is directly elected, rather than appointed by the governor general.[32] Only one-quarter of

---

30 Rainer Knopff and Dave Snow, "'Harper's New Rules' for Government Formation: Fact or Fiction?" *Canadian Parliamentary Review* (Spring, 2013): 25.

31 Ipsos Reid, "Majority (68%) of Canadians from Every Part of Country Supports Governor General's Decision to Prorogue Parliament," 5 December 2008, www.ipsos-na.com/news-polls/pressrelease.aspx?id=4201.

32 Ibid.

respondents were aware that Canada was a constitutional monarchy with the Queen as its head of state.[33] While the Conservative position during this episode may be explained away as an act of political desperation – that the Conservatives did not genuinely believe what they were saying – this chapter and subsequent ones cumulatively suggest that there are larger constitutional aspirations at play. The public relations strategy, I argue, is to exploit public ignorance about parliamentary practice and to shift understandings about constitutional practice in the direction of U.S.-style limited government.

1. Presidentializing the Prime Minister?

The Prime Minister Gets His Way

The product of more than 148 years of constitutional development, political authority is now, more than ever, concentrated in the person of the prime minister. Though nowhere mentioned in our principal constitutional texts, the prime minister wields vast authority in accordance with constitutional convention, including powers formerly exercised by the monarch under the royal prerogative. The concentration of power in the Prime Minister's Office is attributable directly to this inheritance from the British Crown.

Though drawn from the ranks of the House of Commons – and so accountable directly to the electorate of a single constituency – and ultimately responsible to Parliament – which might at its whim withdraw its confidence – the Canadian prime minister is an unusually powerful political figure, much more so than his counterparts in other Westminster democracies.[34] Much has already been written about the concentration of political authority in the prime minister. Usually attributed to Pierre Elliott Trudeau's prime ministership, the number of personnel associated with the office has since exploded, as has authority in the person of the prime minister at the expense of both the House

---

33 Dominion Institute, "In the Wake of Constitutional Crisis, New Survey Demonstrates That Canadians Lack Basic Understanding of Canada's Parliamentary System," 15 December 2008, www.dominion.ca/DominionInstituteDecember15Factum.pdf.

34 Herman Bakvis and Steven B. Wolinetz, "Canada: Executive Dominance and Presidentialization," in *The Presidentialization of Politics: A Comparative Study of Modern Democracies*, ed. Thomas Poguntke and Paul Webb (Oxford: Oxford University Press, 2005), 211.

of Commons and Cabinet.[35] Political aspirations are increasingly subject to control by the prime minister.[36] National leadership conventions, depleted media resources, and public preoccupation with the political heads of state all contribute to making the prime minister the focal point for much of what goes on in Canadian politics. We should add to this list the formal legal controls inherited from the British Crown and over which the prime minister now exercises unfettered discretion. The Senate, though formally equal in power to the lower house in most every respect (discussed in chapter 3), is under the sway of prime ministerial patronage, and so once a sufficient number of appointments to party loyalists have been made, the upper house takes on the complexion of the party in power.[37] There is little, then, "in the way of institutional check, at least inside government, to inhibit his ability to have his way."[38] The prime minister, observe Aucoin, Jarvis, and Turnbull, "is, in short, in charge at all times."[39] Harper and Flanagan conclude (writing while Prime Minister Jean Chrétien was in power) that Canadians live "in something a little better than a benign dictatorship," having generated a "concentrated power structure [in the prime minister] out of step with other aspects of society."[40]

The principal structural constraints on prime ministerial authority reside outside of parliamentary confines. They concern institutional checks associated with the federal division of powers. There is, for instance, the countervailing authority generated by highly concentrated power in the offices of each of the provincial premiers.[41] There also is a

---

35 Thomas A. Hockin, "The Prime Minister and Political Leadership: An Introduction to Some Restraints and Imperatives," in *Apex of Power: The Prime Minister and Political Leadership in Canada*, ed. Thomas A. Hockin (Scarborough, ON: Prentice-Hall of Canada, 1971), 14–15.

36 Bakvis and Wolinetz, "Canada: Executive Dominance and Presidentialization," 211.

37 Thomas J. Bateman, "Prime Ministers and Presidents: Institutional Differences and Political Convergence," in *Canada and the United States: Differences That Count*, ed. David M. Thomas and David N. Biette, 4th ed. (Toronto: University of Toronto Press, 2014), 130.

38 Donald J. Savoie, *Governing from the Centre: The Concentration of Power in Canadian Politics* (Toronto: University of Toronto Press, 1999).

39 Peter Aucoin, Mark D. Jarvis, and Lori Turnbull, *Democratizing the Constitution: Reforming Responsible Government* (Toronto: Emond Montgomery, 2011), 71.

40 Stephen Harper and Tom Flanagan, "Our Benign Dictatorship," *Next City* 2, no. 2 (1996–7): 35.

41 Bakvis and Wolinetz, "Canada: Executive Dominance and Presidentialization," 212.

powerful judicial branch that has the power to confine prime ministerial ambitions. After an active period of invalidating federal exercises
of authority, contemporary courts largely have abandoned this policing function.[42] An unprecedented number of exercises of legislative
authority, at both the federal and provincial levels, have been granted
judicial sanction by the Court. This posture of deference is reinforced
by numerous interpretive doctrines the Court has embraced. There
remains, nevertheless, the threat of an occasional declaration of ultra
vires. Conservative plans for a national securities regulator to supplant
otherwise constitutionally valid provincial schemes suffered such a
fate, to the surprise of many legal commentators.[43] Political parties play
a constraining role on prime ministerial politics, but these tend to fall
away once power is secured. Nevertheless, parties generate countervailing sources of power where rivals can find requisite support with
which to challenge sitting prime ministers, particularly if they hold
positions in Cabinet.[44]

As concerns those matters that fall constitutionally within the scope
of federal authority, the prime minister can get things done – prime
ministerial authority is highly efficient.[45] A combination of concentrated political power and an ability to secure a legislative agenda
gives rise to what Savoie calls "court government." Power is now concentrated in the prime minister and a handful of "selected courtiers"
drawn from the ranks of Cabinet, the bureaucracy, and the private
sector.[46]

---

42 Bruce Ryder, "Equal Autonomy in Canadian Federalism: The Continuing Search for
Balance in the Interpretation of the Division of Powers," *Supreme Court Law Review*
(2d) 54 (2011): 565–600.

43 *Reference re Securities Act* [2011] 3 SCR 837; David Schneiderman, "Making Waves:
The Supreme Court of Canada Confronts Stephen Harper's Brand of Federalism," in
What's Next for Canada: Securities Regulation after the Reference, ed. Anita Anand, 75–94
(Toronto: Irwin Law, 2012).

44 G.W. Jones, "The Prime Minister's Power," in *The British Prime Minister*, ed. Anthony
King (London: Macmillan, 1985), 197, 205.

45 Richard Simeon and Elaine Willis, "Democracy and Performance: Governance in
Canada and the United States," in *Degrees of Freedom: Canada and the United States in
a Changing World*, ed. Keith Banting, George Hoberg, and Richard Simeon (Montreal
and Kingston: McGill-Queen's University Press, 1997), 170.

46 Donald J. Savoie, *Court Government and the Collapse of Accountability in Canada and the
United Kingdom* (Toronto: University of Toronto Press, 2008), 16.

The President Has a Say

The executive in the U.S. constitutional system is not only fundamentally different, it is, one might say, unique in the world.[47] Before turning to a description of that system, it is worth noting that the "favored solution" in Philadelphia was to have Congress choose the executive. This would have been prophetic, as the outlines of a system of parliamentary responsible government were only just beginning to be seen. A proposal that the president be elected via an electoral college appointed by states emerged only very late in the proceedings. This suggests, for Robert Dahl, a "group of baffled and confused men who finally settled on a solution more out of desperation than confidence."[48] Eric Nelson suggests otherwise, that the resulting scheme was the product of a compromise between American Whigs who opposed kingly prerogatives and those who saw in the president an American monarch, one who could "represent the people as a whole and tame the tyrannical proclivities and partialities of the assembly." The president, in Nelson's account, should not be considered equivalent to the British prime minister but, instead, to the British King.[49]

Rather than adopting a method of appointment corresponding to the nascent system of responsible government emerging in Great Britain, the Americans opted for an indirect method of election, a college of electors chosen by states. Contemporary commentators describe the mechanism an "eighteenth-century antique" that is in desperate need of reform.[50] This became clearer following the election fiasco of 2000, resulting in the election of George W. Bush, who received a plurality of electoral college votes but a lower percentage of the popular vote than his opponent, Democratic nominee, Vice President Al Gore.[51]

---

47 Robert A. Dahl, *How Democratic Is the American Constitution?* (New Haven, CT: Yale University Press, 2001), 62.

48 Ibid., 66, 67.

49 Eric Nelson, *The Royalist Revolution: Monarchy and the American Founding* (Cambridge, MA: Harvard University Press, 2014), 186, 203. "The president of the United States does in reality what the king of Great Britain does only in theory" (228).

50 Ronald Dworkin, "Early Responses," in *A Badly Flawed Election: Debating Bush v. Gore, the Supreme Court and American Democracy*, ed. Ronald Dworkin (New York: New Press, 2002), 67.

51 But see Keith E. Whittington, "The Electoral College: A Modest Contribution," in *The Longest Night: Polemics and Perspectives on Election 2000*, ed. Arthur Jacobson and Michel Rosenfeld, 371–90 (Berkeley: University of California Press, 2002).

The electoral college was intended to ensure that only those sufficiently enlightened and disinterested, rather than the mass of citizens,
have the capacity to choose their president. States shall appoint, in the
manner they choose, a number of electors equal to the "whole number of Senators and Representatives to which" the state is entitled in
Congress.[52] As a result of the formula for representation concocted at
the Philadelphia Convention (slaves represented three-fifths of a person), southern slave states disproportionately influenced, via the electoral college, the selection of antebellum presidents.[53] If the method of
selecting independent electors in the eighteenth century was to be delegated to the states, electors mostly now follow results of the popular
vote within their home states.[54] The system remains, however, a "starkly
elitist conception of government that was popular then but which no
politician would dare endorse today."[55]

State interests also have a greater ability to influence political outcomes at the centre than is the case in Canada. Representation in the
Senate, for instance, is allocated along state lines equally, while patterns of party politics aid in ensuring that state interests are taken
into account in the composition and function of the national authority.[56] States remain the "primary training ground for federal officials,"

---

52 US Constitution, art II, s1, cl 2.
53 Akhil Reed Amar, *America's Constitution: A Biography* (New York: Random House,
     2005), 158.
54 Nelson Polsby, "Holy Cow! Preliminary Reflections on the 2000 Election," in *A Badly
     Flawed Election: Debating Bush v. Gore, the Supreme Court and American Democracy*, ed.
     Ronald Dworkin (New York: New Press, 2002), 271.
55 Dworkin, "Early Responses," 67–8.
56 This is associated with the "political safeguards of federalism" argument made ini-
     tially by Herbert Wechsler, "The Political Safeguards of Federalism: The Role of the
     States in the Composition and Selection of the National Government," *Columbia Law
     Review* 54 (1954): 546; also Jesse H. Choper, *Judicial Review and the National Political
     Process: A Functional Consideration of the Role of the Supreme Court* (Chicago: University
     of Chicago Press), 176–84; and updated by Larry D. Kramer, "Putting the Political
     Safeguards Back into the Political Safeguards of Federalism," *Columbia Law Review*
     100 (2000): 215–93. Wechsler argued that the national political process was "intrinsi-
     cally well adapted to retarding or restraining new intrusions by the center on the
     domain of the states. Far from a national authority that is expansionist by nature,
     the inherent tendency in our system is precisely the reverse, necessitating the widest
     support before intrusive measures of importance can receive significant considera-
     tion, reacting readily to opposition grounded in resistance within the states" ("Politi-
     cal Safeguards of Federalism," 558).

while officials at all levels depend on each other for electoral success. In addition, the federal government relies increasingly on state administrators to enforce federal law, which helps to safeguard state political interests.[57] This is augmented by the checking mechanism of the U.S. Supreme Court. Though it left the federal government free to exercise authority under its commerce clause for much of the second half of the twentieth century, since 1995 the Court has made curbing this grant of federal authority a priority. The Court has revived limits to the federal spending power, invigorated the Tenth Amendment as a limit on congressional authority (which "reserves" to the states or to the people all powers not "delegated" to Congress), and significantly narrowed federal authority to enforce limits against states laid down by the Fourteenth Amendment.[58] Many of these doctrinal trends came together in the perfect storm that was the constitutional challenge to President Obama's Affordable Care Act. The majority of the Court, in an opinion by Chief Justice Roberts, declined to find for the federal government on most of these grounds. The chief justice, however, salvaged a key part of the law, joining with the liberal wing of the Court, in holding that the plan's "individual mandate," which ensured the universality of health insurance coverage, was authorized by the federal taxing power.[59]

Determined to check tyrannical abuses of authority, executive power in the American system is separated out from the legislative, or at least "kept at some distance" from each other."[60] So determined were the framers to avoid the executive "corrupting" elected officials, the "ineligibility" and "incompatibility" clauses of the constitution are intended to preclude members of Congress from holding federal executive appointment while serving in elected office.[61] The separation of executive and legislative branches complements well other features of the constitution

---

57 Kramer, "Putting the Political Safeguards Back," 279, 285, 283. Posner and Vermeule go so far as to eschew enforceable legal constraints on executive power. De facto political constraints on the executive, such as elections and the maintenance of credibility, have emerged as substitutes for legal constraints, in Eric A. Posner and Adrian Vermeule, *The Executive Unbound: After the Madisonian Republic* (Oxford: Oxford University Press, 2010), chap. 4.

58 Generally, see Erwin Chemerinsky, *Enhancing Government: Federalism for the 21st Century* (Stanford: Stanford University Press, 2008).

59 *National Federation of Independent Business v Sebelius*, 132 S.Ct. 2566 (2012).

60 Neal Devins and Louis Fischer, *The Democratic Constitution* (Oxford: Oxford University Press, 2004), 83.

61 US Constitution, art I, s 6, cl 2.

that were intended to impede law-making at the centre. Each department would have "a will of its own," wrote Madison in "Federalist No. 51," and so each branch would check the other. It was therefore necessary to furnish each department with "constitutional arms for its own defence." Emblematic of these checking mechanisms is the power of the president to veto acts of Congress and the corresponding ability in Congress to override vetoes by a special majority of two-thirds vote. This enables the executive not only to constitutionally "defend himself," observes Hamilton in "Federalist No. 73," but to "furnish an additional security against the ... passing of bad laws."[62] Though there might be a worry that the executive veto might equally prevent the passing of good laws, Hamilton reassures us, it is better to have no laws than bad ones: "This objection will have little weight with those who can properly estimate the mischiefs of that inconstancy and mutability in the laws, which form the greatest blemish in the character and genius of our governments. They will consider every institution calculated to restrain the excess of lawmaking, and to keep things in the same state in which they happen to be at any given period as much more likely to do good than harm; because it is favurable to greater stability in the system of legislation."[63]

Concerned about the veto's stultifying effect, Levinson wryly observes that if too many cooks can spoil the broth, they also can "effectively, assure that ultimately there will be no broth at all."[64] This is because, as an "institutional" veto player, presidential vetoes act as a prophylactic to policy change. According to Tsebelis's game theoretic account, constitutional systems can enhance policy stability by constitutionally mandating unanimous consent from a range of veto players. This narrows the "winset" of agreement required to upset the status quo,[65] in which case regimes with presidential vetoes render policy change more onerous than in bicameral parliamentary systems.

In theory, executive authority should be limited to those matters outlined in the text of the constitution, and they are few. Executive power is "vested" in the president; he is deemed commander-in-chief; and he

---

62 Alexander Hamilton, James Madison, and John Jay, *The Federalist Papers*, ed. Clinton Rossiter (New York: New American Library, 1961), 321, 442, 443.

63 Ibid., 444.

64 Sanford Levinson, "Federalist No. 73 (Hamilton): Why the Presidential Veto?" (unpublished 2012).

65 George Tsebelis, *Veto Players: How Political Institutions Work* (Princeton, NJ: Princeton University Press, 2002), 19, 21.

is empowered to recommend measures to Congress and to "take care" that laws are "faithfully executed." Power is shared with the Senate in the making of treaties and in major nominations. Though the president has complete authority in choosing nominees for Cabinet and those for judicial and other executive appointment, the Senate has a veto power to "advise and consent" in the making of these appointments.

In practice, the residuum of presidential power beyond the text has been continually contested. Justice Jackson's classic formulation in the Steel Seizure case distinguished between circumstances where the president acts under the express or implied authority of Congress, where "his authority is at its maximum, and those occasions where the President contradicts Congressional authority, when his power 'is at its lowest ebb.'"[66] President Truman's temporary seizure of steel mills in anticipation of a nationwide strike fell into the latter category. There is a third category, however, when the president acts and Congress has not spoken, where "he can only rely upon his own independent powers." This is what Justice Jackson famously called the "zone of twilight in which he and Congress may have concurrent authority, or in which its distribution is uncertain." "In this area," Justice Jackson adds, "any actual test of power is likely to depend on the imperatives of events and contemporary imponderables, rather than on abstract theories of law."[67] A lot of ink has been spilled on exploring this "zone of twilight."[68] Much depends upon the degree to which there is coordination with the legislative branch, which may or may not be willing to play along if controlled by the opposing political party (resulting in the phenomenon of divided government). There is more that can be said about the murkiness of presidential authority, particularly in wartime. We might consider, for instance, the unprecedented power grab by the presidency of

---

66 Presidential authority "includes all that he possesses in his own right plus all that Congress can delegate." Otherwise, "then he can rely only upon his own constitutional powers minus any constitutional powers of Congress over the matter," per Justice Jackson in *Youngstown Sheet & Tube Co v Sawyer*, 343 US 579 (1952) at 635, 637.

67 Ibid.

68 For example, Edward S. Corwin, *The President: Office and Powers, 1787–1957, History and Analysis of Practice and Opinion*, 4th rev. ed. (New York: New York University Press, 1957); Henry Monaghan, "The Protective Power of the Presidency," *Columbia Law Review* 93 (1993): 1–74; Martin S. Lederman and David Jeremiah Barron, "The Commander in Chief at the Lowest Ebb: Framing the Problem, Doctrine, and Original Understanding," *Harvard Law Review* 121 (2008): 689–804.

George W. Bush,[69] accompanied by unnerving claims that the president can ignore the execution of laws duly enacted by Congress on constitutional grounds, including prohibitions on torture, via 127 presidential signing statements concerning 1,000 different provisions.[70]

Removal of the president also is intended to be difficult. Presidents are expected to serve out their full four-year lease at the White House unless subjected to the extraordinary procedure of impeachment by the Senate for high crimes and misdemeanours. Otherwise, presidents are unmovable. They cannot be removed by votes of non-confidence, nor will the president's party act on its own initiative to remove him or her from the post.[71] There is no other safeguard in the case of a failed executive, hence the phenomenon of waiting until the inauguration of President-Elect Obama while the increasingly dismal presidency of George W. Bush waited out the end of a four-year term as an economic crisis was brewing. It is in this respect that the virtue of parliamentary forms of government, working together with the party system, is most pronounced. Successful votes of non-confidence, particularly in minority government situations, can remove unpopular governments. Even when a party is firmly in control of the machinery of government, the transition of executive authority has the potential to occur long before any fixed period of tenure runs out.[72] This occurred, for instance, in the case of Tony Blair, whose declining fortunes, partly as a result of joining the "coalition of the willing" that invaded Iraq in 2003, resulted in his early departure from the prime ministership. Blair's tenancy terminated at No. 10 Downing sometime earlier than did his presidential counterpart at 1600 Pennsylvania Avenue.[73]

---

69 Jack Goldsmith, *The Terror Presidency: Law and Judgment inside the Bush Administration* (New York: W.W. Norton, 2007); Peter Irons, *War Powers: How the Imperial Presidency Hijacked the Constitution* (New York: Henry Holt, 2005); John Yoo, *War by Other Means: An Insider's Account of the War on Terror* (New York: Atlantic Monthly, 2006).

70 Todd Garvey, "Presidential Signing Statements: Constitutional and Institutional Implications," Congressional Research Service 7-5700 (4 January 2012), 7–8; Charlie Savage, *Takeover: The Return of the Imperial Presidency and the Subversion of American Democracy* (New York: Little Brown, 2007), chap. 10.

71 Bruce Ackerman, *The Decline and Fall of the American Republic* (Cambridge, MA: Harvard University Press, 2010), 29.

72 R.H.S. Crossman, "Introduction," in Walter Bagehot, *The English Constitution* (Glasgow: Fontana/Collins, 1963), 54. Crossman adds that the "method employed must always be that of undercover intrigue and sudden unpredicted coup d'etat" (54).

73 Philip Gould, *The Unfinished Revolution: How New Labour Changed British Politics for Ever* (London: Abacus, 2011), 446, 495–6. Gould describes "the so-called coup" having had some success (496, 498). Also see Peter Mandelson, *The Third Man: Life at the Heart of New Labour* (London: HarperPress, 2012), 386–7.

Testing the "-ization" Thesis

It is often said that the president is the most powerful person in the free world. There remains a "profound gap," however, between the perceived power of the president and the presidential ability to get things done.[74] In the early twentieth century, journalist Sidney Low observed that, unlike the American president, an "English Prime Minister, with his majority secure in Parliament," can do almost anything, "for he can alter the laws, he can impose taxation or repeal it, and he can direct all of the forces of the state."[75] This renders claims that there is a convergence of sorts between prime ministerial and presidential offices incongruous. The argument being made, however, is that the "'presidentialization' of politics has become more widespread in more recent years, regardless of formal constitutional characteristics."[76] A cluster of claims usually are associated with the presidentialization thesis (at least as applied to Westminster democracies) having to do, first, with the centralization of policy-making and coordination; second, the marginalization of Cabinet and Parliament; and third, the personalization of party leadership.[77] The first and second factors were characteristic features of British parliamentary democracy by the time Bagehot's *English Constitution* was first published in 1867, writes Richard Crossman. Crossman identified a shift from Cabinet government to prime ministerial government, which had "already before 1867 given him near-Presidential powers."[78] Crossman walked back this controversial claim several years later: the prime minister "has not become in the least Presidential, but he is certainly more powerful than he was," he maintained.[79]

---

74 Simeon and Willis, "Democracy and Performance," 169.

75 Sidney Low, *The Governance of England*, rev. ed. (London: T. Fisher Unwin, 1914), 47.

76 Thomas Poguntke and Paul Webb, "The Presidentialization of Politics in Democratic Societies: A Framework for Analysis," in *The Presidentialization of Politics: A Comparative Study of Modern Democracies*, ed. Thomas Poguntke and Paul Webb (Oxford: Oxford University Press, 2005), 1; Paul Webb and Thomas Poguntke, "The Presidentialization of Politics Thesis Defended," *Parliamentary Affairs* 66 (2013): 646–54.

77 R.A.W. Rhodes, John Wanna, and Patrick Weller, *Comparing Westminster* (Oxford: Oxford University Press, 2009), 86; Poguntke and Webb, "Presidentialization of Politics in Democratic Societies," 5.

78 Crossman, "Introduction," 51.

79 R.H.S. Crossman, *Inside View: Three Lectures on Prime Ministerial Government* (London: Jonathan Cape, 1972), 45. Prime ministerial authority increased by reason of, among other things, "the centralisation of the party machine under his personal rule" and by the "growth of a centralised bureaucracy." See Crossman, "Introduction," 52; Crossman, *Inside View*, 65, 67.

Associated with the phenomenon of presidentialization is the rise of what Michael Foley calls "spatial leadership," where the office of the president is kept at some distance from the operations of ordinary government, exploiting contradictory "insider" and "outsider" roles.[80] Prime Minister Margaret Thatcher was the proverbial outsider who capitalized on the opportunity to govern in the style of spatial leadership. "She gave physical form to that which drives leaders into presidential solitude at the same time that it forces them into presidential prominence as a personalised intermediary between the government and the public," claims Foley.[81] The characteristics of a presidentialized prime minister intensified to "unprecedented levels" under the leadership of Tony Blair.[82]

Taking stock of Crossman's diagnoses in the Trudeau era, Denis Smith is of the view that the Canadian prime minister may be further along the road to being a presidential leader than the British. With singlehanded control over party, Cabinet, and the timing of elections, "it is virtually impossible to replace" an "alert Prime Minister." With so "many weapons of influence and patronage" at hand, he is "virtually as immovable as an American President during his term of office."[83] Herman Bakvis and Steven Wolinetz confirm that there are "distinct signs of presidentialization" at the federal and even at provincial levels. With extraordinary control over the parliamentary caucus, Cabinet, and the federal policy agenda, together with an overriding focus on leadership during party conventions, the Canadian prime minister might provide the best case for the presidentialization thesis. Bakvis and Wolinetz, however, treat the argument as analogous to the prevalence of "executive dominance" and so acknowledge the features they have isolated describe no "new phenomenon."[84] For this reason, Thomas

---

80 Michael Foley, *The British Presidency: Tony Blair and the Politics of Public Leadership* (Manchester: Manchester University Press, 2000), 31.

81 Michael Foley, *The Rise of the British Presidency* (Manchester: Manchester University Press, 1993), 9, 87.

82 Ibid., 110; Michael Foley, "Presidential Attribution as an Agency of Prime Ministerial Critique in a Parliamentary Democracy: The Case of Tony Blair," *British Journal of Politics and International Relations* 6 (2004): 292–311; Graham Allen, *The Last Prime Minister: Being Honest about the UK Presidency* (Thorverton: Imprint Academic, 2003).

83 Denis Smith, "President and Parliament: The Transformation of Parliamentary Government in Canada," in *Apex of Power: The Prime Minister and Political Leadership in Canada*, ed. Thomas Hockin (Scarborough, ON: Prentice-Hall of Canada, 1971), 231, 233.

84 Bakvis and Wolinetz, "Canada: Executive Dominance and Presidentialization," 199, 218.

Bateman prefers to characterize the "convergence" between the offices of president and prime minister as being one about "personalization," where "personality and agenda" combine to overcome party, caucus, senior public service, and Cabinet colleagues.[85]

There are many claims bundled up in the presidentialization thesis, some of which undoubtedly well capture recent developments in parliamentary democracies such as Canada's.[86] Rather than tend to each of these claims singly, I want to cut to the chase and argue that the presidentialization of the Canadian prime minister is improbable only because the prime minister is already so much more powerful than the president.[87] Much of the presidentialization literature relies on questionable empirical claims about the nature of presidential authority. The U.S. president's office is perceived to be a powerful one not because of the office's formal constitutional authority but because, it is said, the president has the "power to persuade."[88] It is the capacity of the president to transform the nation's values and expectations – to engage in "transformational change"[89] – that underscores the power of presidential leadership. The problem, George C. Edwards III explains, is that there is a striking "lack of evidence of the persuasive power of the presidency." Focusing on what he calls the "best test cases," Edwards examines the record of the seemingly most successful presidencies (Presidents Lincoln, F.D. Roosevelt, Johnson, and Reagan). He concludes that whatever successes they had (and they were fewer than usually is assumed), these presidents did not move public opinion. They were more successful at exploiting existing public opinion than "creating it in the first place." "Presidential issue priorities," Edwards observes, "are often a response

---

85 Bateman, "Prime Ministers and Presidents," 117; Keith Dowding, "The Prime Ministerialization of the British Prime Minister," *Parliamentary Affairs* 66 (2013): 620.

86 Indeed, there are other parallels, often overlooked, between parliamentary and presidential systems of government. See Richard Albert, "The Fusion of Presidentialism and Parliamentism," *American Journal of Comparative Law* 57 (2009): 531–77.

87 Richard Heffernan, "Why the Prime Minister Cannot Be a President: Comparing Institutional Imperatives in Britain and America," *Parliamentary Affairs* 58 (2005): 55; Dowding, "Prime Ministerialization of the British Prime Minister," 628.

88 Richard E. Neustadt, *Presidential Power: The Politics of Leadership with Reflections on Johnson and Nixon* (New York: John Wiley & Sons, 1976), 100.

89 Precisely how candidate Barack Obama described the Reagan presidency in contrast to the Clinton presidency. See John Heilemann and Mark Halperin, *Game Change: Obama and the Clintons, McCain and Palin, and the Race of a Lifetime* (New York: HarperCollins, 2010), 205.

to the public rather than a cause of the public's agenda." As for Congress, the persuasive president is less likely to secure support than one who strategically exploits the congressional hand that they are dealt. "Rather than creating conditions for important shifts in public policy," Edwards concludes, "effective leaders are the less heroic facilitators who work at the margins of coalition building to recognize and exploit opportunities in their environments."[90] So it turns out that the U.S. presidency is less powerful and influential and more dependent on existing opinion than the presidentialization literature acknowledges. This renders the analogy even less apt. Because the differences between presidential and parliamentary systems "far outweigh the likenesses by some margin," it is "better to talk of changing styles of leadership, about centralization, than about presidentialization," advise Rhodes, Wanna, and Weller.[91]

It would be imprudent, however, to abandon all efforts at analogizing between presidents and prime ministers. Some lines of inquiry may shed light on changes occurring within parliamentary systems. Responding to claims that such analogies are inapt, Michael Foley alleges that such a stance "runs the risk of foreclosing perspectives and confining analytical imagination at a time of acknowledged change."[92] In his careful parsing of the presidential/prime ministerial analogy, Foley isolates three features of Thatcher's leadership style that well complement developments under Prime Minister Harper's watch. First, Thatcher was able to maximize the power potential within the office and so further personalize it.[93] Second, she conscripted national history to "project herself and her office as an embodiment of national principles and values." Last, Thatcher exploited the vagueness of the unwritten constitution to advance her agenda. This precipitated concerns about a constitutional crisis and need for constitutional reform to curtail executive authority.[94] One can find parallels to each of these elements in Harper's leadership style, from an unprecedented preoccupation with agenda-setting[95] (rebranding federal authority as the

---

90 George C. Edwards III, *The Strategic President: Persuasion and Opportunity in Presidential Leadership* (Princeton, NJ: Princeton University Press, 2009), 9, 17, 55, 79, 187.
91 Wanna and Weller, *Comparing Westminster*, 111.
92 Michael Foley, "Prime Ministerialization and Presidential Analogies: A Certain Difference in Interpretive Evolution," *Parliamentary Affairs* 66 (2012): 659.
93 Foley, *Rise of the British Presidency*, 154.
94 Ibid., 158, 170–2.
95 Fred Fletcher, "The Harper Government's Communication Strategy: The Message, the Message, the Message," *Canada Watch* (Spring 2011): 37–8, 43.

"Harper Government"), conscription of history, in particular military history (i.e., the War of 1812),[96] and exploitation of unwritten constitutional convention and practice (requests for repeated prorogations in the face of political crises), precipitating calls for constitutional reform to curtail the exercise of executive authority.[97]

2. Presidentializing the Prorogation

Harper's New Rules?

Even if the presidentialization thesis fails to entirely convince, the events of November 2008 remain remarkable in the annals of parliamentary democracy, and not merely because a coalition government threatened to assume the controls of government. The history of responsible government in Canada, and elsewhere, reveals that this is entirely within the acceptable parameters of parliamentary practice.[98] Rather, what is extraordinary is that the Harper government claimed that it was illegitimate for a change of government to occur without a new federal election.

Perhaps the claim should be confined to the unusual circumstances where a sovereignist party, the Bloc Québécois, is conscripted to play a supporting role in a proposed coalition government. Though not formally part of the coalition, the Bloc agreed to support the Liberal-NDP coalition on confidence votes for eighteen months. This elicited storms

---

96 Steven Chase and Daniel LeBlanc, "'Little-Known War' of 1812 a Big Deal for Ottawa," *Globe and Mail*, 27 April 2013.

97 Aucoin, Jarvis, and Turnbull, *Democratizing the Constitution*; Peter Russell and Cheryl Milne, *Adjusting to a New Era of Parliamentary Government: Report of a Workshop on Constitutional Conventions* (Toronto: David Asper Centre for Constitutional Rights, 2011).

98 Aucoin, Jarvis, and Turnbull, *Democratizing the Constitution*, 173. For instance, in both 1873 and 1926, governments led by different parties changed hands without an election – interestingly, in both cases prime ministers sought to foreclose parliamentary inquiries into misbehaviour – though in both instances elections were held within three months of the new government taking office. See Eugene A. Forsey, *The Royal Power of Dissolution of Parliament in the British Commonwealth* (Toronto: Oxford University Press, 1968), 133–9, 183. There are other such precedents emanating out of provincial arenas in addition to Australia and Great Britain. There also are instances where a prime minister is ousted by party convention or caucus revolt between federal elections. See Russell, "Learning to Live with Minority Parliaments," 141.

of outrage, some of them confused, about separatists formally partici-
pating in government, or fears of concessions having been extracted,
dangerous to the future of Canada, in exchange for the Bloc's support.
Though legitimately elected to forty-nine parliamentary seats in the
House of Commons, the "Bloc is not a political party like the others,"
remarks historian Michael Bliss. Though other political parties have
played "footsie" with the Bloc – both government and opposition parties have cooperated with them on previous occasions – it is an entirely
different thing to "jump into bed with them," Bliss contends. "The only
way to test Canadians' comfort level with an enhanced status for the
Bloc in the governance of the country is through an election," Bliss
maintained.[99]

As mentioned earlier, Tom Flanagan insists, without qualification, on
a new election whenever there is a change of government. He lays out
this argument in a short editorial opinion in January 2009.[100] Critics, it
is claimed, ignored a Flanagan editorial opinion published one month
earlier.[101] That earlier editorial, allege Rainer Knopff and Dave Snow,
"thoroughly fits into the older consensus" about when dissolution
should occur.[102] This is because, in December 2008, Flanagan claimed
that criteria articulated by Eugene Forsey, that venerable constitutional
authority, had been satisfied by the threat of coalition government and
warranted a new election.[103] What are the parameters of that "older
consensus"? Forsey's authoritative tome, *The Royal Power of Dissolution
of Parliament in the British Commonwealth* (1943), is an exhaustively

---

99 Bliss, "Playing Footsie with the Enemy." Bliss's critique is overblown to the extent
    that he likens the proposed coalition to constitutional reform proposals, like the
    1987 Meech Lake Accord, that were hatched by backroom insiders without much
    thought of consulting the people. "Just as it was finally realized that the [1992]
    Charlottetown Accord had to be taken to the people," Bliss opines, "so the Liberal-
    NDP-Bloc coalition proposal would have to go to the Canadian people before it
    could be legitimately implemented," in Michael Bliss, "Ignoring Our Constitutional
    Tradition," *National Post*, 6 December, 2008. This analogy is inapt. Constitutional
    reform proposals, if successful, permanently change Canada's fundamental law
    and cannot be undone without triggering onerous amending formulae. Successful
    "implementation" of the coalition proposal could work only for a time before mat-
    ters ultimately returned to the electorate for their approval.
100 Flanagan, "Only Voters Have the Right to Decide on the Coalition."
101 Tom Flanagan, "This Coalition Changes Everything," *Globe and Mail*, 8 December,
    2008.
102 Knopff and Snow, "Harper's New Rules," 19.
103 Flanagan, "This Coalition Changes Everything."

researched defence of the governor general's refusal to dissolve Parliament in 1926 at the behest of Prime Minister Mackenzie King, who faced an impending motion of censure.[104] Rather than accede to King's request for dissolution, Governor General Byng called upon Arthur Meighen, leader of the Conservative opposition, to form the government, which fell in less than a week.[105] Resisting the proposition that a prime minister is entitled automatically to dissolution upon demand, Forsey acknowledged there are circumstances in which dissolution could be granted. No government was entitled to dissolve Parliament unless, among other things, some "great new issue of public policy had arisen" or "there had been a major change in the political situation,"[106] though the precedent on this front was mixed.[107] Flanagan contends that by proposing what Dion explicitly rejected during the September 2008 campaign, namely a coalition government, Dion "wrought a *fundamental change* in the political situation because it involved an entire potential government, not just this or that policy" and so satisfied Forsey's "conditions" warranting dissolution and a new election.[108]

Let us accept, for the moment, that a "great issue of public policy" or "major change in the political situation" warrants dissolution (as mentioned, the evidence of established practice is equivocal). Forsey's lawyerly scrutinizing of the record nowhere suggests coalitions could not legitimately arise after an election or that a coalition arising after an election satisfied these conditions. To the contrary, Forsey considers a coalition government, both before and after an election, as a foreseeable

---

104 Forsey, *Royal Power of Dissolution*, 132, 145. This represented – remarkably, given the thoroughness of the work – Forsey's hastily completed doctorate while teaching full-time at McGill University. See Helen Forsey, *Eugene Forsey: Canada's Maverick Sage* (Toronto: Dundurn, 2012), 37.

105 Forsey, *Royal Power of Dissolution*, 131–9.

106 Ibid., 162. In his discussion Forsey treats "some great new issue of public policy" and "major change in the political situation" as interchangeable (265); also Eugene Forsey, "Professor Angus on the British Columbia Election: A Comment," *Canadian Journal of Economics and Political Science* 19 (1953): 228.

107 Forsey, *Royal Power of Dissolution*, 256, 266. Forsey refers to Sir Robert Peel as originating authority for the proposition, later endorsed by Lord John Russell (265, 267). Alpheus Todd affirms that there must be "an important political question … at issue," in *Parliamentary Government in the British Colonies*, 2nd ed. (London: Longman's, Green, 1894), 773–4. Also A.B. Keith, *The King and the Imperial Crown* (London: Longmans, 1936), 177 ("an important change of policy") 265, 267.

108 Flanagan, "This Coalition Changes Everything" (emphasis added).

response to political machinations. For instance, he expressly contemplates coalitions arising in response to repeated dissolutions.[109] More to the point, in his response to Arthur Berriedale Keith's proposal that dissolution be granted automatically upon the prime minister's request, Forsey suggests otherwise.[110] Instead of dissolution, Forsey asks, why should the electorate not "take the consequences [of a prior election] in the form of a coalition or a series of minority Governments?"[111] Coalitions may be short lived, Forsey insists, in which case might "it not be the wish of the House, and also the country, that there should be a new coalition, or a new minority Government with independent support from another party, without a general election?"[112] Forsey contemplates a scenario where two parties might join together after an election: "If two Opposition parties, hitherto at issue on some great question of public policy, drop their opposition to each other and *fuse*, then it certainly seems reasonable for the minority Government to challenge the new, fused party in the country. But if the opposition 'coalition' is merely a temporary arrangement for the purposes of the division lobby; if it expresses no more than purely negative agreement that the existing Government is undesirable; then it may be questioned whether, in all circumstances, it is reasonable that a minority Government should be granted a dissolution."[113]

Australian precedent in 1909 supports Forsey's interpretation of "temporary" arrangements, no more than "purely negative" expressions of opinion, making it unreasonable to accede to a request for dissolution. There the parties were divided over "great questions of public policy: immigration and the land tax, and defence," in which, during the election, there was no prospect of compromise forthcoming between the opposition parties. The governor general appropriately refused Prime Minister Fisher's request for dissolution.[114] The events

---

109 Forsey, *Royal Power of Dissolution*, 93.
110 "Normally ... the electorate should be allowed to decide, for it may be held to take the consequences of returning a dubious verdict in the previous contest," in Arthur Berriedale Keith, *The Constitution of England from Victoria to George VI* (London: Macmillan, 1940), 1:86–7.
111 Forsey, *Royal Power of Dissolution*, 111, 116.
112 Ibid., 111, 116.
113 Ibid., 119–20.
114 Ibid., 37. On the Australian case, see Herbert Vere Evatt, *The King and His Governors: A Study of the Reserve Powers of the Crown in Great Britain and the Dominions* (London: Oxford University Press, 1936), 51–3.

of 2008 resemble the scenario of a temporary coalition rather than one where political parties, formerly in disagreement on some great issue of public policy, change their views and "fuse" into a single new party. It is reasonable to question, therefore, whether a minority government should be granted dissolution in the circumstances of 2008 (though it was prorogation, and not dissolution, that was then in play).

This analysis does not do away entirely with the fundamental objections many had to the Bloc Québécois agreeing to prop up the coalition. Note, however, that they were not to form part of the government. This probably reflected Bloc supporters' preferred course of action. Though they endorsed the coalition in early polling,[115] there were reservations expressed about propping up a government led by the father of the Clarity Act, Stéphane Dion.[116] It was particularly awkward for Harper and his former advisor Flanagan to claim that Bloc Québécois participation raised some great new issue of public policy warranting an election when they had earlier contemplated a formal alliance with the Bloc. In a 1996–7 co-authored essay, Harper and Flanagan call for the construction of a new conservative alliance "at least of the two Anglophone sisters [the Progressive Conservative and Reform Parties] and perhaps ultimately including a third sister." The "third sister" is an allusion to the Bloc Québécois, whose rural supporters they describe as "voters who would not be out of place in Red Deer, except that they speak French rather than English." "It may be that the third sister can never be brought back in," they lament, as "they may never again see merit in a conservative coalition" as they did under John A. Macdonald's party leadership ("a single party in name but a coalition in substance").[117] Conservative opposition leader Stephen Harper even proposed in a letter of 9 September 2004, jointly signed with the Bloc and NDP leaders to Governor General Adrienne Clarkson, that opposition parties might

---

115 Joël-Denis Bellavance, "Les Québécois en faveur d'une coalition," *La Presse*, 1 December 2008.

116 Louise Leduc, "Le Bloc a la benediction des bonzes indépendantistes," *La Presse*, 3 December 2008. For a survey of leading Quebec opinion on the prorogation episode, see Frederic Boily, "La 'crise de la prorogation' vue du Québec," *Constitutional Forum constitutionnel* 18, no. 1 (2009): 21–31. The Clarity Act, enacted in response to the Supreme Court's opinion in the *Quebec Secession Reference* (1998), authorized the House of Commons to determine unilaterally, in the context of any future Quebec referendum, whether a "clear majority" answered a "clear question."

117 Harper and Flanagan, "Our Benign Dictatorship," 54, 55.

be invited to take the reins of government should the minority-led Liberal government, under Paul Martin's leadership, fall.[118] The letter described the opposition parties as "together constitut[ing] a majority in the House," and as "hav[ing] been in close consultation." "We believe," the joint letter continues, "that, should a request for dissolution arise this should give you cause, as constitutional practice has determined, to consult the opposition leaders and consider all of your options before exercising your constitutional authority."[119] Documents proposing a joint speech from the throne were circulating.[120] "Without question," explained the late NDP leader Jack Layton, Harper was prepared to enter into "some kind of relationship with the Bloc."[121] So the Bloc's support hardly satisfied the "great issue of public policy" or "major change in the political situation" standard articulated by Forsey.

Knopff and Snow decline taking a position on whether Forsey's conditions were met in 2008. Instead, they argue that, by reason of Flanagan's engagement with Forsey's scouring of the commonwealth record on dissolution, Flanagan (or those in agreement with him) did not hold to an elections-only rule in the case of the defeat of a minority government. "Harper's new rules," they claim, "turn out to be mythical" – the critics have set up only straw men to knock down.[122] Flanagan's engagement with Forsey's careful account, I have suggested, was superficial and ill informed. It amounted to a denial of precedent, both historical and contemporary, and Forsey's own words on the subject. If not a "new rule," it was a made-up one.

There was even less of an engagement with parliamentary traditions in the Conservative campaign that mobilized opposition to the threatened coalition. Constitutional niceties were cast aside and, instead, Conservatives were content to capitalize on Canada's increasingly personalized form of government by suggesting the prime minister is directly elected by the people. As the Dominion Institute survey suggests, half of Canadians so believed.[123] The nature of Canada's

---

118 Martin, *Harperland*, 183.
119 Brian Topp, *How We Almost Gave the Tories the Boot: The Inside Story behind the Coalition* (Toronto: Lorimer, 2010), 34.
120 Smith, "Several Options Exist under Constitution."
121 Martin, *Harperland*, 183.
122 Knopff and Snow, "Harper's New Rules," 23, 25.
123 Dominion Institute, "In the Wake of Constitutional Crisis, New Survey Demonstrates That Canadians Lack Basic Understanding of Canada's Parliamentary System," 15 December 2008, www.dominion.ca/DominionInstituteDecember15Factum.pdf.

highest office necessitated elections for that high office, Conservatives implored. A change of government from one party to the next could not occur otherwise.

Conservative radio ads declared that Dion "is trying to overturn the election he lost and take power through the back door."[124] The Conservative Party implored supporters to write letters to the editor and to call talk radio to let "people know the current coalition discussions are 'undemocratic' and amount to an 'overturning' of the election, a usurping of power and, of course, an 'attack on Canada.'"[125] The prime minister's chief of staff called upon supporters to "use every single tool and medium at our disposal to communicate to Canadians" how this "affront to democratic will" amounted to an attempt to "seize an unelected mandate" and appended several "communication products" with which to get the message out.[126] Conservative fundraising letters declared, "Liberals have *no mandate* to lead a government ... This back-room deal is so *unprecedented* and so *undemocratic* that Canadians must have their say. This is Canada. *The privilege to govern must be earned, not taken* ... In the last election, Conservatives stood together and spoke out loud and clear about the kind of Canada they wanted. Now we must stand together once again to ensure that the wishes of the voters are respected. Time is of the essence."[127]

One prominent Conservative blogger, mobilizing anti-coalition rallies, claimed that Liberals sought to "overturn the results of the last election and impose a Prime Minister and a Government that Canadians did not vote for."[128] The pro-coalition campaign was not nearly as vocal or as effective. In addition to having to overcome a significant fundraising

---

124 Shane Dingman, "New Conservative Radio Ads Reject Coalition, Push for Election," *National Post*, 2 December 2008.

125 Naheed Nenshi, "Harper Can't Help Himself ... or Can," *Calgary Herald*, 4 December 2008. Gilles Toupin and Joël-Denis Bellavance, "Offensive tous azimuts des conservateurs," *La Presse*, 2 December 2008.

126 Whittington, McCharles, and Campion-Smith, "Tories Blink in Showdown"; "Text of PMO E-mail to MPs on Key Talking Points," *Calgary Herald*, 30 November 2008; Andrew Mayeda, "Harper Restores Cash to Parties," *Calgary Herald*, 30 November 2008.

127 Irving Gerstein, "Letter from Chair, Conservative Fund of Canada," 29 November 2008. Emphasis in the original.

128 P.M. Jaworski, "Stephen Taylor Launches Rally for Canada Website," *Western Standard*, 2 December 2008; "Stand Up for Canada," e-mail from standupforcanada@conservative.ca, 2008.

deficit compared to the Conservative Party's success,[129] there was no effective rebuttal of the dominant Conservative narrative. Radio ads paid for by the Canadian Labour Congress, for instance, focused on the Harper government's quiescent economic agenda that helped to justify the "new coalition government."[130] This hardly responded to the coordinated and concerted campaign that the coalition was illegitimate. In journalist Lawrence Martin's evaluation, it "was a case of one side being able to sell its message, the other side not."[131] I next inquire into just how effective the Conservative ground war turned out to be.

Reading the Newspaper Coverage

By examining reporting in four city newspapers, we can gauge how well Conservative talking points "took." Though readership of the print media is in decline,[132] an examination of two newspapers in Alberta (the *Calgary Herald* and the *Edmonton Journal*), one in Ontario (the *Toronto Star*, Canada's largest circulation newspaper), and one in Quebec (*La Presse*, the largest French-language broadsheet circulation newspaper) enables us to clarify the basis upon which the regions took sides in the coalition controversy. Because Alberta was at "the epicentre of anti-coalition anger,"[133] content analysis of two of Alberta's leading city newspapers was undertaken during the period 27 November to 8 December 2008. Toronto readership, by contrast, was not as angered by the proposed coalition and Montreal readership was the most supportive of the coalition. Both provide a contrast to Alberta-based opposition during this period.[134] A qualitative analysis of 259 stories was undertaken, roughly distributed in equal amounts among the four newspapers – sixty-eight in *La Presse*, seventy-four in the *Toronto Star*, fifty-three in the *Edmonton Journal*, and sixty-four in the *Calgary Herald*. In addition to inquiring into how the coalition was portrayed in these

---

129 Geddes and Wherry, "Inside the Crisis That Shook the Nation," 15.
130 Canadian Labour Congress, "Coalition – YES! The Best Plan for Canada," 2 December 2008, www.youtube.com/watch?v=75djonzjtkI.
131 Martin, *Harperland*, 183.
132 Susan Ruttan, "The Case for Newspapers," *Alberta Views* 11, no. 10 (2008): 29.
133 Petti Fong, "Opinions, Emotions Run High in the West," *Toronto Star*, 5 December 2008.
134 Leger Marketing, "National Poll: Sun-Media," December 2008, www.leger360.com/admin/upload/publi_pdf/081241eng.pdf.

newspapers, it would be of interest to know how accurately Canada's constitutional foundations were represented. Were constitutional niceties explained to readers, or was reporting reduced, as it usually is, to combative imagery between warring sides, each portraying the other as usurper?[135] One study of English-language television newscasts during this period found that television journalism gave equal time to each side's preferred narrative but also equally unfavourable assessments of both the government and opposition positions.[136] With a focus on media frames[137] – on identifying the "broad organizing theme" selected by media outlets[138] – Miljan's study did not evaluate the content of English-language television news, from either a government or opposition perspective. In this part, I turn to a qualitative analysis of select print media in both official languages.

It should come as no surprise to learn that the preponderance of the coverage was not devoted to highlighting Canadian parliamentary traditions. Peter Russell expressed just this concern, in a *Toronto Star* editorial opinion, that there was too "little public knowledge of the constitutional rules that govern our parliamentary system of government" and that "people who should know better" were able to exploit that ignorance.[139] Nor were many distinctions drawn between presidential and prime ministerial forms of government. The *Toronto Star* blurred these lines: columnist Jim Travers described a "quasi-presidential federal politics"[140] while the *Toronto Star* editorial board emphatically declared that "Canada does not have a presidential system."[141] *Edmonton Journal* columnist Paula Simons was one of the only Alberta-based journalists to point out that, in Canada's parliamentary system,

---

135 Florian Sauvageau, David Schneiderman, and David Taras, *The Last Word: Media Coverage of the Supreme Court of Canada* (Vancouver: UBC Press, 2006).

136 Lydia Miljan, "Television Frames of the 2008 Liberal and New Democratic Accord," *Canadian Journal of Communication* 36 (2011): 567–8.

137 Miljan's study compared the proportion of strategic frames, which emphasize conflict, with substantive frames, emphasizing the substance of issues (ibid., 567). On the use of framing in media studies, see Robert M. Entman, "Framing: Toward Clarification of a Fractured Paradigm," *Journal of Telecommunication* 43 (1993): 51–8.

138 W. Lance Bennett, *News: The Politics of Illusion*, 6th ed. (New York: Pearson Longman, 2005), 27.

139 Peter Russell, "Constitution and Precedent Are on Coalition's Side," *Toronto Star*, 3 December 2008.

140 Jim Travers, "Canadian Democracy Is the Big Loser," *Toronto Star*, 2 December 2008.

141 "Harper's Speech Adds Fuel to Fire," *Toronto Star*, 4 December 2008.

"we elect a group of MPs rather than one president."[142] Though there were no such comparative discussions in Montreal-based *La Presse*, journalists and editorialists did enlighten readers about parliamentary traditions and so would have generated some constitutional literacy on the question.[143] For the most part, however, the papers in question chose not to complicate matters too much. Instead, they preferred to rely on the operating assumption – perhaps not an entirely unreasonable one – that readers understood how governments were elected and prime ministers appointed in Canada.

Four dominant narratives emerge in reading the press during this tumultuous week. The first narrative, central to events that precipitated prorogation, concerned the need to address the unprecedented economic crisis. Both sides to the coalition debate appealed to this narrative, though it was the preferred frame for the parliamentary opposition in the period immediately following release of the minority government's fiscal statement. Every single paper published opinion pieces and editorials condemning the government's curiously detached fiscal document.[144] Conservatives were eager to snatch this negative frame away from the opposition. The *Calgary Herald* editorial board, for instance, wrote that the coalition "with Bloc backing would be calamitous for Canada, considering the NDP's and Bloc's fiscal policies."[145] Stephen's Harper's address to the nation on Tuesday evening (3 December 2008) was intended to reassure Canadians that his government was "acting to deal with the crisis" and that, at a "time of global economic instability," it was not the time to make deals with separatists.[146] Opposition leader Stéphane Dion stuck to the economic theme in his counter-address on behalf of pro-coalition forces that same evening (an out-of-focus video, delivered a half an

---

142 Paula Simons, "Harper Keeps His Political Cards Close to His Chest," *Edmonton Journa*, 4 December 2008.

143 For example, Yves Boisvert, "Ce que peut faire Michaëlle Jean," *La Presse*, 3 December 2008; and Sébastien Grammond, "Michaëlle Jean doit dire non," *La Presse*, 3 December 2008.

144 For example, "Flaherty's Update Mere Posturing," *Edmonton Journal*, 28 November 2008; André Pratte, "Irresponsable, M. Harper!" *La Presse*, 28 November 2008; Walkom, "Hard Right Tory Ideology"; but see Carol Goar, "Less Lecturing and More Listening," *Toronto Star*, 28 November 2008.

145 "Do the Right Thing for Canada," *Calgary Herald*, 29 November 2008.

146 Harper, "Opposition Imposing Deal."

hour after it was scheduled for national broadcast).[147] He referred to the "global economic crisis" and the "duty" of the federal government "to act and help Canadians weather this storm" and to act "in a collaborative but urgent manner to protect jobs."[148] His poorly received televised address was almost entirely devoted to economic matters. Only a handful of sentences responded to the narrative of usurpation, to which I turn next.[149]

The second dominant narrative was that of an unprecedented coup d'état or political putsch.[150] This narrative channelled Conservative talking points developed over the weekend as the rumoured coalition began to take form.[151] Prompted by Tory MPs, Alberta newspapers dutifully delivered the indictment. Calgary MP Jim Prentice described the situation as "irresponsible and undemocratic."[152] This was never about an economic update, complained Edmonton MP Rona Ambrose, but a "power grab" that was "deeply disturbing from a democratic point of view."[153] Summarizing the state of public opinion as Christmas time approached in the capital city, an *Edmonton Journal* headline read,

147 Malorie Beauchemin, "Les libéraux se justifient," *La Presse*, 3 December 2008; Glen McGregor, "'Dion and Dion Only' Caused Video Fiasco," *Edmonton Journal*, 7 December 2008.

148 Dion to Michaëlle Jean, 2008, author's collection.

149 "Our system of government was not born with Canada. It is ancient. There are rules that govern it and conventions that guide it. Coalitions are normal and current practice in many parts of the world, and are able to work very successfully. They work with simple ingredients: consensus, goodwill and co-operation. Consensus is a great Canadian value" (ibid.).

150 Barry Cooper, "Coalition Politics Just Means Bigger Drain on Purse," *Calgary Herald*, 3 December 2008; Jason Fekete, "Calgary MPs Fear Fallout in Alberta," *Calgary Herald*, 2 December 2008; Kim Guttormson, "Coalition Talk Prompts Anger, Disbelief; Calgarians Divided on Political Crisis," *Calgary Herald*, 2 December 2008; Sean Myers and Jason Fekete, "Prime Minister Enjoys Strong Support at Home," *Calgary Herald*, 4 December 2008.

151 Former Conservative backbencher Brent Rathgeber reports that "caucus members are [routinely] provided talking points, canned stump speeches, and sample letters to the editors of local newspapers, all designed to reinforce the government's messaging and the caucus member's role in distributing those communications to his or her constituents," in his *Responsible Government: The Decline of Parliamentary Democracy in Canada* (Toronto: Dundurn, 2014), 83.

152 David Akin, Mike de Souza, Andrew Mayeda, and Juliet O'Neill, "Power Play: Opposition Union Aims to End Tory Reign within a Week," *Calgary Herald*, 2 December 2008.

153 Juliet O'Neill, "Liberals, NDP Near Deal," *Edmonton Journal*, 1 December 2008.

"Santa's Opinion Is, It's a Coup."[154] When the narrative was reported in the *Toronto Star*, by contrast, it was fiercely resisted.[155] *La Presse* also sought to dispel confusion about the coup narrative.[156] A number of *La Presse* items, nevertheless, described the coalition as illegitimately engaging in a "putsch" or a "coup"[157] and aspiring to seize power "through the back door."[158]

The third narrative, in some ways the flip side of the second, addressed the loss of political power by Alberta. "Alberta loses," shouted a front page *Calgary Herald* headline.[159] Alberta would largely be left out of the coalition, in which case it will be the "National Energy Programme all over again," predicted political scientist Barry Cooper.[160] Alberta's ouster from the centres of power in Ottawa, it was reported, would threaten the "country's economic engine."[161] The energy sector's response was one of dread. Though not a component of the coalition agreement, the industry feared a potentially punishing carbon tax[162] that posed a devastating threat to the future of the oil patch.[163] Threats of western alienation and a revived separatist movement

154 Ryan Cormier, "Santa's Opinion Is, It's a Coup," *Edmonton Journal*, 3 December 2008; Archie McLean, "How It Might All Shake Down: What a Federal Coalition Could Mean for Alberta," *Edmonton Journal*, 4 December 2008.
155 "Coalition Deserves Chance to Govern," *Toronto Star*, 2 December 2008. The editorial reads, "The suggestion was that the coalition deal was illegitimate and undemocratic, a coup d'etat. It is nothing of the sort. It is the way our parliamentary system works, especially in the immediate aftermath of the election of a minority government" (ibid.).
156 Laurence Bherer, Graciela Ducatenzeiler, Pascale Dufour, Jane Jenson, Éléonore Lépinard, Christine Rothmayr, and Marie-Joëlle Zahar, "Quel 'coup d'État'?," *La Presse*, 7 December 2008; Marissal, "Un coup d'État tranquille."
157 Lysiane Gagnon, "Un putsch, rien de moins," *La Presse*, 2 December 2008; Marc Simard, "Les trois indécents," *La Presse*, 4 December 2008.
158 Christian Paradis, "Il n'y a pas eu de 'Québec bashing,'" *La Presse*, 6 December 2008.
159 "Monstrous Result of an Ill-Conceived Political Coupling," *Calgary Herald*, 2 December 2008.
160 Fekete, "Calgary MPs Fear Fallout in Alberta."
161 Gary Lamphier, "Ottawa Sends the Good, Grey White into Meltdown," *Edmonton Journal*, 4 December 2008.
162 Nigel Hannaford, "Federalist Souls Sold for a Shot at Supreme Power," *Calgary Herald*, 2 December 2008.
163 Charles Frank, "This Is No Time for a Coalition of Losers," *Calgary Herald*, 2 December 2008; O'Neill, "Liberals, NDP Near Deal."

appeared repeatedly, particularly in the *Calgary Herald*,[164] but also in *La Presse* coverage.[165] Less extreme were reactions that Alberta would no longer be well represented at the Cabinet table. The prospects were that Alberta would end up with only one coalition member of Parliament, Edmonton NDP MP Linda Duncan.[166] This is where some difference in tone emerges between the Calgary and Edmonton press – one *Edmonton Journal* columnist viewed this as a potentially positive development for Alberta's capital region.[167]

A fourth narrative concerned (what we might generously call) patriotism. *Calgary Herald* columnist Don Martin pulled on this narrative thread when he wrote that the governor general could not "endorse a separatist-controlled coalition without triggering a crisis in the monarchy, never mind the Constitution."[168] Prime Minister Harper also pushed this button when he began his counter-assault in Parliament on Tuesday, 2 December. Harper accused the coalition of a "betrayal" of the voters, the economy, and the "best interests" of the country.[169] This patriotic trope explains Harper's mistaken complaint about the absence of Canadian flags at the coalition signing ceremony.[170] The prime minister accused opposition leader Dion of ridding the room of Canadian flags before the official signing of the coalition documents. Numerous news organizations took note that Canadian and provincial flags were

---

164 Don Braid, "Harper Following Clark's Old Path," *Calgary Herald*, 2 December 2008; Jason Fekete, "Coalition Could Revive Western Alienation: Separatist Party Urged for Region," *Calgary Herald*, 3 December 2008; Lamphier, "Ottawa Sends the Good, Grey White into Meltdown."

165 Patrick Lagacé, "Les Albertains sont en ta …," *La Presse*, 3 December 2008; and Lagacé, "Stephen Harper, Superstar," *La Presse*, 7 December 2008.

166 Trish Audette and Todd Babiuk, "Only One Albertan in Opposition Ranks," *Edmonton Journal*, 2 December 2008; Renata D'aliesio, "Political Stability Crucial Says Stelmach: Alberta Could End Up with One Coalition MP," *Calgary Herald*, 2 December 2008.

167 Todd Babiuk, "Messy Side of Democracy May Put City NDP MP in New Caucus," *Edmonton Journal*, 2 December 2008. As was the case with many of the relevant political actors, perspectives on the coalition were often based on "calculations of self-interest." See Grace Skogstad, "Western Canada and the 'Illegitimacy' of the Liberal-NDP Coalition Government," in *Parliamentary Democracy in Crisis*, ed. Peter Russell and Lorne Sossin (Toronto: University of Toronto Press, 2009), 164.

168 Martin, "Who Will Blink on the Brink."

169 Akin, Mayeda, and O'Neill, "Harper Seeks to Suspend House."

170 Don Martin, "One Can Only Weep at the Sad Spectacle," *Calgary Herald*, 3 December 2008.

prominently on display,[171] but this fact did not stand in the way of the prime minister's accusations. Typically, the patriotism theme would be conjoined with claims about lack of democratic legitimacy (the second narrative), as Harper did in his address to the nation on the evening of 3 December. "Canadians take pride in our history as one of the world's oldest continuous democracies," Harper declared, and "constant in every case ... is the principle that Canada's government has always been chosen by the people." Here, the "opposition is attempting to impose this deal without your say, without your consent, and without your vote."[172] The opposition leader's rebuttal, broadcast later that same evening, with its emphasis on the economy, did not successfully invoke the patriotism trope. The phenomenon of Bloc-bashing, equivalent to Quebec-bashing for many in *La Presse*,[173] was a central element in this narrative – it is particularly pronounced in the Alberta coverage[174] – and helps to explain some of its success.

Though there is little discussion in the press coverage of pertinent distinctions between presidential and prime ministerial forms of government, there is an occasional reference to parliamentary conventions. *Toronto Star* columnist James Travers argued early on in the crisis that a coalition government "would not be an affront to democracy."[175] The *Calgary Herald* editorial page acknowledged in passing, on two separate occasions, that the coalition is "breaking no rules" of the Westminster system of government.[176] Also in the *Herald*, NDP Finance Critic Thomas Mulcair offered a constitutional lesson, in his response to the Conservative fiscal statement: "I think that anyone who knows the Canadian constitutional system will be able to explain to you that long

---

171 Akin, Mayeda, and O'Neill, "Harper Seeks to Suspend House."
172 Harper, "Opposition Imposing Deal."
173 Beauchemin, "Les libéraux se justifient"; Hugo De Grandpré, "Les médias canadiens se déchaînent," *La Presse*, 3 December 2008; Tommy Chouinard, Karim Benessaieh, and Vincent Brousseau-Pouliot, "Le discours à la nation fait écho au Québec," *La Presse*, 3 December 2008.
174 "Reckless Cause, Reckless Effect in Time of Crisis," *Edmonton Journal*, 2 December 2008: "Installing a coalition Liberal-NDP government led by Stephane Dion – a leader recently roundly rejected by Canadians along with his botched central policy, now propped up by the separatist Bloc Quebecois, would be an insult we cannot tolerate, even for a few months."
175 Jim Travers, "Harper Gives In to Political Temptation," *Toronto Star*, 29 November 2008.
176 "People's Choice," *Calgary Herald*, 4 December 2008.

before talking about an election, if the government loses the confidence of Parliament, there are a lot of other things that will happen before we would have an election, especially so soon after the last one."[177] Helen Forsey, daughter of Eugene Forsey, drawing on her father's work reiterated some of these same lessons in an opinion piece published in the *Edmonton Journal*.[178] Cutting through the cant, *Edmonton Journal* columnist Lorne Gunter acknowledged that it "is part of our parliamentary democracy that opposition parties may attempt to replace a minority government without forcing an election, if they believe they have the votes to do it." If "you think it is unreasonable to have to wait until the end of January to dispatch Stephen Harper from the PMO," Gunter wrote, "then you are permitting your hatred for Harper to blind you to the traditions and conventions of our democratic system."[179] There are few acknowledgments that the Harper government was subtly likening the office of prime minister to that of the directly elected president. The only hint of this is suggested in an *Edmonton Journal* report concerning Monday's stormy parliamentary debate. Taunting each other, Tories reportedly hurled "traitor" insults at Dion while Liberal backbenchers "shout[ed] at Harper, 'You are not the president.'"[180]

What the coverage reveals is, for the most part, a disinterest in the press to instruct Canadians about the parliamentary fundamentals of responsible government. As Conservative talking points get channelled through the rituals of balanced journalistic practice – hearing from one side and then another – there seems to be no countervailing narrative that is as compelling or as effective. But for the few instances already mentioned, there is little instruction about Canadian parliamentary traditions as compared to the compelling and sensational narrative about "undemocratic seizures" of political power and "no change of government without elections." Such instruction, which would have required detailed historical treatment, not amenable to short, sharp, quotable sound bites, simply was not considered newsworthy.

---

177 Canwest News Service, "Confidence: Coalition Government Seen as a Possibility," *Calgary Herald*, 28 November 2008.
178 Helen Forsey, "Gov. Gen. Must Invite Coalition to Govern," *Edmonton Journal*, 4 December 2008.
179 Lorne Gunter, "A Much-Needed Time-Out on the Hill," *Edmonton Journal*, 5 December 2008.
180 Canwest New Service, "Harper Scorns Coalition," *Edmonton Journal*, 3 December 2008.

We can conclude that Harper and the Conservative Party won the war of words in December 2008. The claim that the prime minister is directly elected and that a fresh election needs to be called when a government is overturned took hold and, according to public opinion polling, was particularly successful in Alberta. There was little in the Alberta press – or very much elsewhere, for that matter – to counter these trends. A number of factors contributed to this outcome in addition to the press coverage. The Conservatives could not have buried the prospects for a coalition government, returning triumphantly to Parliament in February 2009, without having prepared the terrain on which to successfully wage their ground war. This included the unpopularity of candidate Dion, the role of the Bloc Québécois in propping up the coalition, the coolness of Michael Ignatieff, the leading contender to succeed Dion in heading up the Liberal Party, to the proposed coalition, and widespread misunderstanding among Canadians about the workings of Canada's parliamentary system of government. So successful was the Conservative campaign in 2008 that the prime minister kicked off the next federal election campaign in March 2011, on the steps of the governor general's residence at Rideau Hall, with references to looming threats of an unstable coalition government.[181] Ultimately, the prime minister and his supporters were proven right. Politics in Canada are personalized around the prime minister. We have, for some purposes, presidentialized the office of the prime minister.

3. The Prerogatives in 2008

It remains only to say a few things about the governor general's decision to accede to the prime minister's request to prorogue. As discussed in the introduction, most Crown prerogatives are under the direct control of the prime minister. There remain in reserve only a handful of personal prerogatives held by the Crown's representative in Canada,

---

181 Prime Minister Harper declared on the steps of Rideau Hall, "Canadians need to understand clearly, without any ambiguity: Unless Canadians elect a stable, national majority, Mr. Ignatieff will form a coalition with the NDP and Bloc Québécois. They tried it before. It is clear they will try it again. And, next time, if given the chance, they will do it in a way that no one will be able to stop." Quoted in Andrew Mayeda, Mark Kennedy, and Althia Raj, "Tories, Liberals Battle for Quebec: Party Leaders Spar over Positions on Coalition Governments," *Edmonton Journal*, 27 March 2011.

such as proroguing and dissolving Parliament and calling upon the prime minister to form the government. Prime Minister Harper called upon Governor General Michaëlle Jean to exercise this power to prorogue in the wake of the December 2008 crisis. Though prorogation is not a prerogative power usually attended by controversy, on this occasion it certainly was.

The controversy turned on the degree to which the governor general was entitled to exercise her discretion in responding to the prime minister's request. In the usual case, the governor general will follow the prime minister's advice.[182] Generalizing from this default rule, Henri Brun insists that the governor general has no discretion to refuse the prime minister but for exceptional circumstances, such as when the prime minister refuses to step down after a defeat, either at the polls or in Parliament, circumstances that Brun likens to a "coup d'état."[183] On the other hand, Andrew Heard maintains that by acceding to the prime minister's request, the governor general "failed to defend Canadian parliamentary democracy."[184] Rather than staying above the political fray, her decision amounted to a "serious intervention in the political process."[185] Other commentary ends up mostly in the middle. Acknowledging that the governor general can exercise her discretion in such circumstances, C.E.S. Franks concludes that she "made the right decision."[186] David Cameron agrees, surmising, "Ultimately, the system worked."[187]

All of these opinions appropriately are informed by the baseline rule that the royal prerogative, including those personally held by the governor general, must be exercised in accordance with the "advice" tendered by Cabinet – that she has "no freedom to select among alternative courses of action." Anything less would not be tolerated in a

182 Heard, "Governor-General's Decision to Prorogue Parliament," 19.

183 Henri Brun, "Michaëlle Jean n'a pas le choix," *La Presse*, 4 December 2008.

184 Heard, "Governor-General's Decision to Prorogue Parliament," 21.

185 Andrew Heard, "The Governor-General's Decision Suspension of Parliament: Duty Done or a Perilous Precedent?," in *Parliamentary Democracy in Crisis*, ed. Peter Russell and Lorne Sossin (Toronto: University of Toronto Press 2009), 60.

186 C.E.S. Franks, "To Prorogue or Not to Prorogue: Did the Governor General Make the Right Decision?," in *Parliamentary Democracy in Crisis*, ed. Peter Russell and Lorne Sossin (Toronto: University of Toronto Press 2009), 46.

187 David Cameron, "Ultimately, the System Worked," in *Parliamentary Democracy in Crisis*, ed. Peter Russell and Lorne Sossin (Toronto: University of Toronto Press 2009), 194.

contemporary democracy such as Canada's.[188] This has not always been the case. Even as mid-nineteenth-century Great Britain was governed by Cabinet, Lord Brougham advised that the opinions of the Crown "if deeply entertained ... [could still] exert a real influence upon the conduct of public affairs." "This is the spirit of the Constitution," he wrote, "which wills that the individual Monarch should not be a mere cipher but a substantive part of the political system and wills it as a check on the other branches of government."[189] Canada's late nineteenth-century authority on such matters, Alpheus Todd, advises that, though the governor general was expected to "defer to the advice of his Ministers, so long as they continue to possess the confidence of the popular chamber," he can refuse to follow that advice. He could do so "if, at any time, he should see fit to doubt the wisdom, or the legality, of the advice tendered to him, or should question the motives" prompting that advice, so as to lead him to believe that it has been motivated by "corrupt, partisan, or other unworthy motives, and not by a regard to the honour of the Crown, or the welfare and advancement of the community at large." In other words, the office possessed "full discretionary powers" that enabled the Crown to "exercise a beneficial influence, and an active supervision over the government of the empire."[190] Such "active supervision" surely is no longer tolerated.

Instead, such discretion as the governor general has will be confined to those rare occasions, such as when there is some question as to who should govern in the Crown's name. Even then, such discretion should be exercised in ways that keep the office out of politics to the greatest degree possible. It is the application of this principle that divides Brun (who insists on near absolute deference to prime ministerial advice) from Heard (who insists that the governor general may act independently of that advice).

Governor General Jean, we are advised, kept the prime minister waiting in Government House for over two hours for her decision. We also know that she discussed with him various matters that would have informed her exercise of discretion, and also broke up her discussion

---

188 Andrew Heard, *Canadian Constitutional Conventions: The Marriage of Law and Politics*, 2nd ed. (Toronto: Oxford University Press, 2014), 39.

189 Henry, Lord Brougham, *Political Philosophy, Part III: Of Democracy, Mixed Monarchy* (London: Charles Knight, 1844), 302.

190 Todd, *Parliamentary Government in the British Colonies*, 816–17, 5; Todd, *On the Position of a Constitutional Governor* (Ottawa, 1848), 5.

to consult with her advisor, Peter Hogg. She extracted, it is reported, two concessions: that Parliament would be recalled in January and that a budget would be introduced shortly afterwards.[191] What the record reveals is that the governor general believed that she could exercise her discretion as she saw fit.[192] I maintain that we should worry, however, about her intervening in political affairs (taking responsibility, that is) without political accountability. As mentioned, it generally is agreed that the governor general is expected to steer clear of political controversies and so should exercise her discretion in ways that minimize her meddling in Canadian parliamentary affairs. The governor general should be guided less by the dictates of political partisanship and more by the principles of democracy and responsible government. Her actions should be guided principally by considerations that do the utmost to respect the will of Parliament and, ultimately, the people. It turns out, conveniently for the governor general, that Parliament is the best available barometer of the people's will as expressed periodically through the electoral process.[193]

Though Prime Minister Harper's minority government had served a mere two weeks and a few days, he had lost the confidence of the House of Commons but without a vote on the floor having taken place. The House had not yet "spoken." Prime Minister Harper asked Ms Jean to prorogue the current session in order to avoid losing that vote of confidence. His request, for this reason, was unusual and unprecedented and should make Canadians feel unease. The only analogous event in the annals of Canadian history is when Prime Minister John A. Macdonald called on a reluctant Lord Dufferin to prorogue Parliament in 1873 in order to forestall a motion of censure associated with the Canadian Pacific Railway scandal.[194] There is little doubt, however, that Ms Jean rightly acceded to his request.

---

191 Steven Chase, "Michaëlle Jean Feared a 'Dreadful Crisis' When Harper Sought Prorogation: Ex-Advisor," *Globe and Mail*, 25 June 2012; Franks, "To Prorogue or Not to Prorogue"; Michael Valpy, "GG Made Harper Work for Prorogation," *Globe and Mail*, 5 December 2008.

192 Eric Adams, "The Constitutionality of Prorogation," *Constitutional Forum constitutionnel* 18, no. 1 (2009): 17–20.

193 Eugene A. Forsey, "The Governor General as Defender of Democracy," in Forsey, *Eugene Forsey*, 318.

194 Barbara J. Messamore, *Canada's Governors General, 1847–1878: Biography and Constitutional Evolution* (Toronto: University of Toronto Press, 2006), chap. 8.

Control over the length of parliamentary sessions rests with the leader of the governing party. It is with good reason that James Mallory described prorogation as "one of the ways by which the Cabinet can control a recalcitrant House."[195] Having formed the government, and with the House lending its confidence following the speech from the throne, Stephen Harper legitimately was entitled to utilize the levers available to prime ministers to steer the course of parliamentary business. This includes advising the governor general when to begin and when to end sessions of the House of Commons. It may also encompass advising on the exercise of the prerogative in cases where votes of confidence are pending. Exercising her discretion in this manner is less problematic than it appears, as prorogation only delays a vote – it does not bar an eventual vote. Playing with the timing of parliamentary sessions, then, is a much less drastic step than to insist on the dissolution of Parliament in order to avoid a vote of non-confidence.

Should the prime minister have lost both the ground war in December 2008 and a subsequent vote of confidence upon Parliament's return in January, constitutional practice should have been guided, again, by the principles of democracy and responsible government. The governor general's obligation was to respect the will of Parliament as expressed in the general election of only several months earlier. She would have been obliged to turn to the opposition party, or any combination of parties sitting in the minority Parliament, to determine whether they had the confidence of the House to govern. Rather than undermining democratic principles, this would have respected them. After all, the outcome of the general election awarded a majority of seats to parties other than the Conservative Party of Canada.

It follows that the governor general should not insist on being satisfied that any alternative governing party or coalition is a "stable" one, as some have insisted.[196] Not only is stability too vague a criterion, the governor general is in no better position to predict the length of a minority government than parliamentarians themselves. The paper trail generated by the proposed coalition – including the text of an agreement and several letters to Ms Jean herself – in the days leading up to the

---

195 James R. Mallory, *The Structure of Canadian Government* (Toronto: Macmillan of Canada, 1971), 222.

196 Peter W. Hogg, "Prorogation and the Power of the Governor General," *National Journal of Constitutional Law* 27 (2009): 198.

decision to prorogue clearly were meant to assuage any doubts on her part that the coalition could govern for at least eighteen months. The voices of parliamentarians in the House, however, should suffice for this purpose as they determine, between elections, who governs. If the alternative proves unstable, then dissolution will follow. Nor does some matter of great public importance warrant the governor general ignoring Parliament's will. For the governor general to do so would be to meddle significantly in the workings of Canadian parliamentary democracy. It would have her discount the legitimacy of democratic expression.

As regards these general outlines, I would go so far as to say that even Mackenzie King would have agreed. King made his infamous request to dissolve Parliament in 1926 in advance of a motion of censure (the "Stevens Amendment").[197] King advised Lord Byng that there was no probability that Arthur Meighen, leader of the opposition, would be capable of securing the confidence of the House, in which case, he advised Lord Byng, Parliament should be dissolved. On this, Byng preferred to accept the word of Meighen, who erroneously advised Byng that he could govern. Meighen's government quickly fell and a general election followed. As King reiterated his position later that year, "When Parliament ceased to be in a position to make a satisfactory decision as to which party should govern, it was then for the people to decide."[198] If Parliament is in a position to make that decision, there is little for the governor general to do other than to follow it.

---

197 Forsey, *Royal Power of Dissolution*, 145.
198 Robert McGregor Dawson, *Constitutional Issues in Canada, 1900–1931* (London: Oxford University Press, 1993), 89.

3 The King's Prerogative vs Parliamentary Privilege: Prorogation 2009

There is no limit to the curiosity of Parliament.

Walter Bagehot[1]

If prime ministers, like presidents, are the product of popular elections, as Prime Minister Harper alleged in 2008, what is the relationship between the head of government and the branches that constitute Parliament? With no distinguishing source of legitimacy, are they coequal? What of Parliament's historic task of calling to account government's misuse of authority? Has this role been rendered redundant? These are just some of the salient questions bobbing to the surface as yet another conflagration threatened to consume the Conservative minority government, only one year after the 2008 constitutional crisis. The government was not likely to fall this time, however. The threat was, instead, public shaming, even the possibility that ministers of the Crown would be expelled from the House. Prorogation, once again, was pulled out of the parliamentary toolkit to save governmental face.

It had been known for some time that detained persons handed over to Afghan authorities by Canadian military personnel could face torture or death. According to the director of the Kandahar office of the Afghanistan Independent Human Rights Commission, approximately 30 per cent of Afghan prisoners had suffered some kind of abuse while in the hands of Afghan security.[2] Canadian transfers to Afghan forces

---

1 Walter Bagehot, *The Collected Works of Walter Bagehot*, ed. Norman St John-Stevas (London: Economist, 1974), 5:320.
2 Graeme Smith, "General Defends Detainee Policy," *Globe and Mail*, 3 June 2006.

halted in November 2007 because of such rumours, only to resume again in February 2008.[3] Constitutional litigation by Amnesty International failed to halt potential Canadian complicity in ongoing rights violations overseas.[4] A Military Police Complaints Commission Inquiry was mired in procedural delay in October 2009 due to government obstruction precipitated, in part, by the evidence of diplomat Richard Colvin. Colvin, having served seventeen months at the Canadian embassy in Kandahar, testified eventually before the Special House of Commons Committee on the Canadian Mission in Afghanistan in November 2009.[5] He divulged that Canadian forces "detained, and handed over for severe torture, a lot of innocent people" and that he had issued warnings about this to his superiors.[6] Colvin's testimony prompted opposition members on the House of Commons Committee to insist on the production of documents linked to his testimony before proceeding with the appearance of government witnesses in rebuttal.[7] The Conservative government responded with vigorous denials and a refusal to produce unredacted (or uncensored) documents.[8]

Liberal MP Ujjal Dosanjh introduced in Parliament a motion for the production of all documents related to Colvin's testimony, in addition to all documents associated with the Amnesty International litigation and the Military Police Complaints investigation.[9] The text of the motion

---

3 Campbell Clark, "Transfers Can Resume, Afghan Minister Says," *Globe and Mail*, 9 February 2009.

4 Paul Koring, "Top Court Won't Hear Appeal on Afghan Detainees," *Globe and Mail*, 22 May 2009.

5 Military Police Complaints Commission, "Commission's Final Report – MPCC 2008-042 – concerning a Complaint by Amnesty International Canada and British Columbia Civil Liberties Association in June 2008" (Glenn M. Stannard, chair), 27 June 2012, www.mpcc-cppm.gc.ca/03/afghan/2012-06-27/index-eng.aspx.

6 Steven Chase, "All Detainees Were Tortured, All Warnings Ignored," *Globe and Mail*, 19 November 2009.

7 Steven Chase and Clark Campbell, "Opposition Aims to Block Diplomat's Testimony," *Globe and Mail*, 24 November 2009.

8 In a stunning about face in December 2009, Canadian military officials acknowledged evidence of torture in 2006. See Steven Chase and John Ibbitson, "MPs Join Forces to Order Release of Afghan Records," *Globe and Mail*, 11 December 2009.

9 Canada, *Debates* (No. 128), 40th Parliament, 2nd Session (10 December 2009), 7877. Interestingly, the motion did not call upon the government to produce any legal opinions regarding these matters, particularly whether international human rights of Charter of Rights violations had occurred, presumably because these would have been considered privileged documents.

replicated a similar one introduced and passed in Special Committee. While the committee had power to direct its own proceedings, a House motion would add the weight of parliamentary might to the demand for production. The motion passed with a bare majority of two votes.[10] Failing to comply with a standing order of the House risked the Conservatives running afoul of Parliament's will and the powerful resources that are available to it, including contempt motions, powers of seizure, even arrest.[11] In short order, the prime minister asked the governor general to prorogue Parliament and not have it reconvene until more than two months later, on 2 March 2010. Canadians rightly suspected that Harper was trying to dodge a bullet.

Other reasons were offered, however. Prime Minister Harper described the last-minute, Christmas-week prorogation – in which thirty bills would die on the order paper – as "routine" and a time to "recalibrate."[12] With an unremarkable speech from the throne delivered on Parliament's return in March, paired with a warmed-over budget shortly thereafter, it became apparent that the prime minister was being disingenuous – that prorogation in December 2009 was precipitated by the government's stubborn resistance to producing unredacted documents to the House of Commons. Public opinion disapproved of prorogation by a margin to two to one.[13] A rare front-page *Globe and Mail* editorial captured the mood well, at least among its well-heeled audience. "Canada's democracy," the editorial alleged, "should not be conducted on the basis of convenience for the governing party."[14] Prorogation in the circumstances diminished democracy, it was argued. Online opposition on Facebook grew into a "growing public uprising."[15]

10 Richard J. Brennan, "MPs Order Release of Afghan Torture Documents," *Toronto Star*, 11 December 2009.

11 Mark Bosc and Audrey O'Brien, eds., *House of Commons Procedure and Practice*, 2nd ed. (Ottawa: House of Commons, 2009), chap. 3, www.parl.gc.ca/procedure-book-livre/Document.aspx?Language=E&Mode=1&sbdid=7c730f1d-e10b-4dfc-863a-83e7e1a6940e&sbpid=976953d8-8385-4e09-a699-d90779b48aa0.

12 Daniel Leblanc, "Harper Suspends Parliament to 'Recalibrate,'" *Globe and Mail*, 31 December 2009; Les Whittington, "PM Downplays Detainee Scandal," *Toronto Star*, 6 January 2010.

13 Gloria Galloway, "Concern over Suspension of Parliament Grows, Poll Finds," *Globe and Mail*, 8 January 2010.

14 "Democracy Diminished, Accountability Divided," *Globe and Mail*, 31 December 2009. See statistics at *Globe and Mail*, "Readership Information," globelink.ca/readership/.

15 Susan Delacourt and Richard J. Brennan, "Grassroots Fury Greets Shuttered Parliament," *Toronto Star*, 5 January 2010.

Rallies opposing prorogation, and a few in support, arose in cities across Canada. The 2009 prorogation even inspired a book of collected poetry.[16]

On what constitutional basis could the government refuse to hand over documents? There is little doubt that proroguing Parliament at the prime minister's behest was, strictly speaking, "constitutional" (just as it was, I argued, in the controversial 2008 prorogation).[17] It was, however, unseemly, if not outright abusive of the Crown's reserve powers, to shut down a House of Commons investigation into charges that Canadians handed over Afghan detainees to face torture in contravention of the Geneva Conventions.[18] As for the government's refusal to hand over unredacted documents, Justice Minister Rob Nicholson claimed that production of documents would sacrifice the safety of soldiers serving abroad and would run afoul of numerous statutory enactments. After receiving legal advice from the Department of Justice, the government abandoned the argument about statutory prohibitions. Instead, the government's argument boiled down to one about the separation of powers: that disclosure would undermine the government's (that is, the executive branch's) obligation to "protect sensitive information that, if disclosed, would compromise Canada's security, national defence and international relations."[19] In so many words, the government claimed an executive privilege that would shield the government from scrutiny by Parliament and its investigative committees. This looked very much like claims to executive secrecy that had been issuing out of the George W. Bush White House during the "war on terror."

It is curious that the government would trot out a doctrine – the separation of powers – not so well rooted in Canada's parliamentary

---

16 Stephen Brockwell and Stuart Ross, eds., *Rogue Stimulus: The Stephen Harper Holiday Anthology for a Prorogued Parliament* (Toronto: Mansfield, 2010).

17 So long as the prime minister had the confidence of the House – and there was no suggestion yet that he would lose this confidence any time soon – and so long as there was a sitting of Parliament at least once a year – the only constitutional requirement in the democratic rights section of the Canadian Charter of Rights and Freedoms (section 5) – then prorogation on this occasion seemed constitutionally defensible.

18 Just as it was unseemly for Prime Minister John A. Macdonald to call upon Lord Dufferin to prorogue Parliament in 1873 in order to halt an inquiry into the Canadian Pacific Railway scandal. See Barbara J. Messamore, *Canada's Governors General, 1847–1878: Biography and Constitutional Evolution* (Toronto: University of Toronto Press, 2006), chap. 8.

19 Canada, *Debates* (No. 128), 40th Parliament, 2nd Session (10 December 2009), 7873.

tradition. Walter Bagehot famously described the executive and legislative branches, in the years preceding Confederation, as almost completely fused, not separated.[20] Peter Hogg declared in his authoritative constitutional text that there simply is no separation of powers in Canada.[21] To be sure, there are separate branches expressly outlined in the parts to the Constitution Act, 1867, but this has always looked more like a textual facade than an accurate portrayal of parliamentary practice.

Nevertheless, the government was insistent that the different branches "respect each other" and not trample on each other's privileges. Canada's 2009 citizenship study guide invoked the same classical formulation, describing Canada's Constitution as exhibiting an "interplay between the three branches of government – the Executive, Legislative and Judicial – which work together but also sometimes are in creative tension."[22] Rather than describing the relationship between legislative and executive branches within parliamentary systems of government – in which the executive is responsible to the legislative branch – this seems to be a warmed-over version of the separation of powers idealized by Montesquieu and put into practice in the U.S. Constitution. The Harper government seemed to be undoing the hard-fought accountability secured by the achievement of responsible government over a century ago.

In this chapter I take up the puzzle of the separation of powers in Canada in order to assess the argument, articulated by the Conservative government and its legal counsel, that the executive branch is not accountable to the legislative. Why would the government have recourse to what is largely a fiction, and why would subsequent discussions regarding the matter continue to be framed in this way? It has something to do, I argue, with the successful career of the separation of

---

20 Bagehot, *Complete Works*, 5:210.
21 Peter W. Hogg, *Constitutional Law of Canada*, student ed. (Scarborough, ON: Thomson Canada, 2008), 221; also Patrick J. Monahan, *Constitutional Law*, 3rd ed. (Toronto: Irwin Law, 2006), 94.
22 Government of Canada, *Citizenship and Immigration Canada, Discover Canada: The Rights and Responsibilities of Citizenship – Study Guide* (Ottawa: Minister of Public Works and Government Services Canada, 2009), 29. McKay and Swift also have recourse to the 2009 citizenship guide as an expression of Canada as a "warrior nation" – an effort to rebrand Canada as militaristic rather than pacific, in Ian McKay and Jamie Swift, *Warrior Nation: Rebranding Canada in an Age of Anxiety* (Toronto: Between the Lines, 2012), 15.

powers concept. Though a version admittedly lurks in the background of Canada's parliamentary tradition, it is subordinate to other dominant tropes having to do, early on, with "mixed" or "balanced" government and, later on, with responsible government. Since the achievement of responsible government, the legislative branch, for most purposes, is intimately connected to the executive branch, both inside and outside of Parliament, and so the formal separation of powers is entirely compromised. The executive, such as it is, can be described more accurately as a "parliamentary executive."[23]

The separation of powers, nevertheless, stubbornly persists in Canadian constitutional parlance, nowhere more on display than in the Afghan detainee episode. In the first part of this chapter, I trace the outlines of the doctrine in the history of political thought addressing principally the separation between the legislative and executive branches (the judicial branch will be mentioned only in passing). As some of the thinkers discussed in this part will be familiar to many (e.g., Locke and Montesquieu), readers may want to push on to the next part, where I move sequentially through the English, Canadian, and U.S. literature to determine the degree to which the separation of powers has been assimilated into constitutional thought and practice. Subsequently, I turn to warring legal opinions issuing out of the Department of Justice in defence of government and those offered by the House of Commons legal counsel in defence of Parliament. As the history in the first part makes clear, Parliament easily wins the contest. Framing the debate in terms of the separation of powers, however, obscures the main contest – one that has been played out in times past between Crown prerogative and parliamentary privilege. The debate, in other words, was fought on terrain that does not well fit what I am describing as Canada's constitutional culture. In the last part, I consider proposals to tame Crown prerogative that settle this ongoing tension to some degree.

We learn that there is only a veneer of separation between the legislative and executive branches. There is, in short, no support for the government's position. We are faced, once again, with the Harper

---

23 A.V. Dicey, "Comparison between English & Other Executives: Parliamentary & Non-Parliamentary Executives," in A.V. Dicey, *General Characteristics of English Constitutionalism: Six Unpublished Lectures*, ed. Peter Raina (Oxford: Peter Lang, 2009), 79–95; and in Dicey, *Lectures on Comparative Constitutionalism*, ed. J.W.F. Alison (Oxford: Oxford University Press, 2014), 274–85. K.C. Wheare, *Modern Constitutions* (London: Oxford University Press, 1960), 37, also favours the term.

government abandoning parliamentary traditions and looking for inspiration, instead, to constitutional practices associated with divided government in the United States.

1. The Career of a Concept

Dwelling in the Middle[24]

Montesquieu famously introduced the "separation of powers" between the executive, legislative, and judicial branches in his discussion of the English Constitution.[25] It is curious that he would offer this as an apt description of the eighteenth-century working English constitution when another, more popular theory of English constitutionalism prevailed at the time, one not easy to reconcile with a theory of functional separation.[26] The prevailing view was that England had a "mixed" or "balanced" constitution where monarchical, aristocratic, and democratic elements come together in Parliament, each serving as a "mutual check" upon each other.[27]

Though traceable back to classical accounts of mixed government,[28] the notion that power can be shared among the three estates is acknowledged by Charles I in "The King's Answer to the Nineteen Propositions," an expedient reply to Parliament's demands in 1642.[29] In the face of entreaties to give up royal authority to the legislature in the

---

24 From Halifax: "True virtue hath ever been thought a trimmer, dwelling in the middle between the two extremes," quoted in Isaac Kramnick, *Bolingbroke & His Circle: The Politics of Nostalgia in the Age of Walpole* (Ithaca, NY: Cornell University Press, 1992), 141.

25 Baron de Montesquieu, *The Spirit of the Laws*, trans. Thomas Nugent (New York: Hafner, 1949), bk 11, chap. 6.

26 Betty Kemp, *King and Commons, 1660–1832* (London: Macmillan, 1957), 82–3.

27 William Blackstone, *Commentaries on the Laws of England* (1765; Chicago: University of Chicago Press, 1979), 1:150.

28 Aristotle, *Aristotle's Politics*, trans. Benjamin Jowett (Oxford: Clarendon, 1916); Polybius, *A Fragment out of the Sixth Book of Polybius* (London: J. Bettenham, 1743); Iain Stewart, "Montesquieu in England: His 'Notes on England,' with Commentary and Translation," *Oxford University Comparative Law Forum* 6 (2002), ouclf.iuscomp.org/articles/montesquieu.shtml#spirit.

29 The answer was authored by the King's advisors, Viscount Falkland and Sir John Colepeper. See W.B. Gwyn, *The Meaning of the Separation of Powers: An Analysis of the Doctrine from Its Origin to the Adoption of the United States Constitution* (The Hague: Martinus Nijhoff, 1965), 25.

naming of councillors, ministers, and judges, Charles I concedes that laws "are jointly made by a king, by a house of peers, and by a House of Commons chosen by the people." The "government," he declares, is "entrusted to the king" with the power to make war and peace, making peers, choosing councillors and judges, etc. This is a "kind of regulated monarchy" that is subject to the power of the House of Commons. The House, Charles I declares, is "solely entrusted" with the power to "levy money" – "the sinews as well of peace and war" – and of impeaching those who have advised the King in violation of the law. The King, after all, can do no wrong – only his advisors can be held to account. Finally, the House of Lords is entrusted with a "judicatory power," the King announces, "an excellent screen and bank between the prince and people, to assist each against the encroachment of the other." The problem with the nineteen propositions sent by the two houses of Parliament, complains Charles, is that they "leave nothing for us [the King] but to look on" which "will return us to the worst kind of minority."[30] Charles's words, Corrine Weston alleges, had an almost "magical effect upon contemporaries."[31] Though opportunistic, the monarch had abandoned the theory of the divine right of kings in favour of a mixed constitution made up of coordinate authorities.

The mixed (or balanced) constitution became the dominant conception of the English Constitution for the next two centuries. That is how the Lord Bolingbroke describes the Constitution in the early eighteenth century, invoking the tropes that would have been widely shared even as between the government, then led by Walpole, and the opposition, led by Bolingbroke:

> A king of Great-Britain is that supreme magistrate, who has a negative voice in the legislature. He is entrusted with the executive power; and several other powers and privileges, which we call prerogatives, are annex'd to this trust. The two houses of parliament have their rights and privileges; some of which are common to both; others particular to each. They prepare, they pass bills, or they refuse to pass such as are sent to them. They address, represent, advise, remonstrate. The supreme judicature

---

30 J.P. Kenyon, *The Stuart Constitution, 1603–1688: Documents and Commentary* (Cambridge: Cambridge University Press, 1986), 18, 19.

31 Corrine Comstock Weston, *English Constitutional Theory and the House of Lords, 1556–1832* (London: Routledge & Kegan Paul, 1965), 24.

resides in the lords. The commons are the grand inquest of the nation; and to them it belongs likewise to judge of national expences, and to give supplies accordingly.

If the legislative, as well as the executive power, was wholly in the king, as in some countries, he would be absolute; if in the lords, our government would be an aristocracy; if in the commons, a democracy. It is this division of powers, these distinct privileges attributed to the king, to the lords and to the commons, which constitute a limited monarchy.[32]

Nearly everyone endorsed the revolution of 1688 and the Act of Settlement between King and Commons. The King, no longer ruling as of divine right, would have only a negative voice. Instead, he was now one of the three estates that comprised Parliament – King, Lords, and Commons – generating a kind of "admirable equipoise" that secured stability and security.[33]

The King had an additional existence outside of Parliament, however, and this is where it could be said that executive authority would lie. The King, with the advice and assistance of council (first the Privy Council and, after 1688, the Cabinet)[34] conducts affairs of state, typically those associated with the royal prerogatives such as those pertaining to the making of war and peace. For this reason, William R. Anson describes the Crown as "bifurcated," between the Crown in Parliament and the Crown in Council.[35]

The shared discourse of the mixed constitution generated a power-sharing arrangement between a "still powerful" King and a "newly powerful" House of Commons through much of the eighteenth century. While this relationship lasted, the theory maintained that the "blend [results in] a balance, an association in which each partner contributes its particular virtue, while inviting the others to check its particular vice."[36] It is noteworthy that, by this account, no body has

---

32 Henry St John Viscount Bolingbroke, *Remarks on the History of England*, 3rd ed. (London: R. Francklin, 1745), 82.
33 Francis Plowden, *A Short History of the British Empire: The Last Twenty Months* (London: G.G. and J. Robinson, 1794), 7.
34 Henry Hallam, *The Constitutional History of England from the Accession of Henry VII to the Death of George II* (London: Ward, Lock, 1893), 731.
35 William R. Anson, *The Law and Custom of the Constitution, Part I. Parliament*, 3rd ed. (Oxford: Oxford University Press, 1897), 41.
36 J.G.A. Pocock, *The Machiavellian Moment: Florentine Political Thought and the Atlantic Republican Tradition* (Princeton, NJ: Princeton University Press, 1974), 362–3.

particular expertise or specialization. All subjects fall potentially within Parliament's grasp. The theory, however, came slowly to be unravelled and unbalanced.[37] The expansion of the franchise, by the Reform Acts of 1832 and 1867, undid the balance such that the mixed or balanced constitutional lost much of its meaning.[38]

If there is little functional division in the mixed regime,[39] under a separation of powers regime, in its ideal formulation, each branch is assigned special purposes and expected not to invade the authority of the other. This has the effect, Diamond observes, of shrinking political space by narrowing the range of subjects capable of political resolution: "The mixed regime idea presupposes politics as a high and all-embracing art, an art aimed at comprehensive justice and hence requiring high, ultimately aristocratic deliberation and statesmanship. The separation of powers aims chiefly at the liberty of each, and therefore can try to limit politics and government to general and equal laws and their fair execution."[40] A political regime premised upon the separation of powers anticipates, then, a limited role for the government in the social life of its people.[41] For this reason, Diamond concludes that the mixed regime and the separation of powers "are about as unlike and unrelated as any two political arrangements can be expected to be."[42]

Diamond perhaps overstates his case. As we learn from the history of political thought, discussed next, the two are not entirely unrelated. It is regrettable, however, that scholars have not been so careful to distinguish between these two sets of ideas from either a historical or theoretical point of view. This might be the effect of the mixed constitution having been lost to the mists of time. The separation of powers, by contrast, has emerged as the victor, generating a better descriptive and normative account of how modern democracies operate.[43] As we see below, almost all involved in the 2009 prorogation sought to explain

---

37 Kemp, *King and Commons*, 1–2, 5.
38 Ibid., 1–2, 5, 145; Weston, *English Constitutional Theory*, 244.
39 Supply, however, was to be initiated and voted upon by the Commons.
40 Martin Diamond, *As Far as Republican Principles Will Admit*, ed. William A. Schambra (Washington: AEI, 1992), 64.
41 Martin Loughlin, *Foundations of Public Law* (Oxford: Oxford University Press, 2010), 390.
42 Diamond, *As Far as Republican Principles Will Admit*, 65.
43 M.J.C. Vile, *Constitutionalism and the Separation of Powers*, 2nd ed. (Indianapolis: Liberty Fund, 1998), 38, 108.

their point of view on the separation of powers. An older frame of reference – one that contrasts the vestiges of monarchical authority with modern democratic theory – better explains the interests that are at stake. I turn next to some of the principal theorists in the history of political thought who worked through the separation of powers and its relationship to prerogative power at its origins. Readers who wish to push beyond this intellectual history are advised to move to "U.S. Origins," where I turn to a discussion of American practice.

The People's House

Discussion of the political theory underlying the separation of powers in early modernity begins appropriately with John Locke.[44] However, Locke was not the first to speak of the matter. After the execution of Charles I, Puritan radicals John Lilburne and his Leveller followers sought to contain unicameral Parliament by invoking functional limitations. Lilburne distinguished between the "law-executing" and "law-making" powers of Parliament, aiming to confine the representative assembly only to the latter. Law-executing powers would be available in courts of law, otherwise "people would be rob'd of their intended and extraordinary benefit of appeales," for "in such cases," wrote Lilburne, "they must appeale to Parliament either against it self, or part of it self; and can it ever be imagined they will ever condemn themselves, or punish themselves?"[45] In the third "Agreement of the People" (1649), co-authored by Lilburne, it was proposed that a committee of Parliament's own members have conduct of "the managing of affairs" in intervals between meetings of the representative assembly, a proposal that sounds something like Cabinet government.[46] Though the Levellers had little success displacing the dominant trope of mixed government,[47] the separation of powers was a "cardinal principle in the constitutional proposals they [the Levellers] were urging the country to accept."[48]

---

44 This is despite Laslett's protestations that Locke would have had no such doctrine in mind. See Peter Laslett, "Introduction," in John Locke, *Two Treatises of Government*, critical edition by Peter Laslett (Cambridge: Cambridge University Press, 1964), 118.
45 William Haller and Godfrey Davies, *The Leveller Tracts, 1647–1653* (New York: Columbia University Press, 1944), 197.
46 Don M. Wolfe, ed., *Leveller Manifestoes of the Puritan Revolution* (New York: Thomas Nelson and Sons, 1944), 405.
47 Weston, *English Constitutional Theory and the House of Lords*, 51.
48 Gwyn, *Meaning of the Separation of Powers*, 43.

Locke learned much from these commonwealth-era proposals.[49] In his *Second Treatise of Government*, Locke distinguishes between those with the power to make laws – the legislative power, which need not always be sitting – and those with the power to execute them – executive power, a power "always in being." Because of a "temptation to human frailty to grasp at Power," resulting in law-making and executing that is "to their own private advantage," Locke observes, in "well order'd commonwealths" these powers "come often to be separated."[50] It was for the purposes of ensuring that laws promoted the common good (Locke's *salus populi*[51]), as opposed to some "distinct interest from the rest of the Community," that functions needed to be separated out.[52]

Idealizing from the English constitutional model, Locke generates an understanding of executive power that renders it subordinate to legislative (or parliamentary).[53] To be sure, the executive has a "share" in law-making (here he seems to be speaking of the Crown-in-Parliament), it is, however, "visibly subordinate and accountable to it" (speaking here of the Crown-in-council).[54] The legislative power thereby becomes

---

49 Ibid., 71.

50 Locke, *Two Treatises*, ¶143–4. There is no separate judicial authority in this account of the separation of powers – the judicial power is subsumed under the legislative branch, whose authority is to "determine all the Controversies, and redress the Injuries, that may happen to any Member of the Commonwealth" (¶90; also discussion in Vile, *Constitutionalism and the Separation of Powers*, at 65). This is not to say that Locke was not concerned with the "dispensation of justice" in the legislative branch. The determination of rights must be done, Locke writes, in accordance with "promulgated laws, and known and Authoris'd Judges" (¶136).

51 *Salus populi est suprema lex*: the welfare of the people is the paramount law. Loughlin associates this idea with the precepts of "prudence" and "droit politique," in Martin Loughlin, *The Idea of Public Law* (Oxford: Oxford University Press, 2003), 387. The maxim is traceable to Cicero's *De Legibus* and emerges as an expression of fundamental law in the mid-seventeenth century. See Cicero, *De Re Publica and De Legibus*, trans. Clinton Walker Keyes (Cambridge: Harvard University Press 1928), 1.3. 8; J.W. Gough, *Fundamental Law in English Constitutional History* (Oxford: Clarendon, 1961) 99.

52 Locke, *Two Treatises*, ¶143–4.

53 Ibid., ¶132. "There can be but one supream Power, which is the Legislative, to which all the rest are and must be subordinate" (ibid., ¶149).

54 Ibid., ¶152. Scholars have not been careful to distinguish between the two locales in which the Crown will be found. Pasquino, for instance, ascribes to Locke the thesis that Parliament and laws were established to limit prerogative, by in Locke's terms "ballancing the Power of Government, by placing several parts of it in different hands" (ibid., ¶107), in Pasquale Pasquino, "Locke on King's Prerogative," *Political Theory* 26 (1998): 203. But Locke very likely is referring here to the Crown in Parliament and the mixed or balanced constitution (also Locke, *Two Treatises of Government*, ¶152).

empowered to curb the executive. Not only is this a defence of parliamentary supremacy, observes Ashcraft, it is also, and more radically, "a
defence of the deposition of kings by that body."[55]

Locke initially separates out what he calls federative power – the
power to wage war and make peace – from executive and legislative
power. As it concerns relations lying beyond the borders of the commonwealth, he likens this power to one available to all in the state of
nature. Generalizing again from the English case, Locke acknowledges
that this power typically will be vested in one person with the sole
discretion to determine its use. Federative power concerns affairs that
are "much less capable to be directed by antecedent, standing, positive
Laws ... and so must necessarily be left to the Prudence and Wisdom
of those hands it is in, to be managed for the public good." As a practical matter, federative and executive powers will be placed in the same
hands and so, for the purposes of his discussion, proceeds to treat
them as united in the body of the executive.[56] Executive power continues to exhibit, however, characteristics of natural power, for it, claims
Harvey Mansfield, "remains [available] wherever political power is
ineffective."[57]

This prudential and natural authority is carried over into domestic affairs in the person of the executive. The reason that authority is
lodged in an executive is that inevitably there is a need for a power that
is "always in being" – a power that has the capacity for efficiency and

---

55 Richard Ashcraft, *Locke's Two Treatises of Government* (London: Unwin Hyman, 1987),
187.
56 Locke, *Two Treatises*, ¶145, ¶132, ¶152, ¶147, ¶148. Indeed, when government was in
its "infancy," Locke observes, "the Government was almost all prerogative" (¶162).
57 Harvey C. Mansfield Jr, *Taming the Prince: The Ambivalence of Modern Executive Power*
(New York: Free Press, 1989), 199. This is reminiscent of Schmitt's commissary
dictatorship: "The justification for dictatorship consists in the fact that, although
it ignores existing law, it is only doing so in order to save it." See Carl Schmitt,
*Dictatorship: From the Origin of the Modern Concept of Sovereignty to Proletarian Class
Struggle*, trans. Michale Hoelzl and Graham Ward (Cambridge: Polity, 2014), xliii. It
is appropriate here to refer to the Schmittian readings of Locke that have proliferated
in the post-9/11 English-language universe: that Locke envisages an executive that
is not reducible to law but can act extra-legally. See Clement Fatovic, "Constitutionalism and Presidential Prerogative: Jeffersonian and Hamiltonian Perspectives,"
American Journal of Political Science 48 (2004): 429–44; Pasquale Pasquino, "Locke on
King's Prerogative"; Loughlin, *Idea of Public Law*, 386; Oren Gross, "Chaos and Rules:
Should Responses to Violent Crises Always Be Constitutional?," *Yale Law Journal* 112
(2003): 1102–4.

dispatch. By contrast, the legislature may be too numerous and too slow to convene and so is not "always in being." "Accidents may happen," Locke warns, and any delay "might endanger the publick."[58] These imminent hazards "in which the ends of political society are most at risk" call for an ability to respond with rapidity and force.[59] This is the advantage of prerogative authority, advises Locke,[60] the paradigmatic instance of the Crown outside of Parliament, which "*is nothing but the Power of doing publick good without rule.*" Prerogative power grants to the executive robust authority over things by which "the law can by no means provide for," "and those must necessarily be left to the discretion of him that has the executive power." It is a power to act "for the public good, without the prescription of the Law, and even sometimes against it."[61]

This looks like licence for the executive to do anything it wishes. However, Locke is not interested in simply legitimating prerogative power. He also is anxious about its unfettered domain of discretion – its potential for arbitrariness[62] – and so identifies criteria for its use and abuse, which turn on contestable conceptions of the public good (*salus populi*).[63] Moreover, the legislature retains the power to "resume it out of those hands, when they find cause, and to punish for maladministration against the laws." Prerogative power "can be nothing," Locke writes, "but the Peoples permitting their Rulers, to do several things of their own free choice" to which they can "acquiesce" "without the least complaint" after it is done.[64] Locke appreciates that prerogative

---

58 Locke, *Two Treatises*, ¶144, ¶152, ¶160, ¶156. "Constant *frequent meetings of the Legislative*, and long Continuations of their Assemblies, without necessary occasion, could not but be burthensome to the People, and must necessarily in time produce more dangerous inconveniences, and yet the quick turn of affairs might be sometimes such as to need their present help" (ibid., 156). However, Locke is not exhibiting a disdain for the legislature. See his instructions to members of the 1681 Oxford Parliament to call for "annual Parliaments to dispatch and provide for those important affairs and businesses that can nowhere else be taken care of." See John Dunn, *The Political Thought of John Locke: An Historical Account of the Argument of the "Two Treatises of Government"* (Cambridge: Cambridge University Press, 1969), 55n3.

59 Dunn, *Political Thought of John Locke*, 150.

60 Ibid.

61 Locke, *Two Treatises*, ¶166, ¶159, ¶160.

62 Ibid., ¶210.

63 Dunn, *Political Thought of John Locke*, 149.

64 Locke, *Two Treatises*, ¶153. This looks like a version of Locke's "tacit consent." See Mansfield Jr, *Taming the Prince*, 203.

authority was not always in the hands of the "wisest and best Princes." Learning from experience that rule by "weak princes" gave rise to "mistake," "flattery," and "use of this power for private ends of their own," the people "declared limitations" on the prerogative. Locke gives licence to the people to continue to do so. It is a "wrong notion of government," Locke concludes, to say that the people have "encroached upon the prerogative" when they have set limits to it, for "they have not pulled from the prince anything that of right that belonged to him," but instead have declared that the power that was to be used for "their good" was used otherwise.[65] In other words, however efficient a power it may usefully be, the prerogative is a grant of trust held by the Crown on behalf of the people, which the people may take away.[66] It is the exercise of this reserve of power in the people that I propose setting in motion in the conclusion to this chapter.

Locke confirms, then, an ability to place limits on the Crown outside of Parliament when exercising royal prerogatives.[67] Yet curbing prerogatives must be difficult to accomplish if the executive has a "share" in law-making authority (when exercising authority as Crown-in-Parliament), in which case, admits Locke, "he is no more subordinate than he himself shall think fit, which one may certainly conclude will be but very little."[68] But the wise Prince, Locke might also say (but does not), will be prudent in exercising his veto for the public good within Parliament, just as he is in exercising prerogatives outside of it.

Even this will not entirely reconcile legislative with executive authority, for among the prerogatives exercised by the executive is the power to dismiss and summon the legislature. This does not give the executive "a superiority" over the legislature but instead amounts to a "Fiduciary

---

65 Locke, *Two Treatises*, ¶164–5, 163. "For the end of government being the good of the community, whatsoever alterations are made in it tending to that end, cannot be an encroachment upon any body, since no body in government can have a right tending to any other end" (ibid., ¶163).

66 John A. Simmons, *The Lockean Theory of Rights* (Princeton, NJ: Princeton University Press, 1992), 218; Mansfield, *Taming the Prince*, 203. I cannot agree with Payne's interpretation that Locke "attacks the notion that to define by positive laws what was prerogative is to encroach upon the prerogative" in Sebastien Payne, "The Royal Prerogative," in *The Nature of the Crown: A Legal and Political Analysis*, ed. Maurice Sunkin and Sebastien Payne (Oxford: Oxford University Press, 1999), 88.

67 Kemp, *King and Commons*, 27.

68 Locke, *Two Treatises*, ¶152.

Trust, placed in him, for the safety of the People."[69] Locke devotes considerable attention to executive power to summon legislatures in chapters 13 and 14 of the *Second Treatise*, underscoring the point that Locke was preoccupied with determining the outer limits of prerogative power to control Parliament.[70] This power was central to the controversy over royal authority in the late seventeenth century, in which, as close advisor to the first earl of Shaftesbury, Locke was directly involved. In the period 1679–81, King Charles II was intent on not having Parliament meet, resolving "never to call another."[71] Shaftesbury, leader of the Whig opposition to the King, complained of the "prorogations, the dissolutions, the cutting short of Parliaments, not suffering them to have time or opportunity to look into anything."[72] Ashcraft has observed that both the argument and the language that Locke deploys in his discussion of the prerogatives mimics that used by Shaftesbury and other radical Whigs in opposition to the refusal of the monarch to summon Parliament.[73]

It turns out that, even if the people can declare limits on prerogative power, little can be done when the legislature is not convened, other than to "appeal to heaven." "Between an Executive Power in being, with such a Prerogative, and a Legislative that depends upon his will for their convening, there can be no *Judge on Earth*," Locke proclaims.[74] Refusing to convene Parliament amounts to the use of "force without Authority," Locke declares; it amounts to being in a "state of war with the People," "for having erected a Legislative, with an intent they should exercise the Power of making laws, either at certain set times, or when there is need of it; when they are hindr'd by any force from, what is so necessary to the Society, and wherein the Safety and preservation of the people consists, the People have a right to remove it by force."[75]

We now have arrived at the "practical objective" of Locke's constitutional edifice: to empower the people to revolt when denied the capacity

69 Ibid., ¶156.
70 Richard Ashcraft, *Revolutionary Politics & Locke's Two Treatises of Government* (Princeton, NJ: Princeton University Press, 1986), 321; Dunn, *Political Thought of John Locke*, 150.
71 Ashcroft, *Revolutionary Politics*, 313.
72 Earl of Anthony Ashley Cooper Shaftesbury, *A Speech Lately Made by a Noble Peer of the Realm* (London: Printed for F.S., 1681) 2.
73 Ashcroft, *Revolutionary Politics*, 315.
74 Locke, *Two Treatises*, ¶165, ¶168.
75 Ibid., ¶155.

to be supreme.[76] For these reasons, it seems erroneous to assign to Locke the view that he was "content" to allow the King to prorogue, dissolve, and summon Parliament as he saw fit, and that he was "quite happy to grant to the king the right to veto acts" of Parliament.[77] Pasquino is correct to observe that many scholars have passed over Locke's discussion of the prerogative "in silence,"[78] though it was a central concern of his *Second Treatise*.[79] Those who have addressed his discussion have tended to ascribe to him a general ambivalence towards,[80] if not endorsement of,[81] this discretionary authority. It is true that Locke identifies advantages to executive discretion – in the granting of pardons, for instance – but it is not true to suggest that he was disinterested in restraining its use. He was not aligning himself with royalists on this front.[82] Locke's seeming ambivalence about the relationship between King and Parliament has befuddled his interpreters, but this ambiguity likely was deliberate and strategic – it unified opposition forces to the King.[83] As if to underscore the point, if any part of Locke's treatise has taken hold, it is this part – it represents the prevailing doctrine in the parliamentary world.

All Mixed Up

Charles-Louis de Secondat, Baron de Montesquieu, was not so interested in preserving or enhancing legislative supremacy. Rather, it appears to have worried him immensely. His aim, instead, was to develop a defence of aristocratic rule ("moderate monarchy") by landed gentry in response to republicanist threats.[84] In the course of

---

76 Ashcroft, *Revolutionary Politics & Locke's Two Treatises of Government*, 191.
77 Paul A. Rahe, *Republics Ancient and Modern*. Vol. 2, *New Modes and Orders in Early Modern Political Thought* (Chapel Hill: University of North Carolina Press, 1994), 245.
78 Pasquino, "Locke on King's Prerogative," 199.
79 Dunn, *Political Though of John Locke*, 150.
80 For example, Loughlin, *Foundations of Public Law*.
81 For example, Rahe, *Republics Ancient and Modern*.
82 See Locke's instructions to members of the 1681 Oxford Parliament reproduced in Dunn, *Political Thought of John Locke*, 55n3.
83 It is for this reason that Ashcroft calls it a "supremely shrewd political manifesto of the radical movement as a whole," in Ashcroft, *Revolutionary Politics*, 321n140.
84 Louis Althusser, *Politics and History: Montesquieu, Rousseau, Marx*, trans. Ben Brewster (London: Verso, 2007), 97; Annelien de Dijn, *French Political Thought from Montesquieu to Tocqueville: Liberty in a Levelled Society?* (Cambridge: Cambridge University Press, 2008), 32; de Dijn, "Was Montesquieu a Liberal Republican?," *Review of Politics* 76 (2014): 21–41.

writing his innovative comparative constitutional treatise, *The Spirit of the Laws*, Montesquieu penned some of the most influential, if opaque, passages on the separation of powers. Purporting to describe England's constitutional system, Montesquieu begins by noting that there is, "in every government ... three sorts of power [or *pouvoir*]: the legislative, the executive in respect of the law of nations [what Locke called "federative" power], and the executive in regard to civil laws," which Locke associates with the "judiciary power,"[85] each of which is described as a "*puissance.*"[86] When the legislative and executive are united in the same person, there is no liberty, he maintained: "There would be an end of everything [*tout seroit perdu*], were the same man or the same body whether of nobles or of the people, to exercise those three powers, that of enacting laws, that of executing the public resolutions, and that of trying the causes of individuals."[87]

Though Montesquieu's formulation includes a judicial branch, it appears that this branch is not as significant as the first two. Montesquieu conceives of the "power to judge" as one exercised by "individuals drawn from the body of the people"[88] – something akin to trial by jury[89] – which renders this power, "as it were, invisible,"

---

85 Montesquieu, *Spirit of the Laws*, 11.6.151. There is controversy over the degree to which Montesquieu misrepresented the state of affairs at the time. Holdsworth describes Montequieu's *Spirit* as "superficial," "inadequate and to some extent misleading," in William Holdsworth, *A History of English Law* (London: Methuen, 1938), 10:718. Stewart, by contrast, claims that Montesquieu was very well acquainted with the English (really British) Constitution and its politics and sought to draw out a model of ideal types, in Stewart, "Montesquieu in England." This is confirmed by his discussion of the "depths of corruption" in Parliament (in a preparatory letter to Mr Domville) in Baron de Montesquieu, *My Thoughts (Mes Pensées)*, trans., ed. Henry C. Clark (Indianapolis: Liberty Fund, 2012), 594; Montesquieu, *Oeuvres Complètes de Montesquieu*, ed. M. André Masson (Paris: Les Éditions Nagel, 1950), 2:593; and also by Montesquieu's avowal, at the end of his discussion in chap. 6, that he does not purport to be answering the empirical question of whether "the English actually enjoy this liberty or not," Montesquieu, *The Spirit of the Laws*, 162; Montesquieu, *Oeuvres Complètes*, ed. Roger Caillois (Paris: Librarie Gallimard, 1951), 2:407. He well understood, in other words, how reality did not comport with his abstract account.

86 Montesquieu, *Oeuvres Complètes*, 2:397. Manin associates "pouvoir" with function and "puissance" with institutional organs of the state, in Bernard Manin, "Montesquieu," in *The Critical Dictionary of the French Revolution*, ed. Francois Furet and Mona Ozouf, trans. Arthur Goldhammer (Cambridge: Belknap, 1989), 732.

87 Montesquieu, *Spirit of the Laws*, 152; Montesquieu, *Oeuvres Complètes*, 2:397.

88 Montesequieu, *Spirit of the Laws*, 153; Montesquieu, *Oeuvres Complètes*, 2:398.

89 Vile, *Constitutionalism and the Separation of Powers*, 113

"in some measure next to nothing," he writes.[90] Yet Montesquieu also insists that judicial power be kept separate from legislative and executive authority. He tolerates the latter two being united, as they were in moderate monarchies on the Continent, in which case, all liberty is not lost when both legislative and executive puissance are joined together.[91] So long as judicial power is at some distance from the monarch, there will be no despotism.[92] However muddled the "separation" (a phrase that Montesquieu does not use), here we have three distinct bodies serving different functions but without any obvious relation to the prevailing idea in England of balanced or mixed government.

Instead, Montesquieu goes on to discuss balanced government as if it were a species of the "three sorts of power" previously mentioned.[93] Seeing as the judicial power is, "in some measure next to nothing," he proceeds to a discussion of the remaining two. The legislative branch, in particular, is in "need of a regulating power" "to check the licentiousness [les entreprises] of the people." Montesquieu recommends that a "legislative body composed of the nobility is extremely proper for this purpose."[94] These are the intermediate powers (pouvoirs) through which the channels of monarchical power flow. The executive, by

---

90 Montesquieu, Spirit of the Laws, 153, 156; Montesquieu, Oeuvres Complètes, 2:398, 401. Further in the chapter, Montesquieu acknowledges that judicial power is assigned to distinct bodies exercising mechanical authority: "National judges are no more than the mouth that pronounces the words of the law, mere passive beings" (Montesquieu, Spirit of the Laws, 159; Montesquieu, Oeuvres Complètes, 2:404).

91 Montesquieu, Spirit of the Laws, 152; Montesquieu, Oeuvres Complètes, 2:397. "Most kingdoms in Europe enjoy a moderate government because the prince who is invested with the first two powers leaves the third to his subjects" (Montesquieu, Spirit of the Laws, 152; Montesquieu, Oeuvres Complètes, 2:397); and, in chapter 7: "Here the three powers are not distributed and founded on the model of the constitution above mentioned; they have each a particular distribution, according to which they border more or less on political liberty; and if they did not border upon it, monarchy would degenerate into despotic government" (Montesquieu, Spirit of the Laws, 162; Montesquieu, Oeuvres Complètes, 2:408).

92 Manin, "Montesquieu," 734. This ambivalence about judicial power may have been strategic. Casting it as a negligible force in English constitutional law may have been for the purposes of allaying fear of "judicial oppression," suggests Gwyn in Meaning of the Separation of Powers, 103.

93 Ville, Constitutionalism and the Separation of Powers, 91.

94 Montesquieu, Spirit of the Laws, 155, 156; Montesquieu, Oeuvres Complètes, 2:401. Loughlin considers that the "landed class" made the whole machine run and not mixed or divided powers, in Idea of Public Law, 24.

contrast, is best left in the hands of the monarch, with the power to share in legislation by exercising a power of refusal, this to ensure preservation of royal prerogatives.[95] Though the legislative branch may not have the power to "stop the executive," "it has a right and ought to have the means of examining in what manner its laws have been executed." The resulting equipoise is described as follows: "Here then is the fundamental constitution of the government we are treating of. The legislative body [corps] being composed of two parts, one checks the other, by the mutual privilege of refusing. They are both checked by the executive power [puissance], as the executive is by the legislative." Montesquieu goes on to say, "These three powers [puissances] should naturally form a state of repose or inaction. But as there is necessity for movement in the course of human affairs, they are forced to move, but still to move in concert."[96] It will be extraordinary, then, when they do move in concert.[97]

It is from this short discussion that a key element of liberal constitutionalism has been derived, and this is somewhat unfortunate – a discussion of which purports to be about three seemingly separate powers turns out to be a description of the mixed constitution operating within the precincts of Parliament. The resulting muddle gives rise to controversy over precisely what Montesquieu intended. Eisenmann, for instance, characterizes the dominant interpretation, which ascribes a separation of powers doctrine to Montesquieu, as the exact opposite of what he proposes.[98] Rather than being separated out, Eisenmann

---

95 Montesquieu, *Spirit of the Laws*, 16, 156, 159; Montesquieu, *Oeuvres Complètes*, 2:247, 404, 405. "Otherwise," Locke writes, "it [the executive] would be stripp'd of its prerogatives," in *Two Treatises*, ¶52.

96 Montesquieu, *Spirit of the Laws*, 158, 160; Montesquieu, *Oeuvres Complètes*, 2:402, 405.

97 Under Montesquieu's system, then, "divided power results in citizens being less governed," observes Pierre Manent in *An Intellectual History of Liberalism*, trans. Rebecca Balinski (Princeton, NJ: Princeton University Press, 1995), 62. In his "Notes on England," for instance, Montesquieu describes the passage of a "miraculous" bill that neither the Lords nor the Commons truly desired passage of in its final form (Stewart, "Montesquieu in England").

98 Charles Eisenmann, "La pensée constitutionnelle de Montesquieu," in Université de Paris, Institut de Droit Comparé, *La pensée politique et constitutionnelle de Montesquieu: Bicentenaire de L'esprit des Lois, 1748–1948* (Paris: Recueil Sirey, 1952), 145; also Michel Troper, "The Development of the Notion of the Separation of Powers," *Israel Law Review* 26 (1992): 6.

maintains, Montesquieu contemplates powers encroaching substantially upon each other, acting together in "concert."[99] Manin similarly insists that Montesquieu envisages powers being moderated by their interplay within the legislative branch.[100]

On the other hand, it seems doubtful that the dominant account is entirely wrong. Montesquieu's discussion opens with an idealized description of three sorts of powers found in "every government." He assimilates doctrines that had wide circulation in Britain that included a version of the separation of powers[101] – not so much an excuse for the ensuing confusion, but it may be that Montesquieu's intermingling of the dual doctrines was, as Gwyn suggests, to maximize the principal object of securing liberty. He "developed the two doctrines separately," Gwyn writes, "showing that they were both necessary for political liberty and taking care as best he could that his statement of one did not conflict with that of the other."[102] Pangle goes so far as to claim the two doctrines are fused in order to "stabilize" and "institutionalize" the "balance of factional power."[103] To the extent that the balanced constitution later become superfluous, it makes sense that his forceful account of the separation of powers generated the prevailing frame of reference for liberal constitutional orders.

English Assimilation

As Montesquieu well knew when he composed the *Spirit of the Laws*, the dominant account of the British Constitution was more of a mixed affair than a partitioned one. "At the same time," Holdsworth admits, "there is an element of truth in Montesquieu's analysis." The principal problem is that Montesquieu exaggerates "the sharpness of

---

99 Eisenmann, "La pensée constitutionnelle de Montesquieu," 155, 158; Althussser, *Politics and History*, 91. It is a fear that any one branch can act to oppress the nobility or revolt against the king, Althusser claims, that animates Montesquieu (93–4).

100 Bernard Manin, "Montesquieu et la politique moderne," in *Lectures de l'Espirit des Lois*, ed. Céline Spector and Thierry Hoquet (Pessac: Presses Universitaires de Bordeaux, 1985), 224; Manin, "Montesquieu," 732.

101 For example, Humphrey Mackworth, *A Vindication of the Rights of the Commons of England* (London: J. Nutt, 1701), 4; Kramnick, *Bolingbroke & His Circle*, 142.

102 Gwyn, *Meaning of the Separation of Powers*, 109.

103 Thomas L. Pangle, *Montesquieu's Philosophy of Liberalism: A Commentary on* Spirit of the Laws (Chicago: Chicago University Press, 1973), 122–3.

the separation."[104] So it turns out there are distinctive executive and legislative branches in the parliamentary tradition, just not as sharply defined as Montesquieu suggests. I turn here to brief discussions of three thinkers (Blackstone, de Lolme, and Paley) who assimilated Montesquieu's normative account into the dominant English one. A great deal has been written about each of them. The emphasis here will be on the place of prerogative power in their understanding of the mixed/separated constitution.

Blackstone aimed to bring together the dominant mixed constitution account with Montesquieu's separation of powers, though without much success.[105] It was for the purpose of "preserving the balance of the constitution that the executive should be a branch, though not the whole, of the legislature," he observed.[106] It was necessary, conversely, to contain legislative power by the other branches (the Lords and Crown), otherwise, it "would soon become tyrannical, by making continual encroachments, and gradually assuming to itself the rights of the executive power." All "the parts of it [Parliament]," Blackstone claims, "form a mutual check upon each other."[107]

---

104 Holdsworth, *History of English Law,* 721. Montesquieu left out, for instance, any discussion of political parties, the emerging Cabinet system, or the professional judiciary. See Sheila Mason, "Montesquieu on English Constitutionalism Revisited: A Government of Potentiality and Paradoxes," *Studies on Voltaire and the Eighteenth Century* 278 (1990): 115. For a defence of Montesquieu in this regard, see C.P. Courtney, "Montesquieu and English Liberty," in *Montesquieu's Science of Politics: Essays on the Science of the Laws,* ed. David W. Carrithers, Michael A. Mosher, and Paul A. Rahe (Lanham, MD: Rowman and Littlefield, 2001), 279–80.

105 Vile, *Constitutionalism and the Separation of Powers,* 121.

106 Blackstone, *Commentaries on the Laws of England,* 149. Bentham complains – and will not be the first to do so – that it is difficult in the *Commentaries* to distinguish between the functions of the executive in contradistinction to the legislative branch, in Jeremy Bentham, *A Fragment on Government,* ed. J.J. Burns and H.L.A. Hart (Cambridge: Cambridge University Press, 1988), 73–4. He also challenges the view that the Lords have an advantage in "wisdom" over the Commons: "The fact is, as every body sees, that either the members of the House of Commons are as much at leisure as those of the House of Lords; or, if occupied, occupied in such a way as to give them a more than ordinary insight into some particular department of Government" (78).

107 Blackstone, *Commentaries on the Laws of England,* 150. Blackstone improves upon Montesquieu's description of the operation of the judicial branch, observes Vile, in *Constitutionalism and the Separation of Powers,* 113. Blackstone admits the "distinct and separate existence of the judicial power," which constitutes "one main preservative of the public liberty." "Nothing therefore is more to be avoided," he concludes, "in a free constitution, than uniting the provinces of a judge" with the legislative or executive (259–60).

The tone of Blackstone's discussion of prerogative power – of the Crown in Council operating in its executive capacity – is, much like the rest of the work, obsequious.[108] Though the prerogatives formerly were considered a subject "too delicate" for commentary, Blackstone maintains that this was never reflected in "the language of our ancient constitution and laws." He admits early on, therefore, that "the limitation of the regal authority was a first and essential principle in all the Gothic systems of government established in Europe." Abuses of its exercise are to be met with "indictments" and "impeachments" of the King's "evil counselors" and "wicked ministers." Though he denies being "an advocate for arbitrary power," he lays down the principle that "in the exertion of lawful prerogative, the king is and ought to be absolute":[109] "He may reject what bills, may make what treaties, may coin what money, may create what peers, may pardon what offences he pleases; unless where the constitution has expressly, or by evident consequence, laid down some exception or boundary; declaring, that thus far the prerogative shall go and no farther. For otherwise, the power of the crown would indeed be but a name and a shadow, insufficient for the ends of government." Prerogative authority, for Blackstone, is "irresistible and absolute." Should its exercise give rise to grievance or dishonour, the only remedy is to "call his advisors to a just and severe account."[110]

Blackstone does improve on earlier accounts by linking the prerogatives to the operation of the balanced constitution in Parliament. Acknowledging that executive power must have its "due independence and vigour," it is hemmed in by "such reasonable checks and restrictions [issuing out of Parliament] as may curb it from trampling on those liberties, which it was meant to secure and establish." If left to itself, prerogative power would "spread havoc and destruction among all the inferior movements: but, when balanced and bridled (as with us) by it's [sic] proper counterpoise, timely and judiciously applied, its operations are then equable and regular, it invigorates the whole machine, and enables every part to answer the ends of its construction."[111] Under

---

108 Blackstone's account of the King's prerogative, observes Loughlin, "highlights its absolutist qualities," in *Foundations of Public Law*, 381.
109 Blackstone, *Commentaries on the Laws of England*, 230–1, 237, 243.
110 Ibid., 244.
111 Ibid., 243.

Blackstone, the Crown is less bifurcated and the balanced constitution, in a novel formulation, operates both inside and outside of Parliament.

The Swiss writer Jean Louis de Lolme is as protective of prerogative power as is Blackstone. De Lolme comprehends prerogative authority, though "at first sight" as vast as that claimed by absolute monarchs, tamed by an incapacity to obtain revenue without Parliament's cooperation. The royal prerogative, "destitute as it is of the power to impose taxes, is like a vast body, which cannot of itself accomplish its motions." So without "touching the prerogative itself, they [Parliament] have moderated the exercise of it." It is this division of legislative power – divided between Crown, Lords, and Commons – that provides stability in English constitutional law. "It is without doubt," he writes, "absolutely necessary, for securing the constitution of a state, to restrain the executive power, but it is still more necessary to restrain the legislative." This is because of its "bare" power to change laws: "If I may be permitted the expression, the legislative power can change the constitution as God created the light."[112] While de Lolme is content with merely cabining unitary executive power, legislative power requires division. De Lolme proceeds to describe the division of Parliament into its three estates, the resulting constitutional "balance," and the merits of its "steady" government consistent with dominant accounts of the mixed constitution.[113]

William Paley, like Blackstone, assimilates the royal prerogative into his account of the balanced constitution but does not embrace Montesquieu's formulation wholeheartedly. Instead, the emphasis remains on a "balance of power, and a balance of interest" within Parliament. "By a balance of power," he writes, "is meant that there is no power possessed by one part of the legislature, the abuse or excess of which is not checked by some antagonist power, residing in another part." For instance, any one of the three estates comprising Parliament could check the other by exercising veto rights. "By the *balance of interest*," Paley continues, "is meant this: – that the respective interests of the three estates of the empire are so disposed and adjusted, that whichever of the three shall attempt any encroachment, the other two

---

112 Jean Louis De Lolme, *The Constitution of England or, An Account of the English Government: In Which It Is Compared Both with the Republican Form of Government and the Other Monarchies of Europe*, new ed. John McGregor (London: Henry G. Bohn, 1853), 67, 68, 156, 157.

113 Ibid., 159; Vile, *Constitutionalism and the Separation of Powers*, 116.

will unite in resisting it."[114] A more nuanced point that James Madison later would develop, each estate had an incentive to protect its own turf and to ensure there was no encroachment by one into the territory of another.[115] In order to promote the advantages of "decision, secrecy and despatch," Paley acknowledges that the "constitution has committed the executive government to the administration and limited authority of an hereditary king." The prerogatives assigned to the Crown, including a power to negative laws framed by the two houses, are "checked" by the "privileges" of Parliament, including, for instance, that of "refusing to fund supplies of money to the exigencies of the king's administration."[116]

In Paley's formulation, Crown prerogative is counterpoised against parliamentary privilege. Yet in practice these "formidable prerogatives," Paley admits, have "dwindled into mere ceremonies." In their stead has arisen the use of "influence ... growing out of that enormous patronage ... placed in the disposal of the executive magistrate." Paley, unlike his predecessors, acknowledges the Crown's influence in Parliament through the use of patronage (or "place" men) as essential to the maintenance of "balance" among the estates. Reform of the manner in which seats in the House are apportioned and members elected would have the tendency of enhancing the authority of the House and of generating "less flexibility to the influence of the Crown."[117] Influence of this sort was essential to Paley for maintaining the balance between Crown, Lords, and Commons. Otherwise, popular assemblies would aggregate all of the power to themselves, just as they did in the American colonies.[118] There is an interesting counterfactual hinted at by Henry Hallam.[119] If placemen – those who had "an office or place of profit under the king," as it was put in the Act of Settlement – had been excluded from the House of Commons (as had been advocated by

---

114 Willam Paley, *The Principles of Moral and Political Philosophy*, 2nd ed. (London: Printed by J. Davis, for R. Faulder, 1786), 309, 311.
115 Weston, *English Constitutional Theory and the House of Lords*, 131.
116 Paley, *Principles of Moral and Political Philosophy*, 307, 309–10.
117 Ibid., 302, 317. Paley quotes these words but without reference. Hume makes a similar argument in "Of the Independency of Parliament," in David Hume, *Essays Moral, Political and Literary* (London: Grant Richards, 1912), 45.
118 Paley, *Principles of Moral and Political Philosophy*, 319; Kemp, *King and Commons*, 64, 143–4.
119 Hallam, *Constitutional History of England*, 734.

parliamentary reformers like Bolingbroke), no minister would have sat in the House. Cabinet government might never have evolved. Instead, we may have seen an entrenchment of the separate branches.[120]

Problems of Cabinet Government

In essays collected in 1867 under the title *The English Constitution*, Walter Bagehot famously dismissed the idea of the separation of powers and placed the Cabinet at the centre of English constitutional practice – a view that continues to influence Canadian constitutional conceptions. Bagehot acknowledges that there have been "two descriptions of the English Constitution which have exercised immense influence": the first is the separation of powers; the second, the balanced constitution. Both, he declares, are "erroneous." Bagehot chooses, instead, a different bifurcation of the English Constitution: that between its "dignified" parts (those that excite and preserve reverence of the population, principally the monarchy) and its "efficient" parts (those parts that make it work).[121]

The "efficient secret of the English Constitution," observes Bagehot, is the "close union, the nearly complete fusion" of the executive and legislative powers. This more-than-partial fusion is achieved via the body of the Cabinet – the "board of control" chosen by the legislature from among persons "it knows and trusts." The Cabinet is the "efficient secret of the English Constitution" and the "connecting link," Bagehot wrote, "a hyphen which joins, a buckle which fastens, the legislative part of the state to the executive part of the state." Farther along in the volume, Bagehot contrasts features of Cabinet government with presidential government. The former purports to divide sovereignty among multiple persons; the latter "is the type of simple constitutions, in which the ultimate power upon all questions is in the hands of the same persons."[122] Bagehot seems not to understand very well the U.S. system of presidential authority. But he does understand that the balanced constitution no longer is an apt description of English constitutional law.

---

120 "Such a separation and want of intelligence between the crown and parliament," Hallam suggests, "must either have destroyed the one, or degraded the other" (ibid., 741).
121 Ibid., 204–5, 206.
122 Ibid., 210, 212, 210, 211, 212, 349.

Lord Grey was of the view that expansion of the franchise would not upset that balance.[123] The object of reform, he maintained, was to "preserve" and "to redress the balance of the Constitution, not to make it incline as much on one side as it had previously done." Nevertheless, Grey agreed with the view that the "common description of the British Constitution ... [as being of the three estates] has ceased to be correct" – that executive and legislative power were now "virtually united."[124] With the passage of the reforms acts of 1832 and 1867, expanding the franchise to all householders and workingmen, the balance had been permanently upset. The Crown could no longer exercise "influence" as Paley understood it – no longer could the King independently choose ministers or manage House membership by exploiting the power of patronage. This was a process that eventually "forced the King out of politics."[125] It amounted to a "great calamity to the whole nation," complained Bagehot in the introduction to the second edition of *The English Constitution*.[126] Balance "lost all meaning," Kemp observes, when the electorate determined both membership in the House and composition of the King's ministers. The balance was not entirely destroyed, however. Executive authority, now in the hands of the prime minister and his Cabinet, was rendered more legitimate and powerful vis-à-vis Parliament.[127]

Albert Venn Dicey, Oxford Vinerian Professor of English Law, also sought to distance English constitutional law from the "dogma" associated with Montesquieu's formulation, "which has undergone a different development on each side of the Atlantic" (referring to France and to the United States). Dicey dismissed Montesquieu as having "misunderstood on this point the principles and practice of the English constitution."[128] Instead, Dicey described the executive in England as being a "parliamentary *Executive*" – meaning a Cabinet government. So it was with "all the Constitutions of such British colonies as

---

123 Weston, *English Constitutional Theory and the House of Lords*, 244.
124 Earl Grey, *Parliamentary Government Considered with Reference to a Reform of Parliament: An Essay* (London: Richard Bentley, 1858), 86, 4, 66.
125 Kemp, *King and Commons*, 111.
126 Bagehot, *English Constitution*, 172. Bagehot was, he wrote, "exceedingly afraid of the ignorant multitude of the new constituencies" (177).
127 Kemp, *King and Commons*, 145, 110.
128 A.V. Dicey, *Introduction to the Study of the Law of the Constitution*, 7th ed. (London: Macmillan, 1908), 333.

enjoy representative government." This "violates the soundest part of Montesquieu's doctrine enjoining the separation of powers," Dicey declared. It was plain that in governing through a committee of the "supreme legislature," the three powers are "blended together."[129]

Dicey proceeded to describe what he calls the "law of the constitution," namely, those "rules enforced or recognised by the Courts."[130] Whenever Parliament speaks, its speaks via statute, entitling the judiciary to review enactments for their conformity with the law of the constitution – a process Dicey associated with the idea of the "rule of law." These rules include not only specific enactments of Parliament but "general principles," which are the result of judicial decisions arising out of individual cases "brought before the Courts."[131] The law of the constitution is contrasted with "conventions" of the constitution, which "make up a body not of laws, but of constitutional or political ethics." These amount, for the most part, to the discretionary powers of the Crown, principally the prerogatives. For Dicey, the prerogatives are the "residue of discretionary or arbitrary authority, which at any given time is legally left in the hands of the Crown." This is an old authority, "in truth anterior to that of the House of Commons," which survives only to the extent that prerogatives have not been disrupted by practice (such as disuse) or by statute.[132]

Like Paley before him, Dicey prefers to contrast prerogative power with parliamentary privileges. There "exists a close analogy: the one is the historical name for the discretionary authority of the Crown; the other is the historical name for the discretionary authority of each House of Parliament." Yet there is no real equivalency of the two. The conventions serve only "one ultimate object": to secure the supremacy of Parliament. No "modern lawyer," writes Dicey, "would maintain that these powers or any other branch of royal authority could not be regulated or abolished by Act of Parliament." For this reason, the "modern code of constitutional morality secures," Dicey

---

129 Dicey, "Comparison between English & Other Executives," 79, 81, 82. This is in contrast to extra-parliamentary executives, like the American presidency (89). Dicey's friend William Anson also saw "no reason why legislative and executive duties should not be discharged by the same person or body of persons" (Anson, *Law and Custom of the Constitution*, 39).
130 Dicey, *Introduction to the Study of the Law of the Constitution*, 26, 413.
131 Ibid., 27, 191.
132 Ibid., 413, 418, 420, 421.

concludes, "though in a roundabout way, what is called abroad the 'sovereignty of the people.'"[133] We might also say that Locke has finally gotten his way.

U.S. Derivation

Though Montesquieu was preoccupied with preserving royal pre-rogatives, American framers were not similarly concerned. The Americans, like the French after them,[134] were content to adopt Montesquieu's tripartite division but without "allowing his (or Locke's) defense of prerogative to outweigh the lessons of their own history."[135] It was, after all, abuse of this discretionary authority through the office of governor that had agitated the colonists in the first instance.[136] For this reason, the first constitution of the United States, the Articles of Confederation of 1777, omitted any reference to the executive, so "radical [was the colonists'] distrust of executive authority."[137] Instead, a Committee of the States was authorized to perform some executive-type functions – such as building and equip-ping a navy and land forces – and only while Congress was in recess.[138] This conciliar body was granted no significant authority, however, such as that of waging war and making peace. Madison subsequently described the executive in the Articles of Confederation as "the worst part of a bad Constitution,"[139] expressing concerns about the absence

---

133 Ibid., 423, 424, 61, 426.
134 Manin, "Montesquieu et la politique moderne," 732.
135 Jack N. Rakove, *Original Meanings: Politics and Idea in the Making of the Constitution* (New York: Vintage Books, 1996), 250. Rakove exaggerates the degree to which Locke was interested in defending the prerogative.
136 Bernard Bailyn, "The Origins of American Politics," *Perspectives in American History* 1 (1967): 52–4; Jack N. Rakove, *Revolutionaries: A New History of the Invention of America* (Boston: Houghton Mifflin Harcourt, 2010), 176–7. Though it should be noted that the colonists called upon the King to exercise his prerogative of disal-lowing parliamentary usurpation of colonial legislative power. See John Phillip Reid, *Constitutional History of the American Revolution: The Authority of Law* (Madison: University of Wisconsin Press, 1993), 158.
137 Merrill Jensen, *The Articles of Confederation: An Interpretation of the Social-Constitutional History of the American Revolution, 1774–1781* (Madison: University of Wisconsin Press, 1962), 179.
138 Articles of Confederation, art 9.
139 James Madison to Caleb Wallace, 23 August 1785, in *Writings*, ed. Jack N. Rakove (New York: Library of America, 1999), 42.

of an executive to enforce laws in his famous "Vices of the Political System of the United States."[140]

Executive authority, however, was not so much at the forefront of Madison's mind during the framing in 1787 – it "claims the 2d place," he declared.[141] As its prerogatives (war and peace) were now in the hands of Congress, it did not deserve much consideration. The framers were therefore puzzled about what do with the executive branch. Their debates were "frustratingly episodic and circular," observes Rakove. Executive branch authority crystallized only as delegates began feeling uneasy about the powers proposed to be wielded by the Senate.[142] The initial, hastily secured consensus that Congress would directly appoint the president – not unlike the nascent parliamentary practice – was transformed into indirect election by the state's electoral college.[143] Madison subsequently defended the scheme in the *Federalist Papers* by invoking the "oracle [Montesquieu] who is always consulted and cited on this subject." Though "he be not the author of this invaluable precept in the science of politics, he has the merit of displaying and recommending it most effectually to the attention of mankind." In defending the complex scheme of checks and balances in the 1787 text, Madison explains that, on "the slightest view of the British Constitution," it could not have been that Montesquieu intended to say the three departments were "totally separate and distinct from each other."[144]

---

140 Ibid. In his discussion of a "want of sanction to the laws, and of coercion," Madison wrote, "If the laws of the States, were merely recommendatory to their citizens, or if they were to be rejudged by County authorities, what security, what probability would exist, that they would be carried into execution? Is the security or probability greater in favor of the acts of Congs. which depending for their execution on the will of the state legislatures, wch. are tho' nominally authoritative, in fact recommendatory only" (72–3).

141 Ibid., 41.

142 Rakove, *Original Meanings*, 253, 256, 267.

143 F.H. Buckley, *The Once and Future King: The Rise of Crown Government in America* (New York: Encounter Books, 2014), 54. Because this compromise was expected to preserve congressional control over appointment by having states vote in the House of Representatives in cases where there was no clear majority (US Constitution, art II, s 1), Buckley concludes that the "separation of powers should thus be demoted from its position as a foundational principle of constitutional interpretation" (61).

144 Alexander Hamilton, James Madison, and John Jay, *The Federalist Papers*, ed. Clinton Rossiter (New York: New American Library, 1961), 301, 302. This must be an example of what Gordon Wood has in mind when he writes that the massive constitutional rethink that occurred in the 1780s often was justified "by ingenious manipulations" of Montesquieu's doctrine. See Gordon S. Wood, *Empire of Liberty: A History of the Early Republic, 1789–1815* (New York: Oxford University Press, 2009), 407.

He did not mean to say, Madison stipulates, "that these departments ought to have no *partial agency* in, or no *control* over, the acts of each other." Rather, the concern was with wholesale exercises of authority by one "department" over another, in which case, it was no violation of the principle to have the branches sharing in, or blending, their authority. The challenge was to avoid "too great a mixture" that would undermine the benefits of separation.[145]

Madison was a close reader of Montesquieu and so folded the balanced constitution, with its tripartite non-functional divisions, back into the mixture. The genius of the Madisonian design is not only the idea of "partial interdependence" of the separate branches, Ostrom observes, but the complex system of "potential veto positions" that are contemplated: "The capacity of such a system to govern depends upon the capacity of each part to reach agreement within the potential veto positions of each other part." The balance of power and of interests (Paley's formulation) get full play in Madison's constitutional edifice.[146]

A single "magistrate" was preferred to generate the "most energy dispatch and responsibility to the office," James Wilson declared at the Philadelphia Convention.[147] But he "did not consider the Prerogatives of the British Monarch as a proper guide in defining the Executive powers."[148] Some of these prerogatives, he noted, "were of a Legislative nature," among them war and peace, and so could properly be allocated to Congress – this was the consensus view.[149] The royal prerogatives therefore were carved up: declarations of war were given to Congress while the conduct of war was within executive authority; the making of treaties is granted to the executive with the advice and consent of the Senate. There is nothing left of the prerogatives, says Rakove, other than to "repel sudden attacks."[150] No inherent executive power otherwise is available to an American president.[151]

---

145 Ibid., 302, 302–3, 307 (emphasis in original).
146 Vincent Ostrom, *The Political Theory of a Compound Republic: Designing the American Experiment*, 2nd ed. (Lincoln: University of Nebraska Press, 1987), 144, 145.
147 Max Farrand, *The Records of the Federal Convention of 1787* (New Haven, CT: Yale University Press, 1966), 1:65.
148 Ibid.
149 Daniel J. Hulsebosch, "The Plural Prerogative," *William and Mary Quarterly* 68 (2011): 587.
150 Jack N. Rakove, "Taking the Prerogative Out of the Presidency: An Originalist Perspective," *Presidential Studies Quarterly* 37 (2007): 95.
151 David Gray Adler, "The Framers and Executive Prerogative: A Constitutional and Historical Rebuke," *Presidential Studies Quarterly* 42 (2012): 376–89.

This has not impeded presidents from claiming vast authority beyond that suggested by the framing and ratification debates. As there is a large literature on this subject, I want to draw on only one of its variants, having its roots in claims to prerogative authority, which will look familiar to observers of executive authority elsewhere. It is what political scientist Richard Pious refers to as the institution of "prerogative governance":

> This involves the unilateral assertion of power to decide and act, an imposition of a chain of command from the White House through the Executive Office of the President and into the departments (in the case of the Pentagon, from the President directly to the Secretary of Defense) and the issuance of self-executing orders to officials in departments, resulting in *faits accomplis* to deal with the issue. Control of information is a crucial component in prerogative governance, whether it involves secrecy, selective leaks, or framing and spin. Routine classification systems are not useful, but sensitive compartmentalized information (that is circulated among a handful of officials) is organized by top presidential staffers. Decision making is concentrated in a small group setting ... Once decisions have been made and implemented, information is kept close.[152]

Of course claims to prerogative governance do not always prevail – they may not receive the sanction of Congress or of public opinion more broadly. The judicial branch, for one, has not endorsed the idea that broad prerogative authority resides within the executive branch. This is made apparent in modern claims to executive privilege, claims that resemble those made by Prime Minister Stephen Harper in response to demands for unredacted documents regarding the treatment of Afghan detainees.

The courts have guarded Congress's inquisitorial role, acknowledging that, in the words of Woodrow Wilson, the "vigilant oversight of administration" was "quite as important as legislation."[153] Claims to

---

152 Richard M. Pious, "Prerogative Power and Presidential Politics," in *The Oxford Handbook of the American Presidency*, ed. George C. Edwards III and William G. Howell, 461–2 (Oxford: Oxford University Press, 2009).

153 Woodrow Wilson, *Congressional Government: A Study in American Politics* (1885; Cleveland: World Publishing, 1965), 195; Morton Rosenberg, "Presidential Claims of Executive Privilege: History, Law, Practice and Recent Developments," Congressional Research Service Report for Congress, 21 August 2008, www.fas.org/sgp/crs/secrecy/RL30319.pdf.

executive privilege, the courts have said, are not absolute but only pre-sumptively privileged. That presumption can be overcome whenever there is an appropriate showing of public need.[154] Typically claims to executive privilege have to do with the "deliberative process" within the executive branch by which policy is made[155] – these are akin to Cabinet confidences in parliamentary systems. The D.C. Circuit Court in In re Sealed Case (1997) distinguished between a "deliberative process privilege," which is a common law privilege and more easily reversed and a "presidential communications privilege" rooted in the constitution, which applies only to "direct decisionmaking by the president" associated with "quintessential and non-delegable Presidential power."[156] The latter, narrowly confined, presumption is overcome only by a test of necessity – the material must be relevant and not otherwise available using due diligence.[157]

Despite the availability of a presidential privilege, presidents and their staff continue to make exaggerated claims to executive privilege. They have been aided by the aggressive interpretation of presidential power by conservative legal scholars who have been promoting the concept of the "unitary executive." Though it takes different forms, the idea is rooted in the separation of powers and the constitution's grant of powers to the president in Article II.[158] The "vesting" of executive power in a single office,[159] accompanied by other specific allocations of authority,[160] generates a "domain of unfettered action" in a wide variety of fields, including unilateral war-making.[161] It has provided cover for a flurry of presidential signing statements[162] and top-down control of

154 Nixon v Sirica, 487 F 2d 750, 717 (1973) (DC Cir).
155 Rosenberg, "Presidential Claims of Executive Privilege," 10.
156 In re Sealed Case, 121 F 3d 729, 746, 752 (1997) (DC Cir).
157 Ibid., 754.
158 Steven G. Calabresi and Christopher S. Yoo, The Unitary Executive: Presidential Power from Washington to Bush (New Haven, CT: Yale University Press, 2008).
159 Rakove shows that this originalist interpretation, which rests on the "vesting clause," is entirely without merit, in Rakove, "Taking the Prerogative Out of the Presidency," 97–8.
160 Ryan J. Barilleaux and Christopher S. Kelley, "Introduction: What Is the Unitary Executive?," in The Unitary Executive and the Modern Presidency, ed. Ryan J. Barilleaux and Christopher S. Kelley (College Station: Texas A&M University Press, 2010), 3.
161 John Yoo, War by Other Means: An Insider's Account of the War on Terror (New York: Atlantic Monthly, 2006), 103.
162 Charlie Savage, Takeover: The Return of the Imperial Presidency and the Subversion of American Democracy (New York: Little, Brown, 2007), 234.

administrative personnel. The unitary executive "discounts," observes Skowronek, "the notion of objective, disinterested administration in service to the government as a whole and advances in its place the ideal of an administration run in strict accordance with the president's priorities."[163]

If traceable back to the first administration of George Washington, it generally is admitted that the Reagan administration promoted the unitary executive and made it a central organizing theme of their two terms in office.[164] As the ranking House Republican on the committee investigating the Iran-Contra affair, Dick Cheney spearheaded a minority report that would have insulated President Reagan from congressional inquiry into his handling of foreign affairs.[165] The framers, Cheney and his fellow dissenters insisted, created a single and unitary executive that granted the president the "primary role of conducting the foreign policy of the United States. Congressional actions to limit the president in this area therefore should be reviewed with a considerable degree of skepticism. If they interfere with core presidential foreign policy functions, they should be struck down."[166] So what if Congress cut off funds to support the Nicaraguan contras and the president sought to replace funding through other means, including from foreign governments? So long as he is operating within spheres of executive authority, the president remains beyond the reach of Congress. "Congress must realize," the minority report declares, "that the power of the purse does not make it supreme." "To the extent that the Constitution and laws are

---

163 Stephen Skowronek, "The Conservative Insurgency and Presidential Power: A Developmental Perspective on the Unitary Executive," *Harvard Law Review* 122 (2008): 2077.

164 Calabresi and Yoo, *Unitary Executive*, 383. Samuel Alito, then deputy assistant attorney general in the Office of Legal Counsel and now U.S. Supreme Court justice, is credited with having drafted a legal memo to Reagan's advisors promoting executive unilateralism via the use of signing statements. See Samuel J. Alito, "Using Presidential Signing Statements to Make Fuller Use of the President's Constitutionally Assigned Role in the Process of Enacting Law," 5 February 1986, www.archives.gov/news/samuel-alito/accession-060-89-269/Acc060-89-269-box6-SG-LSWG-AlitotoLSWG-Feb1986.pdf.

165 Cheney proudly referenced the text in a 2005 interview, in Jane Mayer, *The Dark Side: The Inside Story of How the War on Terror Turned into a War on American Ideals* (New York: Doubleday, 2008), 60.

166 US Congress, *Report of the Congressional Committees Investigating the Iran-Contra Affair*, 100th Cong, 1st sess (November 1987), 469.

read narrowly, as Jefferson wished," they wrote, "the Chief Executive will on occasion feel duty bound to assert monarchical notions of prerogative that will permit him to exceed the law."[167]

This was the same radical view that Vice President Dick Cheney and his legal counsel, Richard Addington (who provided research for the 1987 minority report), brought to the White House of George W. Bush. Cheney and Addington emerged as the "most influential adherents" of the unitarian view,[168] settling on a "strategy of aggressive executive unilateralism."[169] Fuelled by this extravagant theory, the Bush administration repeatedly refused to disclose documentation concerning, among other things, the suspicious firing of nine U.S. attorneys. The District Court for the District of Columbia found no merit to the administration's claim of privilege as regards documents held by the president's legal advisor and chief of staff in this case. The asserted absolute immunity claim, the Court held, "is entirely unsupported by existing case law."[170] Though critical of the Bush administration's excessive claims to secrecy, President Obama continued on in a similar vein, repeatedly invoking the state secrets doctrine to shield the president from Congress's prying eyes.[171]

2. A Canadian Separation of Powers?

What have these eighteenth-century treatise-writers and the U.S. gloss on them to do with Canadian constitutional developments? As discussed in chapter 1, the strategy taken up in Britain's "second empire" was to avoid the pitfalls of overly representative legislative assemblies. The principal cause of the American Revolution, according to political

---

167 Ibid., 457, 465.
168 Barton Gellman, *Angler: The Cheney Vice Presidency* (New York: Penguin, 2008), 97; Bruce P. Montgomery, *Richard B. Cheney and the Rise of the Imperial Vice Presidency* (Westport, CT: Praeger, 2009), 121.
169 Jack Goldsmith, *Power and Constraint: The Accountable Presidency after 9/11* (New York: W.W. Norton, 2012), 37.
170 Committee on the Judiciary, United States House of Representatives v Harriet Miers and Joshua Bolten, Case No. 08-00409 (DDC, 2008), 78.
171 Goldsmith, *Power and Constraint*, 42. Obama, in fact, maintained many of the "war on terror" policies put in place by his predecessor. This is because, argues Jack Goldsmith, these policies had been subject to constraints imposed by watchers of the president, including not only the other branches but also the press, the legal bar, and voters (209).

leadership in Britain, was not metropole mismanagement but an inability to maintain a carefully "balanced" constitution that preserved a "due mixture of the Monarchical, & Aristocratical parts of the British Constitution."[172] Heeding repeated calls for a representative assembly, the plan hatched in 1791 was for an elected lower assembly, analogous to the House of Commons, and a hereditary legislative council, analogous to the House of Lords, made up of "discreet and proper persons."[173] The object, Lord Grenville informed Dorchester, was to give to the upper branch a "greater degree of weight and consequence than was possessed by the Councils in the Old Colonial Governments" so as to counterbalance populist tendencies.[174] In the ensuing parliamentary debates, all sides shared in the discourse of the balanced constitution. Opposition leader Charles James Fox declared that "every part of the British dominions ought to possess a government, in the constitution of which monarchy, aristocracy and democracy were mutually blended and united; nor could any government be a fit one for British subjects to live under, which did not contain its due weight of aristocracy, because that he considered to be the proper poise of the constitution, the balance that equalized and meliorated the powers of the two other extreme branches, and gave stability and firmness to the whole." William Pitt, prime minister and Chancellor of the Exchequer, agreed that "aristocracy was ... the true poise ... of the constitution; it was the essential link that held the branches together, and gave stability and strength to the whole; aristocracy reflected the lustre of the Crown, and lent support and effect to the democracy, while the democracy gave vigour and energy to both, and the sovereignty crowned the constitution with authority and dignity." There ensued a debate over whether the Legislative Council should be hereditary or elected (Fox's proposal). "Aristocracy must be nearer to the Crown than to the democracy," declared Burke, who spoke for many. Fox's proposal, allegedly republican in origin, went down to defeat by a vote of thirty-nine

---

172 "Discussion of Petitions and Counter Petitions *Re* Change of Government in Canada," enclosed with correspondence from William W. Grenville, secretary of state, to Lord Dorchester, governor of Canada, 20 October 1789, in Adam Shortt and Arthur G. Doughty, eds., *Documents Relating to the Constitutional History of Canada, 1759–1791* (Ottawa: J. de L. Taché), 2:983.
173 The Constitutional Act, 1791, 31 George III, c 31, art III.
174 W.P.M. Kennedy, ed., *Statutes, Treaties and Documents of the Canadian Constitution, 1713–1929*, 2nd ed. (Toronto: Oxford University Press, 1930), 186.

to eighty-eight.[175] The transplant, of course, never did take – hereditary nobility never could take root in the forests of North America.[176]
Instead, a theory resembling one of political equality, accompanying
the rise of parliamentary self-government, overtook plans for a home-
grown aristocracy.[177]

Responding to the causes of rebellion in Upper and Lower Canada,
Lord Durham also was desirous of restoring "balance" to British North
America.[178] Durham feared a "general legislature, which ... wields a
power which no single body, however popular in its constitution ought
to have; a power which must be destructive of any constitutional balance." In terms resonant of *The Spirit of the Laws*, Durham declared, "The
true principle of limiting popular power is that apportionment of it in
many different depositaries which has been adopted in all the most free
and stable States of the Union."[179] This appears to be an endorsement
not only of Montesquieu's formulation, that power must check power,
but an endorsement of the iteration adopted by the American framers.
On the other hand, Durham complained of the absence of responsible government in the Canadian provinces.[180] "This entire separation
of the legislative and executive powers of a State, is the natural error
of governments desirous of being free from the check of representative
institutions," he warned. It had been the "wise principle" of the English
Constitution ever since the Revolution of 1688, Durham maintained, to

---

175 E.A. Cruikshank, "The Genesis of the Canada Act," *Ontario Historical Society Papers
    and Records* 28 (1932): 291, 295, 308. It was in the course of these debates in May
    1791 that Fox and Burke had their famous falling out, Fox rising in the House to
    reply with "tears trickling down his cheeks" (275).
176 Jeffrey L. McNairn, *The Capacity to Judge: Public Opinion and Deliberative Democracy
    in Upper Canada, 1791–1854* (Toronto: University of Toronto Press, 2000), 33; F. Mur-
    ray Greenwood, *Legacies of Fear: Law and Politics in Quebec in the Era of the French
    Revolution* (Toronto: Toronto University Press, 1993), 139.
177 McNairn, *Capacity to Judge*, 271.
178 Janet Ajzenstat, "Modern Mixed Government: A Liberal Defence of Inequality,"
    in Janet Ajzenstat, *The Canadian Founding: John Locke and Parliament* (Montreal and
    Kingston: McGill-Queen's University Press), 145–62; also Janet Ajzenstat, *The Politi-
    cal Thought of Lord Durham* (Montreal and Kingston: McGill-Queen's University
    Press, 1988).
179 Earl of Durham, *Lord Durham's Report on the Affairs of British North America*, ed. C.P.
    Lucas (Oxford: Clarendon, 1912), 2:287.
180 Ibid., 2:79, now enshrined in section 54 of the Constitution Act, 1867. See discus-
    sion in Janet Ajzenstat, *The Once and Future Canadian Democracy: An Essay in Political
    Thought* (Montreal and Kingston: McGill-Queen's University Press, 2003), 65–7.

vest "direction of the national policy, and the distribution of patronage, in the leaders of the Parliamentary majority."[181] This exhausts Durham's discussion of the separation of powers in his *Report* and it appears mostly ambivalent.[182] If, in one passage, he appears to embrace the virtues of American constitutional design, in his discussion of responsible government he appears to turn the tables on American constitutional conceptions, the principal threat facing a continuing British presence in North America.

However, Durham was not content merely to grant representative assemblies in Canada authority over all of its affairs. As mentioned in chapter 1, Durham posited a distinction between the internal and external affairs of the colony. The former subjects fell within the ambit of Canadian authority, the latter few subjects fell within the authority of the imperial Parliament.[183] Durham imposed a further limit on Canada's internal affairs by recommending that money votes not be introduced without the prior consent of the Crown.[184] This grant of authority to the executive at the expense of the assembly, together with his recommendation for responsible government, was intended to ensure that the lower house was not too powerful. "The popular house was to have the power to 'balance' the executive, but not the power to govern," Ajzenstat observes.[185] After some delay, responsible government was granted to the colony and with it almost every one of the subjects reserved for the imperial Parliament came under the control of Canada's parliamentary executive. The theory of the mixed constitution was rendered "outdated" as a consequence.[186]

The Constitution Act, 1867 curiously is devoid of references to Cabinet government yet exhibits the anachronism of the mixed governmental

---

181 Durham, *Lord Durham's Report*, 79.
182 Ajzenstat writes that it is "clear that 'balance' as espoused by the British thinkers has the same roots as the American doctrine of the separation of powers" and that Durham, like other Whigs of the period, meant to describe the British Constitution "in that language" (in Ajzenstat, *Political Thought of Lord Durham*, 71). I am less confident than Ajzenstat about this.
183 Durham, *Lord Durham's Report*, 282.
184 Ibid., 286–7. Martin attributes this recommendation to Edward Ellice, in Ged Martin, *The Durham Report and British Policy* (Cambridge: Cambridge University Press, 1972), 47.
185 Ajzenstat, "Modern Mixed Government," 4; Ajzenstat, *Political Thought of Lord Durham*, 61; Ajzenstat, *Once and Future Democracy*, 66.
186 McNairn, *Capacity to Judge*, 240.

frame. Admittedly it is not a comprehensive account of constitutional government in Canada – it is, one might say, "shocking,"[187] even embarrassing,[188] in its disconnect from constitutional reality. The framers must have been aware, however, of Montesquieu's idealized English polity and the American framers' iteration of the tripartite division of powers. The Constitution's preamble declares that it is expedient not only to provide for legislative authority, "but also that the Nature of the Executive Government therein be declared." Very little detail about the executive is provided, however.[189] The 1867 Act then devotes parts of the Constitution to each of "Executive Power" (Part III), "Legislative Power" (Part IV), and "Judicature" (Part VII). The "Judicature" articles in sections 96–101 aim to secure a semblance of judicial independence.[190] Although there is nothing express about a separation of the executive from the legislative branch, section 9 of the 1867 Act declares, "The Executive Government and Authority of and over Canada is hereby declared to continue and be vested in the Queen." A Privy Council is established to "aid and advise" the Queen (section 11), a function performed in actuality by Cabinet.[191] The Queen is also made "commander-in-chief" of land and naval forces (section 15). This is the extent to which the "Crown in Council," that part of the Crown that serves "wholly outside" of Parliament, is described.[192] The other side of the Crown, the Crown in Parliament, is represented in section 17. Under the heading "Legislative Power," it is declared that there "shall be one Parliament for Canada, consisting of the Queen, an Upper House styled the Senate and the House of Commons." This is a throwback to the balanced constitution that, by 1867 in both Britain and Canada, had ceased to meaningfully exist. A separation is therefore established in the constitution between what formally is styled an executive branch under a monarch, whose authority operates only when authorized by the legislative branch. If there is not "nearly complete fusion" here, there is more than mere intermingling.

---

187 R. McGregor Dawson, *The Government of Canada*, 5th ed., rev. Norman Ward (Toronto: University of Toronto, 1970), 58.

188 Anson, *Law and Custom of the Constitution*, 34.

189 Dawson, *Government of Canada*, 60.

190 W.R. Lederman, "The Independence of the Judiciary," part 2, *Canadian Bar Review* 34 (1956): 1139–79.

191 Dawson, *Government of Canada*, 59.

192 Anson, *Law and Custom of the Constitution*, 41.

Unsurprisingly, early Canadian treatise writers incorporated Bagehot's recently published restatement of the English Constitution into their own treatments of Canada's new constitutional order (but without adopting his distinction between the "efficient" and the "dignified" parts). The principal difference between British and American systems of government, observed W.P. Clement, "is in the connection between the law-making and law-executing departments of government."[193] The "will of the law-making body is made to sympathetically affect and control the will of the executive in the administration of public affairs" – no such "cooperation and sympathy" will be found in the United States. Clement proceeds to quote Bagehot at length.[194] Similarly, for A.H.F. Lefroy, the "retention of parliamentary responsible government" represents the "fundamental" difference between the British and U.S. systems.[195] In modern times, Peter Hogg, with an assist from Bagehot, emphatically declares that "in a system of responsible government, there is no 'separation of powers' between the executive and legislative branches of government."[196] There is not even a general separation of powers as between the judicial and the political branches – the latter can confer judicial functions on other bodies just as it can confer non-judicial functions on courts.[197] None of these authors have sought recourse to the now abandoned discourse of the mixed or balanced constitution.[198]

It could be said that the Supreme Court of Canada has endorsed this view. In Re Residential Tenancies Act (1981) Justice Dickson quotes Professor Hogg's formulation approvingly. Justice La Forest similarly

---

193 W.H.P. Clement, *The Law of the Canadian Constitution* (Toronto: Carswell, 1892), 2; Clement, *The Law of the Canadian Constitution*, 2nd ed. (Toronto: Carswell, 1904), 18.

194 Clement, *Law of the Canadian Constitution*, 2nd ed., 18–20; Clement, *Law of the Canadian Constitution*, 15.

195 A.H.F. Lefroy, *Canada's Federal System Being a Treatise on Canadian Constitutional Law under the British North America Act* (Toronto: Carswell, 1913), 742.

196 Hogg, *Constitutional Life of Canada*, 221, 290n53; Monahan, *Constitutional Law*, 94.

197 Hogg, *Constitutional Life of Canada*, 221, 290 n53; also Monahan, *Constitutional Law*, 94. Also J.R. Mallory, *The Structure of Canadian Government* (Toronto: Macmillan of Canada, 1971), 146, citing Bagehot approvingly; and Dawson, *Government of Canada*, 168, invoking Bagehot's Cabinet as "buckle" metaphor.

198 Lefroy quotes several times, however, from the Privy Council decision in *Bank of Toronto v Lambe* [1887] 12 Appeal Cases 575, 587 (JCPC), that the 1867 Act "provides for the federated provinces a carefully balanced Constitution, under which no one of the parts can pass laws for itself except under control of the whole, acting through the Governor-General" (in Lefroy, *Canada's Federal System*, 188).

has declared, "While in broad terms, such a separation of powers does exist,[199] it is not under our system of government rigidly defined."[200] In Douglas College, Justice La Forest ends up endorsing Ontario's measure to "confer non-judicial functions on the courts of Ontario" and conferring "judicial functions on a body which is not a court,"[201] effectively making Hogg's point about there being no real separation of powers as between the judicial and other branches.[202] It could also be said that the Supreme Court has been strategic about its use of the separation of powers. In controversies over broadcasting proceedings in the New Brunswick legislature[203] and authorizing judges to determine hourly rates of counsel appointed as amicus curiae,[204] the Court has relied on the fact that "distinct organs" perform "separate functions" allowing for the "evolution of certain core competencies in the various institutions vested with these functions." The Court's capacity to control rates of pay for legal counsel, for instance, "must be responsive to the proper function of the separate branches of government, lest it upset the balance of roles, responsibilities and capacities that has evolved in our system of governance over the course of centuries."[205] In other cases, the Court has displayed a distinct reluctance to step on the toes of the legislative branch when reviewing budgetary measures[206] and on the toes of the executive branch when asked to interfere in the prerogatives having to do with foreign affairs.[207] In other instances having to do with budgets and the prerogative over foreign affairs, however, it has not been so sensitive.[208]

---

199 See *Fraser v Public Service Staff Relations Board* [1985] 2 SCR 455, 469–70.

200 *Douglas/Kwantlen Faculty Association v Douglas College* [1990] 3 SCR 570, 601.

201 Ibid., 728.

202 An ambivalence toward a separation of powers is revealed in the Court's opinion in *Dolphin Delivery* concerning the application of the Canadian Charter of Rights and Freedoms to court orders made in the course of private litigation. The direction, in section 52 of the Constitution Act, 1982, that the Charter applies to "government" at both federal and provincial levels, speaks to the executive branch of government and not to the judicial branch, Justice McIntyre maintains (in *RWDSU v Dolphin Delivery* [1986] 2 SCR 573, 598).

203 *New Brunswick Broadcasting Co v Nova Scotia (Speaker of the House of Assembly)* [1993] 1 SCR 319.

204 *Ontario v Criminal Lawyers' Association* [2013] 3 SCR 3.

205 Ibid., paras 28, 30.

206 *Newfoundland (Treasury Board) v NAPE* [2004] 3 SCR 381.

207 *Canada (Prime Minister) v Khadr* [2010] 1 SCR 44.

208 *Singh v Minister of Employment and Immigration* [1985] 1 SCR 177; *United States v Burns* [2001] 1 SCR 283.

In the course of his book-length argument for coordinate construction of Charter rights and freedoms as between courts and the legislatures, Dennis Baker provocatively claims the separation of powers has a central place in Canadian constitutional design.[209] He lays no emphasis on the mixed or balanced constitution, however.[210] Instead, drawing on Madison's reading of Montesquieu, which allows for significant inter-branch penetration – what Madison calls "partial agency"[211] – Baker claims that this is "precisely the kind of mixed arrangement between the legislative and executive branches that is found in the Canadian constitution." This is because control over the executive by the legislature branch was behind Canadian proposals for responsible government. As illustrated in chapter 1, control over budgets, patronage appointments, and removal of sitting judges from executive councils – control over many of the prerogatives – lay at the heart of the conflict. It follows, Baker argues, that a legislative/executive separation of functions is "logically necessary for responsible government to work." He places substantial emphasis on section 17 of the 1867 Act: "There shall be One Parliament for Canada, consisting of the Queen, an Upper House styled on the Senate, and the House of Commons." This, he claims, represents continuity with these earlier struggles and so "remains a powerful constitutional statement of the separation principle."[212] Why this is not, instead, a Victorian representation of the mixed or balanced constitution he does not say.

Baker nevertheless acknowledges that the "reality" of the conventions of responsible government "have the effect of centralizing power almost completely in the hands of the executive." Rather than working with this sociological reality, Baker wishes to de-centre what he labels "behavioral" interpretations in favour of a "neo-institutionalist" one that re-centres "forms and formalities."[213] Baker here draws on Harvey Mansfield's account of executive authority, which, though drawing its

---

209 Dennis Baker, *Not Quite Supreme: The Courts and Coordinate Constitutional Interpretation* (Montreal and Kingston: McGill-Queen's University Press, 2010); also Ajzenstat, *Canadian Founding*, 62.

210 Baker, *Not Quite Supreme*, 56.

211 Hamilton, Madison, and Jay, *Federalist Papers*, 302.

212 Baker, *Not Quite Supreme*, 60–1, 63.

213 Ibid., 64, 65, 69. Baker writes, "The fusion error – as I maintain it is – clearly involves the kind of radical depreciation of forms and formalities that one typically finds in stringently 'realist' or 'behavioural' social science" (65).

sources from a rich history of political thought, at bottom is about the executive branch in the United States.[214] There is only a modest grant of formal executive authority in the U.S. Constitution, but it is informally muscular: "Formal weakness," Mansfield paradoxically argues, "enhances his [the executive's] informal strength." For this reason, Mansfield subtitles his book "The Ambivalence of Modern Executive Power" in an attempt to capture the necessity of having both formal weakness and informal strength in the modern executive branch, a necessity that he traces to Machiavelli.[215] Similarly, within the Canadian constitutional context, if informal executive power has a tendency to be overly expansive, it also has the potential to be checked by its formal frailty. Baker empirically informs the argument by taking up two instances where executive power was restrained by the legislative branch, first, in accommodating caucus concerns about the absence of a sunset clause in Canada's anti-terror legislation, and second, in the case of expanding the coverage of species-at-risk legislation. These are rare instances, he admits, where the governing party yielded concessions to backbenchers. They are also testaments to the "formal constitution" and its "moderating demands."[216] The "ambivalent" model of constitutionalism, from this angle, envisages checks on executive excess.

The notion that the Commons can act independently as a check on the executive is not, however, a feature unique to a separation of powers account. For instance, the notion prevailed throughout much of the eighteenth century when the mixed or balanced constitution was the dominant constitutional trope. It is a favourable feature of parliamentary government that the legislature is divided, observes de Lolme.[217] This entitles members to "freely oppose every time they believe it necessary." This is the idea of "independence," which Ajzenstat attributes to the leader of the French-Canadian party in the legislature of Lower Canada, Pierre Bédard.[218] It is the same idea that Bolingbroke develops

---

214 Robert Eden, "Executive Power and Presidency," in *Leo Strauss, the Straussians, and the American Regime*, ed. Kenneth L. Deutsch and John A. Murley, 351–61 (Lanham, MD: Rowman and Littlefield, 1999); Mansfield, *Taming the Prince*, 192. Mansfield writes that just as Locke had in mind the English King when referring to executive power, "today it refers to the American presidency" (192).

215 Mansfield, *Taming the Prince*, xviii, 275, chap. 6.

216 Baker, *Not Quite Supreme*, 72, 77.

217 De Lolme, *Constitution of England*, 158.

218 Ajzenstat, quoting Pierre Bédard, in Ajzenstat, *Canadian Founding*, 139, 138.

early in the eighteenth century, that of "independency" as between the various parts of government.[219] "The independency pleaded for consists in this," Bolingbroke wrote, "that the resolutions of each part, which direct these proceedings, be taken independently and without any influence, direct or indirect, on the others."[220] Bolingbroke also recognizes the mutual dependency of each part on each other by having a "power of control in each."[221] The widespread use of patronage by Walpole in order to manipulate proceedings in the House, he warned, would destroy the constitutional balance by having dependency overtake independency.

Baker's empirical account equally is consistent with the successor to the mixed constitutions, responsible government. After all, the doctrine requires that the executive be responsible to the legislative branch, including backbench MPs in the government caucus who insist upon, for instance, sunset clauses in their anti-terrorism bills or animals on federal property to be covered by their species-at-risk legislation. As in Baker's partial agency account, the executive need not always have its way. It is revealing that Baker prefers not to have recourse to these parliamentary traditions and practice because it would not then set him up to make the argument he really wants to make, which is to have the political branches exercise an independent and moderating influence on the judicial branch by adopting a model of coordinate construction.[222] By resurrecting a model of partial separation to displace "fusion," Baker has to displace dominant forms and practices of Canadian constitutional culture. At the same time, he furnishes the Canadian Constitution with a sketch better representative of dominant U.S. constitutional discourse.

One last concern with Baker's account has to do with his emphasis on "forms and formalities" over empirical realities. Canadian constitutional formalities – for example, that the Queen is the all-powerful

---

219 Kramnick, *Bolingbroke & His Circle*, 145.
220 Lord Viscount Bolingbroke, *The Works of the Late Right Honorable, Henry St John, Lord Viscount Bolingbroke* (London: David Mallet, 1754), 1:341. Gwyn describes Bolingbroke's constitutional theory as illustrating the "complete blending of the ideas of mixed monarchy, checks and balances, and the separation of powers found in several of the descriptions of the English Constitution which appeared later in the century," in Gwyn, *Meaning of the Separation of Powers*, 95.
221 Bolingbroke, *Works of the Late Right Honorable*, 341.
222 Baker, *Not Quite Supreme*, 82

head of state – simply bear no relationship to the constitution as practised. This is because the constitution does not merely comprise text
but is made up of unwritten rules (conventions, mostly, which help
inform constitutional culture) that help determine its general outlines.
An emphasis on forms and formalities omits these critical legitimating
supports and so render Baker's account incomplete, if not misleading.

We might credit Baker with attempting to situate the separation of
powers at the centre of Canada's formal constitutional architecture.
The problem is that even Baker's formal model represents so weak a
separation as to amount not even to a Madisonian "partial agency."
As the tenets of responsible government dictate, those who serve in
the executive are "persons entitled to be so by possessing the confidence of the Assembly."[223] Those who so serve are elevated to its ranks
until Cabinets are shuffled or governments change. The formal model,
in other words, is not one of separate but one of blended branches. We
might as well call it what it is: a "partial," even a "nearly complete,"
fusion of the executive and legislative branches.[224]

3. Duelling Legal Opinions

We are now in a better position to assess the legal arguments that
were made by both sides to the dispute over the production of Afghan
detainee documents. I undertake this task, in this part, by having
recourse to memos sent back and forth between legal counsel in the
lead up to the House of Commons motion of 10 December 2009. By
revealing some of the questionable legal arguments made by the government of Canada, I lend support to the suspicion that prorogation
was prompted by the demands for unredacted government documents
and not to "recalibrate," but this is not my main concern. Instead, my
objective is to show that the dispute concerned an older sort of conflict, one familiar to seventeenth- and eighteenth-century British political actors, between the prerogatives of the Crown and the privileges
of the Commons rather than one concerning the separation of powers.
Because the dispute concerns, what is in substance, old ideas about the

---

223 Earl Grey, *The Colonial Policy of Lord John Russell's Administration* (London: Richard
     Bentley, 1953), 1:213–14.
224 Eric Barendt, "Separation of Powers and Constitutional Government," *Public Law*
     [1995]: 604.

relationship between Crown and Parliament, I turn to old solutions, traceable to Locke, in order to resolve this dispute.

Up until the day before the motion to produce was adopted in the House, the government side had been relying on statutes, such as the Canada Evidence Act, legally barring the government from releasing documents that threatened national security in the course of legal proceedings. As the prime minister and his ministers advised the House, the government could produce only "legally available information."[225] Unredacted documents were simply not the "legally available" ones.

Rob Walsh, law clerk and parliamentary counsel to the House of Commons, took objection to these interpretations in a 7 December 2009 memo.[226] In his opinion, the government had no "credible basis" for reaching the conclusion that the Canada Evidence Act and related statutes barred production of the documents. The House was not the type of "proceeding" (defined to include a court or another body with jurisdiction to compel production) to which these statutes would apply. Inexcusably, a Department of Justice lawyer earlier had appeared before a House of Commons committee (Public Accounts) to say that it did not have the power to compel the production of documents. Walsh was "at a loss to understand" the basis for saying the Canada Evidence Act applies to House of Commons proceedings. In any event, the House had sole jurisdiction to determine whether such statutes applied, opined Walsh.[227] This is consistent with the long-standing legal presumption that a statute does not apply to the Crown unless the statute specifically says so.[228] Nor does the record in Parliament reveal that the statute was intended to apply to House committees.[229] The House of Commons had authority, as part of the law of parliamentary privilege, to compel the production of documents irrespective of statute law.[230] In keeping

---

225 Stephen Harper, in Canada, *Debates* (No. 116), 40th Parliament, 2nd Session (24 November 2009), 7145.

226 Robert R. Walsh to Ujjal Dosanjh, 7 December 2009, 7.

227 Ibid., 3, 6; Bosc and O'Brien, *House of Commons Procedure and Practice*, n261.

228 Peter W. Hogg and Patrick J. Monahan, *Liability of the Crown*, 3rd ed. (Toronto: Carswell, 2000), 274–7.

229 Walsh to Dosanjh, 6.

230 The authoritative treatise by Erskine May defines parliamentary privilege as concerning those fundamental rights necessary for the exercise of Parliament's constitutional functions. See *Erskine May's Treatise on the Law, Privileges, Proceedings and Usage of Parliament*, 23rd ed., ed. William McKay (London: LexisNexis UK, 2004), 75n1.

with the principle of responsible government, Walsh concludes, nothing could be excluded from parliamentary scrutiny.[231]

Carolyn Kobernick, assistant deputy minister in the Department of Justice, fired back on 9 December with a letter to Walsh. "It has come to our attention," she writes, "that you have provided legal advice on the question of the application of the Canada Evidence Act ... and that in the course of that opinion, you have been called upon to speculate as to the legal position of the Department of Justice on this matter." The letter, she writes, is intended to "dispel any ambiguity you may have perceived in this regard."[232]

The letter then continues in the tone of a lecture. There are "several basic constitutional principles" in our system of parliamentary democracy "that must always be borne in mind," she advises. Kobernick proceeds to remind Walsh what they are (we have touched on every one of them in this chapter): the rule of law (an assemblage of ideas, including that "no one is above the law"), parliamentary sovereignty (composed of the Queen, Senate, and House of Commons), responsible government (that the executive is drawn from the ranks of the Commons), and the separation of powers. Concerning the last of these, she writes, "Each of the three constitutional branches of government – the executive, the legislative and judicial branches – must respect the legitimate sphere of action of the other branches."[233]

Government officials, "who are agents of the executive, not the legislative branch," may have a statutory duty of non-disclosure that is explicit (i.e., the Official Languages Act) or implicit (i.e., the Canadian Human Rights Act).[234] Parliamentary committees cannot waive that legal duty imposed on government officials. Instead, "the appropriate recourse ... is to report the matter to the House for its consideration." In the course of the lecture, Kobernick acknowledges that there is no statutory basis for refusing to deliver up unredacted documents (she admits that it is not a "proceeding" within the terms of the Canada Evidence Act) – the statute "has no application," she admits. Rather,

231 Walsh to Dosanjh, 7.
232 Carolyn Kobernick to Robert R. Walsh, 9 December 2009, 1. This is the letter that MP Derek Lee claims intimidates witnesses appearing before the House of Commons Committee and so gives rise to contempt of Parliament, but that is a bit of a stretch. See Parliament of Canada, *Debates* (18 March 2010) 1019.
233 Ibid., 1.
234 *House of Commons v Vaid* [2005] 1 SCR 667.

when making decisions about disclosure, the government will be informed by the "values underlying Parliament's intention in these provisions," namely, "to protect the national security of Canada from harm by the unauthorized disclosure of sensitive information." Having recourse to national security concerns is also consistent, she advises, with conventions that have grown up around the compellability of witnesses in cases of national or public security. This is the parliamentary convention that "injurious information should not be disclosed in a parliamentary setting."[235]

So Kobernick admits that there is no strictly legal basis for refusing to comply with the production of documents order. Instead, she argues that the House of Commons and its committees should respect fundamental principles like the separation of powers and simply yield to the government's superior authority in this matter. In his letter of reply to Kobernick of 10 December, Walsh accepts all four of these fundamental constitutional principles, including the separation of powers.[236] He does take issue, however, with her interpretation that these same statutory provisions should guide the conduct of government officials. Walsh accuses Kobernick of failing to "recognize the constitutional function" of Parliament (acknowledged by Charles I) holding the government to account. Nor does she adequately attend to the law of parliamentary privilege. Instead, she engages with "peripheral legal issues to defend the withholding of evidence."[237] In relation to the House of Commons internal proceedings, it is for the House and its committees to determine "how provisions shall apply."[238] It is not, then, for government to decide what provisions shall apply but for the committee "which

---

235 Kobernick to Walsh, 2, 3. Joseph Maingot, *Parliamentary Privilege in Canada*, 2nd ed. (Ottawa: House of Commons and McGill-Queen's University Press, 1997), 191. This is the relevant passage from Maingot: "With respect to federal public servants who are witnesses before committees of either House, the theory of the compellability of witnesses to answer questions generally may come in conflict with the principle of ministerial responsibility. By convention, a parliamentary committee will respect Crown privilege when invoked, at least in relation to matters of national and public security."

236 Robert R. Walsh to Carolyn Kobernick, 10 December 2009, 4.

237 Ibid., 1–2.

238 Ibid., 3; Vaid, *House of Commons v 2005*, para 34. In circumstances when the Supreme Court of Canada insisted that the Canadian Human Rights Act applied to Parliament, the ruling concerned employment relations and not matters within the realm of parliamentary privilege (in ibid., 4–5).

includes Government members, to consider how it shall proceed."[239] There is a further worry that Kobernick's opinion will lead government officials to infer that they can be "prosecuted or disciplined" for making disclosures before parliamentary committees. To the extent that this is an indirect attempt to intimidate witnesses and interfere with committee proceedings, Walsh warns that it constitutes "parliamentary contempt."

Recognizing that the opposition parties were once again aligned against government, Justice Minister Nicholson announced, shortly after the House resumed sitting in March 2010, that retired justice Frank Iacobucci had been retained to "conduct an independent confidential review" of the requested documents. He was also expected to submit a report to the minister recommending what information would be "injurious" to Canada's interests and whether disclosure, "for the purpose of providing parliamentarians with Government information necessary to hold the Government to account ... outweighs the public interest in non-disclosure." Only a summary of this report would be made publicly available.[240] The government could choose to keep this advice close to its chest because Iacobucci was not retained by the House of Commons with all-party agreement but by the Ministry of Justice alone.

Without much hesitation, only a few days later, representatives from each of the opposition parties moved a question of privilege concerning the production of documents pursuant to House order of 10 December. Liberal MP Derek Lee, an authority on matters of parliamentary privilege,[241] also moved for breach of privilege against the minister of defence, Peter MacKay, for intimidating witnesses and Assistant Deputy Minister of Justice Caroline Kobernick for contempt.[242] With a ruling of prima facie contempt of the House in hand, the opposition could then move to invoke the disciplinary powers of the House, which

---

239 Walsh to Kobernick, 1–2, 3; *House of Commons v Vaid*, para 34. In circumstances when the Supreme Court of Canada insisted that the Canadian Human Rights Act applied to Parliament, the ruling concerned employment relations and not matters within the realm of parliamentary privilege (Walsh to Kobernick, 4–5).

240 Canada, Department of Justice, "Backgrounder: Terms of Reference," 13 March 2010, http://www.marketwired.com/press-release/minister-justice-releases-terms-reference-independent-adviser-review-national-security-1131236.htm.

241 Derek Lee, *The Power of Parliamentary Houses to Send for Persons, Papers & Records: A Sourcebook on the Law and Precedent of Parliamentary Subpoena Powers for Canadian and Other Houses* (Toronto: University of Toronto Press, 1999).

242 Canada, *Parliamentary Debates* (18 March 2010) 1019.

are plentiful.[243] The government responded, first, by claiming the 10 December 2009 motion was procedurally invalid, second, that MacKay and Kobernick merely were expressing matters of opinion, and third, that the privileges of the House are not absolute and unqualified but are subject to competing governmental obligations to protect national security and the public interest.[244] In the course of detailing the content of the latter obligations, Justice Minister Nicholson resorted to the separation of powers, maintaining that the House must respect the equally compelling Crown privilege of protecting the national interest. "Each of the three branches," Nicholson declared, "must respect the legitimate sphere of activity of the others."[245] Not only is the executive branch "entrusted with powers and privileges as well as responsibilities for protecting public interest," etc., but the Crown is also "a constituent part of Parliament." Nicholson claimed that the House was overreaching, as it "alone" could not extend privileges beyond those ordinarily granted to it without the assent of the Crown,[246] an argument that muddied the role of the Crown inside and outside of Parliament. He also continued to rely on the specious argument that the government could only produce documents that were "legally available."[247] He did so with some alacrity, dumping about 8,000 pages of unredacted documents on the opposition in the course of debates over the opposition motion. All parties now awaited the Speaker's ruling on the motion of privilege.

Issuing his ruling at the end of April, Speaker of the House Peter Milliken vindicated Walsh's interpretation of the powers of the House. That is, on matters of substance before the Speaker, Prime Minister Stephen Harper and his government were dead wrong. Speaker Milliken accepted the motion as procedurally valid but, without sufficient evidence, preferred not to move against either Minister MacKay or Assistant Deputy Minister Kobernick. Speaker Milliken expressed concern, however, that Kobernick's letter "could be interpreted as having a 'chilling effect' on public servants who are called to appear before parliamentary committees." As for the main event – the right of the

---

243 Bosc and O'Brien, *House of Commons Procedure and Practice*, n333.
244 Ibid., 1549, 1635.
245 Ibid., 1604.
246 Ibid., 1630.
247 Ibid., 1610. Canada, *Parliamentary Debates* (31 March 2010) 1540, 1549, 1604, 1630, 1610.

House to order the production of documents – Speaker Milliken ruled, with recourse to the usual authorities, that to accept the government's position "would completely undermine the importance of the role of parliamentarians in holding the government to account." Speaker Milliken even replied to the government's claim that the order was a breach of the separation of powers between the executive and legislative branches. "It is the view of the Chair that accepting an unconditional authority of the executive to censor the information provided to Parliament," declared Speaker Milliken, "would in fact jeopardize the very separation of powers that is purported to lie at the heart of our parliamentary system and the independence of its constituent parts."[248] That is, it would undermine the legislature's historic responsibility of holding that separate executive to account "outside" of Parliament.

The Speaker concluded by appealing to both sides to find a way out of the impasse. Some negotiated solution, which would make documents available "without divulging state secrets," could be devised. The appointment of former justice Iacobucci, regrettably, did not amount to an adequate resolution of this dispute in the Speaker's eyes. He accepted that this was a "separate parallel process outside of parliamentary oversight." "Furthermore," he added, "and in my view perhaps most significantly, Mr Iacobucci reports to the Minister of Justice; his client is the government."[249]

Subsequent to the Speaker's ruling, the leaders of two of the opposition parties (the Liberals and the Bloc) joined into a memorandum of understanding (MoU) with the prime minister by which an ad hoc committee, operating under an oath of confidentiality, would have access to all of the documents sought by the House Order of 10 December.[250] In cases where public disclosure of "relevant" and "necessary" documents is sought, matters are referred to a panel of arbiters, comprising former justice Iacobucci, together with a former colleague, retired Supreme Court of Canada justice Claire L'Heureux-Dubé, and retired chief justice of the British Columbia Supreme Court, Donald Brenner. The panel has exclusive authority to determine what documentation

---

248 Canada, *Parliamentary Debates* (27 April 2010) 2041–3.
249 Ibid., 2044.
250 Canada, "Memorandum of Understanding between the Right Honourable Stephen Harper, Prime Minister, and the Honourable Michael Ignatieff, Leader of the Official Opposition, and Gilles Duceppe, Leader of the Bloc Québécois," 15 June 2010, http://www.macleans.ca/wp-content/uploads/2010/06/100615-mou-en-final.pdf.

should be disclosed and how it is to be disclosed.[251] The MoU, however, exempts from disclosure two classes of documents that are not otherwise exempt from parliamentary privilege: Cabinet confidences and information subject to solicitor and client privilege.[252] This explains the refusal of the New Democratic Party to participate in a process that compromised the ordinary privileges of Parliament.

The Missing Link

What is not acknowledged by the Speaker of the House, or the lawyers for either of the two branches, is that the dispute boils down to an old but familiar one between the Crown and Parliament – as Paley and Dicey describe it, between royal prerogative and parliamentary privilege. The prerogatives, that realm of unfettered executive discretion, have been whittled away by statute and by practice to a handful of things that are important, nevertheless. But for a few matters that are reserved for the governor general acting on the advice of her ministers (the "personal" prerogatives concerning such things as prorogation and dissolution), they concern subjects such as treaty-making, diplomacy, the deployment of armed forces – matters concerning the making of war and peace. This is where the focus of the dispute lies. Foreign affairs and national security remain subjects for the exercise of Crown prerogative and so seemingly within the exclusive purview of the prime minister acting in his executive capacity. This remains one of the principal sources for the concentration of authority in the Prime Minister's Office.[253]

Describing the prerogative as absolute and beyond reproach – as "dangers not fit to be communicated to the people" – Charles I was later beheaded. Over the last few centuries, the Lockean view has prevailed:

---

251 An interim report was filed by the Panel of Arbiters in April 2011 and made publicly available, providing details about their methodology. See Canada, "Afghan Detainee Document Review: Report by the Panel of Arbiters on Its Work and Methodology for Determining What Redacted Information Can Be Disclosed," 15 April 2011, para 17, http://beta.images.theglobeandmail.com/archive/01289/Afghan_detainee_do_1289874a.pdf.

252 Canada, "Memorandum of Understanding," para iv.

253 As Payne astutely observes, "What may appear as a bizarre leftover from antiquity, ceases to be so strange when the most significant powers continue to have a functional role to play in government," in "Royal Prerogative," 87.

the people, acting through their representatives, determine the scope of Crown prerogative. After all, the conventions that have been built up around the Crown's prerogatives serve the end of ensuring the supremacy of the House of Commons.[254] They are not about preserving power for its own sake but about serving the needs and demands of the people as expressed through their representatives in the House, of which, significantly, the prime minister remains a member. Those prerogatives continue to exist only to the extent that they have not been disrupted by practice over time or by statute.

It seems a sound proposition from a constitutional point of view to argue, as did the opposition, that the privileges of Parliament trump the prerogatives of the Crown. The House of Commons is entitled to control its own procedure, determine the scope and application of statutes to its own proceedings, and order the production of documents. If met with resistance, these privileges entitle the House to take disciplinary measures such as citing members for contempt, expulsion, and even incarceration until the end of the parliamentary session.[255] No inquiry of the House could take place without this power to "enforce obedience," observes Hallam: "No man would seek to take away this authority from parliament, unless he is either very ignorant of what has occurred in other times and in his own, or is a slave in the fetters of some general theory."[256] It was in these circumstances that the treasurer of the state of New South Wales in 1996 was ordered out of the precincts of the Legislative Council (the elected upper chamber) for failing to comply with an order to produce documents.[257] This precisely was the scenario the prime minister and his Cabinet faced after the motion of 10 December 2009 was approved by the House – potentially suffering the embarrassment of being escorted out of the precincts of Parliament.

As gratifying as this scenario might have been to some, the problem is that it might not have had the effect of forcing the government to deliver up unredacted documents. English and Canadian constitutional authorities are clear that the royal prerogative can be abrogated or abolished only by convention – typically requiring a process of some

---

254 Dicey, *Introduction to the Study of the Law of the Constitution*, 426.
255 Robert Marleau and Camille Montpetit, eds., *House of Commons Procedure and Practice* (Ottawa: House of Commons, 2000), chap. 3, n199; *Erskine May's Treatise on the Law*, 163–6; Hallam, *Constitutional History of England*, 781–90.
256 Hallam, *Constitutional History of England*, 789.
257 Lee, *Power of Parliamentary Houses to Send for Persons*, 216.

duration[258] – or by express terms, and perhaps even by necessary implication, of a statute.[259] Applying these considerations in Khadr (No. 2),
the Supreme Court of Canada preferred not to order the return of Omar
Khadr, a Canadian citizen, who was being held at Guantanamo Bay
for ten years on terrorism and related charges after being captured on
Afghan soil. The Court found a serious breach of Mr Khadr's Charter
rights yet chose not to tread into the realm of foreign affairs by directing the government of Canada to seek his release from U.S. custody.
This was, in part, because the National Defence Act did not have
the effect of abolishing the royal prerogative in the realm of international relations. As the prerogative over foreign affairs had not been
displaced by statute, the Court preferred to defer to "the executive to
make decisions on matters of foreign affairs in the context of complex
and ever-changing circumstances, taking into account broader national
interests." The Court opted to "leave it to the government to decide
how best to respond to this judgment in light of current information, its
responsibility for foreign affairs, and in conformity with the Charter."[260]

4. Taming the Prerogative

How, then, could the House compel the production of unredacted
documents? If, at its "infancy," government "was almost all prerogative," Locke proclaimed, the people are now capable of setting limits on
prerogative authority. This entails no encroachment upon the monarch,
as the power does not, as of right, belong to him. It is instead a trust
exercised on behalf of the people in the pursuit of the public good.[261]
The common law has followed suit, acknowledging the capacity of
Parliament to limit, regulate, and even abolish the prerogatives.[262]

But for the handful of personal prerogatives wielded by the monarch
(previously mentioned), prerogatives are mostly within the purview

---

258 *Duff Conacher v Prime Minister of Canada* [2010] 3 FCR 411 (TD); appeal dismissed
   [2011] 4 FCR 22 (CA). Compare Andrew Heard, "*Conacher* Missed the Mark on
   Constitutional Conventions and Fixed Election Dates," *Constitutional Forum
   constitutionnel* 19 (2010): 21–32, with Roberts Hawkins, "The Fixed-Date Election
   Law: Constitutional Convention or Conventional Politics?," *Constitutional Forum
   constitutionnel* 19 (2010): 33–9.
259 *Ross River Dena Council Band v Canada* [2002] 2 SCR 816, para 4.
260 *Canada (Prime Minister) v Khadr* [2010] 1 SCR 4, para 39.
261 Locke, *Two Treatises of Government*, ¶162; Simmons, *Lockean Theory of Rights*, 218.
262 Dicey, *Introduction to the Study of the Law of the Constitution*, 61.

of Cabinet and so have increasingly become a focal point of reform in parliamentary democracies, most notably in the United Kingdom. In 1989 the Labour Party promised a review of the royal prerogative,[263] and Labour MP Jack Straw declared in 1993 that the "royal prerogative has no place in a modern western democracy."[264] To this end, the House of Commons Public Administration Select Committee recommended in 2004 that prerogative authority be enumerated. A parliamentary committee could then be delegated responsibility to review the scope of the prerogatives with a view to introducing framework legislation to "put in place statutory safeguards where these are required." This was "unfinished constitutional business," the committee declared.[265] The Blair government was not so enthusiastic. It rejected any comprehensive proposal to tame executive exercises of the prerogative, maintaining that it was best to proceed as needed on a case-by-case basis.[266] Parliament's long-standing ability to hold the executive to account would suffice for most other purposes. The House of Lords select committee on the constitution subsequently took as a focal point for reform the prerogative power to deploy armed forces abroad, following upon the controversial commitment to join in President George W. Bush's "coalition of the willing" in Iraq. The select committee declared this royal prerogative "outdated" and called upon government to seek parliamentary approval in advance of its use.[267]

Interest in reining in prerogative authority continued under the newly installed Labour government of Gordon Brown. The government

---

263 United Kingdom, House of Commons, Public Administration Select Committee (PASC), "Taming the Prerogative: Strengthening Ministerial Accountability to Parliament," Fourth Report of Session 2003–04, 16 March 2004, para 14, www. publications.parliament.uk/pa/cm200304/cmselect/cmpubadm/422/422.pdf.
264 Ibid., para 16.
265 Ibid., paras 25, 61. The committee followed the advice of Rodney Brazier, whose paper is appended to the PASC report (ibid., 24–30).
266 United Kingdom, Department of Constitutional Affairs, "Government Response to the Public Administration Select Committee's Fourth Report of the 2003–4 Session, Taming the Prerogative: Strengthening Ministerial Accountability to Parliament (HC422)," July 2004, webarchive.nationalarchives.gov.uk/+/http://www.dca.gov. uk/pubs/reports/prerogative.htm.
267 United Kingdom, House of Lords, Select Committee on the Constitution, *Waging War: Parliament's Role and Responsibility* (London: Stationery Office, 2006), 1:41, 43, http://www.publications.parliament.uk/pa/ld200506/ldselect/ldconst/236/236i. pdf; Rosara Joseph, *The War Prerogative: History, Reform, and Constitutional Design* (Oxford: Oxford University Press, 2013), 182–3.

issued a Green Paper declaring exercises of prerogative authority "no longer appropriate in a modern democracy" and pledged to place that power "on a statutory basis" and "under stronger parliamentary scrutiny and control."[268] Reform of the prerogatives deploying armed forces abroad, ratifying treaties, dissolving Parliament, and overseeing the public service would be sought, as would a review of the prerogative authority exercised by Cabinet ministers.[269] In pursuance of the Green Paper's commitments, the Ministry of Justice undertook a comprehensive review of prerogative power exercised by ministerial authority, the results of which were published in 2009. This was the first exercise of its kind since Chitty catalogued many of the prerogatives some 190 years earlier.[270] The ministry canvassed sixty-four different departments and agencies seeking sources of non-statutory authority that fell within the prerogatives, excluding those concerning foreign affairs. The report took note that the government was moving on a number of fronts to strengthen Parliament's role in the exercise of prerogative authority via a Constitutional Reform and Governance Bill, mentioned below.[271] The ministry document was cautious about interfering with prerogative power, particularly in matters calling for flexible and expeditious decision making. The government was resolved, however, "to increase Parliamentary oversight of control in relation to treaties, war powers, senior appointments and the management of the civil service."[272] For the prime minister, this was an opportunity to "address the question of a written constitution." Were Britons to have one, "it would be fitting," wrote Gordon Brown, "to complete it in time for the 800th anniversary of the signing of Magna Carta in Runnymede in 1215."[273] The

---

268 United Kingdom, Department of Constitutional Affairs, Ministry of Justice, "The Governance of Britain," *Green Paper*, Cm 7170, July 2007, 15, 17, www.official-documents.gov.uk/document/cm71/7170/7170.pdf.

269 Lucinda Maer and Oonagh Gay, "The Royal Prerogative," House of Commons Library SN/PC/03861, 30 December 2009, briefing-papers/SN03861/the-royal-prerogative.

270 Joseph Chitty, *Treatise on the Law of Prerogatives of the Crown and the Relative Duties and Rights of the Subject* (London: Joseph Butterworth and Son, 1820).

271 United Kingdom, Ministry of Justice, "The Governance of Britain: Review of the Executive Royal Prerogative Powers: Final Report," October 2009, para 34, www.peerage.org/genealogy/royal-prerogative.pdf. This included removing the hereditary principle from the House of Lords.

272 Ibid., paras 109, 110.

273 Gordon Brown, "A Vote to Give Politics Back," *Guardian*, 2 February 2010.

constitutional project was scuttled by Brown's election defeat in 2010. The Conservative–Liberal Democratic coalition government that subsequently took power expressed little interest in proceeding on these fronts,[274] though the coalition agreement of May 2010 does constrain prime ministerial discretion in the selection of ministers by requiring consultation with the deputy prime minister.[275]

There were a number of other significant constitutional developments under Tony Blair's prime ministership that limited government by prerogative, including devolution to Scotland, Wales, and Northern Ireland, removal of hereditary peers from the House of Lords, and establishment of a new Supreme Court and judicial appointments commission, prompted by concerns about separating judicial from legislative and executive power (which I examine in more detail in chapter 5).[276] Gordon Brown's legacy was limited to placing the civil service on a statutory footing and codifying the rules for parliamentary scrutiny of treaties.[277] The Conservative–Liberal Democrat coalition abolished the prerogative power of dissolution with a fixed-term election law, imposing elections at five-year intervals subject to limited exceptions. This has the effect of abolishing by statute the personal prerogative of the Crown to dissolve Parliament.[278] This was something the Harper government could not achieve via its fixed election date law without running afoul of the Constitution's amending formulae. Instead, the Canadian law preserved the governor general's discretion.

In the wake of Prime Minister Harper's two controversial prorogations, there have been calls for regulation of the prerogatives in

---

274 United Kingdom, House of Commons, Political and Constitutional Reform Committee, "Issues and Questions: Prime Minister, Prerogative and Power," January 2011, www.parliament.uk/business/committees/committees-a-z/commons-select/political-and-constitutional-reform-committee/news/pm-powers-inquiry/discussion-paper-pm-powers/.

275 United Kingdom, "Coalition Agreement for Stability and Reform, May 2010," www.gov.uk/government/uploads/system/uploads/attachment_data/file/78978/coalition-agreement-may-2010_0.pdf.

276 Robert Hazell, "Constitutional Reform in the United Kingdom: Past, Present and Future," in *Reconstituting the Constitution*, ed. Caroline Morris, Jonathan Boston, and Petra Butler, 83–96 (Heidelberg: Springer-Verlag, 2011); Alan Paterson and Chris Paterson, *Guarding the Guardians? Towards an Independent, Accountable and Diverse Senior Judiciary* (London: CentreForum, 2012), www.centreforum.org/assets/pubs/guarding-the-guardians.pdf.

277 Constitutional Reform and Governance Act 2010, c 25.

278 Fixed-Terms Parliament Act 2011, c 14, s 3.

Canada, focusing particularly upon the powers to prorogue and dissolve Parliament. If there is disagreement over whether a change of government requires the calling of a fresh election, why not try to secure some advance agreement about this matter rather than letting such a question fester into constitutional crisis?[279] Similarly, Parliament could have taken a variety of steps to produce unredacted documents. It could have enacted a specific statute authorizing House of Commons access to documents, partially abrogating the prerogative over foreign affairs with accompanying mechanisms addressing such things as confidentiality, where necessary. Such a precise measure, addressing access to documents in the Afghan detainee case, could have left intact the exercise of the prerogative in all other areas of foreign affairs. Or, as has been suggested, Parliament could codify limited prerogatives such as the power to declare war.[280] More ambitiously, Parliament could consider enumerating and then cabining some or all exercises of the royal prerogative, just as U.K. parliamentary institutions have recommended. It may turn out, as Harris suggests in the case of New Zealand, that much prerogative authority already has been displaced by statute.[281] We have only ourselves to blame to the extent we remain wilfully ignorant about these matters.

Parliament could also curb prime ministerial resort to the power of prorogation. A motion, introduced by NDP leader Jack Layton in March 2010 and narrowly approved by the House of Commons, requires the prime minister to seek authorization from the House in cases where prorogation lasts longer than seven days. With all-party agreement, Mendes suggests, the motion could be elevated to a standing order of the House.[282] Statutory codification remains a delicate constitutional question insofar as the Constitution of Canada requires unanimity for amendments that touch on "the office of the Queen, the Governor General and the Lieutenant Governor of a province." One would want to ensure that only the prime minister's discretion is fettered and not

---

279 Peter Aucoin, Mark D. Jarvis, and Lori Turnbull, *Democratizing the Constitution: Reforming Responsible Government* (Toronto: Emond Montgomery, 2011), 176.

280 Christopher Dunn, "Democracy in the 21st Century: Canada Needs a War Powers Act," *Canadian Parliamentary Review* 30 (Autumn 2007): 2–3.

281 B.V. Harris, "Replacement of the Royal Prerogative in New Zealand," *New Zealand Universities Law Review* 23 (2009): 310.

282 Errol P. Mendes, "Prorogation," memo for the Asper Centre Constitutional Conventions Workshop, University of Toronto, 4 February 2011.

that of actors whom the Privy Council constitutionally advise, in which case, the measure would fall under amendments, unilaterally made, concerning "the executive government of Canada."[283]

Some, however, take the view that the prime minister's advisory role cannot be fettered in summoning, proroguing, or dissolving Parliament, insofar as the prime minister advises the governor general. This is because Parliament "would in fact be affecting the office and powers of the Governor General."[284] Note, first, that amendments concerning only the "office" of the Queen and governor general require unanimity, not measures affecting "powers." The word *powers* is invoked elsewhere in the amending formula as regards other things, indicating that something less than powers or functions is caught by this clause.[285] I suspect that the requirement of unanimity has more to do with maintaining Canada's monarchy, and the contentious question of conversion to a republic, than it is about protecting the Crown's "dignity and efficiency."[286] Furthermore, it simply goes too far to argue that all prerogatives have been constitutionalized – and thereby entrenched – by virtue of the amending formula of the Constitution Act, 1982. This rubs against the entire history of the prerogative in Westminster systems of government and would pointlessly hamper Canada's ability to adapt executive power to current needs. This interpretation would render reform of the prerogatives virtually impossible to achieve (I shall have more to say about the stringency of Canada's amending formula in the

---

283 Constitution Act, ss 41(a), 44.
284 Warren J. Newman, "Of Dissolution, Prorogation, and Constitutional Law, Principle and Convention: Maintaining Fundamental Distinctions during a Parliamentary Crisis," *National Journal of Constitutional Law* 27 (2009): 224; also Patrick J. Monahan, "The Constitutional Role of the Governor General," in *The Evolving Canadian Crown*, ed. Jennifer Smith and D. Michael Jackson (Kingston: Institute of Intergovernmental Relations, 2012), 82; Philippe Lagassé, "The Crown's Powers of Command-in-Chief: Interpreting Section 15 of Canada's Constitution Act, 1867," *Review of Constitutional Studies* 18 (2013): 196–7.
285 Minister of Justice Favreau's 1965 white paper on the amending formula ("The Amendment of the Constitution of Canada") called for unanimity on the "functions of the Queen and Governor General in relation to the parliament or Government of Canada," in *Canada's Constitution Act 1921 & Amendments: A Documentary History*, ed. Anne Bayefsky (Toronto: McGraw-Hill Ryerson, 1989), 1:40. The Victoria Conference formula appears to have introduced the "office of the Queen" language that gets taken up in subsequent versions of the amending formulae (in Bayefsky, *Canada's Constitution Act 1921 & Amendments*, 1:218).
286 Lagassé, "Crown's Powers of Command-in-Chief," 198.

next chapter). Would restricting prime ministerial advice on exercise of the personal prerogatives unconstitutionally confine the Crown's authority? Even if, as a practical matter, no governor general since 1926 has refused to follow the advice of his or her prime minister regarding these matters, the personal prerogatives would remain untouched.[287] Instead, only prime ministerial discretion would be curbed, as was envisaged in the amendment to Canada's Elections Act fixing federal election dates. Similarly appropriate statutory language could be devised that would require majority consent of Parliament before the prime minister advised the governor general to prorogue. The fixed election law, it may be recalled, preserved wiggle room for the prime minister. Nevertheless, it was available to be used as a political club with which to batter the prime minister should he contravene its terms, which occurred when he called an early election in 2008. If all relevant actors honoured the tenor of the law, over time it could rise to the level of a constitutional convention that would be binding politically, though not legally enforceable. This is the means by which the prime minister sought to secure an elected Canadian Senate, the subject of the next chapter.

There have also been calls for the "codification" of the constitutional conventions that govern Canada's parliamentary system. Cabinet manuals that summarize precedent and practice in a publicly accessible way have been produced, to beneficial effect, in New Zealand and the United Kingdom.[288] We have learned recently that an exhaustive Canadian version – a two-volume work of some 1500 pages – was produced in 1968 to assist civil servants in administering "the machinery of government."[289] Rather than have it document Canadian parliamentary habits in precise detail, Russell and Milne explain that the hope is to generate an authority containing "statements about important

---

287 Heard claims that "political practice reveals a very clear willingness on the part of modern Canadian governors to exercise their reserve powers," but these concern matters other than prorogation and dissolution, in Andrew Heard, "The Reserve Powers of the Crown: The 2008 Prorogation in Hindsight," in *The Evolving Canadian Crown*, ed. Jennifer Smith and D. Michael Jackson (Kingston: Institute of Intergovernmental Relations, 2012), 89–90.

288 Fraser Harland, "Constitutional Conventions and Cabinet Manuals," *Canadian Parliamentary Review* 34 (Winter 2011): 26–32.

289 Nicholas A. MacDonald and James W.J. Bowden, "The Manual of Official Procedure of the Government of Canada: An Exposé," *Constitutional Forum constitutionnel* 20 (2011): 37.

principles and practices of parliamentary government in Canada." The exercise, they explain, should amount not so much to codification – it would not result in a compendium of rules having the force of law – but to generating "an authoritative and evolving set of principles and guidelines for those involved in the operation of parliamentary government."[290]

That is not all parliamentarians can do. The exercise of the royal prerogative is subject to the full range of parliamentary procedures including, as we have seen, committee proceedings and Question Period. A British textbook writer observes that these ordinary mechanisms for political control of the prerogative "may in practice" prove to be unsatisfactory.[291] This is a proposition that will hold true in the case of a party in majority control of parliamentary machinery. In circumstances of a minority Parliament, however, the opposition holds in its hands the ultimate rebuke of a failure to comply with the expressed will of the House: a successful motion of non-confidence, in which case, the government would fall.

It is folly to think that a court would be interested in intervening in such matters. It is true that courts have gone so far as to define the scope of the prerogative, but they are unlikely to judge "the appropriateness of its exercise" unless individual legal rights or legitimate expectations, understood in a procedural sense, are affected.[292] Nor are courts likely to interfere in the management of the internal affairs of the House insofar as parliamentarians might seek to enforce their will over a recalcitrant prime minister's. Courts are likely to steer clear of this particular fight, not only out of respect for the political branches, just as the Supreme Court of Canada did in Khadr (No. 2) by refusing to issue a meaningful remedy for the ongoing breach of Omar Khadr's rights while he continued to be held in Guantanamo Bay. They would also be justified in staying out because of the variety of self-help remedies available to the House to rectify breaches of parliamentary privilege.

---

290 Peter Russell and Cheryl Milne, *Adjusting to a New Era of Parliamentary Government: Report of a Workshop on Constitutional Conventions* (Toronto: David Asper Centre for Constitutional Rights, 2011), 5. I took part in the consultation that gave rise to this report.

291 Hilaire Barnett, *Constitutional and Administrative Law*, 7th ed. (Milton Park, Abingdon, Oxon: Routledge-Cavendish, 2008), 129.

292 *House of Commons v Vaid*, para 47.

Such proposals have not had traction among the political parties. There is an unattractive laziness about the status quo, observes Harris – it has proven to be a convenient and resilient source of authority, after all.[293] One significant reason must be that subsequent to these abuses of prerogative power, the Harper government was re-elected to a majority government. The Canadian public seemed much less concerned about maintaining the integrity of parliamentary institutions than did the parliamentary opposition.[294]

Once public opinion began to turn against the prime minister's decision to prorogue, it was no coincidence that by 6 January 2010 there was talk of a "renewed" plan to push for an elected Senate. For the prime minister, talk of Senate elections had the beneficial effect of pushing prorogation off the front pages and returning to a pet theme, the Americanization of the Canadian Senate, long promoted by western-based Reformers. This is the subject to which I turn next.

---

293 B.V. Harris, "Replacement of the Royal Prerogative in New Zealand," 303.
294 Michael Ignatieff, *Fire and Ashes: Success and Failure in Politics* (Toronto: Random House Canada, 2013), 145.

4 A "More Salutary Check"? Electing the Canadian Senate

I do not think the Americans have any particular monopoly on democracy.

Stephen Harper[1]

The prorogation of Parliament in December 2008 – the subject of chapter 2 – was not the only consequential event of that month. Rather, the appointment of eighteen new Conservative senators turned out to be an important political moment in the life of the Conservative government. Among the appointees, former journalists Pamela Wallin and Mike Duffy, together with former national chief of the Congress of Aboriginal Peoples, Patrick Brazeau, were summoned to Senate places that they could hold onto until the ripe old age of seventy-five. In Brazeau's case, this meant that he was entitled to this sinecure for forty years. With much political drama, all three were expelled from the Senate in December 2013 for filing false housing or travel claims. Having abused their privileges, they were ejected, subjected to RCMP investigations, and, as regards Duffy and Brazeau, prosecuted criminally.[2]

---

1 Senate of Canada, "Proceedings of the Special Senate Committee on Senate Reform" (chair: Daniel Hays), 7 September 2006, 2:18.
2 The wrinkle that implicated the prime minister in their wrongdoing is that his chief of staff, Nigel Wright, with the knowledge of others employed in the Prime Minister's Office (PMO), concocted a scheme to cover up Senator Duffy's false expense claims by reimbursing his expenses. The prime minister denied any prior knowledge of this scheme. Senator Duffy initially was to be reimbursed out of Conservative Party coffers. Mr Wright ultimately wrote Senator Duffy a personal cheque for the amount. The prime minister claimed that he had no knowledge of Mr Wright's payment until it was made public, but he did not adequately explain whether he had knowledge of the Conservative Party plan.

The Senate's stature, already low in the public mind, had reached unknown depths.[3]

Why did the prime minister undertake this flurry of Senate appointments in December 2008? Since taking office in 2005, the prime minister refrained from filling vacant Senate seats in the hope that elected senators – elected via provincially administered campaigns – would be the candidates "summoned" to places in the Senate. Though the Queen nominally summons senators, she acts, in accordance with constitutional convention, on the advice of her prime minister.[4] Outside of eager Alberta, no province conducted elections for the nomination of senators. Holding off in making appointments resulted in a large number of places going empty, many of them previously held by Liberal party stalwarts. With the threat of a coalition government looming, these rows of empty seats could be filled by well-connected Liberals, even New Democrats.[5] On the other hand, filling vacant Senate seats immediately meant that Conservatives could regain control of the Senate in short order, by March 2009 to be exact. By filling those places and restoring the tradition of appointments as a patronage plum, the prime minister could ensure that, at least until Senate reform secured a foothold, there would be no Liberal obstructionism issuing out of the upper chambers.

Stephen Harper already had tried to kick-start Senate reform. From 2006 to 2011, on at least eight separate occasions, either in the Senate or in the House of Commons, his government introduced legislation calling for consultative elections or term limits for senators.[6] Progress was impeded because of the doubtful constitutional validity of proceeding by federal statute rather than by constitutional amendment with the consent of a majority of the provinces. One of the last iterations, Bill C-7, "The Senate Reform Act," was referred to the Quebec Court of Appeal by the Quebec government to determine its conformity with the constitutional amending formulae. Before the Court issued a ruling (ultimately, it condemned the federal government for seeking

---

3 Almost 70 per cent of Canadians, according to an IPSOS poll taken in December 2013, disagree with the proposition that the Canadian Senate performs a "necessary and useful political function." See IPSOS, "Most (69%) Canadians Disagree That the Senate of Canada Performs a Necessary and Useful Political Function," 2 January 2014, https://www.ipsos-na.com/news-polls/pressrelease.aspx?id=6376.

4 As the power exercised here is expressly authorized by the Constitution, it does not fall within the realm of Crown prerogative discussed in the other chapters.

5 J. Patrick Boyer, *Our Scandalous Senate* (Toronto: Dundurn, 2014), 348.

6 Prorogation in 2009 killed at least one of those attempts (Bill S-7).

constitutional change outside of the amending formula),[7] the Harper government referred the whole mess to the Supreme Court of Canada, and the Court ruled in April 2014 that the proposed federal law offended the Constitution. Any Senate reform initiative would require substantial provincial consent; unanimity was required in the case of abolition. No unilateral tampering with the Senate's "fundamental nature," the Court pronounced, would be tolerated.[8]

Senate reform has long been a preoccupation of Canadian politicians. W.P.M. Kennedy described Senate reform as "merely a plaything of the parties – one of the standing jokes of electioneering campaigns."[9] "During the last hundred years [since Confederation]," observed historian George Wrong, "there has never been a time when reformers have not attacked the second chambers in what is now Canada as useless or arbitrary and, in either case, requiring change or extinction."[10] What is significant about this recent episode is that the government not only talked about Senate reform, it chose to do something about it.[11]

What it chose to do was to secure a key plank of a proposal – the "elected" part of the Triple-E Senate ("elected," "equal," and "effective") – without attending to other constituent elements of the Senate reform plan, namely, its equal and effective parts. This piecemeal reform proposal did not attend to other elements considered necessary for an elected Senate to succeed. Roger Gibbins, an early adopter of Senate reform, warned that such proposals had the potential to "unravel much of what is valuable and distinctive about the Canadian political system,"[12] if not lead us down "a slippery slope at the bottom

---

7 *Reference re Bill C-7 Concerning Reform of the Senate* (2013) 370 DLR (4th) 711 (Que CA).

8 *Reference re Senate Reform* [2014] I SCR 704.

9 W.P.M. Kennedy, *Some Aspects of the Theories and Workings of Constitutional Law* (New York: Macmillan, 1932), 107.

10 George M. Wrong, "Introduction," in Robert A. MacKay, *The Unreformed Senate of Canada* (London: Oxford University Press, 1926), xiv.

11 There have been a few other initiatives, such as removing lifetime appointment and imposing mandatory retirement at age seventy-five, which were secured by unilateral federal statute. The unsuccessful Victoria Charter, Meech Lake Accord, and Charlottetown Accord, discussed below, contemplated constitutional amendments addressing Senate reform.

12 Roger Gibbins, "Senate Reform: Moving towards the Slippery Slope," *Discussion Paper No. 16* (Kingston: Institute of Intergovernmental Relations, 1983), 45, www.queensu.ca/iigr/pub/archive/DiscussionPapers/discussionpaper16 SenateReformMovingTowardstheslipperyslope1983.pdf.

of which lies American congressional politics."[13] In other words, the Harper proposal failed to recognize that reform of the upper chamber necessitated inevitable changes to address its knotty relationship with the lower one.[14] Realistic Senate reform in a bicameral Parliament must attend to the Senate's powers, its relationship to responsible government, the likelihood of deadlock, and its historically subordinate role in relation to the House of Commons. None of these subjects were on the table during Prime Minister Harper's tenure. Though these defects went unmentioned in the Supreme Court of Canada's ruling, the Court did invoke Canadian constitutional history and practice as reasons to impede the progress of Senate reform.

The focus of this chapter, as elsewhere in this book, is to illustrate how the Harper government persistently mimics highly problematic practices of U.S. constitutional governance – here, the upper chamber represented by the U.S. Senate. The elected Australian Senate could be viewed as a model the Harper government sought to emulate. In an address to the Australian Parliament in 2007, Prime Minister Harper identified himself as the victim of "Senate envy" because Australian senators are elected and not appointed.[15] Yet the Australian Senate is unlikely the preferred model. The closer one looks at the Harper government initiative and its origins in Reform Party proposals for a Triple-E Senate, the clearer it is that the U.S. experience plays a preponderant role in this debate, as it does in other areas. Indeed, it is likely that Senate reformers have preferred to play down these connections. Gibbins hypothesizes that "positive reference to the American experience would hand their opponents the club of anti-Americanism,

---

13 Ibid., 31.
14 David E. Smith, *The Canadian Senate in Bicameral Perspective* (Toronto: University of Toronto Press, 2003), 157.
15 Prime Minister of Canada Stephen Harper, "Prime Minister Harper Addresses Australian Parliament in Canberra, Australia," 11 September 2007, pm.gc.ca/eng/news/2007/09/11/prime-minister-harper-addresses-australian-parliament-canberra-australia. Harper declared, "I can't help but notice, however, that you have done a much better job than us with at least one of our Westminster institutions, the Upper House. As one Canadian political scientist I know likes to say, when we look at Australia, we suffer from 'Senate envy.' Because in Canada, Senators remain appointed, not elected. They don't have to retire until age 75, and may warm their seats for as long as 45 years. By the nature of the system, they're not accountable to voters. So it's a rare pleasure for me to be among Senators who are actually elected by the people they represent."

a club that could and would be used to beat back reform."[16] It would be more accurate to say, as does David Smith, that whatever attraction the Australian Senate has to Canadian reformers, it "pale[s] in comparison to the influence the United States Senate has exercised over debate on Canada's upper house."[17]

Irrespective of influence, it is apparent that an elected Senate would result in a significant change in Canadian constitutional culture. As I argued in chapter 1, Canada's constitutional inheritance is one of muscular legislative authority, subject to a division of legislative powers and a charter of rights. Otherwise, Canadian political power is largely unbounded. Insofar as dividing authority between two levels of government can impede policy innovation, the Canadian experience suggests that federalism and bicameralism do not obstruct, though they may delay, the realization of important legislative objectives. The adoption of an elected Senate is likely to give rise not only to delay but, as U.S. precedent suggests, to policy stasis or gridlock.[18]

The first part of this chapter traces the outlines of Canada's upper chamber, beginning with its pre-Confederation origins in an appointed and, for a short time, an elected legislative council in the provincial Parliament of Canada. Returning to an appointed body at Confederation, it was expected that the upper house would have the capacity to check the lower one principally for the purposes of protecting regional and propertied interests. Its original functions, it turns outs, were not well served by the Senate. Over time, it did come to function as a mechanism for delay, but not one of institutional gridlock that brought legislative process to a standstill. The modern movement towards a Triple-E Senate is canvassed in part 2, providing a backdrop to the sequence of proposals floated by the Harper government. These initiatives contemplate institutional gridlock and not just the interposition of delay. Gridlock is a phenomenon associated with the U.S. model that is canvassed in

---

16 Roger Gibbins, "The Impact of the American Constitution on Contemporary Canadian Constitutional Politics," in *The Canadian and American Constitutions in Comparative Perspective*, ed. Marion C. McKenna (Calgary: University of Calgary Press, 1993), 144.

17 Smith, *Canadian Senate in Bicameral Perspective*, 37.

18 Gridlock is defined as "an inability to change policy," in Manabu Saeki, *The Other Side of Gridlock: Policy Stability and Supermajoritarianism in U.S. Lawmaking* (Albany: State University of New York Press, 2012), 15. Its opposite would be the enactment of some specific policy or the confirmation of some specific nominee. See Josh Chafetz, "The Phenomenology of Gridlock," *Notre Dame Law Review* 88 (2013): 2073.

part 3 It becomes apparent that the expectation was that a reformed Canadian Senate would perform many of the same functions as its U.S. counterpart, including blocking legislative initiatives and making it more difficult for the central government to act. The Harper reforms would have resulted in a newly powerful and legitimate Senate that would render the upper house dissonant with Canadian constitutional culture and its tenets of responsible government.

Unlike other initiatives discussed in this book, where a powerful executive is able to exploit the reservoir of discretion available under the prerogatives, the Harper initiative on Senate reform called for passage of a legislative framework. This raised questions about the law's conformity with the constitutional amending formulae in Part V of the Constitution Act, 1982. The chapter turns finally, then, to the question of whether the federal government is entitled to enact legislation on consultative elections and term limits without seeking the consent of the provinces in advance. For all practical purposes, the opinion of the Supreme Court of Canada in the matter has halted the process, instigating another sort of gridlock. I offer a normative reading of the amending formulae, in the last part, that would have allowed for more innovation and experimentation – more play around the joints – than many of the relevant actors would have tolerated. I hope to make clear that this path to developing new constitutional practice was dangerously piecemeal nevertheless and, paradoxically, vulnerable to failure when the government changed hands.

1. Designing Delay

Legislative Council Complaints

During the "first" British Empire, governors of the British North American colonies were expected to receive advice about local conditions from appointed councils.[19] Pursuant to the Royal Proclamation of 1763, for instance, Governor James Murray sought advice from an executive council composed of the lieutenant governors of Montreal and Three Rivers, the chief justice, surveyor general, and eight other local notables who were the "most considerable of the persons of property"

---

19 Leonard Wood Labaree, *Royal Government in America: A Study of the British Colonial System before 1783* (New York: Frederick Ungar, 1958), 134.

in the colony. Elsewhere, executive councils would be complemented by legislative councils. Alternatively, as in the case of Nova Scotia, the executive council would double as an upper chamber.[20] This was a distinctly colonial style of paternalistic governance seemingly befitting Britain's overseas empire in America.[21]

At the beginnings of the "second" British Empire, elected assemblies, analogous to the House of Commons, were introduced in Upper and Lower Canada in 1791. Hereditary legislative councils made up of "discreet and proper persons," analogous to the House of Lords, complemented representative institutions.[22] As explained in chapter 1, the revolt of the American colonies could be explained by the absence of constitutional equipoise between the elected assembly and monarchic and aristocratic branches, so maintained metropolitan leadership. In what remained of British North America, where "all Governments are feeble and the general condition of things tends to a wild Democracy," what was needed was restoration of the British mixed constitution.[23]

During the course of the debate over the Constitution Act, 1791 (discussed in chapter 3), all parliamentarians agreed that the constitution required a robust aristocratic element that would be represented in the upper chamber. This was "the essential [missing] link that held the branches together," declared Chancellor William Pitt – it was "indispensably necessary," agreed Leader of the Opposition Charles James Fox. The 1791 debate in Parliament turned, instead, on whether the Legislative Council was to be appointed or elected. An elective council with property qualifications "infinitely higher" than those for election to the lower house would guarantee a "true aristocracy." The worry was that election based upon property would "render the poise nearer to the people than it was to the Crown in the British constitution," explained Chancellor Pitt. If honours flowed directly from the imperial Crown, the legitimacy of those appointed would be enhanced, as would be the connection between colony and mother country. Edmund Burke agreed: "In a Monarchy ... the aristocracy must ever be nearer the Crown as the fountain of honour ... as the root of the constitution." An

---

20 Oscar D. Skelton, *The Canadian Dominion: A Chronicle of Our Northern Neighbor* (New Haven, CT: Yale University Press, 1919), 11, 28.

21 Duncan McArthur, "A Canadian Experiment with an Elective Upper Chamber," *Proceedings and Transactions of the Royal Society of Canada*, 3rd ser., 24 (1930): 82.

22 Art III of The Constitutional Act, 1791, 31 George III, c 31.

23 Skelton, *Canadian Dominion*, 32, quoting Governor Carleton.

"elective Council would clearly be a democratic Council," he warned. For fear that it smacked of republicanism, the elective principle was roundly rejected.[24]

As a consequence, those nominated to the legislative council under the authority of the 1791 Constitution Act would receive a lifetime appointment, held during good behaviour, while maintaining a residence within the province. It was expected that some "mark of Honour, such as a Provincial Baronetage either personal to themselves, or descendible to their Eldest Sons, in lineal Succession" would be forthcoming, elevating appointments to a hereditary peerage,[25] but no such aristocracy would materialize in the woods of British North America. Instead, legislative councillors would depend on sinecures held at the pleasure of the Crown. In short, they were at the mercy of gubernatorial patronage, rendering the council vulnerable to partisan attack, a result that did nothing to enhance the honour of the Crown.[26]

Though there would be no hereditary chamber like the House in Lords in Canada, the council system did execute its checking functions well. They were "most effective instruments of government," writes McArthur, "the weight of their influence was exerted definitely for the protection of the imperial interest and for the maintenance of proper safeguards for the vested rights of property and of social and political privilege within the colonies."[27] Legislative Council governance was perhaps *too* effective – the upper chambers in both Upper and Lower Canada repeatedly stood in the way of legislative initiatives originating in their lower chambers. Therefore reformers in both provinces insisted

---

24 E.A. Cruikshank, "The Genesis of the Canada Act," *Ontario Historical Society Papers and Records* 28 (1932): 155–327, 295 (Pitt), 292 (Fox), 293–4, 296 (Pitt), 299 (Burke).

25 Grenville to Dorchester, 20 October 1789, in W.P.M. Kennedy, ed., *Statutes, Treaties and Documents of the Canadian Constitution, 1713–1929*, 2nd ed. (Toronto: Oxford University Press, 1930), 186. See art VI of The Constitutional Act, 1791, 31 George III, c 31. Lucas interprets this proposal as one "honestly designed to meet a defect which had already been felt in new countries, the lack of a conservative element in the Legislature and in the people, the absence of dignity and continuity with the past, and the want of some balance against raw and undiluted democracy which has not, as in older lands, been trained to recognize that the body politic consists of more than numbers," in C.P. Lucas, *A History of Canada, 1763–1812* (Oxford: Clarendon, 1909), 252.

26 Jeffrey L. McNairn, *The Capacity to Judge: Public Opinion and Deliberative Democracy in Upper Canada 1791–1854* (Toronto: University of Toronto Press, 2000), 33.

27 McArthur, "Canadian Experiment with an Elective Upper Chamber," 33.

upon elective legislative councils.[28] Leading Upper Canadian reformer Robert Baldwin, however, disparaged elected upper chambers – it was not a solution to the problem of an abusive and corrupt executive. An elected legislative council, Baldwin feared, would not deal with the primary difficulties of colonial government, failed to "correspond with those [institutions] of the Mother Country," and generated an "additional engine of hostility against the [responsible] executive" for which he was struggling.[29] Only responsible government, Baldwin maintained, would solve the problem by rendering the upper chambers subordinate to, and in harmony with, the lower ones.[30] The achievement of responsible government predictably secured that harmony. For "all practical purposes," observes Robert MacKay, the Canadian government thereafter would "become that of a single chamber."[31]

The Legislative Council continued to experience reputational troubles, even then, due to poor attendance records and what was called "swamping" – the appointment of new members to ensure the passage of legislation.[32] Described as an "expensive farce,"[33] the Hincks-Morin ministry in 1853, inspired by developments in the Australian and Cape colonies, sought to revive the moribund upper chamber by mandating popular election.[34]

To what extent was the U.S. Senate a model for reformers in the 1850s? Senators were not then directly elected but were selected by states via indirect election. The famous Lincoln-Douglas debates, which were held throughout Illinois in 1858, demonstrate how public opinion could sway the votes of state electors. The U.S. model of indirect election

---

28 For example, "Petition of House of Assembly of Lower Canada, 1833" and "The Seventh Report on Grievances, 1835," in Kennedy, *Statutes, Treaties and Documents of the Canadian Constitution*, 266, 303.
29 Baldwin to Lord Glenelg, 13 July 1836, in Kennedy, *Statutes, Treaties and Documents of the Canadian Constitution*, 336–7.
30 Elgin was of the view that an elected upper chamber could more legitimately offset the "excesses" of the lower chamber. See Chester Martin, *Foundations of Canadian Nationhood* (Toronto: University of Toronto Press, 1955), 149.
31 Robert A. MacKay, *The Unreformed Senate of Canada* (London: Oxford University Press, 1926), 26.
32 Shirley E. Carkner Hart, "The Elective Legislative Council in Canada under the Union: Its Role in the Political Scene" (MA thesis, Queen's University, 1960), 224.
33 McNairn, *Capacity to Judge*, 317.
34 Carkner Hart, "Elective Legislative Council in Canada," 224; McArthur, "Canadian Experiment with an Elective Upper Chamber," 85.

was influential enough to prompt an opponent to an elected legislative council in Canada to proclaim that those "who have most loudly clamoured for it ... have turned to the United States Senate as a model."[35]

The movement towards direct election remained unstoppable. Encouraged by Lord Elgin and the Duke of Newcastle, the Colonial Office proceeded by enabling legislation in 1854,[36] allowing for either election or nomination and future changes to the composition of the Legislative Council.[37] Joined by Conservatives in 1855, aiming to wrest control of the nominated council from the hands of reformers,[38] the assembly approved a bill providing for elections that was initially rejected by the appointed Legislative Council. On a second try, the council approved the bill, subject to amendments of a "conservative strain" to which the House was amenable.[39] These included higher property qualifications,[40] life-long tenure for non-elected sitting members, and future replacements would be elected in twelve districts every two years to serve eight-year terms.[41]

Confederation Conundrum

The electoral experiment, also tried in Prince Edward Island from 1862 to 1893, was declared to be less than successful by John A. Macdonald during the Confederation debates.[42] He announced that the "only dissenting voice" opposed to the "nominative principle" was Prince Edward Island. Appointments for life had the advantage of comporting with British constitutional practice, though he admitted there was no prospect of

35 Anonymous, *Arguments against an Elective Legislative Council* (Toronto: Leader and Patriot Office, 1856), 5.
36 This was pursuant to the Union Act Amendment Act, 1854, 17 & 18 Vict, c 118.
37 Carkner Hart, "Elective Legislative Council in Canada," 135.
38 Arthur G. Doughty, *The Elgin-Grey Papers, 1846–1852* (Ottawa: J.O. Patenaude, 1937), 749; Donald Creighton, *John A. Macdonald: The Young Politician* (Toronto: Macmillan of Canada, 1956), 181.
39 Elective Legislative Council Act, 1856; Carkner Hart, "Elective Legislative Council in Canada," 181.
40 MacKay, *Unreformed Senate of Canada*, 28.
41 J.C. Dent, *The Last Forty Years: The Union of 1841 to Confederation* (1881; Toronto: McClelland & Stewart, 1972), 261.
42 Janet Ajzenstat, "Bicameralism and Canada's Founders: The Origins of the Canadian Senate," in *Protecting Canadian Democracy: The Senate You Never Knew*, ed. Serge Joyal (Montreal and Kingston: McGill-Queen's University Press, 2003), 12.

nurturing a landed aristocracy that could comprise a hereditary peerage. Macdonald, nevertheless, admitted that the arguments in favour of the elective principle were "numerous and strong." Though not a "failure," the experiment "did not so fully succeed in Canada." One "great cause" that made it less than successful was the enormity of constituencies that made campaigning difficult, if not costly, contributing to the "increasing disinclination" of quality candidates to stand for office.[43]

It is not surprising to find that both elected and life members of the Legislative Council were not as eager to characterize the experiment as less than successful. In the course of the Confederation debates, G.W. Allen maintained that the elected members of the upper house had maintained its "character ... as a conservative body, free from all violent party feeling, and exercising a wholesome check against ill-considered or hasty legislation."[44] Even Etienne Taché, member of Her Majesty's government, did not want to offend his fellow council members, declaring that "until now the elective principle has worked remarkably well," sending to the upper house "gentlemen who would do honor to any deliberative body in the world."[45] Indeed, elections seemed to have secured precisely the same quality of "gentlemen" as would have invited appointment. Many candidates won places by acclamation,[46] lending credence to the complaint about the vast size of constituencies discouraging quality candidates. Once placed, they also "exhibited little [of the] independence its creators had hoped for."[47]

Legislative Council members, nevertheless, were cautious about condemning the plan for an appointed Senate. For Taché, there was a concern that the elective principle would be carried "too far," as it had been in the United States, where calls arose even for the election of judges. Allen's principal worry was that if the upper house continued only to elect members, "party lines" would become "more closely drawn" and conflict would ensue between upper and lower chambers, even over money bills. There were other evils associated with an elective

43 Canada, *Parliamentary Debates on the Subject of the Confederation of the British North American Provinces* (1865; Ottawa: Edmond Cloutier, 1956), 35.
44 Ibid., 117.
45 Ibid., 240; also W.H. Dickson in ibid., 289.
46 Carkner Hart, "Elective Legislative Council in Canada," 200–1; Michel Morin, "L'élection des membres de la Chambre Haute du Canada-Uni, 1856–1867," *Cahiers de Droit* 35 (1994): 39.
47 Carkner Hart, "Elective Legislative Council in Canada," 209–10.

chamber – the prospect, for instance, of "political intriguers" who would make a "living by and for politics." On the other hand, a wholly appointed upper chamber, David Reesor feared, would culminate in a house of only "political friends" of the party in power and so proposed a higher property qualification for the upper house franchise.[48]

It is clear that delegates in both the lower and upper chambers during the Confederation debates were hesitant about maintaining the elective principle in the Legislative Council. Given the ambivalent ten-year experience, it turns out that the benefits of an elected upper chamber were not so great as to risk losing Confederation. That it was key to obtaining the consent of Nova Scotia and New Brunswick to the Confederation compromise likely settled matters for most – they could not be so insistent on a course of action that would antagonize their maritime partners.[49] Indeed, the mode of representation in the proposed Legislative Council (later renamed the "Senate") – by equal section and in fixed numbers, in contrast to the principle of representation by population operating in the lower house – lay at the "base of the whole compact on which this scheme rests," declared George Brown.[50] It was a "constitutional tranquillizer," observes Kunz, to console the weaker provinces fearing that a numerical majority would overwhelm them in the lower chambers.[51]

The "dimly felt" need was for a check on legislative excesses issuing from the House of Commons.[52] In Ajzenstat's recounting of the debates, we see the framers' insistence in all of the confederating colonies on instituting a system of "admirable checks" as was available to the House of Lords under the English Constitution.[53] This was a part

48 Canada, *Parliamentary Debates on the Subject of the Confederation*, 242 (Taché and Allen), 185 (N.F. Belleau), 166 (Reesor).

49 McArthur, "Canadian Experiment with an Elective Upper Chamber," 88.

50 Canada, *Parliamentary Debates on the Subject of the Confederation*, 89.

51 F.A. Kunz, *The Modern Senate of Canada, 1925–1963: A Re-appraisal* (Toronto: University of Toronto Press, 1965), 317.

52 MacKay, *Unreformed Senate of Canada*, 31. What was required, declares MacKay, was a second chamber "not strong enough to control the Ministry, but which would be sufficiently powerful and sufficiently conscientious and independent to perform those indefinite functions which people dimly felt were required of a second chamber by the British system of government, and no more" (31).

53 Ajzenstat, "Bicameralism and Canada's Founders," 5, quoting James Gray Stevens in *Canada's Founding Debates*, ed. Janet Ajzenstat, Paul Romney, Ian Gentles, and William D. Gairdner (Toronto: Stoddart, 1999), 96.

of the system of checks and balances associated with the mixed constitution. The aim was to check majoritarian impulses that trampled
on "minority political rights" to perform the "vital function of checking the potential for highhandedness in Cabinet and Commons."[54] In
this, they would have been informed by John Stuart Mill's discussion
of upper chambers in his *Representative Government* (see appendix 1 at
the end of this chapter).[55] The threat of populist demagoguery remains
a continuing concern for many, even today.[56] The Canadian government offered such rationales in support of its 1978 Constitutional
Amendment Bill (discussed further below). Upper house membership,
the government's White Paper asserts, is more "conservative" and so
provides more "stability" in the performance of its function as a chamber of "sober second thought." "The unfettered will of the majority,"
we are reminded, "was, and often still is, mistrusted, therefore, not
only by the less populous units of federation but by those who fear
demagogues, charismatic leaders, and indeed just the pressures which
may be brought on the government of the day to act in hasty, ill considered and unwise fashion."[57]

It is revealing of Macdonald's objectives that he proclaimed the
reviled nominative system, prior to the introduction of responsible
government in March 1848, as being "to a great extent successful."[58]
It was a success in comparison to its post-responsible-government
successor, which ceased to be a "substantial check" on the legislative
assembly and so no longer served its constitutional functions.[59] The
new Senate, like the old Legislative Council, would be up to the task,
Macdonald maintained. It would have powers fully equal to meet those
of the commons. It would be disabled only from introducing, but not

---

54 Ajzenstat, "Bicameralism and Canada's Founders," 3, 25.

55 Ibid., 27n19.

56 Walters characterizes the justifications offered in those debates as making "for
    uncomfortable reading today," in Mark D. Walters, "The Constitutional Form and
    Reform of the Senate: Thoughts on the Constitutionality of Bill C-7," *Journal of
    Parliamentary and Political Law* 7 (2013): 40. It is hard to see how drawing on this
    English constitutional tradition is all that embarrassing.

57 Marc Lalonde, "Constitutional Reform: House of the Federation," August 1978, in
    Canada's Constitution Act 1982 & Amendments: A Documentary History, ed. Anne F.
    Bayefsky (Toronto: McGraw-Hill Ryerson, 1989), 1:486.

58 Canada, *Parliamentary Debates on the Subject of the Confederation*, 35–6.

59 Ibid.; Morin, "L'élection des membres de la Chambre Haute du Canada-Uni," 41.

amending, money bills.[60] The Senate would be divided into three (later four) equal divisions in order to protect the "sectional interests" of each region, western Canada, Lower Canada, and the maritime provinces. Each would receive twenty-four seats and no more, in divisions that would "preserve the independence of the Upper House, and make it, in reality, a separate and distinct chamber, having a legitimate and controlling influence in the legislation of the country." There would be no swamping of the upper chamber with appointments to ensure that the government's legislative agenda would move forward. Admittedly, there was the danger of deadlock between the two houses, as had occurred in England, but this did not worry Macdonald. The threat of deadlock preserved upper house independence, authorizing it to stall any "hasty or ill considered legislation." In any event, the new upper chamber would "not stand in the way of the deliberate and understood wishes of the people." Membership would be drawn, after all, from the ranks of the citizens themselves. "Springing from the people, and one of them, he takes his seat in the Council with all the sympathies and feelings of a man of the people,"[61] though with the requisite property qualifications, for men who were to sit in the chamber were expected to be "representative[s] of property."[62]

There was greater likelihood of deadlock were the elective principle adopted, Macdonald explained. Elected members could say, "We as much represent the feelings of the people as you do, and even more so; we are not elected from small localities and for a short period." An

60 Lafleur and Geoffrion in Robert McGregor Dawson, *Constitutional Issues in Canada, 1900–1931* (London: Oxford University Press, 1993), 261–2. Constitution Act, 1867, section 53: "Bills for appropriating any Part of the Public Revenue, or for imposing any Tax or Impost, shall originate in the House of Commons." This is traceable to a British House of Commons resolution of 1678, violation of which is considered an "intolerable breach of privilege." See William McKay, *Erskine May's Treatise on the Law, Privileges, Proceedings and Usage of Parliament*, 23rd ed. (London: LexisNexis UK, 2004), 923. In their legal opinion to the Special Committee of the Senate (chairman: W.B. Ross), Lafleur and Geoffrion opine that the "denial of the right to originate money bills does not involve the denial of the right to amend them," in Dawson, *Constitutional Issues in Canada*, 261. Also see Andrew Heard, *Canadian Constitutional Conventions: The Marriage of Law and Politics*, 2nd ed. (Toronto: Oxford University Press, 2014), 147.
61 Canada, *Parliamentary Debates on the Subject of the Confederation*, 38, 36, 37.
62 J.A. Macdonald quoted in "Notes on the Quebec Conference," by A[ndrew]. A[rchibald] Macdonald, 11 October 1864, repr. in *Documents on the Confederation of British North America*, ed. G.P. Browne (Toronto: McClelland & Stewart, 1969), 133.

elected upper house, representing the transient opinions of the public, could claim "a better right" to represent the "deliberate will of the people on general questions," Macdonald maintained. With life tenure, moreover, "our members would die," resulting in turnover of more membership than occurs in the House of Lords and so resulting in a better reflection of the "state of opinion."[63] Yet the short-lived experience with an elected legislative council had given rise to little, if any, conflict.[64] George Brown admitted that the "apprehension that I and others entertained of a collision between the two elective bodies, and a dead-lock ensuing, has not been realized." That was not to say that an independent streak might not have developed, Brown maintained. The exercise of power, he declared, inevitably "sinks down into a thing of everyday wont."[65]

The importance of the Senate to the Canadian framers is made plain by the oft-mentioned fact that six of fourteen days were spent discussing the matter at the Quebec conference, mostly having to do with its mode of representation.[66] Even this turned out to be inadequate, according to Edward Cardwell, secretary of state for the colonies. The draft project emerging out of Charlottetown and Quebec did not sufficiently account for the possibility of deadlock and the means by which harmony would be restored between the two houses should they become mired in a "decided difference of opinion."[67] It comes as no surprise to learn that, when the Canadians travelled to London to secure passage of the bargain, imperial legal officers insisted on a provision to break anticipated deadlocks. Section 26 of the 1867 Act embodied the solution, providing for the appointment of three or six (now four or eight) additional senators, to be apportioned equally among the divisions. By virtue of section 27, no further appointment could be made until the numbers in each section returned, by attrition, to their ordinary levels.[68]

Christopher Dunkin bemoaned the absence of provincial input in the selection of council members. What he hoped for was what he described

63 Canada, *Parliamentary Debates on the Subject of the Confederation*, 37.
64 Carkner Hart, "Elective Legislative Council in Canada," 224.
65 Edward Whelan, *The Union of the British Provinces* (Charlottetown: G.T. Haszard, 1865), 193.
66 MacKay, *The Unreformed Senate of Canada*, 37.
67 Edward Cardwell to Governor-General Monck, 3 December 1864, in Browne, *Documents on the Confederation of British North America*, 170.
68 David Schneiderman, "On Stacking the Senate," *Policy Options* (November 1991): 34–5.

as a "federal check." This "very near approach[ed] ... the worst system which could be devised" – a "quasi-despotism" – "ridiculously the worst," he declared. As in the legislative councils in times past, "party, political appointments" were likely to prevail.[69] Almost all of the discussion in the Legislative Council, MacKay later observed, "freely admitted" that party considerations would govern appointments.[70]

Sober Interposition

In short order, this is precisely how things turned out. One suspects that Macdonald was alive to these potentialities.[71] He was, after all, the master of manipulating patronage. He distributed posts "in a radically new" and "sophisticated" way to the benefit of party, and was "entirely unapologetic" about doing so.[72] Macdonald proceeded to fill the Senate with partisans; all but five appointments going to non-Conservatives, on every occasion in the pursuit of partisan objectives.[73] The Senate quickly proved to be a useful "tool for party management," advises Jeffrey Simpson: "It enabled a prime minister to remove political deadwood from his Commons contingent, to create openings, to weaken opponents, in short, to sharpen his party's fighting form." Even P.E. Trudeau, who did more to diversify the Senate's gender and complexion, allocated the "lion's share" of appointments to "friends and party stalwarts."[74]

As originally intended, propertied interests were well represented. According to Ross, among the first 304 appointments (until Robert Borden's prime ministership), "the great majority were ... engaged in industrial or professional pursuits." Ross maintains, nevertheless, that the Senate could not be accused of acting on behalf of party interests in

---

69 Canada, *Parliamentary Debates on the Subject of the Confederation*, 494–5.

70 MacKay, *Unreformed Senate of Canada*, 47.

71 Trotter writes that the rejection of election in favour of appointment "may indicate that the creation of positions of honour for these provincial legislative councilors was considered desirable as a means of insuring their support for federation," in Reginald George Trotter, *Canadian Federation: Its Origins and Achievement – A Study in Nation Building* (Toronto: J.M. Dent & Sons, 1924), 113.

72 Richard Gwyn, *John A.: The Man Who Made Us – The Life and Times of John A. Macdonald* (Toronto: Random House Canada, 2007), 1:168.

73 Jeffery Simpson, *Spoils of Power: The Politics of Patronage* (Toronto: Collins, 1988), 315; Laurier in Dawson, *Constitutional Issues in Canada*, 241.

74 Simpson, *Spoils of Power*, 317, 327.

the amendment or rejection of bills.[75] By contrast, MacKay's 1926 study reveals identifiable partisan influences at work: more bills were rejected when the majority in the Senate was opposed to the majority in the Commons. Fewer bills suffered such a fate when the same party was in control of both chambers.[76] The Senate veto, nevertheless, was used with "judicious care," MacKay observes. It was a "better interpreter of public opinion and the better judge of public policy" than the expressed will of the elected branch, he maintains. Indeed, MacKay claims, the Senate "has never defeated the real will of the people or obstructed it when that will was clearly expressed."[77] But it admittedly watches "its political enemies more than its political friends."[78]

As discussed in chapter 3, after the introduction of franchise reform in Great Britain and the ascendance of Cabinet government, the House of Lords no longer had the requisite legitimacy to veto House of Commons legislation. The mixed constitution ceased to have any real salience in English constitutional theory, though lip service continued to be paid to the idea. Now the House of Lords could only "delay" legislation.[79] According to convention codified by the Parliament Act 1911, if the Lords were to reject a bill they would be obliged to pass it if enacted by the Commons in three – and since the 1949 Atlee government, in two – successive legislative sessions.[80]

In light of its diminished constitutional role, in 1918 Viscount James Bryce was tasked to reconsider the functions appropriately served by the House of Lords. Bryce isolated, among them, the capacity to delay: "The interposition of so much delay (and no more) in the passing of a

---

75 George Ross, *The Senate of Canada: Its Constitution, Powers and Duties Historically Considered* (Toronto: Copp, Clark, 1914), 69, 79.
76 MacKay, *Unreformed Senate of Canada*, 117, 189; also J.T. Shaw, MP, quoted in Dawson, *Constitutional Issues in Canada*, 275.
77 MacKay, *Unreformed Senate of Canada*, 134, 135. The Senate has, for instance, never defeated social reform legislation "for which there was a clear public demand" (170). "Those hard-headed politicians of the Quebec Conference," write the Research Committee of the League for Social Reconstruction, "must surely have had their tongues in their cheeks when they presented their particular specimen of their handiwork to a credulous populace," in *Social Planning for Canada* (Toronto: Thomas Nelson & Sons, 1935), 499.
78 MacKay, *Unreformed Senate of Canada*, 137.
79 Corrine Comstock Weston, *English Constitutional Theory and the House of Lords, 1556–1832* (London: Routledge & Kegan Paul, 1965), 257.
80 Iain McLean, *What's Wrong with the British Constitution* (Oxford: Oxford University Press, 2010), 93.

bill in to law as may be needed to enable the opinion of the nation to be adequately expressed upon it."[81] Coincidentally, this is where David Smith ends up in the most recent book-length study of the Canadian Senate. Smith notes that the number of Senate vetoes over time is rather slight: "forty-four for all of the twentieth century, with thirty-nine of those before 1940." What the Senate has been able to do is delay legislation. Because "bicameralism broadens the base of consultation," the quality of government is improved, Smith maintains. Just as "two decisions take more time," he writes, "bicameralism means delay."[82] Thus the Senate has performed a function that helps to define the content of Canada's constitutional culture. As discussed in chapter 1, the system of checks and balances "rarely frustrates the popular will."[83] The experience under Canadian bicameralism has been one more of delay than of gridlock and paralysis.[84]

What ends do Senate-induced delay serve? The Senate has utterly failed in its intended function of watching over sectional or provincial interests.[85] Kunz harshly characterizes this original rationale as "essentially a rhetorical device" intended to assuage less powerful maritime interests – a "psychological rather than a political remedy." Indeed, writes Kunz, this claim has "proved to be one of the enduring myths of political demagogy in Canadian history."[86] "In terms of effective regional representation," observes McCormick, Manning, and Gibson, "the Senate is close to a dead loss."[87] In such matters, the federal Cabinet, provincial premiers, and the judiciary have proven more effective in vindicating rights associated with provincial autonomy. Rights of property, both corporate and individual, have been of much greater interest to senators, as, for instance, when property has been "rendered valueless by changes in public policy." MacKay maintains that security of

81 Viscount Bryce in MacKay, *Unreformed Senate of Canada*, 231.
82 Smith, *Canadian Senate in Bicameral Perspective*, 115, 137, 176.
83 Frederick J. Fletcher and Donald C. Wallace, "Federal-Provincial Relations and the Making of Public Policy in Canada: A Review of the Case Studies," in *Division of Powers and Public Policy*, ed. Richard Simeon (Toronto: University of Toronto Press, 1985), 151.
84 David C. Docherty, "The Canadian Senate: Chamber of Sober Reflection or Loony Cousin Best Not Talked About," *Journal of Legislative Studies* 8 (2002): 34.
85 MacKay, *Unreformed Senate of Canada*, 138.
86 Kunz, *Modern Senate of Canada*, 319.
87 Peter McCormick, Ernest C. Manning, and Gordon Gibson, *Regional Representation: The Canadian Partnership* (Calgary: Canada West Foundation, 1981), 29.

property has always been vulnerable to "organized minorities or individuals seeking their selfish interests, and from majorities seeking short cuts to progress."[88] Echoing a refrain common to Anglo-American legal thought in the early twentieth century, MacKay observes, "Probably at no earlier period in Canadian history were economic groups, whether of capital, of labour, or of agriculture, so well organized as at the present time." MacKay believes the Senate would be more effective than the House of Commons in resisting the selfish interests of group life. He seems oblivious, however, to the advantage that organized business interests have had in Canadian social, economic, and political affairs.[89]

By contrast, the Research Committee of the League for Social Reconstruction (think tank of the Co-operative Commonwealth Federation) (CCF), understood the Senate as having served as a "bulwark for property interests."[90] There was no other option than to abolish it, they concluded, a position to which the successor organization to the CCF, the New Democratic Party, still holds fast. Some fifty years on, Campbell agrees that the Canadian Senate is about ensuring that legislation advances the interests of the Canadian business lobby, via technocratic review and special studies. These senators, Campbell asserts, amount to "a lobby from within" – though in the pay of the public – conferring an "undemocratic advantage to business interests in their efforts to compete with other groups for influence in the policy arena."[91] This is not all that senators do, Campbell admits. They also conduct "social investigations" into such things as aging, poverty, and employment.[92]

All are agreed, however, that the Canadian Senate has not vindicated regional or sectional interests as its framers intended. Instead, it has

---

88 MacKay, *Unreformed Senate of Canada*, 150, 153.
89 Ibid., 155. Such anxieties were given expression via judicial interpretation of the U.S. Constitution and associated with the *Lochner* era. See Howard Gillman, *The Constitution Besieged: The Rise and Demise of Lochner Era Police Powers Jurisprudence* (Chapel Hill, NC: Duke University Press, 1993). Like many thinkers in this era, MacKay is inattentive to how the baseline represented by the status quo represents gains secured in law by already powerful political actors. See Cass R. Sunstein, *The Partial Constitution* (Cambridge, MA: Harvard University Press, 1993), 4.
90 Research Committee of League for Social Reconstruction, *Social Planning for Canada*, 500; Woodsworth in Dawson, *Constitutional Issues in Canada*, 243.
91 Colin Campbell, *The Canadian Senate: A Lobby from Within* (Toronto: Macmillan of Canada, 1978), 2; also Docherty, "Canadian Senate," 32–3.
92 Campbell, *Canadian Senate*, 22. These activities do not amount to "lobbying from within," Campbell cautions (22).

been better suited to performing its original checking function on behalf of a variety of interests in – occasionally to the betterment and other times to the detriment of – Canadian public life. On those rare occasions when the upper house was controlled by a party different from the governing one in the lower house, as MacKay observed, it was more watchful of its political enemies. In the period of 1984–97, when opposing parties controlled each house, the Senate was "more active and influential in Canadian politics than at any other time in its history," and so served well its checking function, though this again was motivated largely by partisan considerations.[93] The question for readers is whether it is advantageous to double down on the Senate's capacity to second-guess, emboldening the capacity of the chamber to stand up to the House of Commons, for this is precisely the motivation behind the Tripe-E Senate proposal, to which I next turn.

2. The Bumpy Road to "Triple E"

Under Construction: A House for the Provinces

If Senate reform has been a preoccupation of Canadian political elites since Confederation, the push towards an elected Senate is of more recent vintage. Romanow, Whyte, and Leeson describe the "epidemic" of constitutional reform initiatives after 1976 as being prompted by two converging forces.[94] First, the emergence of Quebec out of its "great darkness" (*la grande noirceur*)[95] that culminated in the election of the Parti Québécois. Second, Alberta Conservatives consolidating power under Premier Peter Lougheed, around the same time as the Organization of Petroleum Exporting Countries (OPEC) began fixing the price of oil (inspired by measures taken by Khadaffi in Libya), marking the beginning of a power shift away from powerful multinationals to oil-producing provinces.[96]

---

93 C.E.S. Franks, "Not Yet Dead, But Should It Be Resurrected? The Canadian Senate," in *Senates: Bicameralism in the Contemporary World*, ed. Samuel C. Patterson and Anthony Mughan (Columbus: Ohio State University Press, 1999), 121, 140.
94 Roy Romanow, John Whyte, and Howard Leeson, *Canada Notwithstanding: The Making of the Constitution 1976–1982* (Toronto: Carswell/Methuen, 1984), xvii.
95 This is the period associated with the long tenure of Premier Maurice Duplessis from 1936 to 1959 with a five-year interruption (1939–44).
96 John Richards and Larry Pratt, *Prairie Capitalism: Power and Influence in the New West* (Toronto: McClelland & Stewart, 1979), 217–18.

It is hard to fathom how reform of central Canadian institutions –
what is called "intrastate federalism" – could placate autonomy
demands made by successive Quebec premiers. Institutional change,
nevertheless, has been a recurring element of contemporary constitutional reform. Initially, such proposals were preoccupied with augment-
ing provincial representation in the central government via a house of
provincial delegates, a model like that of the German Bundesrat.[97] The
reform contemplated by the Trudeau government's plan, "A Time for
Action,"[98] and introduced in Bill C-60, "The Constitutional Amendment
Bill,"[99] was not quite a replica of the German house.[100] The bill envisaged a comprehensive package of constitutional reform, the first phase
of which would include a proposal for a new House of Federation
secured unilaterally by the federal government. The second phase of
reform, which would include a new division of powers together with
a bill of rights, would be pursued in consultation with the provinces.[101]

In the unilateral phase, a new 118-member upper house was proposed, half of whose membership would be appointed by party leaders
in the House of Commons and the other half by those in the provincial
legislatures.[102] Membership in the new upper house would reflect the
proportionate share of the vote won by each party at election time in
each appointing legislative body. Among other features, the reformed
upper house would have a two-month suspensive veto on House of

97 R.M. Burns, "Second Chambers: German Experience and Canadian Needs," in
  Canadian Federalism: Myth or Reality?, ed. J. Peter Meekison, 3rd ed. (Toronto:
  Methuen, 1977), 211; Canada, Task Force on Canadian Unity, *A Future Together:
  Observations and Recommendations* (Ottawa: Queen's Printer, 1979); Donald V. Smiley
  and Ronald L. Watts, *Intrastate Federalism in Canada* (Toronto: University of Toronto
  Press, 1985), 123; Ronald L. Watts, "Second Chambers in Federal Political Systems,"
  in Ontario, Advisory Committee on Confederation, *Background Papers and Reports*
  (Toronto: Queen's Printer, 1970), 2:353–4.
98 Pierre Elliott Trudeau, "A Time for Action: Toward the Renewal of the Canadian
  Federation" (tabled in the House of Commons, 12 June 1978), in Bayefsky, *Canada's
  Constitution Act 1982 & Amendments*, 1:437–59.
99 In Bayefsky, *Canada's Constitution Act 1982 & Amendments*, 1:364–73.
100 First reading, 20 June 1978. Generally, see Donald V. Smiley, *Canada in Question:
  Federalism in the Eighties*, 3rd ed. (Toronto: McGraw-Hill Ryerson, 1980), 82.
101 Romanow, Whyte, and Leeson, *Canada Notwithstanding*, 8–9.
102 Lalonde, "Constitutional Reform," 485–99. There also is an earlier version of this in
  Senate reform proposed by Fielding in 1923 (referred to by J.T. Shaw, MP, quoted in
  Dawson, *Constitutional Issues in Canada*, 277). The following discussion refers to ss
  64, 67, and 70 of Bill C-60.

Commons legislation, would require a double majority for measures of "special linguistic significance," and would exercise a veto over the appointment of Supreme Court justices and other senior federal officials.

The government was of the view that upper house reform could be achieved via unilateral federal legislation, authorized by what was then section 91(1) of the British North America Act, 1949.[103] Bill C-60's provisions would be "constitutionalized but not entrenched," so reform would not necessitate amendment by the British Parliament.[104] Sufficient doubt was raised by the provinces about the constitutionality of this first phase that the government referred two sets of questions – the first having to do with abolition and the second about replacing the Senate with a new upper house – to the Supreme Court of Canada in 1979.[105]

A unanimous Supreme Court denied the capacity of the federal government to unilaterally abolish and then replace the Senate. The Court ruled that, on the question of abolition, the federal government could not act unilaterally to amend the constitution when it affected federal-provincial relations.[106] Having recourse to the Confederation debates revealed that the Senate was to be the key institution for "protecting sectional and provincial interests."[107] The Court seemed disinterested in assessing whether the Senate actually performed this function (perpetuating what Kunz calls one of the "enduring myths of political demagogy").[108] It was sufficient that this was the original intention. Reference to the "Constitution of Canada" in section 91(1) of the Constitution Act 1867, by contrast, referred to "matters of interest only to the federal government." It could not endow the federal government with authority to abolish an institution that was of interest to all members of the federation. As for erecting a new upper chamber that would, among

---

103 The British North America (No. 2) Act, 1949, 13 Geo VI, c 81 (UK) provided, in its opening words, for the "amendment from time to time of the Constitution of Canada …"

104 Bayefsky, *Canada's Constitution Act 1982 & Amendments*, 342.

105 Romanow, Whyte, and Leeson, *Canada Notwithstanding*, 33.

106 *Re Authority of Parliament in Relation to the Upper House* [1980] 1 SCR 54, 64 ["*Upper House Reference*"]. The Court here drew upon Minister of Justice Guy Favreau's 1965 White Paper, "The Amendment of the Constitution of Canada," in Bayefsky, *Canada's Constitution Act 1982 & Amendments*, 22–48.

107 *Upper House Reference*, 68.

108 Kunz, *Modern Senate of Canada*, 319.

other things, alter senators' qualifications, tenure, and method of selection, the Court summarily dismissed unilateral federal capacity: "It is not open to Parliament to make alterations which would affect the fundamental features, or essential characteristics, given to the Senate as a means of ensuring regional and provincial representation in the federal legislative process."[109]

Though contemplated by the questions asked, there was no real consideration given to a directly elected Senate. This would have been intolerable not to senators, maintained the Special Committee on the Senate, but to members of the House of Commons, who would now be faced with a competing source of federal authority.[110] Election of senators would also have been viewed as inimical to the interests of provincial politicians, particularly those in Quebec, for an elected upper chamber would usurp the authority of provincial governments and rival the power of provincial politicians. This is why provincial control over the upper chamber was viewed as more congenial to Quebec's autonomy demands.[111] Advancing a federalist alternative in advance of the 1980 Quebec referendum on sovereignty-association, the Quebec Liberal Party (QLP) proposed a new intergovernmental institution to replace the Senate, to be called the Federal Council, "formed by delegations from the provinces acting on the instructions of their respective governments" together with non-voting federal delegates. Among other things, the Federal Council would have authority to review measures that affect the "fundamental equilibrium of the federation."[112]

Be Prepared to Stop: The Amending Formulae

Canadian constitutional politics were unalterably changed two years later. The Constitution Act, 1982, entrenched not only a charter of rights (in Part I) together with Aboriginal rights (in Part II) but a new set of amending formulae (in Part V). Section 91(1), at issue in the Upper

---

109 *Upper House Reference*, 70, 78.
110 Senate of Canada, Special Committee of the Senate on the Constitution of Canada, "First Report" from Proceedings, Issue 1 (18 October 1978), 432.
111 As reflected in the Pepin-Robarts Task Force on Canadian Unity in Canada, Task Force on Canadian Unity, *A Future Together: Observations and Recommendations* (Ottawa: Queen's Printer), 97–9; and Quebec Liberal Party proposals (the "Beige Paper"), in Constitutional Committee of the Quebec Liberal Party, *A New Canadian Federation* (Montreal: Quebec Liberal Party, 1980).
112 Quebec Liberal Party, *New Canadian Federation*, 53.

House Reference (1980), was repealed. Amendments to the Constitution would now fall within one of four available processes: a "general" formula, requiring Parliament and two-thirds of the provinces representing more than 50 per cent of the population (section 38); a formula requiring "unanimity" in regard to a list of five subjects (section 41); a "bilateral" amending formula available for amendments affecting one or more but not all of the provinces (section 43); and a federal "unilateral" formula concerning amendments to the "Constitution of Canada in relation to the executive government of Canada or the Senate and House of Commons," replacing section 91(1) (section 44).[113] We can reasonably assume that the framers of Part V had the Upper House Reference in mind, and may even have been guided by the Court's reasons, when drafting its text.[114]

Amendments regarding six matters are expressly identified as falling within the general amending formula (section 42). These include "the powers of the Senate and the method of selecting Senators." Such matters cannot fall within the exclusive purview of Parliament under section 44. Provinces are entitled to opt out of amendments under the general amending formula that amount to a reduction in their legislative authority (section 38[2]).[115] None of the subjects mentioned in section 42, however, are available for provincial opt out. What is reasonably clear is that the general amending formula is meant to be the default rule – it is to apply absent circumstances contemplated by the other formulae.[116] Though the general rule applies, the six matters identified in section 42 serve also as exceptions.

---

113 There is, in addition, a counterpart to the federal unilateral formula that applies to each of the provinces in the Constitution Act, 1982, section 45.

114 Senate of Canada, "Proceedings of the Standing Senate Committee on Legal and Constitutional Affairs" (chair: Donald H. Oliver), 23:86. John McEvoy asked precisely this question: whether section 44 was intended to "overcome" the 1978 reference or be interpreted as "consistent" with it. McEvoy concludes, in the face of conflicting 1981 testimony from Jean Chrétien and Roger Tassé, that the "historical evidence may not be as clear" as he would like (23:86).

115 See Peter W. Hogg, *Meech Lake Constitutional Accord Annotated* (Toronto: Carswell, 1988), 46. The opt-out in section 38(2) reads, "An amendment made under subsection (1) that derogates from the legislative powers, the proprietary rights or any other rights or privileges of the legislature or government of a province shall require a resolution supported by a majority of the members of each of the Senate, the House of Commons and the legislative assemblies required under subsection (1)."

116 Canada, Report of the Special Joint Committee of the Senate and the House of Commons, *The Process for Amending the Constitution of Canada* (chairs: Gérald Beaudoin and Jim Edwards) (Ottawa: Queen's Printer, 1991), 11; *Reference re Senate Reform*, para 36.

Detour Ahead: The Triple-E Senate

The "Triple-E" proposal emerged as a prominent feature of constitutional reform only in the 1980s. Promoted by the Canada West Foundation and the Canadian Committee for a Triple-E Senate, endorsed by a special select committee of the Alberta legislature (1985) and by western premiers at their 1986 meeting in Parksville, BC, it has been branded as mostly a western initiative to assuage demands for better representation in central governing institutions. "The solution to the problem of regional [namely, provincial] representation in national policy would be well served by the creation of an elected Senate," claimed McCormick, Manning, and Gibson.[117] Senate reform, so the argument goes, would have thwarted a number of federal initiatives that enraged the west: the adoption of Trudeau's national energy program (intended to capture profits from Alberta's oil patch) and the awarding of a CF-18 fighter plane maintenance contract to Montreal-based Canadair rather than to its Winnipeg-based competitor.[118]

Proposals canvassed all pertinent details: the distribution of Senate seats, length of terms (renewable or non-renewable), electoral methods (first-past-the-post or proportional representation), constituency size, role in confidence votes, general powers (suspensive or absolute vetoes), authority over financial legislation, special powers over particular subjects (official languages and natural resources), and proposals for resolving deadlocks.[119] The 1987 Meech Lake Accord, designed

---

117 McCormick, Manning, and Gibson, *Regional Representation*, 136.
118 Richards and Pratt, *Prairie Capitalism*, 226–7; Roger Gibbins, "Senate Reform: Always the Bridesmaid, Never the Bride," in *Canada: The State of the Federation*, ed. Ronald L. Watts and Douglas M. Brown (Kingston: Institute of Intergovernmental Relations, 1989), 196. "Western political protest," Gibbins observes, "has always been more concerned with the way in which Ottawa has carried out its institutional responsibilities than with the scope of those responsibilities" – principally Quebec's preoccupation, in Roger Gibbins, "Constitutional Politics and the West," in *And No One Cheered: Federalism, Democracy and the Constitution Act*, ed. Keith Banting and Richard Simeon (Toronto: Methuen, 1983), 121. Yet Alberta was sufficiently concerned with federal incursions into the natural resource sector that it insisted that a version of section 92A (conferring tax authority on the provinces over natural resources) be included in the 1982 constitutional package. On this, see J. Peter Meekison, Roy Romanow, and William D. Moull, *Origins and Meaning of Section 92A: The 1982 Constitutional Amendment on Resources* (Montreal: Institute for Research on Public Policy, 1985).
119 Jack Stillborn, "Forty Years of Not Reforming the Senate," in Joyal, *Protecting Canadian Democracy*, 45–9; Ronald L. Watts, "Bicameralism in Federal Parliamentary Systems," in Joyal, *Protecting Canadian Democracy*, 84.

principally to appease Quebec elites, left an elected Senate off the table. Though it never gained the requisite unanimous consent of all provinces, it was believed that the accord would have spurred on reform by entitling provincial governments to provide lists of names from which the prime minister would fill empty Senate seats (section 25). More troublesome for Senate reformers was Meech Lake's proposed amendment to the amending formula, which would have rendered amendments to the Senate in respect of its "powers" and "method of selecting senators" subject to the requirement of unanimity.[120] By contrast, the Senate proposed in the final text of the Charlottetown Accord went some distance to placate the demands of Triple-E proponents,[121] yet it did not go far enough.[122] The proposal, voted down by popular referendum in 1992, would have allowed for the popular election of senators or, alternatively, election by provincial legislative assemblies, the latter option largely to satisfy Quebec.

For our purposes, the more important reform project was that initiated by the fledgling Reform Party of Canada. With Senate reform already an important plank in the party's platform, a draft constitutional amendment was released in May 1988 and delivered, together with a covering letter from party leader Preston Manning, to the four western premiers.[123] The policy did not change markedly over the next ten years.[124] As Reform's chief policy officer and author of its first "Blue

---

120 David Elton, "The Enigma of Meech Lake for Senate Reform," in *Meech Lake and Canada: Perspectives from the West*, ed. Roger Gibbins, with Howard Palmer, Brian Rusted, and David Taras, 23–31 (Edmonton: Academic, 1988).

121 Ronald L. Watts, "The Reform of Federal Institutions," in *The Charlottetown Accord, the Referendum, and the Future of Canada*, ed. Kenneth McRoberts and Patrick Monahan (Toronto: University of Toronto Press, 2003), 27.

122 David Elton, "The Charlottetown Accord Senate: Effective or Emasculated?," in *The Charlottetown Accord, the Referendum, and the Future of Canada*, ed. Kenneth McRoberts and Patrick Monahan, 37–55 (Toronto: University of Toronto Press, 2003).

123 Leslie F. Seidle, "Senate Reform and the Constitutional Agenda: Conundrum or Solution?," in *Canadian Constitutionalism, 1791–1991*, ed. Janet Ajzenstat (Ottawa: Canadian Study of Parliament Group, 1992), 108.

124 Compare Reform Party statement of "principles and policies" (the party's "Bluebooks") in Reform Party, *Platform & Statement of Principles* (Calgary: Reform Party of Canada, 1988), 6, with Reform Party, *The Blue Book: Principles & Policies of the Reform Party of Canada – 1999* (Calgary: Reform Party of Canada, 1999), 13. The principal change occurs in 1999, when the party declares, anticipating the Harper government proposals, "Until a Triple E Senate is achieved, the Reform Party proposes that new Senators be appointed only from a list of persons chosen by the voters in the province where the Senate vacancy exists" (ibid.).

Book" platform, Stephen Harper had a hand in developing the party's Senate reform proposal.[125]

The Reform Party draft constitutional amendment proposed restoring the Senate's original function of "alleviat[ing] feelings of alienation and remoteness toward national affairs which exist, particularly in the less populous regions of Canada and to each of minority groups."[126] Ten Senate seats would be distributed to each of the ten provinces equally, the Yukon and Northwest Territories allocated four seats. Senators would be elected in districts by a single transferable vote (votes would be distributed in accordance with a candidate's ranking) for six-year renewable terms, at elections held in three-year intervals and on fixed dates. Qualifications were not too onerous – senators had to be over eighteen years of age with residency within their home province for five of the preceding ten years, neither a member of a federal or provincial assembly in the preceding year nor a member of Cabinet, a Crown corporation, agency, or tribunal. The reformed institution's powers were to be fulsome, though no money bills could originate out of, nor need be passed by, the Senate. Nor was it to be an institution in which the government could fall – defeat of government bills would not be treated as votes of non-confidence. The Senate would have the power to thwart legislation, however. Where the House did not concur with recommended changes, a reconciliation committee would be established, based on the West German model, composed equally of ten members from each chamber to mediate differences and "seek a mutually acceptable compromise." Lastly, Senate consent would be required for appointment of justices to the Supreme Court of Canada, officers, directors, or members of any federal Crown corporation, board, commission, agency, or tribunal "having a regional impact." Preston Manning, Reform Party leader, illustrated the effect of the proposed constitutional amendment: "In the view of western Reformers, if the Senate deadlocked over a bill like the Petroleum Administration Act, which was the centrepiece of the national energy program, and could find no way to reconcile the conflicting interests, it would be better for Canada if the legislation was not passed than to have discriminatory legislation passed."[127] This was

---

125 Boyer, *Our Scandalous Senate*, 340; Tom Flanagan, *Harper's Team: Behind the Scenes in the Conservative Rise to Power* (Montreal and Kingston: McGill-Queen's University Press, 2013), 13.

126 Canada, *Debates* (No. 88), 36th Parl., 1st Session (20 April 1998) 5814.

127 Ibid.

to be a powerful Senate. Nor would it be captive of party interests – free votes were expected to be the rule. Though much of the Reform model is drawn from the American experience, Reformers seemed to have overlooked the highly partisan U.S. record.

3. The U.S. Senate: Blocking Change

As in Canada, the delegates at the Philadelphia Convention spent a disproportionate amount of time deliberating on the frame of their new Senate.[128] Also, as in Canada, the compromise between large and small states was critical to the success of the enterprise.[129] The resulting plan, which clearly influenced the Canadians at Confederation, adopted representation by population in the lower chamber and equal representation of states in the upper chamber in order to shield the smaller states from the power of the larger. Unanimous consent of all of the states presumably would be required to deviate from the principle of "equal suffrage in the Senate" (the default rule for amendment otherwise being the consent of three-fourths of the states in Article V).

Appointment to the Senate was accompanied by an unusually lengthy tenure. At a time when the usual practice was to have representatives elected annually, new senators would "enjoy unprecedentedly long, six-year terms."[130] No property qualification was included, though candidates had to be at least thirty years of age (in contrast to the House of Representatives minimum of twenty), a citizen for at least nine years, and an inhabitant of the represented state.[131]

Senators were to be chosen by state legislatures.[132] Madison maintained that this would grant to states "agency in the formation of the

---

128 Elaine K. Swift, *The Making of the American Senate: Reconstitutive Change in Congress, 1787–1841* (Ann Arbor: University of Michigan Press, 1996), 9. They "spent more time and energy deliberating on the Senate than on any other single institution or issue, devoting most of the first seven critical weeks to the upper house and thereafter, though more scattered, the equivalent of another week or two of consideration. In contrast, they focused on the House, executive, and judiciary for a few weeks each, at most, and spent even less time on such vital issues as sectionalism and slavery" (ibid., 9).

129 Jack N. Rakove, *Original Meanings: Politics and the Ideas in the Making of the Constitution* (New York: Random House, 1996), 58.

130 Swift, *Making of the American Senate*, 49.

131 US Constitution, art 1, s 3, cl 3.

132 US Constitution, art 1, s 4, cl 1.

federal government" (what Christopher Dunkin had wished for at Confederation).[133] Like arguments for sectional representation in the Canadian Senate, the scheme would act as a palliative to smaller states being swamped by larger ones with a preponderant voice in the lower house. Otherwise, warned Noah Webster, larger states "would gradually annihilate the small states; and finally melt down the whole United States into one undivided sovereignty."[134] The edifice began to crumble as senators failed, first, to follow instructions from state legislatures and, second, when candidates began canvassing voters for their support.[135] This was a tactic made famous by Republican upstart Abraham Lincoln, when he faced off against incumbent Democrat Stephen Douglas in seven debates "before huge, ardent audiences" throughout Illinois in 1858.[136] Such practices gave way to proposals, by the 1880s, for popular election of senators. The prevailing fear in the late nineteenth century was that the Senate had become "a bastion of privilege, a millionaires' club."[137] Oregon state legislators were the first to undertake to vote for the candidate with the greatest number of test votes in state primary elections, a practice that became the state's constitutional rule in 1910. By virtue of the Seventeenth Amendment, in 1913, election by the "people" of the state became the nationwide rule, "universaliz[ing] a situation which the majority of state legislatures had already created."[138]

The U.S. Senate's powers, like those of the Canadian Senate, are co-equal to those of the House of Representatives in all respects except for money bills.[139] In addition to having a share in the legislative function, it also shares with the executive branch jurisdiction over the appointment of federal officers, including Supreme Court judges, and over foreign policy, by requiring a two-thirds vote in the making of treaties.[140]

---

133 Alexander Hamilton, James Madison, and John Jay, "No. 62," *The Federalist Papers*, ed. Clinton Rossiter (New York: New American Library, 1961), 377.

134 "A Citizen of America," 17 October 1787, in *The Debate on the Constitution*, part 1, ed. Bernard Bailyn (New York: Library of America, 1993), 138.

135 William H. Riker, "The Senate and American Federalism," *American Political Science Review* 49 (1955): 462–3.

136 Harold Holzer, *The Lincoln-Douglas Debates: The First Complete, Unexpurgated Text* (New York: HarperCollins, 1993), 2.

137 Akhil Reed Amar, *America's Constitution: A Biography* (New York: Random House, 2005), 412.

138 Riker, "Senate and American Federalism," 468.

139 "All bills for raising revenue shall originate in the House of Representatives, but the Senate may propose or concur with amendments, as on other bills' (art 1, s 7, cl 1).

140 US Constitution, art 2, s 2, cl 2.

The U.S. Senate also serves a circumscribed judicial function, limited to sitting as a court for the trial of impeachments.[141]

Checking Deficient Legislative Wisdom

The idea of mixed government, together with the separation of powers, shaped thinking about North America's first Senate. The English experience may have been viewed as inapt, what with no property qualifications, the continual turning over of Senate membership, and no distinct class interests to be set off against the House of Representatives. It turns out, however, that Britain's House of Lords was ever-present in the framers' minds.[142] The upper chamber was conceived principally as a means of curbing "pure democracy" – the "monuments to deficient wisdom" that sat in the lower house. As Madison put it, this was a body that would prove to be a "salutary check" on "the impulse of sudden and violent passions" of popular assemblies "seduced by factious leaders into intemperate and pernicious resolutions." What could be worse than the lack of constancy in the law, in the ever-changing mutability of "even good measures," "inconsistent with every rule of prudence," asked Madison.[143] The Senate would offer a "cool and deliberate sense" of propriety, a "temperate and respectable body of citizens" that would "check the misguided career and ... suspend the blow mediated by the people against themselves." This was to be an aristocratic assemblage of the best men, then, with sufficient experience and longevity to prevent the people from "errors and delusions."[144]

It is no coincidence that Madison defended his plan for a Senate at the 1787 convention in the very same terms he used in his famous "Federalist No. 10," addressing the problem of "faction." As discussed in chapter 1, Madison sought not to cure factionalism (it was incurable, he concluded) but to check it, by means of a constitutional design that

---

141 James Bryce, *The American Commonwealth* (London: Macmillan, 1891), 1:93.

142 Swift, *Making of the American Senate*, 20; Gordon S. Wood, *The Creation of the American Republic, 1776–87* (Chapel Hill: University of North Carolina Press, 1969), 554.

143 Hamilton, Madison, and Jay, *Federalist Papers*, 386, 379–80, 378–9, 380. As David Smith maintains in the Canadian context, two heads are better than one. A second chamber "doubles the security of the people, by requiring the concurrence of two distinct bodies in schemes of usurpation or perfidy," in Smith, *Canadian Senate in Bicameral Perspective*, 380.

144 Hamilton et al., *The Federalist Papers*, 380, 384.

divided government and separated branches. This is how he expressed himself on the Senate issue to the delegates in Philadelphia:

> In all civilized Countries the people fall into different classes havg. a real or supposed difference of interests ... There will be particularly the distinction of rich & poor ... An increase of population will of necessity increase the proportion of those who will labour under the hardships of life, & secretly sigh for a more equal distribution of its blessings. These may in time outnumber those who are placed above the feelings of indigence. According to the equal laws of suffrage, the power will slide into the hands of the former ... symptoms of a leveling spirit, as we have understood, have sufficiently appeared in a certain quarters to give notice of the future danger.[145]

By invoking the discourse of faction, passion, and tyranny, it is a fair assessment to claim, as has Swift, that the framers were intent on creating an "American House of Lords."[146] But the proposal went further. It was more about "restraining and separating political power."[147] To be sure, the scheme would grant to states some "agency" in the formation of federal law.[148] It would not be just that, however. This was a chamber that would protect the interests of the minority from the majority's penchant for economic levelling. "Those who framed the document," argues Levinson, "and those who venerate it today, are fundamentally fearful of change and are willing to pay a high price to prevent what they would deem to be unfortunate changes."[149]

It was denied, however, that the Senate would be able to transform itself into "an independent and aristocratic body."[150] It would have no "authority as to awe or influence the House of Representatives," it was

---

145   Max Farrand, *The Records of the Federal Convention of 1787*, revised ed., volume 1 (New Haven: Yale University Press, 1966), 422–3.

146   Swift, *The Making of the American Senate*, 47.

147   Wood, *The Creation of the American Republic*, 559.

148   Hamilton, Madison, and Jay, "No. 44," *Federalist Papers*, 287. This is reminiscent of Madison's "partial agency" that Dennis Baker resurrects in the Canadian context and is discussed in chapter 3. See Dennis Baker, *Not Quite Supreme: The Courts and Coordinate Constitutional Interpretation* (Montreal and Kingston: McGill-Queen's University Press, 2010), 56.

149   Sanford Levinson, *Our Undemocratic Constitution: Where the Constitution Goes Wrong (and How We the People Can Correct It)* (New York: Oxford University Press, 2006), 35.

150   Hamilton, Madison, and Jay, *Federalist Papers*, 389.

claimed.[151] Yet it seems inevitable that things would turn out just that way. According to de Tocqueville, the mid-nineteenth-century U.S. Senate comprised the "elite of the nation" – a laudatory outcome – a large portion of whom are "celebrities of America." In contrast to the more raucous House, he credited this result to the method of indirect election in state legislatures. Popular will passed through states, resulting in a body comprising only those with "elevated thoughts" and "generous instincts."[152] By the late nineteenth century, Bryce would observe that the "Senate now contains many men of great wealth."[153] Today, the Senate continues to be described, as it was in the late nineteenth century, as "a millionaires' club."[154] The movement towards direct election of senators – a move that Stephen Harper hopes to emulate in Canada – generated bastions of independent and forcefully legitimate authority, not only as against the House of Representatives but also as against the centrifugal tendencies of state governments.[155] This has precipitated leading Conservatives in the Tea Party movement to call for the repeal of the Seventeenth Amendment and to restore power to state legislatures to appoint senators.[156] In sum, the U.S. Senate has emerged as one of the most powerful upper houses in the bicameral world – the Australian Senate following a close second.

The Australian Senate apportions seats according to the principle of equal state representation. It is as co-equal to its lower house as, in theory, the Canadian Senate is to the House of Commons. Despite equal apportionment, the Australian Senate is a house divided along party lines – it is not a house that represents states or gives voice to their concerns,[157]

---

151 "Answers to Mason's 'Objections' I," by "Marcus," attributed to James Iredell, 20 February 1788, in Bailyn, *Debate on the Constitution*, 369.

152 Alexis de Tocqueville, *Democracy in America*, trans. Harvey C. Mansfield and Delba Withrop (1835; Chicago: University of Chicago Press, 2000) 191–2.

153 Bryce, *American Commonwealth*, 116.

154 Amar, *America's Constitution*, 412–13; Sanford Levinson, *Framed: America's 51 Constitutions and the Crisis of Governance* (New York: Oxford University Press, 2012), 138.

155 Amar, *America's Constitution*, 414; Riker, "Senate and American Federalism."

156 David Schleicher, "States' Wrongs," *Slate*, 27 February 2014, www.slate.com/articles/news_and_politics/jurisprudence/2014/02/conservatives_17th_amendment_repeal_effort_why_their_plan_will_backfire.html.

157 Douglas Brown, Herman Bakvis, and Gerald Baier, "The Senate in Australia and Canada: Mr Harper's 'Senate Envy' and the Intra vs Interstate Debate," in *The Federal Idea: Essays in Honour of Ronald L. Watts*, ed. Thomas J. Courchene, John R. Allan, Christian Leuprecht, and Nadia Verrelli (Montreal and Kingston: Institute of Intergovernmental Relations / Queen's School of Policy Studies / McGill-Queen's University Press, 2011), 503.

much like the Canadian Senate. No matter what the intention of Senate reformers in Canada, there is little reason to think that a reformed Senate would not also give rise to similar party division[158] – any other outcome is "illusory."[159] Because Australian senators have been elected since 1948 in accordance with a system (proportional representation via single transferable vote) different from that used in the lower house, small parties and independent senators have often held the balance of power, resulting in more division and gridlock between the two houses. Interestingly, the resulting loss of government control over the upper chamber has resulted in greater Senate legitimacy. Coupled with expansive legislative authority, Australian design has resulted in one of the most powerful upper chambers in the world of federalism, second only to that of the United States.[160]

Empirical Lessons

The ingredient common to bicameralism in both the U.S. and Australian systems is the muscular role played by their upper chambers. In game theoretic terms, they perform the role of what Tsebelis calls "institutional" veto player. Each system produces a high degree of policy stability by constitutionally mandating a larger number of veto players, narrowing the "winset" of agreement required to upset the status quo. This is more onerous than other parliamentary systems with highly concentrated authority, such as those in the UK or in Canada. In typical parliamentary systems there is much greater capacity for a single party or coalition of parties to control the agenda, in which case, veto positions are less numerous or less effective. It is easier, that is, to diverge from the status quo where there are fewer or weaker players than in those regimes with a multiplicity of them.[161]

Constitutional design in the United States is meant precisely to prompt a multiplicity of veto points. Bicameralism together with presidentialism, staggered and non-uniform electoral cycles, ensures

---

158   Smith, *Canadian Senate in Bicameral Perspective*, 104.

159   Peter H. Russell, *Two Cheers for Minority Government: The Evolution of Canadian Parliamentary Democracy* (Toronto: Emond Montgomery, 2008), 117 .

160   Campbell Sharman, "The Representation of Small Parties and Independents in the Senate," *Australian Journal of Political Science* 34 (1999): 353–61.

161   George Tsebelis, *Veto Players: How Political Institutions Work* (Princeton, NJ: Princeton University Press, 2002), 19, 21, 2.

that deviations from the status quo are difficult to achieve. Chafetz writes that with power shared among many different constituencies, divided government is "baked into our constitutional structure." "Unified government," he observes, "will be the exception."[162]

Conventional wisdom suggests that divided government is facilitated in the United States by the separation of powers, where the president may be from one party and the majority in Congress from another, making it harder to enact laws.[163] According to David Mayhew's pioneering work, divided government along these lines is not the cause of gridlock in the United States. Mayhew observed that the legislative output of governments elected from 1946 to 1990 did not differ in the production of "important laws" under divided or unified regimes. Mayhew did not account, however, for legislation that was introduced but failed to pass (the "denominator" problem). That is, he isolated legislative outputs but not inputs. Aiming to fill this gap, Edwards, Barrett, and Peake incorporate into their analysis "seriously considered bills that did not become law." They find that potentially important measures fail in times of divided government, when the president's administration opposes adoption, as compared to periods where government is unified. "The pre-Mayhew conventional wisdom," they observe, "is correct: *divided government inhibits the passage of important legislation.*"[164]

Congress is treated as unicameral in many of these studies – intra-branch conflict between Senate and House simply is assumed away.[165] Binder's empirical analysis isolates ideological diversity within Congress as a determinant of gridlock and finds that the greater the distance between House and Senate, the greater the likelihood of its arising.[166] Though distance may not be determined entirely by party division – personal preferences of individual legislators

162 Chafetz, "Phenomenology of Gridlock," 2077.
163 George C. Edwards III, Andrew Barrett, and Jeffrey Peake, "The Legislative Impact of Divided Government," *American Journal of Political Science* 41 (1997): 552.
164 Ibid., 550, 557, 562 (emphasis in original).
165 Sarah A. Binder, "The Dynamics of Legislative Gridlock, 1947–1996," *American Political Science Review* 93 (1999): 522.
166 Ibid., 528. This also is Tsebelis's conclusion. The greater the ideological distance between veto players, he writes, the less likelihood there is of departing from the status quo, in Tsebelis, *Veto Players*, 185.

may also be important[167] – partisan disagreement between legislative chambers is a reliable indicator of the degree to which laws get passed.[168]

Mayhew's recent work parses differences between House and Senate in the treatment of 184 different presidential-led initiatives in the post-war era. He finds that neither chamber has been "chief blocker" of presidential plans – each has "served as nearly equal-opportunity blockers," in spite of the Senate's widespread reputation for being more obstinate and conservative than the House. The U.S. Senate tilts in no discernible partisan direction, Mayhew concludes, but it does tilt towards the "status quo side." It has been more interested in preserving the status quo than even the House – it is the most likely "blocker of a proposed move away from policy stability," he finds.[169] So it turns out that the U.S. Congress is working just as it should, making legislative change difficult, just as the Constitution intended.[170]

In Australia, where the Senate is elected and also constitutionally powerful, we find similar results. Comparing a nine-year period where the Senate was not under government control (1996–2005) with a thirty-month period when the Senate and House were of the same party (2005–7), Bach finds that the total share of House bills that passed without amendments or requests for amendments from the Senate declined by 70 per cent (from 30.8 per cent to 11.9 per cent) during the period of unified government. When of the same party, Bach concludes, the Australian Senate proved to be "much more accommodating and cooperative."[171]

What these analytical and empirical observations confirm is that institutionalizing a powerful veto player has the effect of making

---

167 Manabu Saeki, "Gridlock in the Government of the United States: Influence of Divided Government and Veto Players," *British Journal of Political Science* 39 (2009): 587–607.

168 James R. Rogers, "The Impact of Divided Government on Legislative Production," *Public Choice* 123 (2005): 217–33.

169 David R. Mayhew, *Partisan Balance: Why Political Parties Don't Kill the U.S. Constitutional System* (Princeton, NJ: Princeton University Press, 2011), xvii, 162.

170 David C.W. Parker, "Review of Partisan Balance: Why Political Parties Don't Kill the U.S. Constitutional System," *Forum* 9, no. 3 (2011): article 11.

171 Stanley Bach, "Senate Amendments and Legislative Outcomes in Australia, 1996–2007," *Australian Journal of Political Science* 43 (2008): 421. These results are not unlike those MacKay generated regarding the Canadian Senate from 1867 to 1924, in MacKay, *Unreformed Senate of Canada*, 137.

policy reform difficult.[172] Preservation of the status quo – making laws harder to enact – might seem to be in accord also with the sentiments of Canadian framers. They did not intend the Senate, however, to stand in the way of the "deliberate and understood wishes of the people."[173] The Canadian Senate mostly has gotten out of the way. At most, it has caused delay but not obstruction. It also has caused a great deal of public embarrassment.

4. Return to the Bumpy Road: The Harper Reforms

Under Construction: Myriad Bills

Senate reform proposals initiated by the Harper government were mostly in keeping with its Reform antecedents but with one principal difference: no formal amendment to the Constitution was contemplated. After several failed attempts at constitutional reform (the Meech Lake and Charlottetown Accords), accompanied by widespread feeling of constitutional exhaustion, the first Conservative minority government in 2006 abandoned any hope of securing Senate reform through formal constitutional change. This amounted to a repudiation of Reform Party insistence that Senate reform be taken up only if the provinces and the people so desired it.

Instead, Senate reform would be pursued via more modest, seemingly non-constitutional means. As part of its commitment to democratic reform, the Conservative Party declared in 2006 that it would "creat[e] a national process for choosing elected Senators from each province and territory" and would propose "further reforms to make the Senate an effective, independent, and democratically elected body

---

172 This has not stopped the United Kingdom, however, from contemplating election of the House of Lords. The Wakeham Commission recommended a partially elected upper house – see United Kingdom, Royal Commission on the Reform of the House of Lords, *A House for the Future* (chair: Lord Wakeham), January, 2000, chaps 11 and 12, https://www.gov.uk/government/publications/a-house-for-the-future-royal-commission-on-the-reform-of-the-house-of-lords – which would not "challenge the ultimate authority of the House of Commons" (ibid., 97), while the Mackay report (1999) offered a number of different electoral options. While hereditary peerages have been phased out, there is no consensus on how to move forward, though, according to McLean, the political parties continue to "edge toward election," in McLean, *What's Wrong with the British Constitution*, 239.

173 Canada, *Parliamentary Debates on the Subject of the Confederation*, 36.

that equitably represents all regions."[174] Soon after assuming power, the Conservatives moved modestly by introducing Bill S-4 in the Senate, limiting the terms of new senators to renewable eight-year terms.[175] Prime Minister Stephen Harper defended his choice of eight-year term limits in an exceptional appearance before a Senate special committee. Harper explained that eight-year terms neatly coincided with the length of two consecutive majority governments. This was an amendment in respect of the Senate, he maintained, that could be secured unilaterally by the federal government.[176] This is what the 1984 Molgat-Cosgrove Report also envisaged: nine-year fixed terms instituted without the necessity of seeking provincial consent.[177] The length of the proposed term did not vary wildly with the average tenure – about ten years – for sitting senators.[178]

Two different Senate committees examined Bill S-4. The first, the Special Committee on Senate Reform, pronounced the proposed bill constitutional under section 44 of the amending formulae as it concerned an amendment regarding the Senate not mentioned among the subjects listed in sections 41 and 42.[179] This was precisely the

---

174 Conservative Party of Canada, "Federal Election Platform 2006," 44, www.cbc.ca/canadavotes2006/leadersparties/pdf/conservative_platform20060113.pdf. The 2011 election platform promised to "re-introduce and pass legislation setting term limits for senators; continue to encourage the provinces to work with us to establish a democratic process for selecting senators; appoint those who are selected through democratic processes; and in provinces that do not take us up on our offer, we will fill Senate vacancies with individuals who support our Senate reform goals, including our goal of an elected Senate." See Conservative Party of Canada, "Here for Canada," 63, www.conservative.ca/media/2012/06/ConservativePlatform2011_ENs.pdf.

175 Bill S-4, section 29 (introduced 30 May 2006). It died on the order paper at the conclusion of the first session of the 39th Parliament on 14 September 2007.

176 Senate of Canada, "Proceedings of the Special Senate Committee on Senate Reform," 2:7, 2:11. Prime Minister Harper testified before the Special Senate Committee on Senate Reform that the "formula says that the Constitution of Canada in respect of the Senate can be amended by the Houses of Parliament with four exceptions and this is not one of them" (2:11).

177 Canada, *Report of the Special Joint Committee of the Senate and House of Commons on Senate Reform* (chairs: Gildas Molgat and Paul Cosgrove) (Ottawa: Queen's Printer, 1984), 36.

178 Attorney General of Canada, "Factum in the Matter of a Reference concerning Reform of the Senate," 29 July 2013, 46, http://www.macleans.ca/wp-content/uploads/2013/07/SCC-35203-Factum-Attorney-General-of-Canada.pdf.

179 Senate of Canada, Special Senate Committee on Senate Reform, *Report on Bill S-4, An Act to Amend the Constitution Act, 1867 (Senate Tenure)*, October 2006, www.parl.gc.ca/Content/SEN/Committee/391/refo/rep/rep01oct06-e.htm.

prime minister's view. The Senate Standing Committee on Legal and Constitutional Affairs took the opposite view: eight-year terms were too short and fifteen-year terms were more likely to withstand constitutional scrutiny. The committee maintained that the Supreme Court of Canada's decision in the Upper House Reference remained "good law," even though overtaken by the 1982 amendments, and that the prudent course of action was to refer the question of length of Senate tenure to the Supreme Court of Canada.[180] The Harper government later introduced other versions of the Senate tenure bill. Bill C-19 limited senators to single, non-renewable eight-year terms,[181] while Bill S-7 reiterated the terms of Bill C-19,[182] and Bill C-10 was a carbon copy of Bill S-7.[183]

The government concurrently pressed ahead with the other plank of its Senate reform package, namely, consultative elections.[184] Bill C-43 drew on the workings of the Canada Elections Act (CEA), incorporating rules for counting of votes, third-party advertising, and financing rules all under the supervision of the CEA's chief supervising officer. The object of the Act was to lay down a method for "ascertaining the preferences of electors in a province ... within the existing process of summoning senators." The most constitutionally objectionable feature of the bill was that it entitled the governor general (Cabinet acting under the direction of the prime minister) to *order* that consultative elections be held in conjunction with either a federal or provincial election.[185] Though the elections had the appearance of being merely consultative, the proposed legislation looked like a plan

---

180 Standing Senate Committee on Legal and Constitutional Affairs, *Thirteenth Report*, 12 June 2007, www.parl.gc.ca/Content/SEN/Committee/391/lega/rep/rep13jun07-e.htm.

181 Bill C-19 (introduced 13 November 2007) died on the order paper at the conclusion of the second session of the 39th Parliament on 7 September 2008 in advance of the federal election.

182 Bill S-7 (introduced 13 November 2007) also died on the order paper at the conclusion of the second session of the 39th Parliament on 7 September 2008 in advance of the same federal election.

183 Bill C-10 (introduced 29 March 2010) died on the order paper at the conclusion of the 40th Parliament.

184 Bill C-43, the Senate Appointment Consultation Act, received first reading on 13 December 2006 but did not progress beyond this stage.

185 Bill C-43, ss 12 and 13: "The Governor in Council may order the consultation of the electors of one or more provinces in relation to the appointment of senators to represent those provinces."

to force elections down the throats of unwilling premiers. This was a form of unilateralism not easily tolerated under the existing division of powers.

A few short years later,[186] Bill S-8 was introduced and adopted a more relaxed and so less constitutionally problematic approach. No less detailed in its framework – this time election rules appeared as a schedule to the main bill – it was offered as a form of "guidance" and so weakened the impression that this was meant to be federal diktat. The bill acknowledged that provincial Cabinets would determine whether and when a consultative election would be held. The prime minister was obliged to "consider" nominating senators from the list of names submitted to him by the province as a result of the consultation.[187] Both limbs of the Senate reform plan – terms limits and consultative elections – were conjoined in Bill C-7, the Senate Reform Act, introduced in the House on 21 June 2011. Senate appointments were extended to nine years, and the election process, as outlined in Bill S-8, was attached by way of a schedule to the act.

The Quebec government argued that both consultative elections and nine-year term limits were contemplated by the Constitution's general amending formula and so required, at a minimum, the participation of seven of ten provinces representing more than 50 per cent of the Canadian population. The Quebec Court of Appeal, responding in October 2013 to questions put to it by the Quebec government, unanimously agreed. It is the "method" of selecting senators that is contemplated in section 42(1)(b) of the amending formulae, not merely the formal power of the governor general to summon qualified persons to sit in the Senate. "Selection" includes to the "process leading to appointment."[188] Given the elaborate detail

---

186 Bill C-20, identical to Bill C-43, was introduced the following year (13 November 2007), but died at the end of the second session of the 39th Parliament on 7 September 2008.

187 Bill S-8, section 3: where "a province or territory has enacted legislation that is substantially in accordance with the framework set out in the schedule, the Prime Minister, in recommending Senate nominees to the Governor General, must consider names from the most current list of Senate nominees selected for that province or territory."

188 *Reference re Senate Reform*, para 50. The Quebec Court of Appeal quoted at length, on this point, from Charles-Emmanuel Côté, "L'inconstitutionnalité du projet d'élections fédérales sénatoriales," *Revue québécoise de droit constitutionnel* 3 (2010): 83.

contained in the bill – having "all the attributes of a law regulating elections" – "this was no mere consultative process," the Court reasoned.[189]

With authority now in doubt more than ever, and controversy raging over Senate appointees abusing their privileges, the Harper government referred six questions to the Supreme Court of Canada in February 2013.[190] The federal government asked whether it could unilaterally limit senators' terms (anywhere from eight to nine years and for fixed or renewable terms) and enact enabling legislation, including framework electoral legislation, to facilitate provincial consultative elections. The federal government added questions on removal of the 1867 Act's archaic property and minimum wealth qualifications and, though this does not appear to be a part of the Harper government's agenda, whether the general or unanimous consent of the provinces was required for abolition.

Be Prepared to Stop: The Reference

The Supreme Court had been asked about the amending formulae once before. In the Quebec Secession Reference, the Court was asked to rule on the constitutionality of a unilateral declaration of independence by the province of Quebec. Of course, such a declaration would run afoul of the amending formulae, the Court concluded, but the justices never discussed which of the formulae applied, only that an amendment to the Constitution was required.[191] On this occasion, the Court would have to parse the formulae in order to answer the questions asked.

Two broad approaches would be available to the Court (I offer a third approach in the last part of this chapter). The first is what we might call a "textualist" reading: there are no qualifications to section 44 (the federal "unilateral" formula) beyond those mentioned expressly in sections 41 and 42. These are the matters deemed by the framers to concern the "fundamental features and essential characteristics" of

---

189 *Reference re Senate Reform*, para 68
190 "In the Matter of a Reference by the Governor in Council concerning Reform of the Senate, as Set Out in Order P.C. 2013-70, dated February 1, 2013," www.scc-csc.gc.ca/case-dossier/info/sum-som-eng.aspx?cas=35203.
191 *Reference re Secession of Quebec* [1998] 2 SCR 217, para 84.

the Senate that require provincial participation. The second is what we might call a "normative" reading that looks to pre-1982 Supreme Court decisions to inform the amending formulae's textual directives. In this reading of Part V, section 44 is qualified by the federal principle, requiring provincial consent for those changes affecting the Senate's capacity to represent the regions and minorities and to serve as a chamber of sober second thought. These would be functions caught by the "fundamental features and essential characteristics" previously identified by the Supreme Court in the 1979 Upper House Reference. We might respectively characterize these contrasting approaches, drawing on John Whyte, as those of "black letter" constitutional lawyers as opposed to those guided by the "spirit of the Constitution."[192]

These interpretive choices help to explain the conflicting Senate committee reports regarding Bill S-4 (proposing eight-year term limits). The Special Committee on Bill S-4, reporting in October 2006, heard mostly from witnesses who favoured a textual approach. The normative account found little support among the experts the committee chose to consult. The committee concluded that there was no need for additional constitutional clarity by referring the matter to the Supreme Court and, instead, recommended that reforms be pursued under section 44. By contrast, the "overwhelming weight of testimony" before the Standing Committee on Legal and Constitutional Affairs, reporting in June 2007, described the Upper House Reference as remaining "good law – that section 44 had not expanded Parliament's powers but remained the same as it was pre-1982."[193] For instance, Andrew Heard rejected a literal reading of section 44 (which commences with the words "Subject to sections 41 and 42"), because he could not accept that the list of subjects mentioned in those two sections were the only exceptions to section 44.[194] There must be further, unmentioned limits to section 44, and the Upper House Reference provided appropriate

---

192 Canada, House of Commons, Legislative Committee on Bill C-20, "Evidence" (39th Parl., 2nd Sess., 2008), 6:7.
193 Standing Senate Committee on Legal and Constitutional Affairs, *Thirteenth Report*.
194 "The exceptions" to section 44, Heard wrote subsequently, "must, therefore, be more than just those found in sections 41 and 42," in Andrew Heard, "Constitutional Doubts about Bill C-20 and Senatorial Elections," in *The Democratic Dilemma: Reforming the Canadian Senate*, ed. Jennifer Smith (Kingston and Montreal: Institute for Intergovernmental Relations and McGill-Queen's University Press, 2009), 92.

guidance for identifying them, he suggested.[195] Heard is correct – there must be exceptions to section 44 beyond those listed in sections 41 and 42, because the general amending formula is the default rule for all amendments not falling within the scope of things mentioned in section 44 (amendments that concern "the executive government of Canada or the Senate and House of Commons"). It does not follow, however, that section 44 touches upon the Senate only in its "non-essential characteristics" – there is still good reason to think, legally speaking, that upper house criteria have been overtaken by the express limitations on Senate reform found in section 42. As Peter Hogg formulated the point in his testimony before the Special Senate Committee, "I do not think a court will say that subtracted from the power under section 44 are not only the four matters listed in section 42, but also fundamental or essential changes. That would be an odd way of reading the provisions, I think."[196] Nevertheless, the Senate Standing Committee found Heard's logic "compelling" and concluded that consultative elections effected a major change to the Senate's "essential features," invoking the language of the Upper House Reference.[197]

---

195 Senate of Canada, "Proceedings of the Standing Senate Committee on Legal and Constitutional," 23:76. For example, Heard observed there are matters not mentioned as falling within the general formula (section 42) that had been expressly denied to federal authority previously (under section 91[1]), namely extending Parliament's life beyond five years. As this was not included expressly among the six matters listed section 42, then section 44 could not be taken as exhaustive (ibid.). The length of Parliament, however, is included among the democratic rights in the Charter (section 3). No one seriously proposes that an amendment to the Charter's democratic rights would be subject to section 44 and not to the default rule in section 38. With respect, this is no argument for dispensing with the text. Magnet similarly concluded that the Upper House Reference should control interpretation because the Charter (in section 31) was not intended to "extend" legislative powers (ibid., 23:52). But this clause speaks only to the effect of the Charter (Part I) and not to Part V of the Constitution Act, 1982. Magnet concedes this point in passing and so points to the "marginal notes [which] make clear that nothing changes" (ibid.). With respect, again, the marginal notes reveal nothing about a relationship between section 31 of the Charter and section 44.

196 Senate, "Proceedings of the Special Senate Committee on Senate Reform," 4:37. John McEvoy asked precisely this question: whether section 44 was intended to "overcome" the 1978 reference or be interpreted as "consistent" with it. McEvoy concludes, in the face of conflicting 1981 testimony from Jean Chrétien and Roger Tassé, that the "historical evidence may not be as clear" as he would like (ibid., 23:86).

197 Standing Senate Committee on Legal and Constitutional Affairs, *Thirteenth Report*.

Detour Ahead: The Federal and Provincial Arguments

Questions three and four asked the Court whether the federal government had authority under either section 91 of the 1867 Act or section 44 of the 1982 Act, to undertake consultative elections.[198] Section 91 confers on the federal government legislative authority over twenty-nine different classes of subjects and, in the section's opening words, power to make laws for the "peace, order and good government of Canada" not coming within the classes of subjects exclusively assigned to the provinces (in section 92). If authority were derived from the opening words of section 91, this would look less like an amendment to the Constitution. If done pursuant to the federal unilateral amending formula in section 44, then the amending formulae clearly would be in play. Either source could do the requisite work. It is revealing that the federal attorney general placed no reliance on its authority under section 44 in its written argument (factum).[199] Not a lot, however, turned on this distinction.

The federal government was of the view that consultative elections merely committed the prime minister to consider the results of those elections. At most, it amounted to a "constraint" on the prime minister. The prime minister's constitutional discretion, nevertheless, was preserved. Nor did the proposed legislation alter the power of the governor general to "summon qualified persons" to the Senate under section 24. This was a strictly textualist reading of the Constitution.[200]

Most provinces, by contrast, assumed that the sole question was whether the federal plan was authorized by section 44 and that, in answering the question, this authority be read narrowly. Only Alberta[201] and Saskatchewan admitted that authority for consultative elections

---

198 The questions are drafted differently. Question 3 refers to the enactment of legislation under federal supervision to consult provincial populations on their "preferences" (in C-20), while question 4 refers to the enactment of "framework" legislation for consulting provincial populations under provincial supervision (in C-7). Not a lot turns on these distinctions.

199 This is in contrast to its arguments about limiting length of Senate terms, making them non-renewable and removing property qualifications.

200 Attorney General of Canada, "Factum," paras 130, 140.

201 Alberta, "Factum in the Matter of a Reference concerning Reform of the Senate" (2013) paras 30, 36, http://www.international.alberta.ca/documents/AlbertaFactumBackgrounder.pdf.

could be found in section 91.[202] For the other provinces, any law instituting consultative elections would require provincial consent under
the general amending formula (section 38). Typical of this view was
Ontario's submission that "although the Upper House Reference does
not apply directly to section 44, its reasoning remains sound post-1982"
and that the federal government "cannot unilaterally pass an amendment" that "goes beyond "mere housekeeping" and affects matters of
provincial concern.[203] Heard's expert opinion, tendered on behalf of the
Quebec government, summed up the position well: the 1982 amending
formulae not only stipulated limitations on federal unilateral authority but "also added protection for the fundamental characteristics
of the Senate identified by the Supreme Court in the [Upper House]
Reference."[204]

It followed that, for most of the provinces, the general amending
formula would apply to Harper's plan for consultative elections. This
was a simple argument to make: section 42, requiring provincial participation, expressly includes amendments concerning the "method
of selecting Senators." Yet the proposed federal law, in contrast to Bill
C-60 before the Court in the Upper House Reference, did not purport to
be an amendment to the Constitution. Don't be fooled by talk of consultation, warned the provinces, as elections were not meant to be merely

202 Saskatchewan, "Factum in the Matter of a Reference concerning Reform of the
Senate" (2013), para 57, http://www.justice.gov.sk.ca/Senate-Reform-Reference-
Factum.pdf. The amicus curiae appeared to disagree on the question of whether
elections were authorized by section 91 or amounted to an amendment beyond the
unilateral capacity of the federal government to enact. See Amicus Curiae, "Factum
in the Matter of a Reference concerning Reform of the Senate" (2013) paras 99–125,
www.scc-csc.gc.ca/factums-memoires/35203/FM095_Intervener_Attorney-General-
for-Saskatchewan.pdf. If the legislation was authorized by section 91, however,
the amicus were of the view that the requirement that the prime minister "must
consider" those appointees amounted to an unconstitutional fettering of prime
ministerial prerogative (para 124).

203 Ontario, "Factum in the Matter of a Reference concerning Reform of the Senate"
(2013), para 36, www.scc-csc.gc.ca/factums-memoires/35203/
FM075_Intervener_Attorney-General-of-Ontario.pdf.

204 Procureur Général du Quebec, "Factum in the Matter of a Reference concerning
Reform of the Senate" (2013), para 177, www.scc-csc.gc.ca/factums-memoires/
35203/FM085_Intervenant_Procureur-Général-du-Québec.pdf. Every province
but Alberta that weighed in on this question maintained that the Upper House
Reference informed the limits to section 44. New Brunswick made no submission
on this point.

advisory. They were meant to be "an election, full stop."[205] The prime minister would be bound to consider election results and so his discretion would be fettered.[206] Moreover, ignoring the results of a consultative election would undermine the principle of democracy, one of four underlying constitutional principles the Supreme Court identified in the Secession Reference.[207]

Only Alberta and Saskatchewan, as mentioned, were prepared to accept the federal position that consultative elections did not require provincial participation and so could be secured using section 44 or, alternatively, section 91. Alberta's position mirrored the federal one, claiming that constitutional rules remained intact – the governor general continued to have the constitutional authority to "summon qualified persons." There was no constitutional requirement that unilateral initiatives giving rise to a new practice (or "convention") necessitated provincial participation.[208] For Saskatchewan, because elections were merely consultative and non-binding, the federal government had authority to enact the scheme unilaterally under section 91. After all, prime ministers could refuse to follow the election results – no obvious legal remedy would be available if the prime minister did not do so – and the scheme itself would be "subject to repeal or change by subsequent Parliaments."[209]

On the imposition of term limits, almost every province argued that the general amending formula was triggered, requiring the participation of a majority of the provinces. For British Columbia, for instance, a fixed term of any length altered an "essential characteristic" of the Senate and so could not be achieved unilaterally.[210] Alberta strayed from

---

205 Ontario, "Factum," para 60.
206 British Columbia, "Factum in the Matter of a Reference concerning Reform of the Senate" (2013), para 105, www.scc-csc.gc.ca/factums-memoires/35203/FM130_Intervener_Attorney-General-of-British-Columbia.pdf.
207 Newfoundland, "Factum in the Matter of a Reference concerning Reform of the Senate" (2013), para 52, www.scc-csc.gc.ca/factums-memoires/35203/FM030_Intervener_Attorney-General-of-Newfoundland-and-Labrador.pdf; *Quebec Secession Reference* [1998] 2 SCR 217, paras 61–9.
208 Alberta, "Factum," paras 25, 26.
209 Saskatchewan, "Factum," paras 67–8.
210 British Columbia, "Factum," para 97; also Manitoba, "Factum in the Matter of a Reference concerning Reform of the Senate" (2013), para 17, http://www.macleans.ca/wp-content/uploads/2013/08/SCC-Factum.pdf; New Brunswick, "Factum in the Matter of a Reference concerning Reform of the Senate" (2013), para 36, https://archive.org/details/782208-n-b-senate-reference-factum.

its federal ally by maintaining that fixed terms of any length required general provincial consent.[211] By contrast, Ontario took the view that anything less than a fixed term of nine years and, for Saskatchewan, terms of less than ten years – the maximum length of two Parliaments – triggered the general amending formula.[212]

As for Senate abolition, seven of ten provinces were of the view that the unanimous consent of all provinces would be required. For many this was because it would require removing any mention of the Senate in the amending formulae – any amendment of the amending formula requires unanimity (section 41[e]).[213] British Columbia, Alberta, and Saskatchewan – provinces that have been traditionally most interested in Senate reform – were content with the general amending formula applying in the case of abolition,[214] because abolition of the Senate is not listed among the subjects mentioned in section 41 expressly requiring unanimity.[215] The position of these dissenting provinces on the abolition question turned largely on a textual reading. The unanimity formula should be limited only to the list of matters enumerated in section 41 and only if they "clearly come within the list," otherwise, the general amending formula was the default rule.[216]

Implicit in PEI's submission was the converse proposition: that the list of matters enumerated in section 41 was not exhaustive but incorporated amendments to the "basic structure" of the Constitution, though unmentioned.[217] This was the position adopted expressly by the amicus curiae appointed by the Court. Typically, an appellate court might seek out an amicus ("friend of the court") to assist in judicial deliberations by making arguments that otherwise would not be heard by the court. In the Quebec Secession Reference (2013), for instance, because the government of Quebec boycotted the proceedings, the Supreme Court of Canada appointed Quebec City lawyer André Joli-Coeur as amicus curiae to make arguments that would have been made by the

---

211 Alberta, "Factum," para 37.
212 Ontario, "Factum," para 46; Saskatchewan, "Factum," para 37.
213 For example, Ontario, "Factum," para 69; Manitoba, "Factum," para 37.
214 For example, Alberta, "Factum," para 54.
215 British Columbia, "Factum," para 118.
216 Saskatchewan, "Factum," para 116.
217 Prince Edward Island, "Factum in the Matter of a Reference concerning Reform of the Senate" (2013), para 108.

Parti Québécois government.[218] With all ten provinces intervening in the Senate Reference, it is hard to imagine which arguments the Court anticipated it would be deprived of. Nevertheless, on its own initiative, the Supreme Court took the unusual step of appointing two amici, BC lawyer John Hunter, and McGill Dean of Law Daniel Jutras, who jointly submitted a brief to the Court. Abolition, they admit, is "not a matter specifically listed in Part V." However, it would amount to such a "profound constitutional rearrangement" that it would "merit the highest level of consensus." Classifying the amendment as anything other than requiring unanimity is unsatisfying, argued the amici, as it "fails to provide guidance on whether the dismantling of other institutions of governance not specifically listed in Part V – such as the judiciary or the Crown – would similarly trigger the unanimity requirement."[219] This is a curious argument, as the offices of the Queen, governor general, and lieutenant governors, even the "composition of the Supreme Court of Canada," are expressly mentioned in section 41. Abolition of these institutions would automatically trigger unanimity. The "judiciary" otherwise are not included among the matters listed in section 41, so the presumption would be that the default rule – the general amending formula – would apply. The amicus submission renders the general amending formula no longer the default rule and unanimity the general rule, depending on the degree of the significance of the constitutional rearrangement. In this instance the friend of the court, it turns out, was not helpful.

Road Closure: The Supreme Court Decision

In an admirably clear and concise ruling, the Court accepted every single one of the opposing provinces' submissions. The Court rejected adopting a principally textualist approach in favour of an approach that looked to the Constitution's internal "architecture." Any amendment that "engaged" provincial interests – at its origins, the Senate was intended as a "distinct form of representation for the regions" – was beyond federal unilateral capacity, echoing the unpersuasive mantra that the Senate vindicates regional interests. In so doing, the Court replaced the language of "essential features," from the Upper House

---

218   Bruce Ryder, "The Argument of the Amicus Curiae," in *The Quebec Decision: Perspectives on the Supreme Court Ruling on Secession*, ed. David Schneiderman, 77–82 (Toronto: Lorimer, 1999).

219   Amicus Curiae, "Factum," paras 137, 140.

Reference (1979), with that of "fundamental nature."[220] Any changes to the Senate's fundamental nature triggered the general amending formula and the requirement of substantial provincial consent.

The Court declared that "consultative elections would fundamentally alter the architecture of the Constitution" (the heading of one of the sections in the opinion) and that the language of "method of selecting Senators" encompassed "the entire process by which Senators are selected" and "goes beyond the formal mechanism of appointment."[221]

Regarding senatorial tenure, the Court rejected a "narrow textual approach" in favour of an analysis that attended to changes in the "fundamental nature" of the Senate. Even though the imposition of fixed terms may be functionally equivalent to the length of the typical Senate term, such changes engaged the interests of the provinces and so required their consent under the general formula.[222]

Excising the property requirements from the qualifications of senators engaged only the province of Quebec and so could be achieved under the bilateral formula, while the federal government could unilaterally excise the wealth requirements.

Finally, the Court accepted the amicus argument that abolition of the Senate triggered the unanimity requirement. Though abolition "was not on the minds of the framers" of Part V, and so went unmentioned in the list of subjects requiring unanimous consent, such abolition would "alter the structure and functioning of Part V."[223] As it was proposed that the upper house no longer have a role to play in constitutional change, this amounted to an amendment to the amending formulae, necessitating unanimous consent.

There is a significant problem with the Court's and the opposing provinces' position. I confine my remarks here to the question of consultative elections, the principal plank in Harper's Senate reform agenda, though the ruling on term limits also seems overly harsh.[224]

---

220 *Reference re Senate Reform*, paras 27, 52, 77, 79.
221 Ibid., paras 65, 67.
222 Ibid., paras 73, 77, 79, 82.
223 Ibid., paras 101, 106.
224 John Whyte characterizes as amounting to an unconstitutional amendment the requirement that the prime minister "consider" elected senators for appointment. This amounts to the "constitutional introduction of the Prime Minister's nominating power" together with a "textual addition of a constitutionally prescribed step." I do not consider these statutory directives, for reasons explained below, as rising to the level of constitutional amendment. See John Whyte, "The Federal Senate Proposals: A Challenge to Canada's Constitutional Principles," *Revue québécoise de droit constitutionnel* 5 (2013): 77.

The problem is the collective assumption that, by unilaterally facilitating consultative elections, the federal measure would be "entrenched." Entrenchment means that it would be beyond the ability of any future Parliament to ignore or unilaterally repeal the law. As mentioned, under the terms of section 44, Parliament may unilaterally make laws amending its own constitution. This is in contrast to the "general" and "unanimity" formulae, which require proclamations issued by the "Governor General under the Great Seal of Canada" pursuant to resolutions of the Senate and House of Commons together with the requisite number of provincial legislative assemblies. Though styled an "amendment," an enactment authorized by section 44 is merely ordinary law, enacted unilaterally, undone unilaterally, and, therefore, unentrenched. It is not subject to high procedural barriers in order to secure change.[225] This is why the federal government could argue, in the alternative, that Bill C-7 was authorized by section 91, which enables the passage of ordinary federal law.

Unilateral federal amendments are, following Ackerman, examples of normal politics and not moments of "higher lawmaking."[226] Ackerman develops this distinction in order to explain constitutional change outside of the U.S. Constitution's amending formula in Article V. This duality (normal versus higher) will have salience in other comparative constitutional contexts where sub-national approval is a prerequisite to securing constitutional change – where, in other words, mere unilateral declaration by the national sovereign law-making body is insufficient.[227] This is where the distinction between constitutional amendment and "normal" legislation is instructive outside of the Article V context. It follows that it is only an amendment to the Constitution that is entrenched – enacted with the participation of Parliament and the requisite number of provinces – such that it is beyond the capacity of a future Parliament to unilaterally change. Paradoxically, this is

---

225 This is described more particularly as "de facto" entrenchment "in which the possibility of amendment is virtually impossible because of exceptionally high procedural barriers to change." See Melissa Schwartzberg, *Democracy and Legal Change* (Cambridge: Cambridge University Press, 2007), 12.

226 Bruce Ackerman, *We the People: Foundations* (Cambridge, MA: Harvard University Press, 1991).

227 Donald S. Lutz, "Toward a Theory of Constitutional Amendment," in *Responding to Imperfection: The Theory and Practice of Constitutional Amendment*, ed. Sanford Levinson (Princeton, NJ: Princeton University Press, 1995), 264.

what rendered Harper's plan for Senate reform vulnerable. Without seeking to entrench such changes in the Constitution using the general amending formula, it could be that the law would not endure beyond his tenure as prime minister.

Such are the perils of pursuing Senate reform by initiating a top-down alteration in practice (unlike the U.S. experience, which was initiated from the bottom up) that, it was hoped, would evolve into a new constitutional convention. After all, the Harper initiative was not about instantaneously securing Senate reform. Instead, the expectation all along was that a practice would develop over time into a constitutional convention. The Senate bill, observes Walters, was intended to "modify constitutional practice or convention while leaving the *law* of the Constitution untouched."[228] Conventions arise when repeated patterns of behaviour, Jennings writes, "create precedents which others tend to follow, and when they have been followed long enough they acquire the sanctity and respectability of age." It is not sufficient that there be a practice of some duration, for there is also the requirement that those following the rule feel obliged to do so.[229] The hope was that a practice would develop, as it did around indirect election to the United States Senate giving rise to the Seventeenth Amendment to the U.S. Constitution. Similarly, the expectation of Senate reformers was that the practice of Senate elections would prove so popular and commonplace that, not only would a constitutional convention arise,[230] but sufficient consensus could be secured subsequently to amend the Constitution in accordance with the general amending formula. If a highly unusual method to kick-start a convention,[231] there seems to be no constitutional impediment to doing so by statutory declaration of one party.

---

228 Walters, "Constitutional Form and Reform of the Senate," 45.
229 W. Ivor Jennings, *Cabinet Government*, 3rd ed. (Cambridge: Cambridge University Press, 1959), 2, 130.
230 Walters argues that no "true" constitutional convention could arise if it produced an elected but unreformed Senate, in Walters, "Constitutional Form and Reform of the Senate," 49. There are "grave doubts about whether appointing elected senators to an otherwise unreformed Senate would really enhance democracy in Canada" (57). This seems to amount to a new rule against unconstitutional constitutional conventions. The fact is that academics cannot pick and choose what matters rise to convention; instead, the relevant actors do.
231 Heard, *Canadian Constitutional Conventions*, 1–12; Geoffrey Marshall, *Constitutional Conventions: The Rules and Forms of Political Accountability* (Oxford: Clarendon, 1984), 8–10.

It followed that the law would have little practical effect if no provinces, or very few of them, were willing to participate in consultative elections. Provincial governments, upon whose cooperation the proposed scheme depended, could have chosen to cooperate or not, and provincial positions could have evolved from one government to the next. There was, for this reason, much fluidity associated with the initiative. By pursuing non-constitutional means to secure Senate reform, the prime minister could not, and his party may not, have remained in power long enough to ensure that it would stick. It was as if the prime minister had invited the premiers to kick a ball around in his backyard and only the premier of Alberta showed up to play. Even then, Prime Minister Harper inevitably would be moving out and another resident moving in. Without triggering formal constitutional change, the entire plan was vulnerable to reversal in short order. Such was the irony of a prime minister seeking to move Canadian constitutional culture in an American direction with nothing more than a majority in Parliament. If constitutional culture represents widely shared understandings of the relationship between citizen and states and between the institutions of state, something more will be called for.

End of the Road: Misreading the Amending Formulae

Many of the provinces treated an elected Senate as irreversible – a fait accompli. Even the Supreme Court assumed that no future prime minister would "defeat this purpose by ignoring the results of costly and hard-fought consultative elections."[232] This also is the assumption upon which many scholars staked out their positions.[233] It simply was unbelievable, Whyte observed, "that a government would initiate a nonbinding electoral scheme for the Senate" without not being bound by its results.[234] Whyte's analysis is persuasive insofar as the prime minister

---

232 Reference re Senate Reform, para 62.
233 John W. Whyte, "Senate Reform: What Does the Constitution Say?," in The Democratic Dilemma: Reforming the Canadian Senate, ed. Jennifer Smith (Kingston and Montreal: Institute for Intergovernmental Relations and McGill-Queen's University Press, 2009), 107. John Whyte argued forcefully that it "cannot be the case that those seeking to justify an initiative to democratize the Senate can find constitutional justification for their reform through promising never to be bound by the democratic process that they so badly want and that they claim to be so uniquely legitimate" (105).
234 Ibid., 107.

initiating the change continues to wield power – it is less persuasive once he leaves office, particularly if this follows upon a change in the party in power. Walters also argued forcefully that the real purpose of the Senate reform bill was to make it "politically difficult, perhaps even impossible for future prime ministers to depart from" the new practice. It would amount to a "done deal," declared Walters, and would "evaporate" the constitutional right of the provinces to participate in a decision about whether to have an elected Senate.[235] But provincial governments alone would have determined whether the Harper initiative would succeed. The federal principle would not be sidelined. Rather, it was indispensable to the success of the scheme. Despite the use of a "unilateral" amending formula, it simply could not have succeeded unilaterally. An elected Senate could be secured only if a sufficient number of provinces participated, and a future prime minister, of whatever party, was willing to play along. Scholars who are critics of the constitutionality of the Senate reform bill assumed all of this was a foregone conclusion. They forgot that politics would determine this outcome and not law.

There are several additional good reasons not to restrict parliamentary capacity to kick-start innovative constitutional practices via ordinary legislation. This moves us into the realm of normative argument and offers a counter-narrative to the reading offered by the Court and its supporters. First, Canada has burdensome amending formulae – constitutional change is not easy to achieve. It is, in James Bryce's late nineteenth-century nomenclature, a "rigid" constitution in this respect.[236] Because amendment is so difficult to secure, we might want to encourage a reading of the amending formulae that gives it some play around the joints, making experimentation by relevant political actors easier to manage. If one purpose of constitutionalism is to generate an ability to regulate our political lives through law, this should include an ability to reflect upon and even reform self-governing institutions

---

235 Walters, "Constitutional Form and Reform of the Senate," 47, 49, 61. Walters relies on unwritten "constitutional principles" (the "democracy" and "federal" principles) identified in the *Quebec Secession Reference* (1989), to come to this conclusion (ibid., 60). Though the Supreme Court has adopted differing views about the use of these principles, its most recent statements suggest that the use of principles is to be confined to circumstances such as those arising in the context of a threat of unilateral secession by a constituent unit of the federation.

236 James Bryce, *Modern Democracies* (New York: Macmillan, 1921), 2:10.

without too much difficulty. Every constitution, Habermas advises, "is a living project that can *endure* only as an ongoing interpretation continually carried forward" through the guise of legislation.[237]

Second, as the Charlottetown and Meech Lake processes revealed, proposals for meaningful change to Canada's constitutional design are more than likely to fail. This holds true for any future constitutional proposals for Senate reform, including abolition. This helps to explain the Harper government's tepid response to the Supreme Court ruling: no future constitutional change will be contemplated. Whyte acknowledges that the wishes of other constituent units – Quebec's demands, for instance, for further jurisdictional authority over such things as culture, immigration, and foreign affairs – are likely to resurface during negotiations. That such obstructionism could hijack or derail the process, Whyte claims, might be good for us.[238] Failure to grasp the importance of the federal principle at stake in this debate, Whyte maintains, is a failure to grasp the "spirit" of the Constitution and "its fundamental importance to Canada as a good state."[239] It is, however, a recipe for perpetual stalemate. It means being forever stuck with an institution without the requisite legitimacy to "represent" Canadians never mind govern them. Such an interpretive form of constitutional rigidity appears self-defeating. The practical result will be the upkeep of a discredited regime.[240] It is, in short, an indefensible form of gridlock.

Third, Canada's amending formulae are seriously deficient. Only governments are relevant actors in Part V amendments – there is no mention whatsoever of consulting the people, for instance.[241] What our amending formulae contemplate is essentially the same highly undemocratic process as that adopted to amend the Constitution in 1982 and enlisted again by the premiers and prime minister at Meech Lake in 1987. The architects of the 1992 Charlottetown Accord decided that a Canada-wide consultation via referendum was appropriate in light of the Meech Lake Accord's spectacular collapse. Consulting the people then presumably did not

---

237 Jürgen Habermas, *Between Facts and Norms: Contributions to a Discourse Theory of Law and Democracy*, trans. William Rehg (Cambridge, MA: MIT Press, 1926), 126.

238 Whyte, "Senate Reform," 109.

239 Canada, House of Commons, Legislative Committee on Bill C-20, *"Evidence"* (39th Parl., 2nd Sess.) 5:7.

240 See IPSOS, "Most (69%) Canadians Disagree."

241 Alan Cairns, *Charter versus Federalism: The Dilemmas for Constitutional Reform* (Montreal and Kingston: McGill-Queen's University Press, 1992), 88.

run afoul of the constitutional amending formula – at least the Supreme Court of Canada assumed that it did not[242] and would not today.

What options remain open to political actors now that the courts have closed the prime minister's path to Senate reform? Judicial opinion raises doubts about the constitutionality of any tinkering with the Senate. The Quebec Court of Appeal declared that changes to the "process leading to appointment" of senators required broad provincial consent.[243] The Supreme Court of Canada appeared to double down on this point. They declared that the "entire process by which Senators are 'selected'" is constitutionally insulated from change by the general amending procedure.[244] It is hard to see, then, how other forms of consultation – other than informal and non-transparent forms – would also not run afoul of the amending formulae.

This is the problem for Liberal leader Justin Trudeau's proposal – described by many as "bold" and "brave"[245] – of having a non-partisan nominating body recommend names of persons to summon to the Senate.[246] Trudeau describes the process as one that would be developed in consultation with "experts and informed by other non-partisan appointment processes, such as that of the Supreme Court Justices and Order of Canada recipients."[247] Why wouldn't Trudeau's proposal also run afoul of the amending formulae?

A somewhat lively debate ensued, in the days after the Supreme Court released its opinion in the Senate Reference, about whether the ruling precluded Trudeau's consultation initiative. According to the NDP, the Supreme Court opinion precludes the Trudeau plan for consultative panels.[248] Contrariwise, the Liberal Party reading is that an

---

242 *Haig v Canada (Chief Electoral Officer)* [1993] 2 SCR 995.

243 *Reference re Bill C-7*, para 50.

244 *Reference re Senate Reform*, para 65.

245 Tim Harper, "Trudeau Won the Day, But That's It," *Toronto Star*, 30 January 2014; John Ivison, "Timing of Bold Move Curious," *National Post*, 30 January 2014; Jeffery Simpson, "A Senate Idea Worth Considering," *Globe and Mail*, 31 January 2014.

246 Susan Delacourt and Tonda MacCharles, "Liberal Ouster Raises Stakes on Senate Reform," *Toronto Star*, 30 January 2013.

247 Kelly McParland, "Trudeau Gambit Could Use Some Sober Second Thought," *National Post*, 30 January 2013. On the same day as the announcement of his proposal, Trudeau expunged Liberal senators from the Liberal Party parliamentary caucus (something the official opposition New Democrats had earlier proposed). However newsworthy, it did not give rise to similar constitutional problems.

248 Lawrence Martin, "Supreme Court Decision Puts Trudeau in a Bind," *Globe and Mail*, 29 April 2014.

appointments panel is possible, so long as the process is "less formal" (as in, less transparent).[249] When consulted by the Canadian Press, several constitutional experts described the NDP interpretation as "highly doubtful,"[250] because, the experts said, the executive consults on other appointments and has even established advisory panels in the case of judicial appointments. However true, these other appointment processes are not subject to directives outlined in the amending formulae as interpreted by the Supreme Court. In other words, these other appointments are not constitutionally insulated from innovation and experimentation.[251]

It is true that the Supreme Court began its opinion by acknowledging that the Court's conclusions were "tied to specific questions" and that it was not the Court's role to "speculate on the full range of possible changes to the Senate."[252] Yet the Court was not so careful in its reasoning, making entirely plausible the NDP's reading of the decision that precludes even modest changes along the lines of the Trudeau proposal. The Court's incautious and maximalist reading of the amending formulae was to my mind reckless. At the very least, it is unhelpful.

In both the Harper and Trudeau proposals, there remains the problem of pursuing piecemeal reform without thinking more seriously about the relationship between the two houses. In either case, there would be an all-powerful Senate – of either elected officials or appointed distinguished persons – potentially standing in the way of a majority expression of the people's representatives. Under either option, members of the Senate are expected to feel less uncomfortable about stepping on the toes of the lower chamber. There are interlinkages between the upper and lower chambers that these proposals dare not broach, probably because Canadians do not have a clear idea about

---

249 Ibid.

250 Joan Bryden, "Baloney Meter: Trudeau's Senate Plan," National Newswatch, 1 May 2014, http://www.nationalnewswatch.com/2014/05/01/baloney-meter-trudeaus-senate-plan/#.U2I26fldVig. The Canadian Press described the claim as "a lot of baloney" on their baloney meter, meaning that the statement is mostly inaccurate but contains elements of truth (ibid.).

251 The best argument for the constitutionality of the Trudeau proposal runs something like this: irrespective of the amending formula, consulting an advisory panel would not "affect the independence of Senators or otherwise affect the Senate's role as a complementary chamber of sober second thought" (see Reference re Senate Reform, para 88).

252 Reference re Senate Reform, para 4.

what a reformed Senate should look like. Such is the danger of enhancing the legitimacy of the Senate without engaging the citizens and the provinces in advance. It entirely undermines the democratic thrust of the initiative. It looks more like change for its own sake without regard for the impact such a change could have on Canada's constitutional culture.[253]

The Supreme Court ruling in the Senate Reference does have the merit of elucidating aspects of that culture. One could say that the Court was driven to its conclusion about the constitutionality of proposed consultative elections by the Senate's role in Canadian constitutional culture. It was intended to be a "complementary legislative body" with "independence from the electoral process" and not a "perennial rival of the House of Commons."[254] This was to be a body with a defined constitutional role that would "never set itself in opposition to the deliberate and understood wishes of the people."[255] This helps to explain, the Court concludes, why there is no mechanism for deadlock between the two chambers (the Court does not mention section 26 and the potential appointment of extra senators). The proposed consultative elections, they conclude, "would fundamentally modify" Canada's constitutional architecture – it would give the Senate the "democratic legitimacy to systematically block the House of Commons, contrary to its constitutional design."[256]

The Court certainly got much of this right. In practice, the Harper government proposal for Senate reform would result in a serious shift away from a mostly cooperative relationship – occasioning, at most, delay in the legislative agenda – to one of institutional gridlock. The Senate would evolve from being a "complementary legislative body" to a "perennial rival of the House of Commons."[257] This needn't always be the case, however. In periods where the same party controls both

---

253 John Whyte offers the resulting imbalance in favour of a powerful Senate as an argument against Parliament's authority to enact Bill S-8. By contrast, I have argued that this is a matter for the political branches, as instructed by the electorate, to work out amongst themselves. See Whyte, "Federal Senate Proposals," 70–1.

254 *Reference re Senate Reform*, paras 54, 57, 58.

255 Ibid., para 27, quoting John A. Macdonald.

256 Ibid., para 60.

257 *Reference re Senate Reform*, para 58; also Peter Aucoin, Mark D. Jarvis, and Lori Turnbull, *Democratizing the Constitution: Reforming Responsible Government* (Toronto: Emond Montgomery, 2011), 51.

lower and upper houses – where there is the absence of "divided government," so to speak – we might expect less bicameral deadlock. Even then, in circumstances where the upper house does not serve as a confidence chamber there might be a loosening of party control, even party allegiances. An elected senator's institutional loyalty may lie elsewhere than with the prime minister of the ruling party.[258] It is noteworthy that many of the proposals for Senate reform are intended to disrupt rigid party control, by employing different voting mechanisms, attending to the timing of elections, differing geographic bases of representation, and more free votes.[259] The point is not that gridlock is inevitable, only that it is highly plausible (given the U.S. and Australian experiences), and that a discussion about the proper institutional role of each house deserves to be taken up broadly, not via piecemeal reform. The Court might be viewed as having done Canadians a favour – generating an opportunity for sober second thought, we might say. It did more than delay matters, however. It has also tied our hands. Senate reform will continue to be our standing constitutional joke.

Appendix 1: A Note on J.S. Mill and Upper Chambers

Janet Ajzenstat advises that those who contributed to the Confederation debates would have been familiar with the arguments in Mill's *Representative Government* (1910).[260] In Mill's text, she writes, the framers would have found a "classic defence" of the second chamber as a guarantor against "despotism" that complemented well their original expectations for a second chamber.[261] Yet Mill was not that enamoured with second chambers. In the opening of the chapter entitled "Of a Second Chamber," he wrote that he was inclined to think "that if all other constitutional questions are rightly decided, it is but of secondary importance whether the Parliament consists of two Chambers or only of one."[262] That is, if appropriately designed, a single chamber could avoid despotic government without the cumbersome "delay" that would ensue from second chamber review. What Mill sought to

---

258 Docherty, "Canadian Senate," 42.
259 Smiley and Watts, *Intrastate Federalism in Canada*, 133–5.
260 Ajzenstat, "Bicameralism and Canada's Founders," 27n19.
261 Ibid., 7.
262 John Stuart Mill, *Utilitarianism, Liberty, Representative Government* (London: J.M. Dent & Sons, 1910), 324.

prevent was the "evil effect produced upon the mind of any holder of power" of "having only themselves to consult." "It is important that no set of persons should, in great affairs, be able, even temporarily, to make their *sic volo* ["I so order"] prevail without asking any one else for his consent." A second chamber conceivably could act as a "center of resistance" to this form of despotism. Ultimately, for Mill, upper houses were ineffectual to perform this task; instead, the "moderating power in a democratic constitution must act in and through the democratic house."[263]

Mill advances a scheme of proportional representation (PR) so that those who are on the losing side of majority politics ("first-past-the-post") get representation. It would "give reality to the electoral rights of the otherwise virtually disenfranchised minority."[264] Mill had high hopes for the quality of representatives that such a system would attract to stand for election, whose skill and moral power would ensure them an "active part" in public business.[265] It is not within the scope of this discussion to address the merits or demerits of PR. Rather, it is to take from Mill the intuition that it is lower chamber design that should be uppermost in our minds, particularly when the overriding concern in these pages has been the concentration of power in the Prime Minister's Office. "The character of a representative government is fixed by the constitution of the popular House," wrote Mill. "Compared with this, all other questions relating to the form of government are insignificant."[266] It is reform of the constitution of the executive branch, then, that should be priority number one.

263 Ibid., 325–6.
264 Ibid., 262.
265 Ibid., 269.
266 Ibid., 331.

5 Appointing Justices: Supreme Court Nominees and the Press

I share many of the concerns of my colleagues and allies about biased "judicial activism" and its extremes. I agree that serious flaws exist in the Charter of Rights and Freedoms, and that there is no meaningful review or accountability mechanisms for Supreme Court justices.

Stephen Harper[1]

Within one week of the release of the Supreme Court of Canada's decision in the Senate Reference, the prime minister of Canada decided it was an opportune time to tarnish the reputation of the chief justice of the Supreme Court, Beverley McLachlin. The prime minister, working jointly with the Minister of Justice Peter MacKay, decided that she should be politically punished for the Court having handed down a number of embarrassing legal defeats to the government. According to *National Post* columnist John Ivison, this string of defeats was provoking "visceral" "frustration" in the Conservative Cabinet.[2] In addition to the Senate Reference loss, the Court also ruled that the prime minister's nominee, Federal Court of Appeal Justice Marc Nadon tapped to replace retiring Justice Morris Fish from Quebec, was constitutionally ineligible for appointment. According to the Supreme Court's interpretation of criteria laid down in the Supreme Court Act, judges filling Quebec seats on the Court had to be either a Quebec judge (from Quebec superior or appellate courts) or a member of the Quebec bar. Mr Nadon was neither.

1 Stephen Harper, "Why I Hate Gag Laws," *Globe and Mail*, 13 June 2000.
2 John Ivison, "Tories Incensed with Top Court," *National Post*, 1 May 2014.

The Prime Minister's Office (PMO), and later the minister of justice, alleged that Chief Justice McLachlin had acted "inappropriately" by attempting to contact the prime minister about a forthcoming matter before the Court, namely, the eligibility of Justice Nadon for appointment to the Court.[3] The chief justice, however, is routinely consulted about nominees to fill Supreme Court seats. The PMO must have thought that it could cleverly exploit the untransparent, behind-the-scenes intrigue that leads up to a Supreme Court nomination. In a statement released the following day, the chief justice denied that there was ever any attempt to contact the government regarding a pending legal dispute. Instead, the chief justice explained that in July 2013 she sought to "flag" the potential ineligibility of a judge sitting on the Federal Court of Canada to take a Quebec seat.[4] This was three months before any legal action contesting the Nadon nomination was initiated.[5]

It turned out to be a feeble (and feeble-minded) attempt at a political takedown. The prime minister's dates did not match up with the alleged impropriety and the government had never objected to the Chief Justice sitting in on the Nadon hearing. As a consequence of leaked confidential documents, we know that on the list of six candidates circulating to replace Justice Fish, four of those names were Federal Court judges, one of which was Nadon's, all of which were of questionable eligibility.[6] The decision to initiate this little tiff involved a puzzling calculation, particularly in light of the fact that these rulings were issued by a Court stocked with Prime Minister Harper's own nominees. The entirely fabricated quarrel revealed a number of things: the prime minister's vindictive personality, his Reform Party roots, and the weakness of the process he has instituted for the nomination of Supreme Court justices.

Though his allegations about the chief justice's conduct were without factual foundation – indeed, he appeared to climb down from them[7] – from a political point of view, Harper's wariness of the Supreme Court

---

3 Sean Fine, "Harper Says Chief Justice Tried to Discuss Court Case with Him," *Globe and Mail*, 2 May 2014.
4 *Reference re Supreme Court Act*, ss 5 and 6 [2014] 1 SCR 433.
5 Tonda MacCharles, "Stephen Harper Changes Version of Events around Phone Call by Beverley McLachlin," *Toronto Star*, 14 May 2014.
6 Sean Fine, "High-Court Drama," *Globe and Mail*, 24 May 2014.
7 The prime minister admitted that he knew of the eligibility problem and therefore didn't see the need to speak to the chief justice personally when she attempted to contact him (ibid.).

is at least understandable. The Court is unquestionably one of the most powerful institutions in the land. While the judiciary has been policing constitutional limits between the federal and provincial governments since Confederation, the entrenchment of constitutional rights has dramatically increased the judicial role in Canadian public life.[8] This has given rise to what has been called – and these are terms upon which even opposing sides of the ideological spectrum are agreed – a "Charter revolution."[9] An unprecedented focus has been placed on the nine justices who sit on the Supreme Court of Canada, Canada's final court of appeal.

Judicial appointment to high courts in Canada is formally within the jurisdiction of the Crown in Canada (pursuant to section 96). As a practical matter, authority is entirely centralized in the parliamentary executive, namely, in the Prime Minister's Office, with assistance from his Cabinet colleagues (principally, the minister of justice).[10] Though the establishment of a "general court of appeal" is contemplated by the 1867 Act (in section 101), the authority to appoint turns out to be an inheritance of the residue of unfettered discretion associated with the royal prerogative, which included high court appointments, that ultimately passed on to the democratically elected and responsible authority in the House of Commons.[11] Once appointed, judges have security of tenure ("on good behaviour") and a semblance of independence ("salaries are fixed and provided for by Parliament"). These

---

8 It cannot be correct to say, as does Manfredi, that in the pre-Charter era the "only arenas for resolving conflicts among competing policy positions were the legislature and the executive," in Christopher Manfredi, "On the Virtues of a Limited Constitution: Why Canadians Were Right to Reject the Charlottetown Accord," in *Rethinking the Constitution: Perspective on Canadian Constitutional Reform, Interpretation, and Theory*, ed. Anthony A. Peacock (Don Mills, ON: Oxford University Press, 1996), 56. Minorities have had recourse to litigation to promote equality while business actively sought to restrain government regulation under the federal division of powers. See David Schneiderman, "The Old and the New Constitutionalism," in *Re-inventing Canada: Politics for the 21st Century*, ed. Janine Brodie and Linda Trimble (Toronto: Pearson Education Canada, 2003), 246–8.

9 F.L. Morton and Rainer Knopff, *The Charter Revolution and the Court Party* (Peterborough, ON: Broadview, 2000); Lorraine Weinrib, "Canada's Constitutional Revolution: From Legislative to Constitutional State," *Israel Law Review* 13 (1999): 33–50.

10 Irwin Cotler, "Comment juger un juge?," *La Presse*, 4 October 2013.

11 Jacob Ziegel, "Merit Selection and Democratization of Appointments to the Supreme Court of Canada," in *Judicial Power and Canadian Democracy*, ed. Paul Howe and Peter H. Russell (Montreal and Kingston: McGill-Queen's University Press, 2001), 139.

"essential features" of the Supreme Court have been entrenched in the Constitution since 1982.[12]

Until the recent flap over the Nadon appointment, such appointments have flown well below the radar for most of the Supreme Court's life, despite the fact that the Supreme Court's constitutional authority has contributed to shaping Canada's national political conversation.[13] It is surprisingly rare that a Supreme Court decision will define a ballot box question at federal or provincial levels.[14] Little media attention has been paid to judicial appointments, nor have appointments shaped debates within the precincts of Parliament. Conservative legal activists have not successfully organized themselves, as they have in the United States, into peak organizations that mobilize support around like-minded appointees to high court positions.[15] Despite efforts from both left and right wing critics of the Court,[16] there is no viable competing counter-narrative waiting in the wings. Characterization of the Canadian Court as a counter-majoritarian institution simply has not taken hold.[17] It is partly for this reason that appointees have been labelled as non-ideological and apolitical, at least so the legal community maintains. Even Knopff and Morton, critics of the Supreme Court's approach to Charter interpretation, admit that the "'politicization of the judiciary' has not occurred in Canada and does not loom large on the horizon."[18]

---

12 *Reference re Supreme Court Act*, para 94.
13 Numerous instances come instantly to mind, from striking down R.B. Bennett's New Deal legislation to Robert Bourassa's language of commercial signs law.
14 They are not usually "wedge issues" in Canadian political life. See Peter W. Hogg, "Appointment of Thomas A. Cromwell to the Supreme Court of Canada," in *The Democratic Dilemma: Reforming Canada's Supreme Court*, ed. Nadia Verrelli (Montreal and Kingston: McGill-Queen's University Press, 2013), 19. That is not to say that Supreme Court decisions have not befuddled Parliamentarians. See, for example, the Court's ruling in *R v Morgentaler* [1988] 1 SCR 30 (SCC). On this episode, see Janine Brodie, "Choice and No Choice in the House," in *The Politics of Abortion*, ed. Janine Brodie, Shelley A.M. Gavigan, and Jane Jenson, 57–116 (Toronto: Oxford University Press, 1992).
15 Steven M. Teles, *The Rise of the Conservative Legal Movement: The Battle for the Control of the Law* (Princeton, NJ: Princeton University Press, 2008).
16 Joel Bakan, *Just Words: Constitutional Rights and Social Wrongs* (Toronto: University of Toronto Press, 1997); Morton and Knopff, *Charter Revolution and the Court Party*.
17 Florian Sauvageau, David Schneiderman, and David Taras, *The Last Word: Media Coverage of the Supreme Court of Canada* (Vancouver: UBC Press, 2006), 24–6.
18 Rainer Knopff and F.L. Morton, *Charter Politics* (Toronto: Nelson Canada, 1992), 135.

Appointments have served political functions, nevertheless. The constitutionally entrenched presence of three civilian-trained lawyers from Quebec, for instance,[19] and practices regarding provincial and regional representation on the Court,[20] help lend legitimacy to Supreme Court decision-making.[21] Judges also undoubtedly have brought to bear, in their decision-making, political outlooks that, on occasion, have bubbled to the surface. This is more likely to occur in vexing constitutional cases where a high court's freedom to manoeuvre can be characterized as capacious as that of a legislature's.[22] For this reason, one reliably expects Quebec appointees on the Court to decide federalism disputes in ways that preserve jurisdictional autonomy for the provinces, a policing function associated with "classical federalism," though this will not always be the case.[23]

Though calls to reform the appointment process have been longstanding, they intensified with the passage of the Charter of Rights and Freedoms. Now more than ever, judicial authority was actively shaping the Canadian polity (though not as profoundly as some have claimed[24]), hence a closed and secretive process appeared intolerable.

---

19 *Reference Re Supreme Court Act*, para 91.
20 W.R. Lederman, *Continuing Canadian Constitutional Dilemmas: Essays on Constitutional History, Public Law and the Federal System of Canada* (Toronto: Butterworths, 1981), 219. Heard evinces ambivalence about whether these practices have risen to the level of "obligatory" constitutional convention, in Andrew Heard, *Canadian Constitutional Conventions: The Marriage of Law and Politics*, 2nd ed. (Toronto: Oxford University Press 2014), 164.
21 Quebec, *Report of the Royal Commission of Inquiry on Constitutional Problems* (chair: Tremblay, 1956), 3:294; C. Neal Tate and Panu Sittiwong, "Decision Making in the Canadian Supreme Court: Extending the Personal Attributes Model across Nations," *Journal of Politics* 51 (1989): 913. The Supreme Court does not, the Tremblay Commission declared, "enjoy the complete confidence of the people" of Quebec (3:296).
22 Richard A. Posner, *How Judges Think* (Cambridge, MA: Harvard University Press, 2008), 82.
23 It is hard to generate good empirical support for this phenomenon. Russell maintains that Quebec judges were more likely to uphold Quebec lower court decisions as a bloc in the Jehovah's Witnesses cases during the Duplessis era, in Peter H. Russell, *The Supreme Court as a Bilingual and Bicultural Institution* (Ottawa: Queen's Printer for Canada, 1969), 1:203. As an exemplar of a classical-federalist judge from Quebec, see Swinton's discussion of Jean Beetz, in Katherine E. Swinton, *The Supreme Court of Canada and Canadian Federalism: The Laskin-Dickson Years* (Toronto: Carswell, 1990), chap. 9.
24 David Schneiderman and Kate Sutherland, "Conclusion: Toward an Understanding of the Impact of the Charter of Rights on Canadian Law and Politics," in *Charting the Consequences: The Impact of Charter Rights on Canadian Law and Politics*, ed. David Schneiderman and Kate Sutherland (Toronto: University of Toronto Press, 1997), 345.

The "monopoly enjoyed by the executive branch," declared Beatty, "can [no longer] be defended."[25] "At the risk of oversimplification," writes Morton, "Canada now has an American-style Supreme Court with an unreformed British-style appointments system."[26] It was now only a question of when Canada's appointments process would align itself to the new political reality. With the election of Conservative Prime Minister Stephen Harper, a new process of judicial interviews of Supreme Court of Canada nominees before an ad hoc committee of the House of Commons was inaugurated. This has resulted in five nomination hearings since 2006.[27] The committees have no formal constitutional authority, but the process is intended to roughly approximate Senate judicial confirmation hearings in the United States.[28]

---

25 David Beatty, *Talking Heads and the Supremes: The Canadian Production of Judicial Review* (Toronto: Carswell, 1990), 263.

26 F.L. Morton, "Judicial Appointments in Post-Charter Canada: A System in Transition," in *Appointing Judges in an Age of Judicial Power: Critical Perspectives from around the World*, ed. Kate Malleson and Peter H. Russell (Toronto: University of Toronto Press, 2006), 57.

27 Justice Marshall Rothstein was the first nominee to appear before the special committee in March 2006, Justices Karakatsanis and Moldaver appeared jointly in October 2011, Justice Wagner appeared before the committee in 2012, and Justice Nadon, whose appointment was annulled by the Supreme Court of Canada in extraordinary legal proceedings, appeared in October 2014. A sixth nominee, Justice Cromwell, was appointed on 22 December 2008 while Parliament was not in session (it had been prorogued), despite announced plans to have him appear before a special committee (5 September 2008). The House was prorogued at the time because the prime minister's minority government faced a motion of censure initiated by the opposition parties for failing to disclose documents that were demanded by the House of Commons but denied on the grounds of "executive privilege." A seventh nominee, Mr Justice Clément Gascon, was appointed in June 2014 to replace Justice Nadon. In order to expedite the process, the Harper government decided to forego hearings and chose Justice Gascon from a short list provided by the government of Quebec (a process contemplated by the failed 1978 Meech Lake Accord). Stephen Harper's eighth nominee to the Court, Justice Suzanne Côté, also was appointed in November 2014 without appearing before a House of Commons Committee.

28 It should be noted that there are various methods of selection for different U.S. courts. According to Grossman, there is "partisan election, nonpartisan election, executive appointment (with or without legislative confirmation), election by the legislature, and variations of the so-called merit selection or 'Missouri Plan'" entailing a nomination commission and a subsequent uncontested election (more in the nature of a referendum), in Joel B. Grossman, "Paths to the Bench: Selecting Supreme Court Justices in a 'Juristocratic' World," in *The Judicial Branch*, ed. Kermit Hall and Kevin T. McGuire (New York: Oxford University Press, 2005), 145.

The innovation undoubtedly has opened up Supreme Court nominations to greater public scrutiny but according to many in the legal community, it also imperils the prestige and independence of Canada's apex court. After all, justices are not like politicians. They are constrained by techniques associated with legal methods and legal reasoning, typically by having recourse to such things as facts, text, and persuasive precedent.[29] Drawing attention to the discretionary component in judicial decision-making risks attracting politicized portrayals of a partial court, its members seemingly subject to the same vicissitudes as, and no better than, ordinary politicians. To the extent that the media channel the political dimension of judicial decision-making, this further imperils the legitimacy of the Court as impartial and independent.

This chapter examines an innovation that is intended to emulate U.S. constitutional practice. I begin by tracing the evolution of judicial nomination processes to the Supreme Court of Canada, culminating in the new process taken up by Prime Minister Harper since his first appointment of Justice Marshall Rothstein to the Court in 2006. The origins of this policy, I maintain, are traceable to Reform Party proposals (linked with Senate reform plans discussed in chapter 4) intended to emulate U.S. Senate judicial confirmation hearings. The U.S. Senate is constitutionally obliged to provide "advice and consent" on presidential appointments to the U.S. Supreme Court (Article II, section 2, paragraph 2). The utility of such hearings, beginning at least with the confirmation hearing of nominee Robert Bork, has been in doubt for some time, a record that is examined in part 2. In part 3, I turn to the Canadian experience. What utility have Canadian nomination hearings served and what have Canadians learned as a consequence of the new appointment process? By examining print journalism in selected Canadian cities regarding the first five nomination processes, we glean an answer to these questions. The fear among many critics of the new process is that judicial nominations would become politicized. The findings suggest that newspaper coverage has emphasized a "legal frame" (judges "apply" law using the tools of legal reasoning) over a "political" one (judges "make law" using the tools of political bargaining) and

---

29 For discussions about why this is not uniformly the case, see Richard Bellamy, *Political Constitutionalism: A Republican Defence of the Constitutionality of Democracy* (Cambridge: Cambridge University Press, 2007); and Jerome Frank, *Law and Modern Mind* (Garden City, NY: Anchor Books, 1963).

so has turned out to be mostly favourable to the individual nominees and to the Court.[30] It turns out that the more citizens are exposed to the workings of their high court, the more they approve of what they see. Lastly, in part 4, I canvass alternative methods of appointment, ones that are currently employed in other familiar jurisdictions. This comparative exercise, which closes the chapter, is meant to underscore the variety of alternatives available that can improve appointment processes while avoiding pitfalls associated with U.S.-style judicial confirmation hearings.

It is, in some ways, an opportune moment to reconsider once again the nomination process. It seems that the prime minister no longer has an interest in requiring that nominees appear before a special committee of the House of Commons. The nominations of Justices Clément Gascon and Suzanne Côté, both from Quebec, were made without any prior public hearings. This is because, grumbled Minister of Justice Peter MacKay, of the leak of confidential documents concerning the short list of six candidates that resulted in the botched appointment of Marc Nadon.[31] Having failed to tarnish the reputation of the chief justice and having seen the confidential short list leaked afterward, in a fit of spite the government has abandoned its innovative course of action.

The discussion suggests that nomination hearings have not well served those seeking a more open and public Supreme Court appointment process. Instead, there is only the appearance of change – one that leaves the appointment process essentially intact. This might mollify those who have been worried about the politicization of the Court. As the recent spat between the prime minister and chief justice suggests, continued opacity in the appointment process does not serve anyone very well. Thoughtful reform of the appointments process, as in the institutions discussed elsewhere in this book, is overdue.

---

30 This draws on the framing analysis undertaken in Sauvageau, Schneiderman, and Taras, *Last Word*, which contrasts "issue" (here, legal) framing with "strategic" framing. The latter focuses on "words of war and conflict," while the former draws on "the cool and detached discourse of law" (92).

31 Sean Fine, "Harper Appoints New Judge, Passes Over Public Hearing," *Globe and Mail*, 28 November 2014; Peter MacKay, letter to the editor, *Globe and Mail*, 2 December 2014.

1. The Discredited Canadian Process

Granting the governing party exclusive authority to appoint risks rendering Canada's highest court a sinecure for political patronage.[32] Historically there has been a close connection between appointment and affiliation with the political party in power.[33] As regards federal judicial appointment to all levels of court, over the decades "politics was a major factor – if not *the* major factor – in the selection of federal judges in Canada."[34] But political payback has been on the decline. From 1978 to 1985, the Canadian Bar Association (CBA) concluded that "political favouritism has not had an influence on appointments" to the Supreme Court of Canada. The CBA acknowledged, however, that federal ministers of justice "always" give some consideration to political affiliation.[35] This is not to say that high court decision-making in Canada is highly politicized. As mentioned, despite efforts by scholarly critics, and complaints about left-wing bias issuing out of conservative political movements, decision-making by the Supreme Court of Canada generally is portrayed as non-partisan and of a high quality.[36] This is how apex courts around the world, increasingly an audience for the Canadian justices, also appear to view the court's record.[37]

The suspicion of partisanship has been borne out somewhat by a small set of empirical studies. They concern mostly federal judicial appointments across a spectrum of courts, including trial and appellate courts (appointments that are authorized under section 96). Risk's study of appointments between 1945 and 65 revealed that "all but a few

32 William H. Angus, "Judicial Selection in Canada: The Historical Perspective," *Canadian Legal Studies* 3 (1966): 220–51.

33 Martin Friedland, *A Place Apart: Judicial Independence and Accountability in Canada* (Ottawa: Canadian Judicial Council, 1995), 236.

34 Martin Friedland, "Appointment, Discipline and the Removal of Judges in Canada," in *Judiciaries in Comparative Perspective*, ed. H.P. Lee (Cambridge: Cambridge University Press, 2011), 52.

35 Canadian Bar Association, *Report of the Canadian Bar Association Committee on the Appointment of Judges in Canada* (Ottawa: Canadian Bar Foundation, 1985), 57.

36 Irwin Cotler, "The Supreme Court Appointment Process: Chronology, Context and Reform," *University of New Brunswick Law Journal* 58 (2008): 131–2.

37 Claire L'Heureux-Dubé, "Evidence before the Standing Committee on Justice, Human Rights, Public Safety and Emergency Preparedness" (no. 8), 30 March 2004, www.law-lib.utoronto.ca/conferences/judiciary/background.htm; Adam Liptak, "U.S. Court Is Now Guiding Fewer Nations," *New York Times*,17 September 2008.

[appointees] … were affiliated with the party in power at the time they were appointed, and most were actively engaged in politics."[38] This discouraging result was mitigated somewhat by seeking pre-screening advice, after 1967, from the Canadian Bar Association's Judicial Appointments Committee. By 1973, a post in the office of the minister of justice was dedicated to work on candidates' dossiers.[39] Even if the quality of appointments "improved" in the 1970s, Russell and Ziegel observe that, between 1984 and 1988, 47.4 per cent of federal judicial appointments "had a known association with the Conservative Party," then in power under Prime Minister Brian Mulroney.[40] After 1988, modest innovation was instituted in appointments to section 96 courts, other than the Supreme Court. Candidates were to be screened by judicial advisory committees comprising representatives of the bench and bar, in addition to provincial attorneys general and parliamentarians, with the power to rate nominees.[41] After these reforms were instituted, Riddell, Hausegger, and Hennigar observe that of 723 judges appointed from 1989 to 2003, 30.6 per cent were "probable donors to the party that appointed them in the five years prior to their appointment or within the year of appointment."[42] The numbers across both Conservative and Liberal federal administrations were nearly constant.

---

38 Quoted in John Willis, "Methods of Appointing Judges: An Introduction," *Canadian Legal Studies* 4 (1967): 217.

39 Canada, Department of Justice, *A New Judicial Appointments Process* (Ottawa: Ministry of Supply and Services Canada, 1988), 2, 3.

40 Peter H. Russell and Jacob Ziegel, "Federal Judicial Appointments: An Appraisal of the First Mulroney Government's Appointments and the New Judicial Advisory Committees," *University of Toronto Law Journal* 41 (1991): 19. By "known political association," the authors contemplate "major involvement with a party [which] includes running for elected office under the party's banner, serving as a party official or 'bagman,' and active participation in election or leadership campaigns," together with "minor involvement or association with a party includes minor constituency work, financial contributions, and close personal or professional associations with party leaders" (18).

41 Jacob Ziegel, "Judicial Appointments in Canada: The Unfinished Agenda," University of Toronto Faculty of Law, Faculty Workshop, 19 March 2012, 5.

42 Tory Riddell, Lori Hausegger, and Matthew Hennigar, "Federal Judicial Appointments: A Look at Patronage in Federal Appointments since 1988," *University of Toronto Law Journal* 58 (2008): 657. "Probable donors" were judges whose first last and middle name (or middle initial) matched the Elections Canada Contribution to Political Parties list or whose first and last name matched where the name was uncommon. "Possible donors" were those whose first and last name matched but were a "common enough name to leave doubt as to whether the donor was the same person as the appointed judge" (56).

Yet nominees do not simply channel political preferences of the appointing government. In contrast to studies in the United States that employ an "attitudinal model,"[43] which purport to predict judicial outcomes based on the ideology of the appointing president, the policy preferences of the appointing authority is not as reliable a predictor of judicial outcomes in Canada. Alarie and Green find that there is "not at all a strong relationship between the party of the prime minister who appointed the judges and their subsequent voting preferences."[44] Hausegger, Riddell, and Hennigar prefer to rely upon "political affiliation" as a predictor rather than the "party of appointment" in their study of Ontario Court of Appeal decision-making. They find that political affiliation has "some influence" on judicial behaviour in criminal cases.[45] Not only is there a weak connection between purported policy preference and voting outcomes, Canadian Supreme Court justices are likely to agree more often in divisive cases than their U.S. counterparts, and when they do disagree, voting patterns are harder to predict than in the United States.[46] By contrast, Ostberg and Wetstein claim that when the justices disagree, "ideological tensions [as determined by editorial opinion in leading newspapers] play a much stronger role in shaping their voting behaviour."[47] Songer concurs that, in cases where the Court is divided, "the actual behaviour of the justices is related to the party of the appointing prime minister."[48] In a later co-authored study, Songer et al. offer a different conclusion. In contrast to the U.S. data, they write, the party of the appointing prime minister "does not

---

43 Harold J. Spaeth and Jeffrey A. Segal, *Majority Rule or Minority Will: Adherence to Precedent on the U.S. Supreme Court* (Cambridge: Cambridge University Press, 1999); Jeffrey A. Segal and Harold J. Spaeth, *The Supreme Court and the Attitudinal Model Revisited* (Cambridge: Cambridge University Press, 2002).
44 Benjamin Alarie and Andrew Green, "Policy Preference Change and Appointments to the Supreme Court of Canada," *Osgoode Hall Law Journal* 47 (2009): 28; also C.L. Ostberg and Matthew E. Wetstein, *Attitudinal Decision Making in the Supreme Court of Canada* (Vancouver: UBC Press, 2007), 226.
45 Lori Hausegger, Tory Riddell, and Matthew Hennigar, "Does Patronage Matter? Connecting Influences on Judicial Appointments with Judicial Decision Making," *Canadian Journal of Political Science* 46 (2013): 677–8.
46 Benjamin Alarie and Andrew Green, "Should They All Just Get Along? Judicial Ideology, Collegiality and Appointments to the Supreme Court of Canada," *University of New Brunswick Law Journal* 58 (2008): 74.
47 Ostberg and Wetstein, *Attitudinal Decision Making in the Supreme Court of Canada*, 19.
48 Donald Songer, *The Transformation of the Supreme Court of Canada: An Empirical Examination* (Toronto: University of Toronto Press, 2008), 209.

provide a very satisfactory prediction of the career voting patterns of the Canadian justices."[49] The studies offer ambivalent, if not conflicting, results. Almost all are agreed, however, that the diminished salience of ideology to forecast Canadian Supreme Court decision-making, as compared to the U.S. Court, is likely due to the less rigid ideological divide between the principal political parties and a less politically charged appointment process.[50]

There are few constraints on the appointing authority. By statute, nominees to the Supreme Court must have served on a lower court or must have had a minimum ten years of legal practice. Civilian-trained judges from Quebec are constitutionally guaranteed three seats on the nine-person Court and are required to be sitting Quebec judges or members of the Quebec bar.[51] Further regional needs constrain Supreme Court appointments that have likely risen to the level of constitutional convention:[52] two justices must be from western Canada, three from Ontario, and one from Atlantic Canada. Ethnicity and gender also have become factors in recent appointments to the Court. However, the executive still enjoys unfettered discretion.[53] It was a significant development, then, when the prime minister introduced a public interview for nominees to the Supreme Court of Canada.

These developments were portended by concessions made by the short-lived Paul Martin government to shore up the democratic deficit in Parliament. Among his proposals was one to "provide healthy opportunity" to review the "qualifications of candidates" appointed to senior positions "by the appropriate standing committee, before final confirmation."[54] According to Thomas Axworthy, Martin's proposals were intended to attract "core supporters in the Liberal caucus" who had been

49 Donald R. Songer, Susan W. Johnston, C.L. Ostberg, and Matthew W. Wetstein, *Law, Ideology, and Collegiality: Judicial Behaviour in the Supreme Court of Canada* (Montreal and Kingston: McGill-Queen's University Press, 2012), 131.

50 Alarie and Green, "Policy Preference Change and Appointments to the Supreme Court of Canada," 44; Ostberg and Wetstein, *Attitudinal Decision Making in the Supreme Court of Canada*, 217.

51 *Reference Re Supreme Court Act*, para 91.

52 These "essential features" of the Court's composition might even be constitutionalized and so require consent of the provinces to change. See discussion in the Supreme Court's opinion in ibid., paras 91, 94.

53 Ziegel, "Judicial Appointments in Canada," 5.

54 Paul Martin, "The Democratic Deficit," *Policy Options* (December 2003), 12, http://policyoptions.irpp.org/issues/kyoto/the-democratic-deficit/.

disillusioned by the centralization of authority in the PMO under Prime Minister Jean Chrétien.[55] Martin's initiative also coincidentally resembled proposals advanced by Preston Manning's Reform Party. To this end, Justice Minister Irwin Cotler appeared before the House of Commons Standing Committee on Justice and Human Rights with a mandate to reconsider the appointments process. He praised the quality of past appointments while bemoaning the fact that a lack of transparency "has led some to believe, understandably so, that the process is both secret and partisan."[56] Changes to the appointment process clearly were afoot.

In 2004, the Standing Committee on Justice and Human Rights agreed, issuing its report entitled *Improving the Supreme Court of Canada Appointments Process*. The committee found that the process "by which Justices are appointed to the Court is largely unknown and lacks credibility in the eyes of many." A majority of the committee recommended that the minister of justice appear in public in order to explain the process of filling vacancies and to speak to the qualifications of the next nominee. The committee recommended that, when a vacancy is to be filled, an ad hoc advisory committee composed "of one representative of each of the parties with official standing in the House of Commons," along with "representation from the provinces, members of the judiciary and the legal profession, and lay members," be established to prepare a shortlist for the prime minister's consideration.[57] Recommendations would not be binding, so the prime minister's authority would remain intact. When the next two nominees came up for appointment (Rosalie Abella and Louise Charron), Justice Minister Irwin Cotler appeared before the House of Commons Standing Committee on Justice for two hours in order to speak to their credentials.[58] Though wholly novel, it seemed inadequate to many.[59] In their

---

55 Thomas S. Axworthy, "The Democratic Deficit: Should This Be Paul Martin's Next Big Idea?" *Policy Options* (December 2003), http://policyoptions.irpp.org/issues/paul-martin/the-democratic-deficit-should-this-be-paul-martins-next-big-idea/.

56 Irwin Cotler, "Evidence before the Standing Committee on Justice, Human Rights, Public Safety and Emergency Preparedness" (no. 7), 30 March 2004, www.law-lib.utoronto.ca/conferences/judiciary/background.htm.

57 Canada, "Improving the Supreme Court of Canada Appointments Process," *Report of the Standing Committee on Justice, Human Rights, Public Safety and Emergency Preparedness* (chair: Derek Lee) (May 2004), 1, 5, 8.

58 Cotler, "Supreme Court Appointment Process."

59 The initial process is described as a "sham" in a *Globe and Mail* editorial published in advance of the Wagner hearing. See "Harper v. Harper," *Globe and Mail*, 4 October 2012.

2004 dissenting report, Conservative Party members of the Standing Committee on Justice called, instead, for parliamentary ratification of Supreme Court nominees.[60]

The origins of the Conservative Party position are traceable back to its antecedents in the Reform Party of Canada. This was a populist western-based political movement for which Stephen Harper was chief policy officer and the principal architect of the party's "Blue Books" (the party's rolling "Statement of Principles and Policies" on which it ran election campaigns). Prompted by the Supreme Court's decision in Morgentaler,[61] striking down the Criminal Code's therapeutic abortion regime,[62] the Reform Party opted to frame the Supreme Court's work principally in political, not legal, terms. The Reform Party narrative was that Parliament had abdicated its responsibilities in favour of an unaccountable liberal-minded Court operating under the undue influence of "special" interests such as, in this instance, pro-choice feminists. In its 1990 Blue Book, the party declared that it supports "a more stringent and more public ratification procedure for Supreme Court Justices in light of the powers our legislators are handing to the courts."[63] A new reformed senate – the "Triple E-Senate," namely, a Senate that was elected, effective, and equal – would have carriage of the ratification process.[64] The edifice was clearly modelled upon U.S. constitutional text and practice.

Judges were not focused primarily upon "interpretation" of the law. Instead, they were "making or rewriting" the law, complained Reform Party Leader Preston Manning.[65] Canadian judges, David Frum announced in the *Wall Street Journal*, were recklessly imposing their

---

60 Canada, "Improving the Supreme Court of Canada Appointments Process," 16.

61 *R v Morgentaler* [1988] 1 SCR 30.

62 Morton, "Judicial Appointments in Post-Charter Canada," 61; F.L. Morton, "The Meaning of Morgentaler: A Political Analysis," in *A Time to Choose Life: Women, Abortion and Human Rights*, ed. Ian Gentles, 168–85 (Toronto: Stoddart, 1990).

63 Reform Party of Canada, *Building New Canada: Reform Party of Canada Principles and Policies 1991* (Calgary: Reform Party of Canada, 1991), 7.

64 According to the Draft Constitutional Amendment prepared by legal experts and ratified by the party in May 1988 (see discussion in chapter 4). See Leslie F. Seidle, "Senate Reform and the Constitutional Agenda: Conundrum or Solution?," in *Canadian Constitutionalism, 1791–1991*, ed. Janet Ajzenstat (Ottawa: Canadian Study of Parliament Group, 1991), 108.

65 Preston Manning, "Parliament Not Judges, Must Make the Laws of the Land," *Globe and Mail*, 16 June 1999.

"visions of radical equality upon their recalcitrant society."[66] Alberta Municipal Affairs Minister Steve West charged that the Charter "should be scrapped once and for all."[67] Even Alberta Court of Appeal Justice John McClung expressed outrage. In the course of issuing his reasons for judgment in the Vriend case, testing the conformity of Alberta's human rights code with the Charter by omitting sexual orientation as an actionable ground of discrimination, Justice McClung wrote about "crusading ... ideologically determined judges" and the "rights euphoric, cost-scoffing left ... the creeping barrage of the special-interest constituencies that seem now to have conscripted the Charter."[68] Such statements deploy a conventional political frame. Allegations of judicial activism were contrasted with approaches that stuck closely to framers' original intentions: when constrained by originalism, judges "appl[ied] the law, not their personal policy predilections."[69] Directing his ire at the Supreme Court of Canada, Judge Robert Bork declared that the Court has abandoned "constraints that distinguish a court from an elected body" – precisely the complaint Bork would issue in response to organized resistance to his own nomination (discussed below).[70]

Book-length accounts of this phenomenon were offered by political scientists F.L. Morton and Rainer Knopff. They hypothesized that a "Court Party" – a "loose coalition of interests" comprising Charter activists, non-governmental lawyers, and law professors – was influencing outcomes in Charter cases.[71] If they had a point – that groups mobilize to provide structures of support for rights litigants[72] – they

---

66 David Frum, "Canada's Reckless Supreme Court," *Wall Street Journal*, 15 November 1999.

67 Diana Coulter, "Call Sounded to Scrap Charter of Rights," *Vancouver Sun*, 23 April 1994.

68 *Vriend v Alberta* (1996) 132 DLR. (4th) 595, 606–16 (Alta CA), quoted in F.L. Morton, "Canada's Judge Bork: Has the Counter-Revolution Begun?," *Constitutional Forum constitutionnel* 7 (1996): 121–5.

69 Knopff and Morton, *Charter Politics*, 40. Framers' intent is a legitimate resource for judicial interpretation in the United States but not so in Canada, according to the Canadian Supreme Court; see *Re BC Motor Vehicle Act* [1985] 2 SCR 486.

70 Robert H. Bork, *Coercing Virtue: The Worldwide Rule of Judges* (Toronto: Vintage Canada, 2002), 73.

71 Knopff and Morton, *Charter Politics*; Morton and Knopff, *Charter Revolution and the Court Party*, 27.

72 See Alan C. Cairns, "Constitutional Minoritianism in Canada," in *Canada: The State of the Federation 1990*, ed. Ronald L. Watts and Douglas M. Brown, 71–96 (Kingston: Institute of Intergovernmental Relations, 1990); Charles R. Epp, *The Rights Revolution: Lawyers, Activists, and Supreme Courts in Comparative Perspective* (Chicago: University of Chicago Press, 1998).

were hazy about the means by which the Court Party had its way with the Court. Morton and Knopff appear to place special emphasis on judicial education programs and the role of law clerks. No systematic review of judicial education programs was undertaken.[73] Instead, these programs were pejoratively labelled "indoctrination centres for Court Party orthodoxy"[74] solely because some concern gender issues.[75] We are left wondering what percentage of these programs is devoted to gender equality and why judges would be susceptible to a message Morton and Knopff find so reprehensible. Is there anything to be learned, for instance, from the fact that Prime Minister Harper's failed nominee to the Supreme Court, Justice Marc Nadon (whose nomination is discussed below), was chair of the Federal Court of Appeal's Education Committee?[76] Nor is there much explanation about how law clerks – recent law school graduates employed to assist judges for one year in a variety of tasks – are able simply to take over judicial functions. All that is referred to are a couple of revealing anecdotes and a law review article by a former clerk.[77] With this meagre evidence in hand, they conclude that law clerks, channelling the scholarship of their left-wing law professors, are having a "significant impact" on judicial outcomes.[78] Emmett Macfarlane, having interviewed five current and former Supreme Court of Canada justices and twenty-one former clerks, agrees that clerks "wield tremendous influence" and have

---

73 It might be difficult to gain access to some of this material. See the experience related by Robert Ivan Martin, *The Most Dangerous Branch: How the Supreme Court of Canada Has Undermined Our Law and Our Democracy* (Montreal and Kingston: McGill-Queen's University Press, 2003), 9–10. There is, however, a brief but informed discussion about judicial education programs in Friedland, *Place Apart*, chap. 8.

74 Morton and Knopff, *Charter Revolution and the Court Party*, 125.

75 Ibid., 125–7; Morton, "Judicial Appointments in Post-Charter Canada," 61.

76 Prime Minister of Canada Stephen Harper, "Backgrounder: The Honourable Mr Justice Marc Nadon," 30 September 2013, pm.gc.ca/eng/news/2013/09/30/honourable-mr-justice-marc-nadon.

77 Morton and Knopff, *Charter Revolution and the Court Party*, 110–13; Lorne Sossin, "The Sounds of Silence: Law Clerks, Policy Making and the Supreme Court of Canada" *UBC LR* 30 (1996): 279–308. There is a larger U.S. literature on this subject. See, e.g., Todd C. Peppers, *Courtiers of the Marble Palace: The Rise and Influence of the Supreme Court Law Clerk* (Stanford: Stanford University Press, 2006); and Paul J. Wahlbeck, James F. Spriggs II, and Lee Sigelman, "Ghostwriters on the Court? A Stylistic Analysis of U.S. Supreme Court Opinion Drafts," *American Politics Research* 30 (2002): 166–92.

78 Morton and Knopff, *Charter Revolution and the Court Party*, 110.

a "significant influence" on judicial outcomes.[79] Whatever variety of functions clerks perform, it is extremely unlikely that they determine outcomes or channel their law professors' political preferences as they go about their work.[80] In an unpublished study, Fletcher, Choudhry, and Schneiderman[81] compare the attitudinal values of former Supreme Court clerks, legal academics, and government lawyers in order to test the hypothesis that law clerks are channelling their left-wing professors' egalitarian agenda. They find that law clerks "do not share the egalitarian preferences of the professoriate; nor do they share their political outlook generally."[82] It turns out that students chosen to clerk at the Supreme Court of Canada are more conservative than both law professors and Charter litigating government lawyers. The problem is that accounts like Morton and Knopff's lack credible evidence to support their claim that clerks systematically influence judicial outcomes.[83] The whole of it amounts to a simplistic, yet familiar, framing of the judicial function popular among social conservatives, which aims to distinguish between the course of judicial activism – that of politics – and that of judicial restraint – which looks more like law.[84]

Conservative thinkers are seeking to frame the Supreme Court's work in the language of politics. From this angle, insofar as the Court strays from original intentions, the Court is engaging in politics – it is acting like a "de facto third chamber of the legislature."[85] The preferred perspective of judges, lawyers, and law professors is to think of judicial decision-making within a legal frame, with an emphasis on

---

79 Emmett Macfarlane, *Governing from the Bench: The Supreme Court of Canada and the Judicial Role* (Vancouver: UBC Press, 2013), 107.

80 Donald Songer, *The Transformation of the Supreme Court of Canada: An Empirical Examination* (Toronto: University of Toronto Press, 2008), 138.

81 Joseph F. Fletcher, Sujit Choudhry, and David Schneiderman, "Political Agendas among Law Clerks and Their Professors?" paper prepared for the 2010 APSA Meetings, Washington DC.

82 Ibid.

83 Peppers, *Courtiers of the Marble Palace*, 206. Peppers adds that, in the United States, the "necessary conditions for the exercise of influence by law clerks have rarely, if ever, existed on the Supreme Court" (206).

84 The view is naive because it assumes that "application" does not require "inventiveness" that is associated with "judicial activism." Jerome Frank likens the view that judges have no power to "change existing law or make new law" as the "direct outgrowth of a subjective need for believing in a stable, unalterable legal world – in effect, a child's world," in Frank, *Law and Modern Mind*, 38.

85 Morton and Knopff, *Charter Revolution and the Court Party*, 58.

the legal reasons being offered, having recourse to the usual stock of judicial tools like text, structure, precedent, and common law rules and presumptions. The legal community fears that the more Canada moves towards a judicial confirmation process, the more likely the political will overtake the legal frame.

The Conservative Party (successor to the Reform Party – the product of a marriage between the two warring conservative forces, the Reform/Alliance Party and the Progressive Conservative Party of Canada), was less vocal about judicial activism but equally insistent on adopting a confirmation process. In their May 2004 dissenting report, as mentioned, the Conservative Party committee members declared that "Parliament and the legislatures are no longer the only bodies involved in legal policy making, if they ever were" and insisted upon parliamentary ratification of the nominee.[86] In its 2005 inaugural policy conference, the Conservative Party adopted this resolution: "A Conservative Government will ensure that nominees to the Supreme Court of Canada will be ratified by a free vote in Parliament, after receiving the approval of the Justice Committee of the House of Commons."[87] Though neither of these events has occurred – there have been no free votes and nominees have appeared only before ad hoc House committees – there is little evidence that Prime Minister Harper has evolved much in his thinking in this regard. A former colleague insists that the prime minister does not dislike the Charter of Rights as much as is often supposed. He has always been a Charter of Rights "enthusiast," maintains Harper's former associate at the National Citizen's Coalition, Gerry Nicholls. He is not one of those who "still held old school conservative notions about the supremacy of parliament or were suspicious of 'judicial activism.'"[88] Yet, as the epigraph to this chapter indicates, Harper has written that he shares "many of the concerns of [his] colleagues and allies about biased 'judicial activism' and its extremes."[89]

Once in power, the Harper government (in minority and subsequently in majority governments) embraced public interviews before

86 Canada, "Improving the Supreme Court of Canada Appointments Process," 16.
87 Conservative Party of Canada, "Policy Declaration," 19 March 2005, http://www.cbc.ca/bc/news/060119_CPM.pdf.
88 Gerry Nicholls, "Harper and the Charter: Setting the Record Straight," Hill Times, 23 April 2012.
89 Harper, "Why I Hate Gag Laws"; Kirk Makin, "The Coming Conservative Court: Harper to Reshape Judiciary," Globe and Mail, 15 May 2011.

an ad hoc committee of the House of Commons. In announcing the new process that would be adopted for Justice Rothstein's nomination, the first nomination to kick-start the process, Prime Minister Harper reaffirmed his preference for judges who were "prepared to apply the law rather than make it" and who would avoid being "inventive" in their rulings.[90]

2. U.S. Senate Judiciary Committee: Anti-Model?

Renovation of the appointment process has been resisted, in large part, out of fear that politics would pollute not only judicial appointments to, but decision-making by, the Supreme Court of Canada. The Canadian Bar Association (the national body representing lawyers) expressed strong opposition to any form of parliamentary review of candidates in its 2004 submission to the House of Commons Standing Committee on Justice: "Candidates should not be subjected to a congressional type process of public examination and review. This would politicize the appointment process and detract from the principle of the independence of the judiciary."[91] Retired Supreme Court of Canada justice Claire L'Heureux-Dubé testified to similar effect, stating that her "real worry [is] that there will be [a] process putting a candidate right in front of the public with the media in attendance, not looking for the best qualities generally, but looking for the failures, the little things."[92] Canada's merit-based system is not broken, Chief Justice McLachlin declared, so why fix it?[93]

For many, U.S. Senate confirmation hearings represent the anti-model. Falling within executive branch authority, nominations are transmitted to the Senate for its "advice and consent" and sent on to its Committee on the Judiciary. It was only in 1939 that Judiciary Committee hearings were made public and only after 1950 that Supreme Court nominees began to appear regularly before senators.[94] Initially, judicial

---

90 See Sean Gordon, "MPs to Vet Selection of Judge to Top Court: Harper's Choice to Be Named Thursday Critics Fear Drift to 'Political Judiciary,'" *Toronto Star*, 21 February 2006.

91 Canadian Bar Association, "Supreme Court of Canada Appointment Process," March 2004, www.cba.org/cba/submissions/pdf/04-10-03-eng.pdf.

92 L'Heureux-Dubé, "Evidence before the Standing Committee on Justice."

93 David Gambrill, "Chief Justice Says No to Electing Judges," *Law Times*, 23 June 2003.

94 Lee Epstein and Jeffrey A. Segal, *Advice and Consent: The Politics of Judicial Appointments* (New York: Oxford University Press, 2005), 88.

confirmation hearings would take a day or two – today, they take several intense months.[95] Committee proceedings have been described as "leav[ing] blood on the floor,"[96] a "battleground where groups wage holy war and the tactics reflect a take-no-prisoners approach to combat."[97] So dysfunctional are Senate confirmation hearings, the argument goes, that they deter judges from permitting their names to go forward.

A number of preconceptions shape impressions about the U.S. experience. It usually is assumed that it was the failed 1987 nomination of former Yale law professor Robert Bork by President Ronald Reagan that ramped up the duration and intensity of questioning of nominees by senators. Instead, it was the confirmation hearing of Chief Justice William Rehnquist, the year before, that generated the greatest dialogue between senators and the nominee and now remains continually at high levels.[98] Abortion became a preoccupation of senators only after Sandra Day O'Connor's nomination in 1981 but does not dominate hearings today.[99] Abortion, nonetheless, dominates newspaper coverage of Supreme Court judicial appointments in ways that is out of proportion to the number of questions senators ask and the Court's own docket.[100]

The Bork hearings did, however, inaugurate the politically divisive era of judicial confirmation hearings.[101] Bork's prickly reputation was notorious, having served as acting attorney general and President Richard Nixon's hired gun in the firing of Watergate Special Prosecutor Archibald Cox. Bork's approach to constitutional interpretation, purporting to be constrained by framers' intent, seemed to prefer only

---

95 Benjamin Wittes, *Confirmation Wars: Preserving Independent Courts in Angry Times* (Lanham, MD: Rowman and Littlefield, 2006), 41.

96 Stephen L. Carter, *The Confirmation Mess: Cleaning Up the Federal Appointments Process* (New York: Basic Books, 1994), 95.

97 Richard Davis, *Electing Justice: Fixing the Supreme Court Nomination Process* (Oxford: Oxford University Press, 2005), 6.

98 Lori A. Ringhand and Paul M. Collins, Jr, "May It Please the Senate: An Empirical Analysis of the Senate Judiciary Committee Hearings of Supreme Court Nominees, 1939–2009," *American University Law Review* 60 (2011): 598–632.

99 Ibid., 617; Paul M. Collins, Jr, and Lori A. Ringhand, *Supreme Court Hearings and Constitutional Change* (Cambridge: Cambridge University Press, 2013), 122–3.

100 Michael Evans and Shanna Pearson-Merkowitz, "Perpetuating the Myth of the Culture War Court? Issue Attention in Newspaper Coverage of U.S. Supreme Court Nominations," *American Politics Research* 40 (2012): 1028.

101 Grossman, "Paths to the Bench," 144.

certain rights. If principled, his seemed to be the wrong principles and not within the governing "constitutional consensus."[102] It was feared that his judicial approach would undo women's abortion rights and almost "every major civil rights advance" of the last thirty years. Difficult and awkward questioning from even Republican senators, together with an unrelenting media campaign, resulted in a 9:5 rejection by the Senate Judiciary Committee and a Senate vote defeat (58:42). The problem, Bork maintained in his final statement to the Senate Committee, is that where "judicial nominees are assessed and treated like political candidates, the effect will be to chill the climate in which judicial deliberations take place, to erode public confidence in the impartiality of courts, and to endanger the independence of the judiciary."[103]

The Clarence Thomas nomination resulted in his confirmation, partly by having learned lessons from the Bork hearings. An African-American candidate, Thomas built his "career as a civil rights basher" and was cynically offered as the candidate to fill the seat formerly occupied by the lion of the civil rights movement, Justice Thurgood Marshall.[104] Very little was revealed in advance about Thomas's approach, or knowledge of, constitutional law. Thomas even denied that he had ever thought about the constitutionality of abortion, even though he was enrolled as a student at Yale Law School the year Roe v Wade was decided.[105] It became apparent that he was not very well qualified for the job after an initial set of hearings. Additional hearings, prompted by the credible complaints of sexual harassment when he headed up the Equal Employment Opportunities Commission, entirely unravelled.[106] Thomas barely survived the Senate confirmation

---

102 Collins and Ringhand, *Supreme Court Hearings and Constitutional Change*, 205, 202.
103 Robert H. Bork, *The Tempting of America: The Political Seduction of the Law* (New York: Free Press, 1990), 287, 302–8. Bork is quoted in Grossman, "Paths to the Bench," 156.
104 Margaret A. Burnham, "The Supreme Court Appointment Process and the Politics of Race and Sex," in *Race-ing Justice, En-gendering Power: Essays on Anita Hill, Clarence Thomas and the Construction of Social Reality*, ed. Toni Morrison (New York: Pantheon Books), 302.
105 Epstein and Segal, *Advice and Consent*, 97.
106 These allegations were made by Thomas's former employee, then Oklahoma law professor Anita Hill, who was characterized by the members of the Senate judiciary committee as a woman scorned. Stephen Carter, who is a long-time personal friend of Anita Hill, believes the charges: "The notion that she would invent such a story is ludicrous," in Carter, *Confirmation Mess*, 140. See David Brock's *mea culpa* regarding his book-length hatchet job on Anita Hill, in *Blinded by the Right: The Conscience of an Ex-Conservative* (New York: Crown, 2002), chap. 5.

vote (52:48). The national trauma associated with the Thomas hearings lingers as Thomas continues to sit as an associate justice on the U.S. Supreme Court.

Admittedly, the messiness associated with the Bork and Thomas confirmation hearings is atypical. Still, they are intense affairs in which no aspect of the candidate's life goes unexamined in the run-up to the confirmation hearing.[107] They amount to an "exhaustive examination" of the candidates' public and private life. From nomination to appointment, on average, the process goes on for months.[108] The hearings themselves have evolved into an occasion for senators to lecture at length on constitutional matters in nationwide gavel-to-gavel coverage.[109] At the same time, since the Bork hearings, nominees are reluctant to reveal anything about their ideological proclivities.[110] The process "rarely offers significant insights into the views or judging philosophy of future Justices." Instead, it has become a "charade of obfuscation" by the nominees, "aided and abetted by the Senators from both sides of the political aisle."[111] Indeed, there has been a discernible "downward trend in nominee candor," though "not as dramatic" a decline as some assume.[112] Little but platitude is offered to seal the confirmation deal. Candidates have been known to spend days preparing for hearings before "murder boards"[113] – mock hearings in which more than a dozen volunteers role play to help prepare the nominee for the tough questioning to come. It is reported that Chief Justice Roberts participated in ten such "mock hearings of two to three hours each at the Justice Department" in advance of his Senate Committee hearings.[114] In sum,

---

107 Epstein and Segal, *Advice and Consent*, 93.

108 Davis, *Electing Justice*, 31, 67.

109 Elisabeth Bumiller, "But Enough about You Judge; Let's Hear What I Have to Say," *New York Times*, 11 January 2006; Davis, *Electing Justice*, 120. At the Alito hearings, Senator Joseph Biden is reported to have had the "highest ratio of words per panel- list to words per nominee ... [he] managed to ask five questions in his 30 minute allotment," in Bumiller, "But Enough about You Judge."

110 Geoffrey R. Stone, "Understanding Supreme Court Confirmations," *Supreme Court Review* 9 (2010): 435.

111 David A. Yalof, "Confirmation Obfuscation: Supreme Court Confirmation Politics in a Conservative Era," *Studies in Law, Politics, and Society* 44 (2008): 169.

112 Dion Farganis, "'No Hints, No Forecasts, No Previews': An Empirical Analysis of Supreme Court Nominee Candor from Harlan to Kagan," *Law & Society Review* 45 (2011): 554.

113 Davis, *Electing Justice*, 119.

114 Elisabeth Bumiller, "Lengthy Practices Prepare Court Nominee for His Senate Hearings," *New York Times*, 1 September 2005.

observed the Twentieth-Century Fund Task Force on Judicial Selection convened the year following the Bork nomination, the confirmation process "is dangerously close to looking like the electoral process."[115] This precisely is where political scientist Richard Davis ends up: the judicial selection process, he writes, "has all the trappings of an election campaign" but without an electorate, an outcome that he describes as "an untenable situation."[116]

Although there is a correlation between qualifications and Senate approval, Senate roll call votes reveal that partisanship and ideology mostly determine outcomes: the more compatible the candidate is with senators' own views, the more likely candidates will receive their support. If a candidate can "help further their own goals, primarily those that serve to advance their chances of reelection, their political party, or their policy interests," then the candidate will be confirmed. Presidents nominate candidates for precisely the same partisan and ideological reasons.[117] There is the power, as well, to block Supreme Court nominations via Senate filibuster (requiring a supermajority, and not a simple majority, of votes), a threat that helped to sabotage President Johnson's nomination of Abe Fortas.[118] Use of the filibuster has become pervasive, holding up a variety of judicial nominations to federal lower courts.[119] So gridlocked was the Senate along partisan lines that the Democratic majority invoked the "nuclear option," and in November 2013 modified the rules regarding executive and judicial branch nominees so that only a simple majority was required. U.S. Supreme Court nominees, however, were exempt from the rule change.[120]

There is evidence that confirmation hearings prove somewhat helpful in eliciting "varying testimony and useful insights into nominees' interpretive views."[121] Senate hearings typically "involve concrete discussion of judicial decisions" of mostly recent vintage. Questions are

---

115 Grossman, "Paths to the Bench," 159.

116 Davis, *Electing Justice*, 9.

117 Epstein and Segal, *Advice and Consent*, 113, 3.

118 Davis, *Electing Justice*, 79.

119 Thomas E. Mann and Norman J. Ornstein, *It's Even Worse Than It Looks: How the American Constitutional System Collided with the New Politics of Extremism* (New York: Basic Books, 2012), 91–8.

120 Jeremy W. Peters, "Senate Vote Curbs Filibuster Power to Stall Nominees," *New York Times*, 21 November 2013.

121 Michael Comiskey, "The Supreme Court Appointment Process: Lessons from Filling the Rehnquist and O'Connor Vacancies," *PS: Political Science & Politics* 41 (2008): 356.

asked and answered about past precedent without, at the same time, violating judicial norms about proffering opinions concerning disputes likely to arise before the Court.[122] So important is past Supreme Court precedent to the confirmation process that Collins and Ringhand maintain that hearings "function as a formal mechanism through which the Court's [prior] constitutional choices are ratified as part of our constitutional consensus." Confirmation hearings provide a forum for identifying "common understandings" of that past.[123] For this reason, and in contrast to the many negative portrayals of the U.S. confirmation process in circulation, Collins and Ringhand see much to celebrate.[124]

Empirical analysis reveals that public confirmation of Supreme Court nominees, even controversial ones that attract a lot of attention by the press and outside groups, do not necessarily undermine the legitimacy of the nominee or the Supreme Court. Samuel Alito's nomination to replace Justice Sandra Day O'Connor was a particularly contentious but well-managed process in which advocacy groups spent more than U.S.$2 million to sway public opinion.[125] Gibson and Caldeira's study of the Alito nomination suggests that such nominations, though susceptible to being captured by political processes, are capable of keeping some distance from politics, because of a reservoir of "institutional loyalty," sometimes called "diffuse support," that can be drawn upon whenever attention becomes focused on the Court, as it did during the Alito confirmation hearings. The reservoir of institutional loyalty is

122 Anna Batta, Paul M. Collins, Jr, Tom Miles, and Lori A. Ringhand, "Let's Talk: Judicial Decisions at Supreme Court Confirmation Hearings," *Judicature* 96 (July/August 2012) 96: 8, 15; see also Paul M. Collins, Jr, and Lori A. Ringhand, "The Institutionalization of Supreme Court Confirmation Hearings," April 2013, 18, www.psci.unt.edu/~pmcollins/Collins%20Ringhand%20MPSA%202013.pdf. Not only is past precedent discussed but, since 1986, every Supreme Court nominee (but for Clarence Thomas) was asked at least ten questions about the nominees' prior decisions. See Margaret Williams and Lawrence Baum, "Supreme Court Nominees before the Senate Judiciary Committee," *Judicature* 90 (2006): 76.

123 Collins and Ringhand, "Institutionalization of Supreme Court Confirmation Hearings," 3, 8.

124 Post and Siegel go so far as to propose that nominees be asked about how they would have decided past cases, in Robert C. Post and Reva B. Siegel, "Questioning Justice: Law and Politics in Judicial Confirmation Hearings," *Yale Law Journal Pocket Part* 115 (2006): 38–51, http://www.law.yale.edu/documents/pdf/Faculty/Siegel_Questioning_Justice.pdf.

125 Collins and Ringhand, "Institutionalization of Supreme Court Confirmation Hearings," 39.

premised upon the conception that judges are not like politicians; that they engage in principled legal reasoning and not expedient political bargaining. So long as nominees are able to reinforce these pre-existing conceptions, "opponents will find it difficult to substitute an alternative frame centered on ideology and partisanship." The upshot of the contested Alito nomination battle was that the more "people paid attention to the confirmation battle, the more supportive they were of the Court."[126] Relatedly, Gibson has found that, in the context of judicial elections in Kentucky, electoral campaigns do not "damage" the legitimacy of Kentucky courts. Campaigns, instead, help to build legitimacy by making judges accountable while reinforcing the message that judges are "principled" and not self-interested political actors.[127] Whether the reputation of courts as forums of principle will survive the tsunami of campaign finance contributions remains to be seen.[128]

There was little or no consideration given to the empirical evidence as Canadian debates unfolded. Instead, there were fears that the public judicial interview process would backfire and turn nasty. Even worse, there was the lingering suspicion that this was precisely the intended effect: to forever politicize the Supreme Court appointment process so that it looked more like that in the United States. The object of the next part is to test this hypothesis by undertaking a qualitative and quantitative analysis of print journalism regarding the first five nominations. The findings suggest that newspaper coverage emphasized a "legal frame" (judges "apply" law) over a "political" one (judges "make law"). The analysis reveals that the media – among the principal purveyors of constitutional culture – have portrayed the individual nominees, and the Court more generally, in a favourable light.

3. Nominations and the Press

The media turn out to have a critical role to play in determining whether concerns about politicization become actualized or assuaged. According to Spill and Oxley, "Public perceptions" of the U.S. Supreme Court and

126 James L. Gibson and Gregory A. Caldeira, *Citizens, Courts, and Confirmations: Positivity Theory and the Judgments of the American People* (Princeton, NJ: Princeton University Press, 2009), 39–40, 66, 95, 113.

127 James L. Gibson, *Electing Judges: The Surprising Effects of Campaigning on Judicial Legitimacy* (Chicago: Chicago University Press, 2012), 130, 134.

128 Adam Liptak, "Judges on the Campaign Trail," *New York Times*, 28 September 2014.

its justices are "based largely upon the media's portrayal."[129] The high regard in which the U.S. Supreme Court is held (the phenomenon of diffuse support) usually is attributed to "apolitical" media coverage in which there is "little or no discussion of the underlying rationale" for the Court's decisions.[130] Though the media do not control the message[131] – and "work hard" to present news accounts that distance their work from those with political power – they are "the final arbiter of what is likely to be interesting."[132] If the press are central in the determination of whether the framing of news accounts will emphasize either a legal or a political lens, the stakes are rather large.

Baird and Gangl's controlled study of court reporting vignettes reinforce the predominant "myth of legality" that helps to sustain the U.S. Supreme Court's legitimacy.[133] Spill and Oxley's study of newspaper and television news coverage during the 1998 term reveals that a political frame was dominant in television news broadcasts – brief and punchy, with an emphasis on winners and losers, characteristic of sporting events (a standard journalistic convention[134]) – while newspaper reporting was more nuanced, providing information about the "political nature of the decision" and "the role that attitudes and ideology play in the final outcome." Reporting of such fine details, they hypothesize, "clearly undermines faith" in the non-political nature of courts and judicial decision-making.[135] A study of newspaper and television reporting of Supreme Court of Canada decision-making revealed

129 Rorie L. Spill and Zoe M. Oxley, "Philosopher Kings or Political Actors: How the Media Portray the Supreme Court," *Judicature* 87 (2004): 24.

130 Vanessa A. Baird and Amy Gangl, "Shattering the Myth of Legality: The Impact of the Media's Framing of Supreme Court Procedures on Perceptions of Fairness," *Political Psychology* 27 (2006): 598.

131 Stuart Hall, Chas Critcher, Tony Jefferson, John Clarke, and John Roberts, *Policing the Crisis: Mugging, the State, and Law and Order* (Houndmills: Macmillan, 1978), 59.

132 Timothy E. Cook, *Governing with the News: The News Media as Political Institution*, 2nd ed. (Chicago: Chicago University Press), 5, 7.

133 Baird and Gangl, "Shattering the Myth of Legality," 606.

134 Linda Greenhouse, "Telling the Court's Story: Justice and Journalism at the Supreme Court," *Yale Law Journal* 105 (1996): 1551.

135 Spill and Oxley, "Philosopher Kings or Political Actors," 29. On the constraints of television news reporting of the U.S. Supreme Court proceedings, see Elliott E. Slotnick and Jennifer A. Segal, *Television News and the Supreme Court* (Cambridge: Cambridge University Press, 1998), chap. 3. On print reporting, see Greenhouse, "Telling the Court's Story"; and Chester A. Newland, "Press Coverage of the United States Supreme Court," *Western Political Quarterly* 17 (1964): 15–36.

no such difference – newspapers, though supplying greater amounts of information, were no less likely to emphasize a conflict or battle frame associated with raw politics.[136]

The judicial nomination process reveals a similar set of dynamics occurring outside the confines of the courtroom. This renders the process unstable, from a legal point of view. Beyond the control of judicial institutions and press information officers who help to shape positive images of the Court and its justices,[137] appointment processes are susceptible (so the U.S. record suggests) to resembling political campaigns.[138] The political frame, Canadian legalists surmise, is likely to predominate, in spite of the empirical findings, previously mentioned, which indicate that exposure to the discourse of law underscores the distance of judicial decision-making from self-interested politics. I have already mentioned Gibson and Caldeira's analysis of the Alito nomination, which supports the hypothesis that exposure to the high court of principle reinforces the separation of law from politics.[139] Farnsworth and Lichter's study of selected nomination battles on television and in the *New York Times* yields similar findings. They find that assessments of judicial nominees are unusually positive when compared to news coverage of politicians – coverage of nominees is far more positive than coverage of senators asking the questions, for instance – even when nominees attract an unusual amount of negative coverage, as in the Thomas nomination.[140]

---

136 Sauvageau, Schneiderman, and Taras, *Last Word*. The Canadian study confirmed findings in the United States that reporting of high court decision-making, particularly on television, often is uninformative and uninformed, though more in-depth reporting can be anticipated where high court cases have local salience. See Clifford A. Jones, "Voting from the Bench: Media Analysis of Legal Issues in the 2000 Postelection Campaign," *American Behavioral Scientist* 46 (2003): 654–5; Valerie Hoekstra, "The Supreme Court and Local Public Opinion," *American Political Science Review* 94 (2000): 178–89; and Donald P. Haider-Markel, Mahalley D. Allen, and Morgen Johansen, "Understanding Variations in Media Coverage of U.S. Supreme Court Decisions: Comparing Media Outlets in Their Coverage of *Lawrence* v. *Texas*," *Press/Politics* 11 (2006): 64–85.

137 Sauvageau, Schneiderman, and Taras, *Last Word*, 202–3; Richard Davis, *Decisions and Images: The Supreme Court and the Press* (Englewood Cliffs, NJ: Prentice Hall, 1994), 53.

138 Davis, *Electing Justice*, 9.

139 Gibson and Caldeira, *Citizens, Courts, and Confirmations*, 39–40.

140 Stephen J. Farnsworth and S. Robert Lichter, "The Mediated Supreme Court Nomination Process: News Coverage of Confirmed and Non-Confirmed Nominees," paper presented to the Annual Meeting of the American Political Science Association, Philadelphia, 2006, citation.allacademic.com/meta/p_mla_apa_research_citation/1/5/1/9/8/pages151987/p151987-6.php.

Bogoch and Holzman-Gazit's study of nomination coverage in two leading Israeli newspapers also found that, for the most part, reports on judicial nominations tended to focus on legal/professional qualifications. It was only in 2008, when the mechanics of the nomination process attracted substantial political heat, that a political frame became predominant.[141]

Methodology

The object of this part of the chapter is to explore what Canadians learned during five different nomination processes: what did they learn about judges and courts and how do they appear to differ from politicians and legislatures? I answer these questions by undertaking content analysis – both qualitative and quantitative – of print coverage in six different newspapers.[142] The papers selected for the study represent a cross-country sample of tabloid (T) and broadsheet (BS) newspapers in both official languages. In the French language, *Le Journal de Montréal* (T) and *La Presse* (BS) were selected for coding. In the English language, a regional selection of the Toronto-based *Globe and Mail* (Canada's "national newspaper" with a business bent) (BS), the *Toronto Sun* (T), the *Winnipeg Free Press* (BS), and the *Calgary Herald* (BS) were also analysed. The four nominations yielded a set of 166 individual reports. If it is correct to claim that the first hearing (Justice Rothstein's) "galvanized the Canadian media,"[143] our analysis reveals a dropping off of media interest by the time of the fourth nomination hearing (Justice Wagner's) six years later (see figure 5.1).[144]

Content analysis of straight-up journalism, signed op-eds, and editorials was undertaken to answer questions such as how did the media

---

141 Bryna Bogoch and Yifat Holzman-Gazit, "Promoting Justices: Media Coverage and Judicial Nominations in Israel," *Oñati Socio-Legal Series* 4, no. 4 (2014): 639–40, http://ssrn.com/abstract=2478756.

142 In the interests of full disclosure, I have been interviewed by some of the journalists covering Supreme Court appointments and, on occasion, I am quoted in these news reports. I do not believe this is of any consequence to the content analysis undertaken here.

143 Jacob Ziegel, "A New Era in the Selection of Supreme Court Judges?," *Osgoode Hall Law Journal* 44 (2006): 548.

144 Coverage of the Rothstein and the Karakatsanis/Moldaver joint hearings were televised live on cable news. By the time of Wagner's appointment, the live hearing could be followed only over the Internet on the Canadian Public Affairs Channel.

Figure 5.1. Amount of Coverage

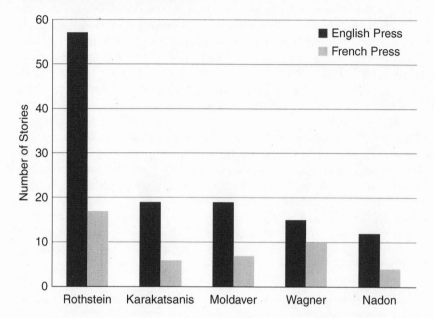

portray the Supreme Court and judicial review (addressing "tone") and how was the appointment process itself portrayed? The overall object is to gauge the dominant frame – frames reflect the way in which media select, organize, and make sense of the world[145] – through which the stories were told. A coding sheet is attached as appendix 2.[146]

It would be useful to ask at this juncture what purposes were served by the new interview process. Peter Hogg, professor emeritus of

---

145 William A. Gamson and David Stuart, "Media Discourse as a Symbolic Contest: The Bomb in Political Cartoons," *Sociological Forum* 7 (1992): 55–86; Stephen D. Reese, "Prologue – Framing Public Life: A Bridging Model for Media Research," in *Framing Public Life: Perspectives on Media and Our Understanding of the Social World*, ed. Stephen D. Reese, Oscar H. Gandy, Jr, and August E. Grant, 7–20 (Mahwah, NJ: Lawrence Erlbaum Associates, 2001).

146 The methodology draws on that deployed in Sauvageau, Schneiderman, and Taras, *Last Word*. Three University of Toronto law students collected and coded stories. In the case of disagreement between the three coders (typically on questions concerning "tone") the author resolved the coding dispute. The coding sheet (see appendix 2) and coding instructions are abridged and adapted versions of those used in the earlier study.

constitutional law at Osgoode Hall Law School and one of Canada's leading authorities on the Constitution, was retained to advise the Committee during the first two sets of public hearings. He provides an answer to this question in a recently published paper. The impetus for the hearings, Hogg advises, was the "democratic notion that important decisions should be transparent." The benefits flowing from the new process, he adds, will be in helping Canadians better "understand the appointment process and the judicial function and to learn about the qualifications of the person nominated for appointment."[147] The interview process had the benefit, then, of improving knowledge of judges and courts and improving citizens' literacy in the ways in which judges decide cases, particularly constitutional ones. Its principal impetus we might characterize as having to do with notions of "accountability." For many legalists, this is what threatens judicial "independence." Americans, Gibson writes, favour more accountability over independence.[148] It seems clear that the Conservative initiative was intended to move Canadians further along the accountability continuum, in an American direction.[149]

Before turning to the content analysis, I should foreground the discussion with a little more detail about the hearings. A short list of six candidates (selected from a much longer list prepared by the minister of justice, following informal consultations) was recommended to the prime minister by an all-party committee of five members, with the Conservative party having a majority of three votes. In other words, the ruling party has not given up control over the process.[150] For each nomination (or in the case of the joint nomination of Moldaver and Karakatsanis in 2011), a special House of Commons committee was convened with representatives from political parties in the House of

---

147 Hogg, "Appointment of Thomas A. Cromwell," 20–1.
148 Gibson, *Electing Judges*, 132. Grossman proposes a somewhat similar binary, between a "professional-independent" model (which he associates with the civil law tradition) and a "responsive-accountable-political" model (which he associates with U.S. practice) in "Paths to the Bench," 146.
149 On the balance between independence and accountability, see Peter H. Russell, "Conclusion," in *Appointing Judges in an Age of Judicial Power: Critical Perspectives From Around the World*, ed. Kate Malleson and Peter H. Russell (Toronto: University of Toronto Press, 2006), 426–31; and Shimon Shetreet, "Judicial Independence and Accountability: Core Values in Liberal Democracies," in *Judiciaries in Comparative Perspective*, ed. H.P. Lee, 3–23 (Cambridge: Cambridge University Press, 2011).
150 Ziegel, "Judicial Appointments in Canada," 12.

Commons, but controlled, again, by the ruling Conservative Party. According to Conservative panel member Brent Rathgeber, among the official criteria were superior intellectual ability, professional capacity, and writing skills. Among the unofficial criteria were "judgments supporting the government's law and order agenda; and, most importantly, judicial deference."[151] Perhaps this helps to explain why the prime minister did not turn the matter over to the House of Commons Standing Committee on Justice and Human Rights, which had reported earlier on reforming appointments and presumably had a better feel for the dossier. Members of these ad hoc committees did not lack expertise entirely – a number of committee members had participated in the process by which a short list of candidates was generated. With the ruling party in control, and committee members of all parties having something of a stake in endorsing the candidate, little drama was expected.

The truncated timing between announcement and appointment contributed to defusing the drama. The first nomination of Marshall Rothstein lasted just under one week, with an announcement on Thursday (23 February 2006), a full-day hearing the following Monday, and appointment the next Wednesday. The joint nomination of two justices, Andromache Karakatsanis and Michael Moldaver, was even more abridged with an announcement on Monday (17 October 2011), an afternoon hearing two days later, and appointment two days after that. Richard Wagner's nomination followed a similar pattern with a Tuesday announcement (2 October 2012), a Thursday afternoon hearing, and appointment the very next day. Similarly, Marc Nadon, whose appointment would be ruled unconstitutional in an extraordinary Supreme Court ruling the following year,[152] was nominated on Monday (30 September 2013), appeared at a hearing the following Wednesday, and was appointed the next day. The condensed timing between nomination, hearing, and appointment ensured that committee members would have little time to prepare for their encounters with nominees. Nor would it provide any opportunity for individuals or interest groups to provide meaningful feedback if they were so inclined. The hearings were just window dressing, complained Kathleen Mahoney. "I don't know who this fellow is," she observed regarding Nadon. "I'm

---

151 Brent Rathgeber, *Irresponsible Government: The Decline of Parliamentary Democracy in Canada* (Toronto: Dundurn, 2014), 201–2.
152 *Reference re Supreme Court Act*, ss 5 and 6.

just Googling him right now."[153] Though it is unlikely that, with a more drawn-out process, organized opposition to the nominees would have been mobilized (outside of the established party system in the House of Commons, that is), the stunted process ensured that "external forces"[154] could not possibly have had time to percolate. So disillusioned was the press by the time of the Wagner nomination, the *Globe and Mail* editorialized that, if the prime minister believed that the nomination process needed fixing, he "should believe in the process he created and give it time to work."[155] Responding to these criticisms during the Nadon hearing, Justice Minister Peter MacKay defended the manufactured short time line by comparing the nomination process to an expedited legal proceeding: "As a lawyer you're very often called before the court on short notice, and expected to make a case."[156]

Another factor that significantly dampened the proceedings was anxiety associated with "demeaning the dignity" or "embarrassing" the nominees. Anxious about this possibility, one committee member (NDP member of Parliament and lawyer Joe Comartin) even threatened to boycott the Rothstein proceedings.[157] In order to assuage these concerns and to help guide committee members, Peter Hogg was retained to guide the ad hoc House of Commons Committee on appropriate questions to ask of judicial nominees at the first two hearings. Though committee members were not obliged to follow a protocol, they respected the spirit of Professor Hogg's guidelines.[158] This was, he declared in his opening statement at the Rothstein hearing, a historic opportunity to prove the critics of the interview process wrong: "This Committee has the opportunity to demonstrate that the Canadian virtues of civility and moderation can make an open and public process work."[159] Hogg advised the committee members about the norms of judicial propriety: they could not forecast opinions about future or controversial cases.

153 Sean Fine, "New Supreme Court Judge Prepares for Vetting," *Globe and Mail*, 2 October 2013.
154 Davis, *Electing Justice*, 27.
155 "Harper v. Harper," *Globe and Mail*, 4 October 2012.
156 Sean Fine, "Nadon Skates through Nomination Hearing," *Globe and Mail*, 3 October 2013.
157 Janice Tibbetts, "Critics Seek to Cancel Judge's TV Appearance," *Winnipeg Free Press*, 25 February 2006.
158 Hogg, "Appointment of Thomas A. Cromwell," 21.
159 Peter W. Hogg, "Appointment of Justice Marshall Rothstein to the Supreme Court of Canada," *Osgoode Hall Law Journal* 44 (2006): 537.

Though committee members were "free to ask any questions at all,"[160] they should focus on whether the candidate had the "right stuff" to be a Supreme Court judge: "Does he have the professional and personal qualities that will enable him to serve with distinction as a judge on our highest court?"[161] Hogg added, in the 2011 joint hearings, that committee members should expect answers to "general questions on how the nominees reach decisions – they are both experienced judges, of course – how they interact with colleagues, their professional lives and work, and any other matters that in your view bear on their ability to be a wise member of our highest court."[162] These were more or less the same guidelines recommended by the committee's next advisor, Jean-Louis Baudouin, former judge of the Court of Appeal, who was retained for the Wagner and Nadon hearings. Only they were not merely guidelines, they were now "rules" to be followed by committee members: "Rules have been defined, and they must be followed," he declared. Warning parliamentarians to "stay away from the American model, which more closely resembles an aggressive cross-examination than a conversation or dialogue," committee members were advised to steer clear of Nadon's prior decisions, subjects that could or might be before the Supreme Court, and even "questions of a very personal nature – except, perhaps, about golf."[163]

The result, on every occasion, was rather unilluminating, drawing ridicule from some of the press corps who described the Rothstein hearing, under questioning by his "political fan club," as "a coronation"[164] and a "love-in."[165] Press grumbling carried over into the joint Moldaver/Karakatsanis hearings, which were described as too rushed, overly "genteel,"[166] and "akin to a meet and greet."[167] They elicited

160 Canada, "Evidence before the Ad Hoc Committee on the Appointment of Supreme Court of Canada Justices," 19 October 2011, 1550.
161 Hogg, "Appointment of Justice Marshall Rothstein," 538.
162 Canada, "Evidence before the Ad Hoc Committee," 1550.
163 Canada, Department of Justice, Ad Hoc Committee on the Appointment of Supreme Court of Canada Justices, "Transcript," www.justice.gc.ca/eng/news-nouv/ja-nj/2013/doc_32972.html.
164 Don Martin, "Supreme Gathering Resembled Coronation," *Calgary Herald*, 28 February 2006.
165 Paul Samyn, "It Was Like a Love-in," *Winnipeg Free Press*, 28 February 2006.
166 "Genteel Grill," *Winnipeg Free Press*, 19 October 2011.
167 Kirk Makin, "Grilling of Top Court Nominees Akin to a 'Meet-and-Greet,' Experts Say," *Globe and Mail*, 19 October 2011.

little about the judges' "perspectives on law, except in the most general way," observed a *Globe and Mail* editorial.[168] Justice Nadon was "lightly grilled" by the committee, its members going "out of their way to avoid the kind of ruthless inquisition endured by nominees to the U.S. Supreme Court," observed a Canadian Press report.[169] In the case of Justice Wagner, he suffered polite but superficial questioning. One of the only questions that dug deep into his "judicial philosophy" – a question concerning the limits of constitutional growth associated with the Canada's "living tree" doctrine (a.k.a. the "living constitution") – was easily deflected by the nominee. Answering the question, he replied, could disqualify him from sitting in some future case. The "Hogg effect" successfully framed the hearings in judicial terms and so neutralized attempts at portraying the nominees as anything other than qualified legalists.

Law versus Politics

With such tight time frames, limited terms of engagement, and few distractions, the legal frame inevitably would prevail in the reporting. Even the basic distinction between law and politics, between judicial activism and restraint, was not dominant in the coverage of the five appointments. It simply was not a preoccupation for the journalists. In this regard, it can be said that the narrative originating out of the Reform Party policy shop was not widely taken up.[170] It turns out that it was a preoccupation for the nominees themselves. Each of the nominees made the point, either in formal comments to, or in response to questions from, the committee and dutifully picked up by the press, that judicial reasoning was unlike political bargaining. Responding to the special Committee in the French language, Justice Karakatsanis declared, "Le pouvoir judiciaire, c'est un pouvoir d'appliquer et d'examiner les lois avec les dispositions de la Charte et la jurisprudence. Ce n'est pas de créer les lois."[171] According to a journalistic account, "Both Karakatsanis

---

168 "Probing Progress," *Globe and Mail*, 21 October 2011.
169 Steve Rennie, "New Supreme Court Nominee Marc Nadon Testifies at Parliamentary Committee," *Winnipeg Free Press*, 2 October 2013.
170 If the distinction likely was to arise, it would be in editorials and op-eds penned, for instance, by law professors insisting that law is not like politics.
171 Hugo de Grandpré, "Un candidat à la Cour suprême s'excuse de ne pas parler français," *La Presse*, 19 October 2011.

and Moldaver indicated they were well aware that their job involves applying the law, whereas Parliament's role is to create law – no doubt scoring points with Conservatives who have long complained about an overly activist judiciary."[172] The following observation was elicited from nominee Wagner during his short two hour meeting: "The courts apply the law and maybe for some people the application of the law is the creation of the law – I don't think it is."[173] Justice Nadon made the same point during his opening statement: "We're not another Parliament," he declared. "It's not up to us to say this is not a good law, it ought to be changed." Nadon acknowledged, however, that the Charter of Rights and Freedoms had altered the judicial role, which "sometimes allows us to indicate if a law needs to be changed."[174] It is revealing that, among our sample of newspapers, only the *Globe and Mail* reported on this dimension of the Nadon hearing.

A Political Process?

This is not to say that the coverage was empty of politics. First, much of the coverage centred on the process and so took on a political hue: the make-up of the advisory committee, the discretion available to the prime minister, and perceived splits within the federal political parties were all the subject of reporting and commentary. This is unsurprising: after all, the process is led by elected politicians, while journalists, who ordinarily cover the political beat, mostly were the ones filing the stories.

---

172 Tobi Cohen, "Top Court Nominee Comes under Fire for Lack of French," *Calgary Herald*, 19 October 2011.

173 One journalist observed that "Judge Wagner also asserted that judges need to remember their place in a democracy: 'The creation of law is for you, Members of Parliament to do,' he said. 'It is not up to judges.'" See Bruce Cheadle, "MPs Get to Know Richard Wagner, Canada's Newest Supreme Court Nominee," *Calgary Herald*, 4 October 2012.

174 Fine, "New Supreme Court Judge Prepares for Vetting"; Jessica Murphy, "MPs Grill Top Court Nominee Richard Wagner," *Toronto Sun*, 4 October 2012. In an exchange with MP Robert Goguen, Judge Nadon had this to say about the separation of powers between the judicial and other branches: "I think the separation of powers is still there. If there are no charter issues, the mandate of the courts is to apply the law as enacted by the Parliament of Canada. I don't think any judge will suggest otherwise" (Canada, "Backgrounder"). It is revealing that Judge Nadon makes no mention of the federal division of powers here or anywhere else in his hearing. It was as if the law of Canadian federalism was not a matter within the purview of Canada's highest court.

This was prevalent during the Rothstein hearings[175] and particularly pronounced during the joint Moldaver/Karakatsanis hearings. The decline in coverage by the time of the Wagner and Nadon hearings – no live broadcast was available other than via the Internet – suggests that even journalists ordinarily covering the political beat found the politics of judicial nominations rather dull.

The fact that the coverage attracted so little political heat is credited largely to the approach adopted by the prime minister. A reader of the English-language coverage would have been left with the impression that Prime Minister Harper should be praised for having taken a nonpartisan approach to the appointment process. As a *Globe and Mail* editorial put it, "Claims of some critics that [Harper] would try to hijack the court for some narrow ideological purpose have proven abysmally wrong"[176] – an observation the editorial board repeated during the following year's nomination process.[177] Criticism of the tepid line of questioning permitted by the committee members occasionally is bemoaned. But the nomination process is described mostly in positive terms. The prime minister emerges unscathed, if not smelling like roses. Only with the Nadon nomination – a less credible candidate whose chief qualification appears to have been ideological compatibility with the government – did the prime minister's positive impression decline (see figure 5.2).

There is evidence, then, of ideology, if not partisanship, determining the choice of candidate. For instance, readers would have been left with the impression that Justice Karakatsanis was appointed, in part, because of her close connection to Finance Minister Jim Flaherty. She previously served as Flaherty's deputy when he was Ontario attorney general.[178] Such questions clearly rose to the surface during the Nadon process, a candidate who was on no one's short list of Supreme Court nominees from Quebec in 2013.[179] Judge Nadon wrote the sole dissenting opinion in

175 The *Globe and Mail*'s Kirk Makin, for instance, who reported regularly on the Supreme Court, is not found in our database of Rothstein stories in 2006.
176 "Probing Progress"; Lorne Sossin, "Picking Judges Injudiciously," *Globe and Mail*, 18 October 2011.
177 "A Role Player, While Balance Waits," *Globe and Mail*, 3 October 2012.
178 Christie Blatchford, "New Top Court Judge Known for Plain Talk," *Calgary Herald*, 18 October 2011; Kirk Makin, "Harper's Picks Highlight New Direction," *Globe and Mail*, 18 October 2011.
179 For example, Sean Fine, "Former Professor Contends for Top Court," *Globe and Mail*, 30 September 2013.

Figure 5.2. Tone of Reference to the Prime Minister

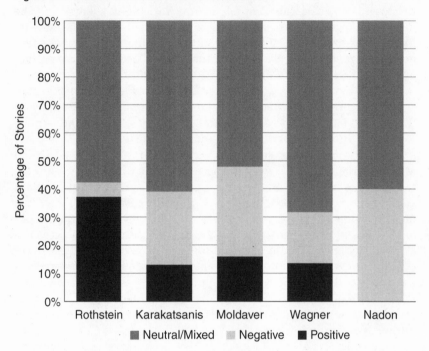

Khadr (No. 2) (2009) at the Federal Court of Appeal, concerning an application for a declaration that Omar Khadr's constitutional rights under section 7 of the Charter continued to be violated while in U.S. custody at Guantanamo Bay. Canada had "met its duty to protect Mr Khadr," Nadon declared.[180] The two Federal Court of Appeal justices affirmed the trial judge's remedy to direct the minister to seek Mr Khadr's repatriation. On further appeal, the Supreme Court agreed that Khadr's constitutional rights continued to be violated. They chose, however, not to issue a remedy. As the prerogative over foreign affairs had not been displaced by statute, the Court preferred to defer to "the executive to make decisions on matters of foreign affairs in the context of complex and ever-changing circumstances, taking into account broader national interests."[181]

---

180 *Khadr v Canada (Prime Minister)* [2010] 1 FCR 73, para 98 (Fed CA).
181 *Canada (Prime Minister) v Khadr* [2010] 1 SCR 44, para 39. The Federal Court of Appeal drew the opposite inference because the Crown had adduced no evidence that requesting Khadr's return would damage U.S.-Canada relations.

In effect, the Supreme Court of Canada agreed with Nadon on the remedial point, but it is significant that Justice Nadon was the sole judge among thirteen who found no Charter violation.[182] It was this that likely brought him to the attention of the Conservative government – little else would have. Nadon sat as a Federal Court judge for twenty years – having previously practised admiralty law for twenty years in Montreal[183] – and elected to be supernumerary (semi-retired) in July 2011. He clearly was beginning to wind down his judicial career. Several of the news reports mentioned Nadon's dissent in the Khadr case in the context of discussing his qualifications for the job.[184] There was nothing "remarkable" – despite the prime minister's claim[185] – about Judge Nadon's qualifications other than his defence of executive prerogative in the Khadr case.

LANGUAGE

Not all appointments went as smoothly as the Prime Minister's Office would have hoped. In some ways, Justice Moldaver's process went off the rails as the result of language issues. Though this was far less a concern to the English-language press, where Justice Moldaver was a media favourite, it was decidedly an issue in the French-language press, because Justice Moldaver lacked French-language skills and this deficiency proved embarrassing for the candidate. It also proved disconcerting for the NDP representative on the House of Commons Committee (Joe Comartin) who complained about the candidate's unilingualism yet sat on the advisory committee that approved the short list of candidates. Moldaver's unilingualism played out in both *Le Journal de Montréal* and in the much larger coverage generated by *La Presse* – "Un Candidat Juge Unilingue Anglophone" announced a *La Presse* headline.[186] Because it was the second such appointment of

182 Yves Boisvert, "Une politisation de la Cour suprême?," *La Presse*, 2 October 2013.
183 Canada, "Backgrounder: The Honourable Mr Justice Marc Nadon."
184 Boisvert, "Une politisation de la Cour suprême?"; Canadian Press, "Harper Nominates Federal Court of Appeal Judge Marc Nadon for the Supreme Court," *Winnipeg Free Press*, 1 October 2013; Hugo de Grandpré, "Cour supreme: Harper nomme un autre home du Québec," *La Presse*, 1 September 2013; Sean Fine, "Harper Appoints Nadon to Top Court," *Globe and Mail*, 1 October 2013; Fine, "Nadon Skates through Nomination Hearing."
185 Staff writer, "Harper Officially Appoints New High Court Judge," *Winnipeg Free Press*, 4 October 2013.
186 Hugo de Grandpré, "Un Candidat Juge Unilingue Anglophone," *La Presse*, 17 October 2011.

a unilingual justice since 2006 – Justice Rothstein also was unilingual, had undertaken to become fluent on the job, and failed to do so – it compounded the impression that this was part of a larger federal trend.[187] Moldaver's unilingualism was mentioned in all six news articles and editorial items published in *La Presse* during this appointment process. It was mentioned far less frequently in the English-language press.

This focus on language also dominated coverage during the Rothstein nomination. Both *Le Journal de Montréal*[188] and *La Presse*[189] were preoccupied with the nominee's ignorance of both the French language and the civil law. After acknowledging this deficiency, however, Yves Boisvert and Nathaélle Morissette in *La Presse* essentially admitted that Rothstein would make an excellent addition to the Court.[190] Though there were many elements to the Nadon nomination that would have been of interest to its francophone readers, language should not have been one of them. After all, Nadon was appointed to fill one of three Quebec seats on the Court and so was fluently bilingual. Yet coverage of the hearing in *La Presse* focused principally on a very brief exchange regarding the value of bilingualism at the Supreme Court (see figure 5.3).[191]

So politics entered into reporting of the nomination process, but not as predicted – in ways that did damage to the federal Conservative Party, the credibility of New Democrats, and possibly the institutional reputation of the Supreme Court of Canada. This should not be surprising. If one views Canada's nomination process as offering a new "political opportunity structure" to intervene in national political discourse,[192] it is predictable that distinctive Canadian political preoccupations, like language, will become channelled through it. Once having begun down this path, politicization of the appointment process, one might say, is unavoidable. The question remains what other political issues get channelled in future nomination processes.

---

187 The Conservatives earlier had opposed legislation mandating bilingual Supreme Court justices (Bill C-232 passed in the minority House of Commons but stalled in the Senate), appointed a unilingual auditor general, and earlier a unilingual Rothstein.

188 Laurent Soumis, "Le Juge Rothstein Passe le test," *Le Journal de Montréal*, 28 February 2006.

189 Yves Boisvert, "Un Processus Utile se Sans Danger," *La Presse*, 28 February 2006.

190 Ibid.; Nathaélle Morissette, "Harper Choisit Marshall Rothstein," *La Presse*, 24 February 2006.

191 Stéphanie Marin, "Le juge Nadon, candidat à la Cour supreme, a compare en comité," *La Presse*, 2 October 2013.

192 Charles Tilly and Sidney Tarrow, *Contentious Politics* (Boulder, CO: Paradigm, 2007), 49.

Figure 5.3. Focus of Coverage

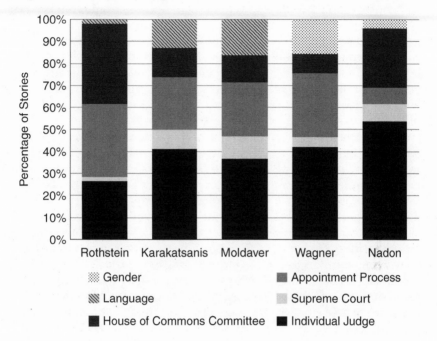

GENDER

The politics of gender were an obvious candidate in this regard. The nomination of Justice Richard Wagner provided just such an occasion. Justice Wagner's rapid rise through the ranks of the judiciary was noted, as were the Conservative Party political connections of his father (Claude Wagner) who served in Prime Minister Joe Clark's Cabinet,[193] but these were mostly non-issues. What was contentious was that Wagner was replacing Justice Marie Deschamps, so there was some expectation that the prime minister would appoint another woman to the seat (to maintain a near parity of four female justices). That this did not occur emerged as a major sub-theme in the reporting. Many articles profiling Wagner made some mention of gender, even those in

193 Claude Wagner also served in the Quebec Liberal Party Cabinet of Jean Lesage in the 1960s. See Tobi Cohen, "Despite Conservative Ties, Richard Wagner Seen as Good Choice for Supreme Court," *Calgary Herald*, 2 October 2012.

popular tabloids such as the *Toronto Sun* and *Le Journal de Montréal*. The *Sun* concluded one of its two reports with a quote from feminist tax law professor Kathleen Lahey. Conveying profound disappointment, Lahey claimed that Wagner's appointment "reduces the diversity and equity reflected in the Court, and sends the message that the wisdom and expertise of woman lawyers and judges is still not valued equally with that of men in 21st-century Canada."[194] This is reproduced in the French language in a *Journal de Montréal* report published on the same day.[195] The first few paragraphs of the only *Winnipeg Free Press* story on the Wagner nomination, entitled "Harper Selects Richard Wagner for Supreme Court, Urged to Pick Woman Next Time") quoted at length from New Democrat MP Françoise Boivin (opposition justice critic) who emphasized the importance of maintaining gender parity on the court – it was as important as guaranteeing three seats on the court for Quebec, she insisted.[196] Nevertheless, Boivin was satisfied with Wagner, given the strength of his personality and expertise in the civil law.[197] Besides, there would be an upcoming opportunity to appoint more women from Quebec due to pending retirements.[198] There was a noticeable, if marginal, difference in French-language coverage. It was a little more sensitive to gender dynamics on the court. *La Presse* devoted a whole story to the issue, observing that the politics of gender "unleashed less passion" than the issue of bilingualism.[199] Overall, however, the question of gender was treated as minor and remediable.

The issue returned to the surface during the Nadon nomination, the next appointment available to Prime Minister Harper. Gender returned prominently in the initial report in *La Presse*[200] and in the Canadian Press report in the *Winnipeg Free Press*. The latter asked pointedly "why he

---

194 Kristy Kirkup, "Prime Minister Nominates Judge Richard Wagner as New Supreme Court Justice," *Toronto Sun*, 2 October 2012.

195 Agence QMI, "Harper recommande un juge québécois," *Le Journal de Montréal*, 2 October 2012; also Stéphanie Marin, "Stephen Harper soumet la candidature de Richard Wagner à la Cour suprême," *La Presse*, 2 October 2012.

196 Keith Blanchfield, "Harper Selects Richard Wagner for Supreme Court, Urged to Pick Woman Next Time," *Winnipeg Free Press*, 2 October 2012.

197 Agence QMI, "Harper recommande un juge Québécois."

198 Bruce Cheadle, "MPs Get to Know Richard Wagner, Canada's Newest Supreme Court Nominee," *Calgary Herald*, 4 October 2012.

199 Marin, "Stephen Harper soumet la candidature de Richard Wagner à la Cour supreme."

200 De Grandpré, "Cour supreme."

[Harper] hasn't done more to address the so-called gender imbalance on the country's highest court."[201] Even NDP Leader Thomas Mulcair carefully waded into the controversy, calling on the government to "be more careful in future in terms of the male-female representation on the court."[202] Asked about his contribution to diversity on the Court by MP Irwin Cotler during the hearing, with particular reference to maintaining an equitable gender balance,[203] Nadon replied cynically, "Am I the ethnic candidate that fits perfectly? I'll let others answer that."[204]

A Personalized Process?

The overwhelming message readers would have received is that the nominees exhibited the ideals of judicial propriety: they had, in Peter Hogg's words, "the right stuff" (see figure 5.4). Justice Moldaver is described in laudatory terms as a "judge with moxy,"[205] of enhancing the criminal law expertise on the Court[206], and having a "fine nose for even the faintest odour of B.S."[207] Sporadic mention is made of Justice Moldaver's complaint about criminal trial lawyers "trivializing" the Charter by excessively invoking the Charter rights of criminal accuseds, but this is looked upon as an advantage, at least among columnists like Yves Boisvert and Christie Blatchford.[208]

Justice Karakatsanis seemingly was of less interest to the media. With a shorter judicial tenure on the Ontario Court of Appeal (eight years

201 Canadian Press, "Harper Nominates Federal Court of Appeal Judge Marc Nadon for the Supreme Court," *Winnipeg Free Press*, 1 October; also Sean Fine, "Harper Appoints Nadon to Top Court"; Jessica Murphy, "MPs Vet Supreme Court Nominee," *Winnipeg Free Press*, 3 October 2013.
202 Canadian Press, "Harper Nominates Federal Court of Appeal Judge Marc Nadon."
203 Cotler asked, "Some people wanted this appointment to be used to maintain the balance between men and women at the court. What elements of diversity do you think you contribute to the judiciary? Why is diversified training desirable?" In Canada, Department of Justice, Ad Hoc Committee on the Appointment of Supreme Court of Canada Justices, "Transcript," 2013, www.justice.gc.ca/eng/news-nouv/ja-nj/2013/doc_32972.html.
204 Fine, "Nadon Skates through Nomination Hearing."
205 Robert Marshall, "A Judge with Moxy," *Winnipeg Free Press*, 22 October 2011.
206 "Even Good Judges Need Public Scrutiny," *Globe and Mail*, 18 October 2011.
207 Christie Blatchford, "Holy Smokes! A Supreme Who's a Star," *Winnipeg Free Press*, 19 October 2011.
208 Yves Boisvert, "Deux nouveaux juges à la Cour suprême," *La Presse*, 17 October 2011; Blatchford, "Holy Smokes!"

as a trial judge), she is touted for bringing more diversity to the Court. There are reported grumblings in the Toronto legal community about having overlooked other more qualified candidates on the Ontario Court of Appeal. Nonetheless, she is reported to have just the right judicial temperament.

From Calgary to Montreal, Justice Wagner is touted as an outstanding candidate. Quoting faithfully from the prime minister's press conference, Wagner is described as an "exceptional candidate who possesses the aptitude and qualifications to serve Canadians well."[209] The tone of the reporting is overwhelmingly positive, one could say glowing, and any concerns about Conservative party ties or gender composition on the Court are dismissed as unimportant or an issue for another day.[210] Even Justice Nadon is lauded for his "able stick-handl[ing]" of the questions. He is a golfer and a bookworm and was once drafted as a teen to the Detroit Red Wings, declared Jessica Murphy in the *Winnipeg Free Press*. "In fact," she continued in her second lead sentence, "the most controversial revelation in Wednesday's grilling by MPs of Marc Nadon, 64, was that he still backs the Motor City team."[211] With reason, the *Globe and Mail*'s headline declared "Nadon Skates Through Nomination Hearing."[212] It turns out that this was not the most controversial aspect of the hearing. During the course of his opening statement, Nadon declared, "In fact, I was drafted by the Detroit Red Wings when I was 14."[213] This turned out to be untrue. Both bloggers and the Red Wings organization refuted Nadon's claim the day after the hearings, leading Nadon to admit that he used the word *drafted* "in the way in which it was used in those days, loosely termed to say that I would be part of the organization. The exact details I never knew exactly."[214] This raised further questions about Nadon's

209 Agence QMI, "Harper recommande un juge Québécois."
210 Cohen, "Despite Conservative Ties, Richard Wagner Seen as Good Choice for Supreme Court."
211 Murphy, "MPs Vet Supreme Court Nominee." The Wagner hearing also is curiously described by Murphy as a "grilling" (Murphy, "MPs Grill Top Court Nominee Richard Wagner"). For reasons mentioned above, the hearings have not risen to such heated levels.
212 Fine, "Nadon Skates through Nomination Hearing."
213 Ad Hoc Committee on the Appointment of Supreme Court of Canada Justices, "Transcript."
214 Jessica Barrett, "New Justice's NHL Draft Claim Refuted by Experts," *Calgary Herald*, 4 October 2013.

qualifications. If you cannot be clear about such things, warned NDP committee member Françoise Boivin, this did not portend well for a career on the Supreme Court.[215] The tabloid press seized on this error, the *Toronto Sun* warning, "In Canada, it's never a good idea to stretch the truth about hockey."[216]

There was a serious question about his qualifications that could have been raised but which was a non-issue between his nomination and appointment. It concerned the question of whether a sitting Federal Court judge was eligible for promotion to sit as a judge from Quebec under the Supreme Court Act. Accompanying the announcement of his nomination on the Monday was a legal opinion tendered by former Supreme Court justice Ian Binnie.[217] The opinion addressed this constitutional question, finding no impediment, smoothing the path for Justice Nadon's elevation. In the following year, the Supreme Court of Canada ruled the appointment unconstitutional.[218] Only one journalist – the reliable Yves Boisvert in *La Presse* – took note of the controversy.[219]

Given the absence of a salient political frame with which to report on the prospective nominees (outside of Justice Moldaver's unilingualism), the press chose to focus on personality and personal biography. As Bogoch and Holzman-Gazit find in their study of Israeli high court appointments, there was substantial "media personalization," with a heightened focus on individual candidates rather than on the Court as an institution.[220] A focus on the human side of nominees satisfies media "imperatives," observes Davis – it enhances "visual attractiveness and sustains audience interest."[221] In contrast to their findings,

---

215 Ibid.; "Marc Nadon officiellement nommé à la Cour suprême du Canada," *La Presse*, 4 October 2013.

216 Jessica Murphy, "Top Court Nominee Backtracks on NHL Draft Comment," *Toronto Sun*, 4 October 2013; Agence QMI, "Nomination officielle du juge Marc Nadon à la Cour suprême," *Le Journal de Montréal*, 4 October 2013.

217 Also reportedly consulted were retired Supreme Court Justice Marie Deschamps and Professor Peter Hogg.

218 *Reference re Supreme Court Act*, ss 5 and 6. In addition, the federal government amended the Supreme Court Act to clear up any confusion on this point. This enactment was also ruled unconstitutional (in ibid.).

219 Boisvert, "Une politisation de la Cour suprême?"

220 Bogoch and Holzman-Gazit, "Promoting Justices," 646; Gideon Rahat and Tamir Sheafer, "The Personalization(s) of Politics: Israel, 1949–2003," *Political Communication* 24 (2007): 67.

221 Davis, *Electing Justice*, 102.

Figure 5.4. Tone of Judge

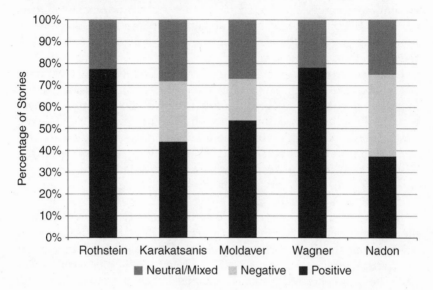

however, elements of "media privatization" also were present, with a focus on "personal characteristics and personal life of individual candidates."[222] The hearings were replete with references to the candidates' backgrounds, often coming from humble origins, and their rise to the top.[223] A life steeped in learning, delivered with a tinge of humour[224] (see figure 5.4) helped frame the dominant message that these all were outstanding and well-qualified candidates, best captured by a *Toronto Sun* headline regarding the Rothstein nomination: "He's Human – Who Knew?"[225]

222 On media privatization, see Rahat and Sheafer, "The Personalization(s) of Politics," 68.
223 See their biographical treatments in the *Toronto Star*, where Moldaver is described as a "nice Jewish boy," in Kate Allen, "'Nice Jewish Boy' Had Blue Collar Beginnings," *Toronto Star*, 15 November; and where Karakatsanis is described as rising up from working-class roots, in Tracey Tyler, "From Prohibition Lane to Highest Court in the Land," *Toronto Star*, 15 November 2011.
224 Ziegel, "New Era in the Selection of Supreme Court Judges?," 549.
225 Greg Weston, "He's Human: Who Knew?," *Toronto Sun*, 28 February 2006.

Rahat and Sheafar associate media privatization with attempts to depoliticize issues.[226] With a focus fixed firmly on the personal, readers would have learned little about decision-making under the Charter of Rights and Freedoms, structures of analysis, or the role the judiciary in Canada's constitutional system.[227] There was hardly any discussion, for instance, of Supreme Court cases already decided, old or new. During the Wagner hearing, there was mention of judicial independence (he is described as a "fervent advocate"),[228] though this is left largely unexplained. It is hard to maintain, then, that an "important educational function" was served by the nomination hearings.[229] In their collective swooning over the candidates, the press corps effectively depoliticized the high court's judicial functions.

A Big "Love-In"?

Overall coverage might best be described as a big "love-in."[230] One can surmise that the journalists liked what they saw because the justices did not exhibit the sort of behaviour one typically finds on Parliament Hill. This is in accord with what we found in our 2008 study of media reporting of the Supreme Court of Canada[231] and with the empirical work undertaken in the United States showing that the more people get to know about the U.S. Supreme Court, via the Senate confirmation process, for instance, the more that they like it.[232] The more the press frames the U.S. Supreme Court's work in political terms, the less the public likes it.[233] The more legalistic the Court appears, however, and the less it demonstrates bargaining associated with political

226 Rahat and Sheafer, "The Personalization(s) of Politics," 67.
227 Writing about the Rothstein hearings, and this could be said about all four nominees, Plaxton observes, "There was a remarkable failure to push Justice Rothstein to say anything about how judges go about interpreting the broad, open-ended rules" of the Charter, in Michael Plaxton, "The Neutrality Thesis and the Rothstein Hearing," *University of New Brunswick Law Journal* 58 (2008): 99.
228 Murphy, "MPs Grill Top Court Nominee Richard Wagner."
229 Ziegel, "New Era in the Selection of Supreme Court Judges?," 555; also Adam Dodek, "Reforming the Supreme Court Appointment Process, 2004–2014: A Ten-Year Democratic Audit," *Supreme Court Law Review*, 2nd ser., 67 (2014): 111–77.
230 Samyn, "It Was Like a Love-in."
231 Sauvageau, Schneiderman, and Taras, *Last Word*.
232 Gibson and Caldeira, *Citizens, Courts, and Confirmations*.
233 Baird and Gangl, "Shattering the Myth of Legality."

processes, the more that readers hold the Court in high esteem. Gibson and Caldeira confirm the hypothesis that "anything that causes people to pay attention to courts," even controversial confirmation processes, "winds up reinforcing institutional legitimacy through exposure to the legitimizing symbols associated with law and courts." This is a consequence of the "positivity bias" (or diffuse support), the reservoir of institutional goodwill associated with the Court that is wakened whenever attention is focused on the Court. "To know Courts is to love them, or at least respect them," they conclude.[234]

So tepid and apolitical were these processes that Justice Wagner recommended that their scope be enlarged to include federal appointees to provincial courts of appeal. "It might surprise you," he declared to the *Globe and Mail*'s Kirk Makin, "but I liked the process."[235] This vote of confidence confounded many court watchers, but it should not have. Wagner was praised to the sky for his intelligence and humanity. Even the unilingual Justice Moldaver was lauded in the francophone press as being a fine judge. We can similarly conclude that the more the Canadian press corps come to know justices on the Supreme Court, the more they like them. They are not like politicians, after all. The danger inherent in Justice Wagner's proposal, however, is that it will harden a process with little public utility and even less legitimacy.

4. Foreign Experiences

If the appointment process is to be reformed, having recourse to comparative appointment processes may prove to be useful.[236] Rather than mimicking dysfunctional practices close at hand, it might be preferable to reach further afield. Some foreign experiences may prove to be more workable than others in the Canadian context. By way of conclusion, I explore a few of those candidates here.

---

234 Gibson and Caldeira, *Citizens, Courts, and Confirmations*, 3, 122.

235 Kirk Makin, "Supreme Court Judge Warns of 'Dangerous' Flaws in the System," *Globe and Mail*, 13 December 2012. Such appointments also are a matter within federal competence under section 96 of the Constitution Act, 1867.

236 Carl Baar observes that comparative study, "like a liberal education, is always good for you," in "Comparative Perspectives on Judicial Selection Processes," in Ontario Law Reform Commission, *Appointing Judges: Philosophy, Politics and Practice* (Toronto: Ontario Government, 1991), 143.

The Continental practice of training a professional cadre of judges early in their legal careers seems a poorer fit. In the civil service model, which operates in jurisdictions like France and Italy, the judiciary controls its own method of selection by conducting entrance examinations and determining promotion via appointment councils. Though merit remains the single overriding criterion, concerns arise about lack of transparency, diversity, and accountability.[237] On the other hand, a return to exclusive prime ministerial discretion, as persists in Singapore and Australia, would be a retrograde step.[238]

The experience that could prove most useful is that of judicial appointment councils. This is a method of appointment associated with the "Missouri plan," where a nomination commission, made up of lawyers and laypersons, screens applicants and forwards a short list of names to the appointing authority, which then chooses the nominee.[239] Nomination councils were recommended for appointments to the Supreme Court in 1985 by the Canadian Bar Association and Canadian Association of Law Teachers.[240] This is the process adopted by Ontario for provincial judicial appointments in 1994, which, according to one assessment, has "improved the overall quality" of the provincial court judiciary, if not making it more representative.[241] Choosing a nominee

---

237 Nuno Garoupa and Tom Ginsburg, "Guarding the Guardians: Judicial Councils and Judicial Independence," *American Journal of Comparative Law* 57 (2009): 103–34.

238 Ibid., 113; Elizabeth Handsley, "'The Judicial Whisper Goes Around': Appointment of Judicial Officers in Australia," in *Appointing Judges in an Age of Judicial Power: Critical Perspectives From Around the World*, ed. Kate Malleson and Peter H. Russell (Toronto: University of Toronto Press, 2006), 123.

239 The nominee holds office for at least one year, after which, at the time of the next general election, voters can approve retention of the judge, who continues to sit through the remainder of the term. See Robert A. Schroeder and Harry A. Hall, "Twenty-Five Years' Experience with Merit Judicial Selection in Missouri," *Texas Law Review* 44 (1966): 1091.

240 Canadian Association of Law Teachers, "Recommendations for Consideration at the Annual Meeting of the Association at the Université de Montréal on Saturday, June 1st, 1985," in *Judicial Selection in Canada: Discussion Papers and Reports* (prepared for the Canadian Association of Law Teachers Special Committee on the Appointment of Judges, 1987), 66; Canadian Bar Association, *Report of the Canadian Bar Association Committee on the Appointment of Judges in Canada* (Ottawa: Canadian Bar Foundation, 1985). As to the differences between their recommendations on Supreme Court appointments, see the discussion in Friedland, *Place Apart*, 239. This roughly is the scheme in place in many U.S. state jurisdictions (the "Missouri Plan"), with the qualification that the state electorate votes whether to retain judges after a probationary period (253).

241 Friedland, *Place Apart*, 246.

from among a short list of candidates has been the practice ever since the Paul Martin administration. This indicates that there has been some movement toward a nominating council, and it would be advantageous to move further along this route. Both the South African and United Kingdom experiences will prove instructive.

The Constitutional Court of South Africa is composed of eleven judges, all of whom are South African citizens, appointed for twelve-year terms with mandatory retirement at age seventy. The Judicial Service Commission (JSC), established under the new South African Constitution of 1996 (section 178), is granted constitutional authority to nominate judges for appointment to the Court, in addition to lower courts. A twenty-three-person body, composed of judicial, legal, legislative, and civil society representatives, chaired by the chief justice, solicits applications for membership in South Africa's Constitutional Court, generates a short list, and then conducts interviews of potential candidates, the transcripts of which are made publicly available. A list of nominees (three names more than the number of vacancies) is offered to the president of the republic, who makes the selection after consulting with the leadership of political parties represented in the National Assembly. Appointees are constitutionally required to be "qualified" and "fit and proper persons." In addition, the Constitution declares the "need for the judiciary to reflect broadly the racial and gender composition of South Africa must be considered when judicial officers are appointed" (section 174[2]). The appointment of president and deputy president to the Constitutional Court is singled out for separate consideration in the Constitution. The president undertakes the selection process, after requisite consultation, without a list of nominees presented by the JSC (section 174[3]).[242] Though the JSC's proceedings otherwise are closed to the public, the process, it is said, has resulted in both an impressive diversity and quality of appointment.[243]

There remain concerns that JSC is top heavy with political appointees. Of its twenty-three members, Corder advises, "fifteen are selected more for their broadly political views than their standing as lawyers,

---

242 See the discussion in Hugh Corder, "Appointment, Discipline and Removal of Judges in South Africa," in *Judiciaries in Comparative Perspective*, ed. H.P. Lee (Cambridge: Cambridge University Press, 2011), 102.

243 Francois Du Bois, "Judicial Selection in Post-Apartheid South Africa," in *Appointing Judges in an Age of Judicial Power: Critical Perspectives from around the World*, ed. Kate Malleson and Peter H. Russell, 280–312 (Toronto: University of Toronto Press, 2006).

of whom at least twelve are likely to be loyal in the first instance to the ruling party in Parliament."[244] The institutional capacity of the JSC to engage with nominees over such things as "judicial philosophy" is in doubt.[245] Nor is there any transparency in the process by which the short list of nominees is generated.[246] Gender diversity has been slow to achieve, despite the constitutional injunction to consider gender composition[247] – only two women now sit on the Constitutional Court.[248] By contrast, the constitutional injunction to take race into account has been enthusiastically embraced,[249] with candidates even asked to self-identify according to racial classifications.[250] According to one JSC member, who has since resigned, the JSC continually overlooks qualified white male candidates.[251]

If there are worries in South Africa that the nominating commission is overrepresented by the political branch and so lacks independence, there is the converse worry in the United Kingdom that judges have too much independence and control over the appointment of their peers. Until 2005, the Lord Chancellor, the chief legal officer in government

244 Corder, "Appointment, Discipline and Removal of Judges in South Africa," 101.
245 Susannah Cowen, "Judicial Selection in South Africa," research paper for Democratic Governance and Rights Unit, University of Cape Town, 2010, 18, www.dgru.uct.ac.za/usr/dgru/downloads/Judicial%20SelectionOct2010.pdf.
246 Dennis M. Davis, "Judicial Appointments in South Africa," Advocate 23, no. 3 (December 2010): 40–3, www.sabar.co.za/law-journals/2010/december/2010-december-vol023-no3-pp40-43.pdf; Yonaton T. Fessha, "Constitutional Court Appointment: The South African Process," in The Democratic Dilemma: Reforming Canada's Supreme Court, ed. Nadia Verrelli (Montreal and Kingston: McGill-Queen's University Press, 2013), 231.
247 Yvonne Mokgoro, "Judicial Appointments," Advocate 23, no. 3 (December 2010): 43–8, www.sabar.co.za/law-journals/2010/december/2010-december-vol023-no3-pp43-48.pdf.
248 University of Cape Town [UCT], Democratic Governance and Rights Unit, "Submission and Research Report on the Judicial Records on Nominees for Appointment to the Constitutional Court February 2013," 2013, 5, www.dgru.uct.ac.za/usr/dgru/downloads/JSC%20submission%20print%20Feb%2013_printfinal.pdf.
249 Pierre de Vos, "Judicial Transformation: South Africa's Appalling Non-Commitment," Daily Maverick, 22 January 2013, www.dailymaverick.co.za/opinionista/2013-01-22-judicial-transformation-south-africas-appalling-non-commitment/#.U3z8gV4ipuY.
250 Cowen, "Judicial Selection in South Africa," 94.
251 Niren Tolsi, "JSC's Izak Smuts Resigns after Transformation Row," Mail & Guardian, 12 April 2013, mg.co.za/print/2013-04-12-izak-smuts-resigns-after-transformation-row.

and member of Cabinet, had sole jurisdiction over judicial appointments in the United Kingdom.[252] The new process was inaugurated with the establishment of a new "Supreme Court" to replace the House of Lords as the final court of appeal in the country.[253] Both the formation of the court and a new appointment process were prompted by the belief that insulating the process from the Lord Chancellor's influence would enhance the separation of powers between the executive and judicial branches.[254] Vacancies on the high court are now filled by a five-member judicial selection commission, which solicits names and nominates one candidate for appointment. The selection commission is an ad hoc body composed of the president and deputy president of the Supreme Court, in addition to representatives of appointment commissions for lower courts from England, Scotland, and Wales, of whom at least one must be a layperson.[255] Appointments are made on the basis of "merit," but candidates are expected to demonstrate "social awareness and understanding of the contemporary world."[256] Practically speaking, the Lord Chancellor is left with one of two choices as a consequence: either the first nominee is accepted or rejected, on the basis of suitability for office; if rejected, the second name put forward by the commission must then be accepted.[257]

252 United Kingdom, House of Lords, Special Committee on the Constitution, 25th Report of Session 2010–12, *Judicial Appointments: Report* (London: Stationery Office, 2012), 7, www.publications.parliament.uk/pa/ld201012/ldselect/ldconst/272/272.pdf.

253 U.K., Constitutional Reform Act 2005, c 4.

254 Alan Paterson and Chris Paterson, *Guarding the Guardians? Towards an Independent, Accountable and Diverse Senior Judiciary* (London: CentreForum, 2012), 19, www.centreforum.org/assets/pubs/guarding-the-guardians.pdf; Lord Woolf in United Kingdom, House of Lords, Select Committee on the Constitution, "Judicial Appointment Process: Oral and Written Evidence" (2011), 129–30, www.parliament.uk/documents/lords-committees/constitution/JAP/JAPCompiledevidence28032012.pdf.

255 House of Lords, *Judicial Appointments: Report*, 8.

256 Lord Phillips of Worth Matravers, "Judicial Independence and Accountability: A View from the Supreme Court," lecture, University College London, 8 February 2011, www.ucl.ac.uk/constitution-unit/events/judicial-independence-events/lord-phillips-transcript.pdf.

257 Kate Malleson, "Appointment, Discipline and Removal of Judges: Fundamental Reforms in the United Kingdom," in *Judiciaries in Comparative Perspective*, ed. H.P. Lee, 117–33 (Cambridge: Cambridge University Press, 2011); Paterson and Paterson, *Guarding the Guardians?*, 26.

As a consequence of the new selection process, Supreme Court judicial personnel have a considerable role to play in the choice of their successors. Twenty-one of the twenty-six individuals involved in the appointment of a Supreme Court justice, advise Paterson and Paterson, will be members of the judiciary, twenty of them senior judges. The danger is one of a "self-perpetuating oligarchy."[258] Nor has diversity in appointments kept pace with developments abroad.[259] With control over the identity of their successors, the process has swung perhaps too far in the direction of judicial independence. Some therefore have called for pre-appointment hearings, following recent Canadian innovations, to enhance democratic accountability. Malleson advises, after the Rothstein hearings, that the Canadian special committee hearings were "widely regarded" as having been "a success."[260] Paterson and Paterson also recommend the adoption of a Canadian model of parliamentary hearings, which "increase both accountability and legitimacy – as it has in Canada – without posing a threat to judicial independence."[261] But the House of Lords Select Committee on the Constitution pointedly rejected such reform in its 2012 report: "We are against any proposal to introduce pre-appointment hearings for senior members of the judiciary. However limited the questioning, such hearings could not have any meaningful impact without undermining the independence of those subsequently appointed or appearing to prejudge their future decisions. In the United Kingdom, judges' legitimacy depends on their independent status and appointment on merit, not on any democratic mandate."[262]

Nor would the Lords accept a greater role for the Lord Chancellor in the selection process or being offered a shortlist from which to choose a nominee, for fear of "politicizing" the process.[263] It is clear that the

---

258 Paterson and Paterson, *Guarding the Guardians?*, 26, 29.
259 Lady Justice Arden in United Kingdom, House of Lords, Select Committee on the Constitution, "Judicial Appointment Process: Oral and Written Evidence," 2011, 9–11, www.parliament.uk/documents/lords-committees/constitution/JAP/JAPCompiledevidence28032012.pdf.
260 Kate Malleson, "The Effect of the Constitutional Reform Act 2005 on the Relationship between the Judiciary, the Executive and Parliament," appendix 3 to the House of Lords, Select Committee on the Constitution, *Sixth Report*, July 2007, www.publications.parliament.uk/pa/ld200607/ldselect/ldconst/151/15102.htm.
261 Paterson and Paterson, *Guarding the Guardians?*, 71.
262 House of Lords, *Judicial Appointments: Report*, para 46.
263 Ibid., paras 26, 37.

Lords had in mind the U.S. process for appointment and not the comparatively tame Canadian version.

Both of these comparative experiences are far from perfect. But they are instructive. They have the merit of better informing how reform initiatives might develop here. The problem is that Canadian initiatives have been shaped by Reform Party proposals of the late 1980s, inspired by U.S. Senate practices. It may be time, then, to look seriously at a judicial nominating commission model. The balance to be struck between political and judicial representation on such a commission will have to be worked out and may be different from the South African or the UK models. Nevertheless, a transparent judicial nomination council would be a significant improvement over the status quo. If there is anything to be learned from the fabricated attack on the chief justice by the PMO, it is that, to the extent that both sides can provide conflicting accounts about the process of judicial appointment, the Canadian model is disturbingly flawed.

Appendix 2: Coding Sheet for Judges

1	**Coder**	Name of coder
2	**caseid**	Case ID
3	**Medium**	Medium
1	Television	
2	Newspaper	
4	**tvid**	If TV, which network?
1	CTV	
2	CBC	
3	TVA	
4	Radio Canada	
99	NA	
5	**npid**	If newspaper, which one?
1	*Calgary Herald*	
2	*Winnipeg Free Press*	
3	*Globe and Mail*	
4	*Toronto Sun*	
5	*La Presse*	
6	*Le Journal de Montréal*	
99	NA	
6	**datsto**	Date of story, dd.mm.yy

7	**judgenom**	Name of judge nominated
1	Rothstein	
2	Karakatsanis	
3	Moldaver	
4	Wagner	
5	Nadon	

8	**apptsta**	Appointment status at time of article
1	Pre-hearing	
2	Hearing	
3	Post-hearing	

9	**locanp**	Location print article in paper
1	Front page (with or without inside turn)	
2	Politics section	
3	Other	
99	NA	

Headlines

10	**mfoh**	Main focus of principal headline
1	Judge	
2	Supreme Court	
3	Process	
4	Other	

11	**faih**	First actor in principal headline
1	Judge	
2	Supreme Court	
3	Stephen Harper	
4	Special Committee	
5	Opposition	
99	Other	

12	**judgetone**	If judge is main focus of principal headline, what is tone?
1	Positive	
2	Negative	
3	Neutral/mixed	
99	NA	

13	**courttone**	If court is main focus of principal headline, what is tone?
4	Positive	
5	Negative	
6	Neutral/mixed	
99	NA	

14   **commtone**

1   Positive
2   Negative
3   Neutral/mixed
99   NA

If House of Commons is main focus of principal headline, what is tone?

15   **maintopi**
1   Individual judge
2   Supreme Court
3   Appointment process
4   House of Commons
        Committee
5   Language
6   Gender
7   Ethnicity
8   Judicial activism
9   Judicial restraint
10   Judicial independence
11   Separation of powers
12   U.S. Senate confirmation
        process
13   Other

Main topic of story (select one)

16   **secontopi**
1   Individual judge
2   Supreme Court
3   Appointment process
4   House of Commons
        Committee
5   Language
6   Gender
7   Ethnicity
8   Judicial activism
9   Judicial restraint
10   Judicial independence
11   Separation of powers
12   U.S. Senate confirmation
        process
13   Other

Secondary topic of story (select one)

Tone

17   **tonescc**
1   Positive
2   Negative
3   Neutral/mixed
99   NA

Tone of references to Supreme Court

18	**tonejud**	Tone of references to judge
1	Positive	
2	Negative	
3	Neutral/mixed	
99	NA	

19	**tonecom**	Tone of references to House of Commons Committee
1	Positive	
2	Negative	
3	Neutral/mixed	
99	NA	

20	**tonepm**	Tone of references to government or prime minister
1	Positive	
2	Negative	
3	Neutral/mixed	
99	NA	

21	**genre**	Genre
1	Hard news	
2	Editorials	
3	News analysis	
4	Columns, opinion pieces, commentary	
5	Direct excerpts	
6	In brief	
7	Feature	
8	Personality profile	
9	Other (cite)	

22	**lawpol**	Frame: Law versus politics distinction
1	Judges apply law	
2	Judges make law	
3	Judges are like politicians	
4	Judges are not like politicians	
5	Other	
99	NA	

Conclusion

If constitutions are living things, then constitutional culture is always in transition. Its elements are potentially in movement, even as they linger long enough for us to comprehend their shadowy outlines. I have argued that the Harper initiatives were intended to move constitutional culture further along in a U.S. direction, with an emphasis on limited and divided government. He has sought to do so by exploiting Canada's constitutional malleability via discretionary prerogatives and control over the parliamentary legislative agenda. In the light of the Canadian ability to more easily translate public preferences into law, the Harper initiatives threatened a constituent element of Canada's constitutional culture.

Subject to the federal division of powers and the Charter of Rights and Freedoms, Canadian constitutional culture enables both levels of government to contemplate a wide variety of policy innovations. In turn, this culture has enabled a diversity of ideological commitments to be given expression through social and economic policy.[1] In this way, Canadian constitutional design is more democratic to the extent that it accommodates political change and keeps open a range of achievable political goals.[2] By contrast, we might describe the U.S. experience as

---

1 On such a notion of pluralism, see David Schneiderman, "Canadian Constitutionalism, the Rule of Law and Economic Globalization," in *Participatory Justice in a Global Economy: The New Rule of Law?*, ed. Patricia Hughes and Patrick A. Molinari, 65–85 (Montreal: Les Éditions Themis, 2004). W.H. New makes similar claims about Canadian culture more generally in his *Borderlands: How We Talk about Canada* (Vancouver: UBC Press, 1998), 46.

2 Adam Przeworski, *Democracy and Market: Political and Economic Reforms in Eastern Europe and Latin America* (Cambridge: Cambridge University Press, 1991), 33.

less democratic. In the United States, democracy is considered untrust-worthy, and politics is characterized as the product of competition among special interests. Constitutionalism shields the market from political authority. To the extent that the Harper government shifts con-stitutional culture in an American direction, it will foreclose political alternatives, checking further our capacity for self-government.

We might say that Conservative success has been uneven. Debate continues about the degree to which the prime minister has shifted Canadian political culture in a more conservative direction. We can say there has been even less success in moving constitutional culture in a U.S. direction (though the use of the interrogative in the title of this book suggests that the question should be kept open). Proposals have been stalled (judicial appointments) or abandoned (Senate reform), while the measure of success in other areas can be evaluated only with the pas-sage of time. There can be little doubt, however, that Canada's consti-tutional path will continue to intersect, even converge, with that of our neighbour. Indeed, it could be said that an ongoing element of Canadian constitutional culture is this need to keep constantly in mind the salient differences and similarities between Canada and the United States.

In doing so, and as Canadians move further away from their British roots, they lose sight of interesting developments occurring in the United Kingdom, and elsewhere, that are worth further study. Not that this book has been about re-situating Canada, once again, in the periph-ery to Britain's centre. Rather, the hope is that, by reflecting on Canada's past, we might better understand the possibilities for developing new constitutional practices; that, in this past, we might find resources for better ascertaining the way forward. The object has not been to merely adjust or modernize imperial inheritances but to move towards "new, yet to be articulated" models.[3] "A tradition doesn't exist to bury you," Margaret Atwood observed in 1972, "it can also be used as material for new departures."[4] The aim here has been to expose Canada's consti-tutional traditions in order to inform debate about the direction that future reform might take.

Even if the Harper initiatives were discordant with elements of Canadian constitutional culture, this does not mean we should cling to

---

3 Ian Angus, *Identity and Justice* (Toronto: University of Toronto Press, 2008), 9.
4 Margaret Atwood, *Survival: A Thematic Guide to Canadian Literature* (Toronto: House of Anansi, 2012), 278.

an inadequate status quo. We should have a "clear apprehension both of the deficiency of what is," advises Tawney, "and of the character of what ought to be."[5] By such measure, reform of the institutions and practices discussed in this book certainly is in order. Though we may be "born into past commitments and inherit them," observes John Whyte, this does not mean stasis.[6] Political order, Whyte maintains, does not "imprison citizens in a fixed state" but cultivates opportunities to consider the merits of both constitutional maintenance and constitutional change.[7] That is the work of statecraft.

Edmund Burke ordinarily is associated with preservation of the status quo, which he so eloquently defended in the eighteenth century.[8] I suggest drawing on another side of Burke that complained about societies being expected to conform to some fixed idea of constitutional order. This principally was Burke's complaint about British obstinacy in the face of an impending revolt in America. He implored Parliament to "govern America according to their nature, and to [their] circumstances; and not according to our own imaginations; nor according to abstract ideas of right."[9]

Undoubtedly, constitutions must accommodate innovation. "A state without means of some change," Burke observed in his *Reflections on the French Revolution*, "is without the means of conservation." Correction with the aim of conservation could be endorsed but not change for its own sake. Reformers, Burke maintained, should proceed cautiously with constitutional change, motivated not by abstractions but in order to advance a constitutional project worth preserving. It would require more understanding and experience in the practical science of government than "any person can gain in his whole life."[10] Uday Singh Mehta's verdict is that Burke's attention to "local conditions" made his

---

5 R.H. Tawney, *The Acquisitive Society* (New York: Harcourt, Brace, 1920), 2.

6 John D. Whyte, "Nations, Minorities and Authority," *University of New Brunswick Law Journal* 40 (1991): 49. The following two paragraphs draw on David Schneiderman, "Edmund Burke, John Whyte, and Themes in Canadian Constitutional Culture," *Queen's Law Journal* 31 (2006): 578–97.

7 John D. Whyte, "A Review of Samuel L. LaSelva, the Moral Foundations of Canadian Federalism," *McGill Law Journal* 42 (1997): 189.

8 C.B. Macpherson, *Burke* (Oxford: Oxford University Press, 1980), 4.

9 Edmund Burke, *Works of the Right Honourable Edmund Burke* (London: Bohn's British Classics, 1856), 1:456.

10 Edmund Burke, *Reflections on the Revolution in France*, ed. F.G. Selby (London: Macmillan, 1898), 23, 67.

non-parochial version of liberalism favourable to conditions of pluralism and openness: "an openness to the world, to its unavoidable con-
tingencies, surprises, and ambivalences."[11]

This capacity to adjust accords well with a distinctive feature of
Canadian constitutional culture I have identified, namely, an ability
to be responsive to expressions of the popular will. This is the merit
of British parliamentary practice, observed Montesquieu: its errors
are capable of correction, they "never last long."[12] The institutionally
muscular state associated with parliamentary sovereignty is open to
change, to pluralism, even to its own disintegration.[13] This is not to
deny that the objectives of destruction and assimilation of others were,
at times, important imperial and Canadian objectives. Rather, it is to say
that those aspects of Canadian constitutional culture worth preserving,
in the face of integrationist pressures, are associated with the idea of
openness. They are about keeping the conversation going.[14] Instead of
agonizing over the content of Canadian identity,[15] Canadians should
seize on this constitutional culture of openness and imagine alternative futures that are inclusive and more democratic than what we have
recently experienced.[16]

Two paradoxes follow upon an insistence that we maintain this
Canadian constitutional culture of openness. The first is the phenomenon of executive dominance. This is a feature that is worth

---

11 Uday Singh Mehta, *Liberalism and Empire: A Study in Nineteenth-Century British Liberal
Thought* (Chicago: University of Chicago Press, 1999), 41–2.

12 Baron de Montesquieu, *Considerations on the Causes of the Greatness of the Romans and
Their Decline*, trans. David Lowenthal (Indianapolis: Hackett, 1965), 88; Montesquieu,
Oeuvres Complètes, ed. Roger Caillois (Paris: Librarie Gallimard, 1951), 2:116. On how
England was in mind when Montesquieu wrote this passage, see Paul A. Rahe, *Mon-
tesquieu and the Logic of Liberty: War, Religion, Climate, Terrain, Technology, Uneasiness of
Mind, the Spirit of Political Vigilance, and the Foundations of the Modern Republic* (New
Haven, CT: Yale University Press, 2009), 48.

13 *Reference re Secession of Quebec* [1998] 2 SCR 217.

14 Simone Chambers, "New Constitutionalism: Democracy, Habermas, and Canadian
Exceptionalism," in *Canadian Political Philosophy: Cotemporary Reflections*, ed. Ronald
Beiner and Wayne Norman (Don Mills, ON: Oxford University Press, 2001), 69.

15 Frank H. Underhill, *The Image of Canada* (Fredericton: University of New Brunswick,
1962), 21.

16 It is to move beyond Dennis Lee's bleak prospect for Canada: "They dawdle
about … form[ing] a destiny, still incomplete, still dead weight, still demanding
whether Canada will be." See Dennis Lee, *Civil Elegies and Other Poems* (Toronto:
House of Anansi, 1972), 34.

domesticating, not preserving. In the course of the book's argument, I have suggested legislative initiatives that can tame executive authority, such as codifying a number of the royal prerogatives. Other initiatives could be envisaged, but it is clear that, as I have argued in almost every chapter, the mass of discretion inherited by the prime minister associated with the prerogatives, together with the concentration of political power in the office leader of the governing party, is dangerously excessive. Such initiatives will be in tension with the preservation of muscular parliamentary authority. We should view taking such initiatives as furthering the project of parliamentary self-government rather than undermining it.

The second paradox associated with a constitutional culture of openness is vulnerability to further American influence. In chapter 1, I described another kind of openness associated with the American constitutional project. This openness represents a strategy of encompassing the globe in an ever-expanding project of liberty.[17] It is premised on the assumption that every citizen of every other state has the potential – and presumably the desire – to become "American." The openness associated with this project of U.S. empire is distinctly different from the culture of openness I associate with the Canadian constitutional experience. Rather than imposing a limited legislative program based on the U.S. model, the Canadian culture of openness is attentive to the dangers of shutting down political possibilities. Yet the culture of openness I have described also makes Canadians vulnerable to the influence of the constitutional project issuing out of the United States. These integrationist pressures continue apace and make their appearance in subtle ways in our legal and political life. It makes Canada vulnerable to the political influence of those within Canada who have as their project a shift in constitutional culture in a U.S. direction.

We should be on guard for those peddling poor imitations. What is called for, instead, is constitutional reflexivity. To be sure, this is not about preserving past practice for its own sake. Rather, it is about being attentive to those parts of our constitutional past that are worth preserving while envisaging the adoption of new practices under conditions of transparency about alternatives and in open debate. Canadians should not unthinkingly embrace familiar U.S. models that impose

---

17 Michael Hardt and Antonio Negri, *Empire* (Cambridge, MA: Harvard University Press, 2000), 166.

new constitutional limits. We should instead consider the possibility of a constitution of differing hues – red, white, green, pink, and pastels of various shades.[18] Constitutional change, even of an informal kind, calls, as it did for Burke at the time of the French Revolution, for "a vigorous mind, steady persevering attention, various powers of comparison and combination, and the resources of an understanding fruitful in expedients."[19] My hope is that this book generates these kinds of resources for thinking through and beyond the current impasse towards a more democratic future, all in the interest of keeping the conversation going.

---

18 See Joyce Wieland, *Confedspread*, 1967.
19 Burke, *Reflections on the Revolution in France*, 23.

Index

Page references followed by *fig* indicate figures.

Bagehot on, 139; Blackstone on, 135–6; Canadian treatise writers on, 153, 155; Dick Cheney on, 147–8; in colonial Canada, 149–50; De Lolme on, 137; Dicey on, 140–2; Durham on, 150–1; Levellers on, 124; Locke on, 124–30; Madison on, 35–6, 142–4; Speaker Milliken on breach of, 164; *vs.* mixed regime, 123–4; Montesquieu on, 120, 130–4; Paley on, 137–9; Supreme Court of Canada on, 153–4, 154n202. *See also* prorogation of Parliament (2009)

Shaftesbury, Anthony Ashley Cooper, Lord, 129

Sheafer, Tamir, 279

Siegel, Reva, 13

Simons, Paula, 101

Simpson, Jeffrey, 191

Skocpol, Theda, 66

Skowronek, Stephen, 147

Smith, David, 180, 193, 205n143

Smith, Denis, 90

Smith, Goldwin, 31, 71

Smith, Peter, 44, 45

Smith, William, 54

Snow, Dave, 79, 94, 98

Songer, Donald, 244

South Africa: nomination of judges to Constitutional Court, 282–3

Spill, Rorie, 258, 259

Spirit of the Laws (Montesquieu), 15, 131, 132nn90–1, 134, 150

Stamp Act (1765), 51

Stepan, Alfred, 28

Straw, Jack, 168

Summary of Colonial Law, A (Clark), 58

Supreme Court of Canada: on amending formulae, 229–30; on application of Human Rights Act to Parliament, 161n238, 162n239; appointment of amici curiae by, 221, 222; composition of, 238, 245, 245n52; controversy over Justice Nadon nomination to, 234–5, 245, 277; as counter-majoritarian institution, 237, 249; criticism of mechanism of appointment to, 228–39; Harper on accountability of, 234; law clerks' role in, 249–50; Khadr ruling, 167, 174, 270–1; libertarianism of, 32; media reporting of, 259–60, 260n136; Morton and Knopff on, 250–1; on prerogative power, 167, 174, 270–1; Quebec federalism disputes in, 238; Quebec Secession Reference, 97n116, 215, 220, 221, 227n235; Reform Party's criticism of, 248; role in Canadian public life, 235–6, 236n8; ruling on federal capacity to abolish or replace Senate, 197–8; ruling on Nadon's nomination, 277; Senate Reference, 222–3, 229–31; on separation of powers, 153–4, 154n202, 167, 174; studies of, 249–50; Upper House Reference, 197, 213, 216, 219, 219n204; Van der Peet decision, 11

Supreme Court of Canada appointment process: appointment of political donors, 243, 243n42; "attitudinal" model, 244–5; benefits of, 263, 263n148; Canadian Bar Association on political favouritism in, 242; on constitutional requirement of justices from Quebec, 235, 238; in comparative perspective,

of democracy in, 54–5; executive power in, 25, 85n57; federalism in, 69–70; labour movement, 66; range of political ideas in, 68n232; scholars on constitutional democracy in, 8; separation of powers in, 85–6. *See also* constitutional culture, American

Upper House Reference, 215–16, 219, 219n204

U.S. Congress: legislative process in, 210; presidential authority and, 86, 147–8; probability of conflict between chambers in, 209–10. *See also* President of the United States; U.S. Senate

U.S. Constitution: amending formula, 224; on congressional authority, 64, 64n210, 70; electoral college, 84; *vs.* English constitution, 24; and gridlock, 4, 180, 209, 256; as "inclusive" project, 19; jurisdiction stripping, 73; link to British model, 37; Madison on bill of rights in, 34–5; main principles of, 33–4; as model of limited government, 33, 34; possibilities for political change under, 65; on presidential power, 37, 146–7; on property rights, 39–40, 65–6; replacement of Articles of Confederation by, 33; on role of upper chamber, 36; on separation of powers, 35, 85–6; southern state influence in, 84; Seventeenth Amendment to, 204; veto players in, 86, 208–9, 209n166

U.S. Senate: authority of, 204–5; as elite of the nation, 207; House of Lords as model for, 206; legislative function of, 204; Madison on,

205n143; method of election, 204, 225; Philadelphia Convention's deliberations on, 203, 203n128; principle of "equal suffrage" in, 203; purpose of, 205; representation of states in, 84–5, 203–4; Tea Party's efforts to change process of election to, 207; veto position of, 208–9. *See also* President of the United States; U.S. Congress

U.S. Senate confirmation hearings, 252–3, 259

U.S. Supreme Court: decision on Affordable Care Act, 85; federal commerce clause authority and, 69–70, 85; judicial appointments to, 21, 253, 256, 260; Lochner decision, 67; media coverage of decisions of, 259; nomination process, 253–5, 255n109, 256–8, 257n122; popular perception of, 258–9; public attention to nominations to, 257

Verba, Sidney, 12
Vermeule, Adrian, 85n57

Wagner, Claude, 273, 273n193
Wagner, Richard: announcement of nomination to Supreme Court, 264; on judicial role, 268, 268n173; nomination hearing, 239n27, 261, 262*fig*, 264, 265, 267, 268, 269, 270*fig*, 273*fig*, 273–4, 276, 278*fig*, 279, 280
Wallace, Donald, 69
Wallin, Pamela, 176
Walsh, Rob, 159, 160, 161–2
Walters, Mark, 225, 227, 227n235
Warren, Earl, 18
Watson, William, 68
Webster, Noah, 204